ACCA

Strategic Professional

Advanced Taxation (ATX – UK) FA2024

Exam Practice Kit

For exams in June 2025, September 2025, December 2025 and March 2026

BPP

Sixth edition 2024

ISBN 9781 0355 2563 8

Previous ISBN 9781 0355 1327 7

eISBN 9781 0355 2567 6

British Library Cataloguing-in-Publication Data

A catalogue record for this book is available from the British Library

Published by

BPP Learning Media Ltd
BPP House, Aldine Place
142–144 Uxbridge Road
London W12 8AA

learningmedia.bpp.com

Your learning materials are printed on paper obtained from traceable sustainable sources.

The contents of these learning materials are intended as a guide and not professional advice. Although every effort has been made to ensure that the contents of this book are correct at the time of going to press, BPP makes no warranty that the information in this book is accurate or complete and accept no liability for any loss or damage suffered by any person acting or refraining from acting as a result of the material in these learning materials.

We are grateful to the Association of Chartered Certified Accountant for permission to reproduce past examination questions.

Contents

Question index

Topic index

Listed below are the key ATX – UK syllabus topics and the numbers of the questions in this Kit covering those topics. We have also included a reference to the relevant Chapter of the BPP ATX – UK Course Book, the companion to the BPP ATX – UK Exam Practice Kit, in case you wish to revise the information on the topic you have covered.

If you need to concentrate your practice and revision on certain topics or if you want to attempt all available questions that refer to a particular subject, you will find this index useful. (M denotes a question from a particular mock exam.)

Syllabus topic	Question numbers	Course Book chapter
Capital tax advice	2, 3, 4, 6, 7, 9, 10, 16, 20, 21, M1 Q3, M3 Q3, M4 Q2	13
Chargeable gains – companies	2, 3, 5, 6, 8, 12, 33, 34, 35	16
Chargeable gains – computation for individuals	4, 8, 9, 10, 17, 21, 24, 26, 28, 29, M1 Q1, M2 Q2, M3 Q1, M3 Q3, M4 Q1, M4 Q3	7
Chargeable gains – shares/ securities for individuals	10, 21	8
Chargeable gains – reliefs for individuals	4, 6, 8, 9, 15, 19, 20, 22, 24, 25, 28, 29, M1 Q1, M1 Q3, M2 Q2, M3 Q1, M3 Q3, M4 Q1	8
Companies – administration, winding up	11, 31	20
Companies – corporation tax computation	1, 2, 3, 5, 6, 8, 9, 10, 11, 12, 29, 30, 32, 33, 34, 35, M1 Q2, M2 Q3, M3 Q2, M4 Q1	16
Companies – close and investment	1, 9, 36, M2 Q2, M2 Q3	21
Companies – groups and consortia	1, 2, 3, 5, 6, 8, 10, 12, 32, 33, 34, M2 Q1, M3 Q2	19
Companies – losses for single company	7, 9, 30, 31, M3 Q2	17
Companies – overseas aspects	1, 2, 8, 12, 32, 33, 34, M1 Q2, M4 Q1	22
Companies – personal service	17	4
Companies – repurchase of own shares	31	20
Companies – tax administration	2, 3, 6, M2 Q3	16
Corporate tax advice	1, 3, 5, M2 Q1, M4 Q1	25
Employment income	4, 7, 8, 14, 15, 23, 24, 35, M4 Q3	4
Ethics	1, 2, 3, 4, 5, 6, 7, 8, 9, 10, 11, 12, M2 Q1, M1 Q1, M3 Q1, M4 Q1	1

Syllabus topic	Question numbers	Course Book chapter
Income tax computation	4, 6, 7, 8, 9, 12, 13, 16, 27, 28, M1 Q3, M3 Q3	2
Inheritance tax	2, 4, 6, 7, 9, 10, 11, 13, 16, 17, 18, 19, 20, 21, M2 Q1, M1 Q3, M3 Q1, M4 Q2	11, 12
Losses for sole traders and partnerships	4, 7, 9, 14, 23, 26, 27, 29, M2 Q2, M1 Q1	15
National insurance contributions	4, 6, 8, 9, 12, 14, 24, 27, 28, 35, M2 Q3	4,14
Overseas personal tax	7, 10, 11, 13, 17, 19, 20, M3 Q3, M4 Q3	9
Owner managed business tax advice	4, 5, 6, 7, 9, 11, 14, 23, 24, 26, 27, 28, 35, M2 Q2, M2 Q3, M3 Q2	18
Partnerships	7, 14, 26, 27	15
Property income	8, 13, 16	5
Share schemes	8, 12, 13, 15, 22, 26	4,6
Sole traders	3, 4, 6, 8, 11, 25, 29, M3 Q1, M4 Q2	14
Stamp taxes	3, 5, M4 Q1	24
Pensions and tax efficient investments	4, 14, 15, 16, 17, 18, 28	3
Personal tax administration	19, M2 Q1, M1 Q1	10
Personal tax planning	8, 12, 18, M1 Q1, M1 Q3, M4 Q2, M4 Q3	6
Value added tax	1, 2, 3, 5, 6, 7, 9, 11, 12, 23, 24, 25, 27, 28, 30, 31, 32, M2 Q1, M2 Q2, M1 Q2, M3 Q1, M4 Q1	23

About this BPP Exam Practice Kit

The Section B 25-mark questions in the exam typically focus on one main syllabus area. The 25-mark questions in this Kit have been grouped according to the section of the syllabus (Parts A–D) to which they mainly relate.

The Section A 50-mark questions in the exam cover a number of different syllabus areas, so the 50-mark questions in this Kit are found in a single bank of questions.

There are also four mock exams which provide you the opportunity to refine your knowledge and skills as part of your final exam preparations.

As an ACCA Approved Content Partner BPP Learning Media gives you the opportunity to use revision materials created by BPP's expert team of Subject Matter Experts who have years of experience authoring Professional Qualification Content. The Subject Matter Experts ensure the content covers the depth and breadth of the syllabus and provides excellent support for your revision.

BPP Learning Media do everything possible to ensure the material is accurate and up to date when sending to print. In the event that any errors are found after the print date, they are uploaded to the following website: www.bpp.com/learningmedia/Errata

Selecting questions

We provide signposts to help you plan your revision.

- A full **question index**
- A **topic index** listing all the questions that cover key topics, so that you can locate the questions that provide practice on these topics, and see the different ways in which they might be examined

Attempting mock exams

There are four mock exams that provide practice at coping with the pressures of the exam day. We strongly recommend that you attempt them under exam conditions.

All the mock exams reflect the question styles and syllabus coverage of the exam.

Question practice

This is the most important thing to do if you want to get through. Many of the most up-to-date exam questions are in this Kit. Practice doing them under timed conditions, then go through the answers and go back to the Course Book for any topic you are really having trouble with. Come back to a question a week later and try it again – you will be surprised at how much better you are getting. Be very ruthless with yourself at this stage – you have to do the question in the time, without looking at the answer. This will really sharpen your wits and make the exam experience less worrying. Just keep doing this and you will get better at doing questions and you will really find out what you know and what you don't know.

Practising as many exam-style questions as possible in the ACCA CBE practice platform will be the key to passing this exam. You must do questions under timed conditions and ensure you produce full answers to the discussion parts as well as doing the calculations.

Also ensure that you attempt all mock exams under exam conditions.

ACCA have launched a free on-demand resource designed to mirror the live exam experiences helping you to become more familiar with the exam format. You can access the platform via the Study Support Resources section of the ACCA website, navigating to the CBE question practice section and logging in with your myACCA credentials.

Videos can be viewed online by accessing your ebook version on VitalSource.

The exam

Approach to examining the syllabus

The Advanced Taxation (ATX – UK) syllabus is assessed by a 3 hour 15 minute computer based exam (CBE). The pass mark is **50%**. All questions in the exam are **compulsory**.

The questions will be scenario-based and may involve consideration of more than one tax, some elements of planning and the interaction of taxes.

Throughout the exam, you will be expected to identify issues, as well as demonstrate detailed knowledge of the tax system. In line with this emphasis on practicality, questions may require you to address 'the UK tax consequences' of a given situation without indicating which particular taxes to consider. It is up to you to identify the relevant taxes, and the issues in respect of those taxes, before beginning your answer.

Calculations are normally only required in support of explanations and advice, and not in isolation. Again, it is often up to you to decide what calculations to produce in order to do this in the most efficient manner. Advice on how to approach a given problem may be provided in the question.

You will be expected to undertake both calculation and narrative work. There is no specific allocation of numerical calculation versus narrative balance within Taxation (TX – UK) and Advanced Taxation (ATX – UK). However, in practice, Taxation (TX – UK) is mainly computational whereas Advanced Taxation (ATX – UK) is mainly narrative. In both exams, your ability to explain your treatment of tax issues and to present your opinions is vital. It is important to note that this does not mean that you need to have perfect grammar or spelling; it means that you need to make yourself understood.

Tax rates, allowances and information on certain reliefs will be given in the exam. You should familiarise yourself with the information provided so that you know how to find it quickly in the exam.

Computer-based exams

All ACCA papers are computer-based examinations (CBEs). The CBE exams for Applied Knowledge modules can be taken at any time; these are referred to as 'exams on demand'. The Applied Skills and Strategic Professional exams can be sat in September, December, March and June of each year; these are referred to as 'exams on sitting'. Advanced Taxation is an 'exam on sitting'. Computer-based examinations must be taken at an ACCA CBE Licensed Centre.

The exam is formatted as follows.

	Format of the exam	Marks
Section A	One compulsory case-study question worth 50 marks. The 50 marks will comprise of 35 technical marks, 5 ethics marks and 10 professional skills marks. All four professional skills will be examined in Section A. • Includes ten professional marks covering all four of the professional skills • Requires you to analyse the information provided and use any guidance given to help address the requirements • As this question is half the exam, it requires careful time management using the number of marks allocated to each requirement to determine how much time to spend on each part • Will deal with a number of different taxes • May have coverage of technical taxation topics new in Advanced Taxation (ATX – UK), such as international aspects, stamp taxes, tax planning and interaction of taxes • Usually also includes application of technical aspects from Taxation (TX – UK) • Will have five marks on ethical issues	50

	Format of the exam	Marks
Section B	Two compulsory 25-mark questions Both questions: • Will contain 20 technical marks with five professional skills marks containing a minimum of two professional skills from analysis and evaluation, scepticism and commercial acumen. Communication skills will not be examined in Section B. • May have coverage of technical taxation topics new in Advanced Taxation (ATX – UK), such as international aspects, stamp taxes, tax planning and interaction of taxes • Usually also include application of technical aspects from Taxation (TX – UK)	50
		100

Remote invigilated exams

In certain geographical areas it may be possible for you to take your exam remotely. This option, which is subject to strict conditions, can offer increased flexibility and convenience under certain circumstances. Further guidance, including the detailed requirements and conditions for taking the exam by this method, is contained on ACCA's website at:

accaglobal.com/an/en/student/exam-entry-and-administration/about-our-exams/remote-exams/remote-session-exams.html

Analysis of past exams

The table below provides details of when each element of the syllabus has been examined in the ten most recent sittings and the question number in which each element was examined. Note that the exams pre June 2023 were under the previous exam format where Section A contained two questions – Questions 1 (35 marks) and 2 (25 marks) – and Section B contained two 20-mark questions (3 and 4). Under the previous exam format there were only four professional skills marks, all within question 1 of each exam.

*		Mar/June 2024	Sept/Dec 2023	Mar/Jun 2023	Sept/Dec 2022	Mar/Jun 2022	Sept/Dec 2021	Mar/Jun 2021	Sept/Dec 2020	March 2020	Sep/Dec 2019
	ETHICS										
1	Ethics, tax avoidance schemes	1(a)	1(a)	1(a)	1(a)	1(a)	1(a)	2(a)	1(a)	1(d)	1(a)
	PERSONAL TAX										
2	The income tax computation		3(c)			2(a) 4(c)	2(a)	2(c)			
3	Pensions and tax efficient investment products			3(c)						3(d) 4(c)	
4	Employment income	3(c)				2(b)	2(a) 4(b)	4(a)	4(c)		
5	Property income			3(c)		4(b)				4(b)	
6	Personal tax planning	2(c) 3(c)					2(a)				
	CAPITAL TAX										
7	Capital gains tax computation	1(b) 3(b)	1(b) 3(b)	1(b)	2(c) 3(b)	2(c) 3(a)	3(b) 4(a)	2(b)	2(a)	1(b) 2(a) 3(d)	
8	Capital gains tax – shares and reliefs	1(b)	1(b) 3(b)	1(b)	1(b) 3(b)	3(a)	1(b) 3(b)	4(b)	2(a) 3(b)	1(b) 2(a)	2(b)
9	Overseas personal taxation	3(a) (b)	3(a) (c)		2(b) 2(c)	2(a) 2(c)	2(b) 4(c)	2(b) 2(c)	2(a) 2(c)	1(a) 1(b)	2(a) 2(c)
10	Personal tax administration			1(d)							
11	Inheritance tax computation	2(a)	1(c)		2(a)	2(d) 4(a)	2(c)	2(b)	1(d)	1(c)	2(b)
12	Inheritance tax: further aspects	2(a)			4(c)		4(a)	2(b) 4(c)	2(c)	4(a)	2(b)
13	Capital tax planning	2(a)	1(b)	1(b) 3(a) 3(b)				2(b)		1(c)	
	OWNER-MANAGED BUSINESS TAX										
14	Sole traders		1(b)		2(d) 3(a)		3(c)	1(b)	2(b)	3(a) 3(b)	

*		Mar/June 2024	Sept/Dec 2023	Mar/Jun 2023	Sept/Dec 2022	Mar/Jun 2022	Sept/Dec 2021	Mar/Jun 2021	Sept/Dec 2020	March 2020	Sep/Dec 2019
15	Sole trader losses and partnerships	2(b)		1(c)	3(a)	1(d)	3(a)		3(a)		4(b)
16	Corporation tax for single companies	1(a)	2(a) 2(c)	2(a)	1(b)		3(c)	1(a) 3(b)	4(d)	2(b)	3(a) 3(c)
17	Losses for single companies		2(b)								
18	Owner-managed business tax planning		2(a) 2(c)	1(c) 1(d)				3(a)	4(c)	3(b)	1(b) 1(c) 4(a)
	CORPORATE TAX										
19	Corporate groups and consortia	1(a)	2(b)		1(b)	3(b)	1(b)		1(b)	2(b)	
20	Administration, winding up, purchase of own shares					1(b)		1(a)			
21	Close companies and investment companies				4(a) 4(b)			3(a)	4(a) 4(b)		1(c)
22	Overseas aspects of corporation tax	1(a)		2(b)	1(c)		1(c)		1(b)	2(c)	3(b)
23	Value added tax	1(a)	1(b)	2(c)	1(b) 3(c)	1(c)	1(d)	1(b)	1(c) 3(c)	2(b) 3(c)	1(c) 4(c)
24	Stamp taxes	1(a)			1(b)						
25	Corporate tax planning	1(a)									

*Covered in Course Book chapter

IMPORTANT! The table above gives a broad idea of how frequently major topics in the syllabus are examined. It should **not** be used to question spot and predict, for example, that Topic X will not be examined because it came up two sittings ago. The examining team's reports indicate that they are well aware that some students try to question spot. The examining team avoid predictable patterns and may, for example, examine the same topic two sittings in a row.

Passing the ATX exam

Videos can be viewed online by accessing your ebook version on VitalSource.

https://www.accaglobal.com/gb/en/student/exam-support-resources/professional-exams-study-resources/p6/syllabus-study-guide.html

https://learningmedia.bpp.com/pages/resources-for-students

Revising ATX

Firstly, we must emphasise that you will need a good knowledge of the **whole syllabus**. This means **learning/memorising the rules** in order to be able to answer questions. The examining team has commented that it is a **lack of precise knowledge** that causes many candidates problems in the exam.

All the questions in Section A and Section B are compulsory and any part of the syllabus can be examined in any question. However, there are certain topics which are particularly important.

- The **calculation of income tax payable**, including the **restriction of the personal allowance** and **tax reducers**
- **Personal pension schemes**, in particular the **annual allowance** and the **annual allowance charge**
- **Taxation of an unincorporated business** including loss reliefs.
- The **calculation of benefits from employment** so that you can make sensible comparisons between **remuneration packages**. Make sure you can advise on **tax free benefits** too. The rules for **share schemes** and on **termination payments** should be known very well
- The **structure and mechanics of inheritance tax** (eg types of transfer, nil rate band, seven year cumulation, residence nil rate band)
- The **exemptions** and **reliefs available for the different taxes**, in particular **for capital gains tax** (eg business asset disposal relief, gift holdover relief, rollover relief) and **inheritance tax** (eg spouse exemption, business property relief). **Exemptions and reliefs** are the **foundation of any tax planning**
- The **computation of corporation tax**, including dealing with **loan relationships, intangible assets, and research and development expenditure**
- **Close companies** including the position of **participators**
- All aspects of **corporation tax groups** including the impact of loss relief, chargeable gains groups, the effect of group VAT registration and stamp taxes groups. You should pay particular attention to the impact on **corporate restructuring**
- For **value added tax,** the **rules on land and buildings**, the **capital goodsscheme**, **special VAT schemes** available for small businesses so that you can advise if and when they might be appropriate, and the **partial exemption rules**
- **Overseas aspects** of income tax, CGT, IHT, corporation tax and VAT
- **Tax administration**, including filing dates, penalties and interest for all taxes
- **Ethical considerations** when acting for clients

accaglobal.com/gb/en/student/exam-support-resources/professional-exams-study-resources/p6/examiners-reports1.html

Gaining the easy marks

Your technical knowledge (including knowledge brought forward from Taxation) should enable you to score a small number of relatively easy marks. There are likely to be a small number of marks available in certain requirements for definitions or explanations that don't have to be related to the scenario. However, don't assume that you can ignore all the scenarios and still pass! The level of marks available in ATX for knowledge alone (without application) is around 20-30% and so is nowhere near enough to pass the exam.

Professional marks are available in Section A and Section B questions, and some of these should be easy to obtain. For example, there are likely to be marks available for presenting your answer in section A in the format, style and tone, requested (eg a report).

Essential skills areas to be successful in Advanced Taxation (ATX – UK)

We think there are three areas you should develop in order to achieve exam success in Advanced Taxation (ATX – UK):

(a) **Knowledge application**; technical knowledge accounts for a high percentage of the marks in the ATX – UK exam and it is essential to have a good knowledge of all syllabus areas.

(b) **ATX – UK Professional skills**; these are worth 20% of the marks in the ATX – UK exam and are explained in detail in this section.

(c) **Exam success skills**; these are general skills required in the application of good exam technique and apply to any exam.

At the revision and final exam preparation phases, these should be developed together as part of a comprehensive study plan of focused question practice.

These skills are shown in the diagram below.

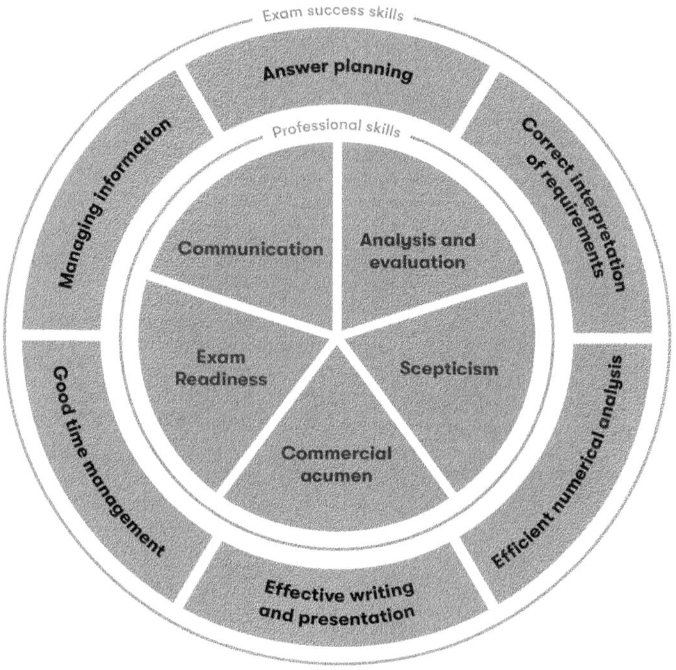

ATX – UK professional skills

In your exam 20 marks will be available for demonstrating the professional skills that would be expected from a proficient tax professional. Professional skills marks should not be thought of as being separate from the technical content of an answer; they are earned by providing comprehensive and relevant responses to the technical requirements.

There are four professional skills – these skills are important and are worth 20 marks in the exam, a brief summary of each skill is given below.

ACCA professional skill: Definition	Three aspects of each professional skill
Communication To express yourself clearly and convincingly through an appropriate medium, while being sensitive to the needs of the intended audience	• Inform target audience using clear format • Persuade with logical argument • Appropriate use of technology

ACCA professional skill: Definition	Three aspects of each professional skill
Commercial acumen To show awareness of the wider business and external factors affecting businesses, and use commercially sound judgement and insight to resolve issues and exploit opportunities	• Practical considerations • Recognise constraints • Awareness of alternative opportunities to those suggested
Analysis and evaluation To appraise information objectively and to draw logical conclusions, recognising the impact on relevant stakeholders	• Consider the relevance or significance of data • Assess impact on stakeholders • Apply analysis to the taxpayer in the question
Scepticism To probe, question and challenge information and views presented to you, to fully understand business issues and to establish facts objectively, based on ethical and professional values	• Question validity of approaches • Challenge opinions • Identify new information needed

Professional skills marks should not be thought of as being separate from the technical content of an answer; they are earned by providing comprehensive and relevant responses to the technical requirements.

All of the professional skills will be examined in Section A of the exam, which is a single 50-mark case study. 10 of the 50 marks will be allocated to demonstrating professional skills marks.

Section B will consist of two compulsory scenario-based 25-mark questions. **Each B question will allocate 5 marks to professional skills,** so 10 marks in total will be available for professional skills marks in Section B. Each question will contain a **minimum of two professional skills from Analysis and Evaluation, Scepticism and Commercial Acumen**.

These are covered in more detail in the Skills Checkpoints in the ATX – UK Course Book.

Videos can be viewed online by accessing your ebook version on VitalSource.

Exam success skills

Passing the ATX – UK exam requires more than applying syllabus knowledge, it also requires the development of excellent exam technique through question practice.

We consider the following six skills to be vital for exam success.

Exam success skill 1

Managing information

Questions in the exam will present you with a lot of information. The skill is how you handle this information to make the best use of your time. The key is determining how you will approach the exam and then actively reading the questions.

Advice on developing this skill

To avoid being overwhelmed by the quantity of information provided, you must take an **active approach** to reading each question.

Active reading means focussing on the question's requirements first, highlighting key verbs such as 'evaluate', 'analyse', 'explain', 'discuss', to ensure you answer the question properly. Then, when you have an understanding of what the question will require you to do, read the rest of the question, highlighting important and relevant information, and making notes of any relevant technical information you think you will need.

Computer-based exam

In a computer-based exam (CBE) the **highlighter tool** provided in the toolbar at the top of the screen offers a range of colours:

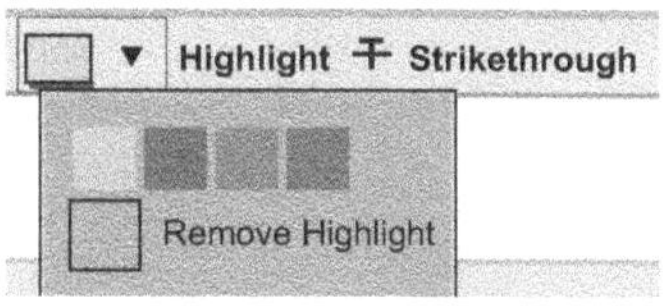

This allows you to choose **different colours to emphasise different aspects of a question**. You could use a different colour for information relevant to each sub-part of a question or you could use a different colour for each tax. You need to try out a few options and see what works best for you.

The **strikethrough function** allows you to delete areas of a question that you have dealt with - this can be useful in managing information if you are dealing with numerical questions because it can allow you to ensure that all numerical areas have been accounted for in your answer.

The CBE also allows you to **resize windows** by clicking on the bottom right-hand corner of the window as highlighted in the following section:

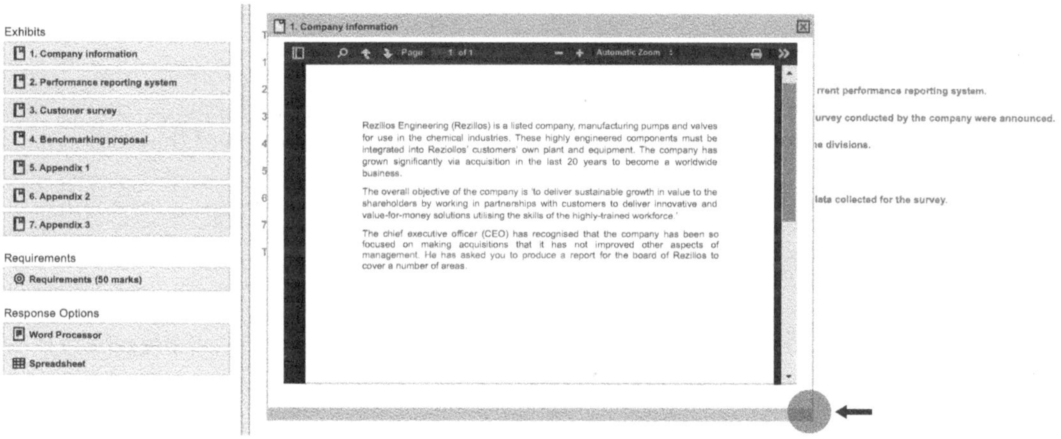

This functionality allows you to **display a number of windows at the same time**, so this could allow you review:

- the question requirements and the exhibit relating to that requirement, at the same time, or
- the window containing your answer (whether a word processing or spreadsheet document) and the exhibit relating to that requirement, at the same time.

Exam success skill 2

Correct interpretation of the requirements

The active verb used often dictates the approach that written answers should take (eg 'explain', 'discuss', 'evaluate'). It is important you identify and use the verb to define your approach. The **correct interpretation of the requirements** skill means correctly producing only what is being asked for by a requirement. Anything not required will not earn marks.

Advice on developing this skill

This skill can be developed by analysing question requirements and applying this process:

Step 1 Read the requirement

Firstly, read the requirement a couple of times slowly and carefully and **highlight the active verbs**. Use the active verbs to define what you plan to do. Make sure you identify any sub-requirements within a requirement – this is **often signalled by the use of the word 'and'** within a requirement.

Important active verbs for ATX – UK include the following:

Advise

This requires you to provide someone with useful information, or to **tell them what you think they should do** based on a consideration of the issues presented in a scenario.

Calculate

This means to ascertain by computation; to make an estimate of; evaluate; perform a mathematical process. The ACCA advise you to provide a description alongside your numerical calculations.

Conclude

This means the result or outcome of an act or process or event, final arrangement or settlement. The ACCA advise you to end your answer well, with a clear decision.

Discuss

This will require you to consider and debate/argue about the pros and cons of an issue. The ACCA advise you to write about any conflict and to compare and contrast.

Evaluate

This will require you to present **a 'balanced' discussion** of an issue looking at both the positive and negative issues. Where numbers feature in a question, an evaluation will require you to use the numbers provided to create a value from which a **judgement** can be made.

Explain

This involves making an idea clear and could require you to, for example, show logically how a concept is developed or to **give the reason** for an event. The ACCA advise you not just to provide a list of points. You should add in some explanation of the points you're discussing.

Identify

This means to recognise something.

Recommend

If you are asked to 'recommend' then you are expected to use details presented in the scenario to create **a logical and justified** course of action.

State

This means to explain something precisely so it is important that you focus on the exact scenario.

A full list of ACCA verbs can be found here:

accaglobal.com/ca/en/student/sa/study-skills/verbs-fundamentals.html

Step 2 Read the rest of the question

By reading the requirement first, you will have an idea of what you are looking out for as you read through the case overview and exhibits. This is a great time saver and means you don't end up having to read the whole question in full twice. You should do this in an active way – see Exam success skill 1: Managing Information.

Step 3 Read the requirement again

Read the requirement again to remind yourself of the exact wording before starting your written answer. This will capture any misinterpretation of the requirements or any missed requirements entirely. This should become a habit in your approach and, with repeated practice, you will find the focus, relevance and depth of your answer plan will improve.

Exam success skill 3

Answer planning: Priorities, structure and logic

This skill requires the planning of the key aspects of an answer which accurately and completely responds to the requirement.

Advice on developing this skill

All exam questions will contain a brief bulleted summary of the key areas covered which is intended to give you a broad awareness of the subjects being examined in order to assist you with your planning.

Everyone will have a preferred style for an answer plan. For example, it may be a mind map, bullet-pointed lists or simply highlighting the question. If you are sitting your exam in-centre then you will be able to plan either using the scrap paper provided or the on-screen scratchpad. If you are sitting your exam via remote invigilation only the on-screen scratchpad will be available for your planning. Choose the approach that you feel most comfortable with that works with how you are sitting your exam, or, if you are not sure, try out different approaches for different questions until you have found your preferred style.

For a discussion question, highlighting the question is likely to be insufficient. It would be better to draw up a separate answer plan in the format of your choosing (eg a mind map or bullet-pointed lists).

Make sure you take note of the date assumption given in the question. You will need to be aware of the date's potential significance in terms of the overall timeline and its relevance to the sequence of events being provided within the scenario. You should also make note of what output you will need to produce. The 50-mark question could involve different clients and so more than one type of document may be requested.

In a computer-based exam you can use the copy and paste functions to copy the question requirements to the beginning of your answer. This will allow you to ensure that your answer plan addresses all parts of the question requirements.

Copying and pasting simply involves highlighting the relevant information and either right clicking to access the copy and paste functions, or alternatively using Ctrl C to copy and Ctrl V to paste.

Exam success skill 4

Efficient numerical analysis

This skill aims to maximise the marks awarded by making clear to the marker the process of arriving at your answer. This is achieved by laying out an answer such that, even if you make a few errors, you can still get some credit for your calculations. It is vital that you do not lose marks purely because the marker cannot follow what you have done.

Advice on developing efficient numerical analysis

It is important to use the spreadsheet provided to produce a clear and efficient numerical analysis.

It is **not a sensible idea** to perform calculations on a calculator and then manually transfer them to the spreadsheet because this will not **show the marker where numbers have come from.**

It is important to remember that, in an exam situation, it is difficult to get every number 100% correct. It is important that you do not spend too long on any single calculation. If you are struggling with a solution then make a sensible assumption, state it and move on.

Using a spreadsheet allows you to **show the marker how numerical values have been calculated**, because the basis for a calculation is displayed if the marker clicks onto a cell.

Clear labelling should also help to show the marker what the numbers are intended to mean.

If your calculations are fairly straightforward there is no need to provide a detailed explanation however, a **workings section** will sometimes be a useful feature of a spreadsheet answer if more detailed calculations are involved. The workings will reduce the likelihood of errors being made if calculations are complex.

Keep your workings as **clear and simple as possible** and ensure they are cross referenced to the main part of your answer. Where it helps, provide brief narrative explanations to help the marker understand the steps in the calculation. This means that if a mistake is made you should not lose any subsequent marks for follow-on calculations.

Spreadsheet short-cuts

You can also use useful spreadsheet short-cuts to improve the efficiency of your numerical analysis. For ATX – UK this is no more complex than using the standard tools that you should be used to within Excel. The basic mathematical functions and the 'sum' function should be sufficient.

It is also really helpful to link cells together in your formulae. For example, rather than re-typing in your taxable non-savings income you can simply use the cell reference where your taxable non-savings income is and apply your tax rate directly to the linked cell to calculate the tax thereon. This will mean that if you later correct a mistake in your taxable non-savings income figure, the correction should automatically feed through your figures. You will see examples of effective use of the spreadsheet function in the answers to some of the Mocks at the back of this Exam Practice Kit.

Exam success skill 5

Effective writing and presentation

Written answers should be presented so that the marker can clearly see the points you are making, presented in the format specified in the question. The skill is to provide efficient written answers with sufficient breadth of points that answer the question, in the right depth, in the time available.

Advice on developing this skill

Step 1 Use headings

Using the headings and sub-headings from your answer plan will give your answer structure, order and logic. This will ensure your answer links back to the requirement and is clearly signposted, making it easier for the marker to understand the different points you are making. Underlining your headings will also help the marker.

Step 2 Write your answer in short, but full, sentences

Use short, punchy sentences with the aim that every sentence should say something different and generate marks. Write in full sentences, ensuring your style is professional.

Step 3 Do your calculations first and explanation second

Questions often ask for an explanation with suitable calculations. The best approach is to prepare the calculation first then add the explanation before the calculation. Performing the calculation first should enable you to explain what you have done. In the CBE format it is very easy to add the explanation in above your calculations (if they are all in the word processor) or to prepare your calculations in the spreadsheet first and then write about them in the word processor afterwards.

Exam success skill 6

Good time management

This skill means planning your time across all the requirements so that all tasks have been attempted at the end of the 3 hours 15 minutes available and actively checking on time during your exam. This is so that you can flex your approach and prioritise requirements which, in your judgment, will generate the maximum marks in the available time remaining.

Planning time

In ATX – UK it is **crucial to spend time on planning before starting to write your answer**. This allows time for a candidate to immerse themselves in the question scenarios. Approximately 20% of your time should be allocated to planning to ensure that you are able to assimilate the key features of the scenario before starting to write.

For a 50-mark question, planning time should be 50 marks × 1.95 × 0.2 = **20 minutes.**

For a 25-mark question, planning time would be 25 marks × 1.95 × 0.2 = **10 minutes per question.**

Writing time

For time management purposes, candidates should allocate time based on the **technical marks available.** Professional skills marks should not be thought of as separate requirements as they are earned by providing **comprehensive and relevant responses to the technical requirements.**

Writing time can be calculated by **multiplying the technical mark allocation for each requirement by 1.95 minutes** (as the 20% of time spent planning is exactly offset by the extra 20% of marks available for professional skills marks).

So, time planning for a 25-mark question with, for example, a 12 mark part a and an 8 mark part b (and 5 professional skills marks) should be as follows:

Total time: 25 marks x 1.95 minutes per mark = 49 minutes

Planning time: 49 minutes x 0.2 = 10 minutes

Writing time: part a = 12 x 1.95 minutes per mark = 23 minutes

Writing time: part b = 8 x 1.95 minutes per mark = 16 minutes

At the beginning of a question, work out the amount of time you should be spending on each requirement and **note the finishing time for each requirement- either in your word processor answer (to delete later) or in the scratch pad.**

Keep an eye on the clock

Aim to attempt all requirements, but be ready to be ruthless and move on if your answer is not going as planned. The challenge for many is sticking to planned timings. Be aware this is difficult to achieve in the early stages of your studies and be ready to let this skill develop over time.

Avoid discussing issues at great length, remember that the Strategic Professional Options examinations are normally marked on the basis of **one mark per point, possibly with an extra mark for more fully developing the same point.**

If you find yourself running short on time and know that a full answer is not possible in the time you have, consider recreating your plan in overview form and then add key terms and details as time allows. Remember, some marks may be available, for example, simply stating a conclusion which you don't have time to justify in full.

Questions

Section A questions

1 Forti Ltd group (ACCA specimen exam (FA21), amended to FA24) (98 mins)

You should assume that today's date is 1 December 2025.

You work for a firm of accountants. One of your firm's clients is the Forti Ltd group of companies. Emma is one of the shareholders of Forti Ltd and is also a client of your firm.

Your manager has asked you to set out some notes in preparation for a forthcoming meeting with Forti Ltd and Emma and they require advice on:

- Brawn Ltd's corporation tax computation for the year ended 31 March 2025;
- Whether Forti Ltd is a close company;
- Matters to be considered in connection with some intra-group sales;
- The VAT annual accounting scheme; and
- Some personal tax queries from Emma.

The following exhibits provide information relevant to the question;

(1) Schedule prepared by a tax assistant

(2) Email from Emma

(3) Vyc Ltd – information from client files

(4) Email from your manager – work to be carried out

This information should be used to answer the question **requirements** within your chosen **response option(s)**.

Required

You should assume that today's date is 1 December 2025.

Carry out the work required as set out in the email from your manager.

Note. The split of the mark allocation is shown in Exhibit 4 – Email from your manager. **(40 marks)**

Professional marks will be awarded for the demonstration of skill in communication, analysis & evaluation, scepticism and commercial acumen in your answer.

(10 marks)

(Total = 50 marks)

Exhibit 1: Schedule prepared by a tax assistant

Brawn Ltd – Corporation tax computation for the year ended 31 March 2025

	Notes	£	£
Tax adjusted trading income	1, 2		240,800
Sale of Marussia Ltd – Proceeds	3	484,000	
Less:			
– Indexed cost		(396,300)	
– Annual exempt amount		(3,000)	
			84,700
			325,500

	Notes	£	£
Less:			
– Losses transferred from:			
– Marussia Ltd (£60,000 × 5/12)	4		(25,000)
– Eagle Ltd (£52,500 × 20%)	5		(10,500)
Taxable total profits			290,000
Corporation tax @ 25%			72,500

Notes.

1 The treatment of the following items of expenditure needs to be checked.

	£	
The cost of establishing a company share option plan (CSOP)	6,000	Disallowed
The cost of entertaining overseas customers	4,000	Disallowed
Accrued management bonuses to be paid on 1 February 2026	7,000	Allowed

2 The tax adjusted trading income is after deducting a total of £48,000 in respect of research and development expenditure. The expenditure consisted of salaries paid to Brawn Ltd staff of £21,000 and payments for subcontracted labour of £27,000.

3 Marussia Ltd was purchased on 1 August 2024. On 1 November 2024, Brawn Ltd signed a contract to sell Marussia Ltd for £484,000, and the sale took place on 31 December 2024. Accordingly, the substantial shareholding exemption was not available. The sale of Marussia Ltd resulted in a degrouping charge of £21,500. This has been included as a chargeable gain in the corporation tax computation of Marussia Ltd.

4 Marussia Ltd made a tax adjusted trading loss of £60,000 in the year ended 31 March 2025.

5 Eagle Ltd made a tax adjusted trading loss of £52,500 in the year ended 31 March 2025 and did not pay a dividend.

6 During the year ended 31 March 2025, Brawn Ltd began selling components to Gordini Co. Are there any issues which need to be considered in respect of these sales in relation to Brawn Ltd's corporation tax liability?

Exhibit 2: Email from Emma

To: Tax manager

From: Emma

Date: 1 December 2025

Subject: Gift of Vyc Ltd shares

Hi

Our family company, Vyc Ltd, has had another excellent year and its value continues to increase. On 1 July 2026, I will give my son, Edward, 10,000 ordinary shares in the company. Edward has spent most of the last few years travelling in Asia and I am hoping that this gift of shares will persuade him to return to the UK.

I appreciate there may be a UK inheritance tax (IHT) liability if I die within seven years of this gift. Please explain the circumstances which would result in the maximum IHT liability on this gift and provide me with a calculation of the amount which would then be due.

I also wanted to check in with you about some potential gains that I'm going to make shortly on the disposal of some investment properties I own. Because I'm going to reinvest the money in other properties, I don't see the need for me to disclose these gains to HMRC – is that OK?

Many thanks

Emma

Exhibit 3: Vyc Ltd – information from client files

Vyc Ltd is an unquoted manufacturing company, which is registered in the UK. It does not own any assets other than those which are used in its trade.

The shareholders in Vyc Ltd are set out below. The shareholdings have not changed for many years.

	Number of shares
Emma	35,000
Bill (Emma's husband)	19,000
Lily (Emma's Daughter)	10,000
Charlotte (Emma's sister)	20,000
Louis (Charlotte's Husband)	16,000
	100,000

You should use the following values for an ordinary share in Vyc Ltd when carrying out this work.

Shareholding	Value per share £
Up to 25%	10
26% to 50%	13
51% to 74%	19
More than 75%	22

On 1 October 2021, Emma made a cash gift to her daughter, Lily. This resulted in a transfer of value after deduction of exemptions of £280,000. This is the only gift Emma has made. When explaining the maximum inheritance tax (IHT) liability, you should focus on the date on which Emma's future death may occur and the availability of business property relief.

Exhibit 4: Email from your manager – work to be carried out

Forti Ltd group

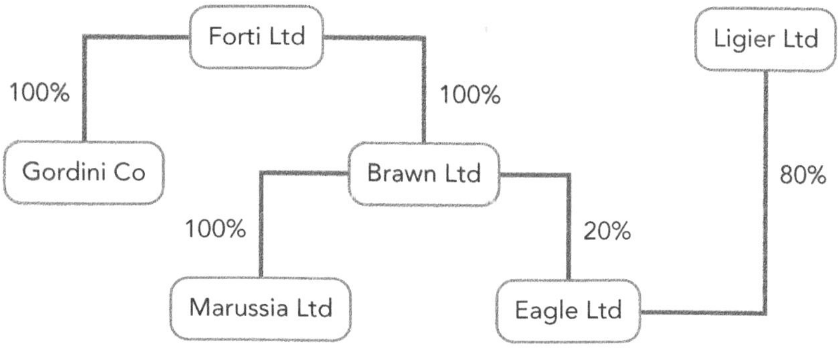

Forti Ltd has an issued share capital of 120,000 ordinary shares. It is owned by 12 shareholders, each of whom owns 10,000 ordinary shares.

All six of the companies are trading companies. Gordini Co is resident in and trades in the country of Arrowsia; it does not carry out any activities in the UK. The other five companies are all resident in the UK. There is no double tax treaty between Arrowsia and the UK.

The only changes to the group structure in recent years relate to the purchase and subsequent sale of Marussia Ltd as set out in Note 3 to the attached schedule.

Ligier Ltd has no links to the Forti Ltd group other than its shareholding in Eagle Ltd.

Please can you set out some notes for me in preparation for a forthcoming meeting with Forti Ltd and Emma which covers the following matters:

(a) **Brawn Ltd – Review of the corporation tax computation**

I attach a schedule detailing the corporation tax computation for Brawn Ltd for the year ended 31 March 2025. This schedule has been prepared by an inexperienced tax assistant.

I can confirm that the substantial shareholding exemption is not available and that the figures given for the indexed cost of Marussia Ltd in the schedule, the degrouping charge in note 3, and the tax adjusted trading losses referred to in notes 4 and 5 have all been calculated correctly.

Review the computation and related notes in order to identify any errors and prepare a revised schedule showing calculations of the correct taxable total profits and the corporation tax liability. You should include notes explaining the errors you have identified and the changes you have made.

Note. Ignore value added tax (VAT). **(12 marks)**

(b) **Other corporate matters**

(i) Brawn Ltd will only be a close company if Forti Ltd is a close company. Set out the matters which need to be considered in order to determine whether or not Forti Ltd is a close company. **(5 marks)**

(ii) Set out the matters which need to be considered in connection with the sale of components to Gordini Co referred to in note 6 to the schedule. **(3 marks)**

(c) **Value added tax (VAT) annual accounting scheme**

The management of the Forti Ltd group have asked for advice on the annual accounting scheme.

State the conditions which must be satisfied by any company wishing to operate the annual accounting scheme and explain the operation of the scheme. **(5 marks)**

(d) **Emma's gift of the Vyc Ltd shares**

Prepare notes allowing us to answer Emma's queries set out in her email to us. I've provided some background information on Vyc Ltd that you might need from our client files. **(10 marks)**

(e) **Emma's potential gains**

Explain the implications for Emma, and our firm, if Emma fails to report her gains to HM Revenue & Customs. **(5 marks)**

2 Hahn Ltd group (Sep/Dec 2016, amended) (98 mins)

You should assume that today's date is 1 September 2025.

Your manager has had a meeting with Sophie Rogers, the finance director of Hahn Ltd. Both Sophie and Hahn Ltd are clients of your firm.

Sophie would like some advice in respect of:

- Some corporate tax issues in relation to Frit Ltd regarding rollover relief, group use of a trading loss, corporation tax payments and related payment dates;
- Group VAT registration;
- A VAT refund; and
- Inheritance tax.

The following exhibits provide information relevant to the question:

(1) Extracts from a memorandum following a meeting with Hahn Ltd;

(2) Email from Sophie regarding her inheritance; and

(3) Email from your manager – work to be carried out.

This information should be used to answer the question **requirements** within your chosen **response option(s)**.

Required

You should assume that today's date is 1 September 2025.

Respond to the instructions in the email from your manager.

Note. The split of the mark allocation is shown in Exhibit 3 – Email from your manager. **(40 marks)**

Professional marks will be awarded for the demonstration of skill in communication, analysis & evaluation, scepticism and commercial acumen in your answer.

(10 marks)

(Total = 50 marks)

Exhibit 1: Extracts from the memorandum – dated 1 September 2025

Hahn Ltd group

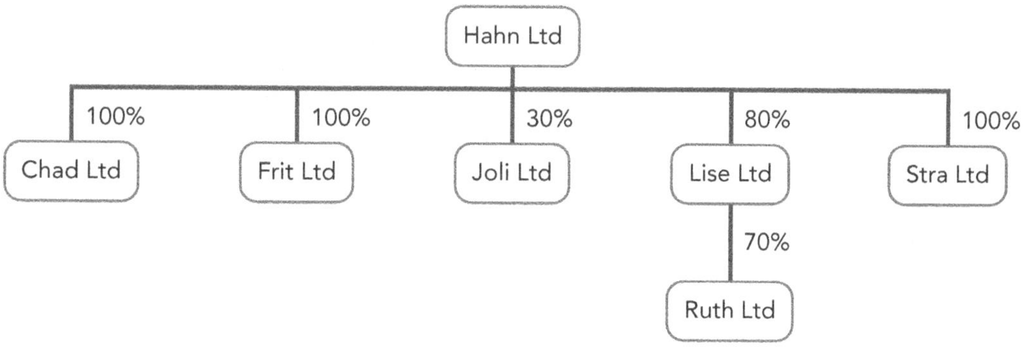

Notes.

1 All of the companies are UK resident trading companies with a year end of 31 March.

2 All of the companies are registered for the purposes of value added tax (VAT).

3 With the exception of Chad Ltd, all of the companies have been members of the Hahn Ltd group for many years.

4 Hahn Ltd has today purchased Chad Ltd from Zeno Ltd. Prior to its disposal to Hahn Ltd, Zeno Ltd had owned Chad Ltd, and six other wholly-owned subsidiaries, for many years.

5 Joli Ltd is not a consortium company.

Budgeted results for the year ending 31 March 2026

	Hahn Ltd	Chad Ltd	Frit Ltd	Joli Ltd	Lise Ltd	Ruth Ltd	Stra Ltd
	£'000	£'000	£'000	£'000	£'000	£'000	£'000
Tax adjusted trading profit/ (loss)	180	675	(540)	410	375	320	38
Chargeable gains	–	–	65	–	–	–	–
Trading loss brought forward	–	–	–	–	–	–	28
Capital loss brought forward	–	–	31	–	–	–	–
Assets purchased which qualify for rollover relief	–	–	14	–	–	6	10

Notes.

1 The budgeted results include £94,000 of sales made by Hahn Ltd to Stra Ltd. The arm's length price of these sales would be £104,000. Both of these figures are exclusive of VAT. No tax adjustments have been made in respect of these sales. The Hahn Ltd group is a large group for the purposes of the transfer pricing rules.

2 Frit Ltd's chargeable gain will be in respect of the sale of a building to an unconnected third party for £125,000. The building is a qualifying business asset for the purposes of rollover relief.

3 None of the companies will receive any dividends in the year ending 31 March 2026.

4 Frit Ltd will not be able to carry its loss back to the year ended 31 March 2025.

5 All of the companies, with the exception of Frit Ltd and Stra Ltd, were required to pay their corporation tax liabilities for the year ended 31 March 2025 by instalments.

VAT

(1) The Hahn Ltd group is considering registering as a VAT group. Frit Ltd makes some exempt supplies, such that it is a partially exempt company. The other six companies all make standard rated supplies only. Stra Ltd uses both the annual accounting scheme and the cash accounting scheme.

(2) Today, Chad Ltd received a refund of VAT from HM Revenue & Customs (HMRC). The company has not been able to identify any reason for this refund.

Exhibit 2: Email from Sophie regarding her inheritance – dated 1 September 2025

To: Manager
From: Sophie Rogers
Date: 1 September 2025
Subject: Inheritance from my mother

Sadly my mother died on 31 July 2025. She left the whole of her estate, with the exception of a gift to charity, to me. I attach a computation of the inheritance tax due which I have prepared but I recognise that this is not an area that I am confident with. I'd be most grateful if you could review my calculation and let me know what you think?

Thanks

Sophie

Mother's lifetime gift

	£
1 June 2021 – Gift of cash to Sophie	30,000

Mother's chargeable estate at death on 31 July 2025

	£	£
Freehold property – Mother's main residence		530,000
UK quoted shares		400,000
Chattels – furniture, paintings and jewellery	40,000	
Less items individually worth less than £6,000	(25,000)	
		15,000
Cash		20,000
		965,000
Less gift to charity		(70,000)
Annual exemption		(3,000)
Chargeable estate		892,000
Less nil rate band	325,000	
Gift in the 7 years prior to death (£30,000 – £6,000)	(24,000)	
		(301,000)
		591,000
Inheritance tax (£591,000 × 40%)		236,400

Exhibit 3: Email from your manager – work to be carried out

Please prepare a memorandum for the client files which addresses the following issues:

(a) **Frit Ltd**

(i) **Chargeable gain of Frit Ltd**

Calculate the additional amount which would need to be spent on assets qualifying for rollover relief, such that the unrelieved gain would be fully covered by Frit Ltd's brought forward capital loss. **(3 marks)**

(ii) **Relieving the trading loss of Frit Ltd**

(1) Prepare explanations, together with supporting calculations, to show how the trading loss of Frit Ltd should be allocated between the companies in the group. The group's priority is its cash flow position and the need to minimise the corporation tax payable by instalments.

When preparing these calculations, you should assume that the whole of the chargeable gain of Frit Ltd will be relieved by rollover relief.

(2) Prepare a schedule setting out the amounts of corporation tax payable by Hahn Ltd, and the companies it controls (ie not Joli Ltd) in respect of the year ending 31 March 2026, together with the related payment dates.

(19 marks)

(b) **Group registration for the purposes of VAT**

By reference to the specific information in my memorandum only, set out the matters which will need to be considered when deciding which of the companies should be included in a group registration **(5 marks)**

(c) **Chad Ltd – refund of VAT**

Prepare a summary of the actions which we should take, and any matters of which Chad Ltd should be aware, in respect of the refund of VAT. **(5 marks)**

(d) **Sophie – Inheritance tax**

Finally, could you prepare some notes for me for a call with Sophie to discuss her inheritance tax calculation? I've got a junior to check and I can confirm that all of the arithmetic, dates and valuations are correct. In addition, there were no other lifetime gifts, and none of the assets qualified for business property relief.

I'd like you to review the computation and identify any errors. You should explain each of the errors you find and calculate the value of the inheritance which Sophie will receive after inheritance tax has been paid. **(8 marks)**

Thanks,

Tax manager

3 Heyer Plc group (Mar/Jun 2017, amended) (98 mins)

You should assume that today's date is 1 June 2025.

Your manager has asked you to take charge of some work in connection with the Heyer plc group of companies. The Finance Director of Heyer plc has also introduced your firm to Farina and Lauda, potential new clients, who are partners in the FL Partnership.

In addition to some ethical considerations about becoming tax advisers to Farina and Lauda, advice is required on:

- Corporate group planning
- Group restructuring
- Capital allowances for the PL Partnership and whether Lauda should disclaim incorporation relief.

The following Exhibits are set out below:

(1) Heyer Plc group – schedule of information from the client files

(2) FL Partnership – notes from a telephone call with Farina and Lauda

(3) Email from your manager – work to be carried out

This information should be used to answer the question **requirements** within your chosen **response option(s)**.

Required

You should assume that today's date is 1 June 2025.

Respond to the instructions in the email from your manager.

Note. The split of the mark allocation is shown in Exhibit 3 – Email from your manager. **(40 marks)**

Professional marks will be awarded for the demonstration of skill in communication, analysis & evaluation, scepticism and commercial acumen in your answer. **(10 marks)**

(Total = 50 marks)

Exhibit 1: Heyer Plc group – schedule of information from the client files

Group structure

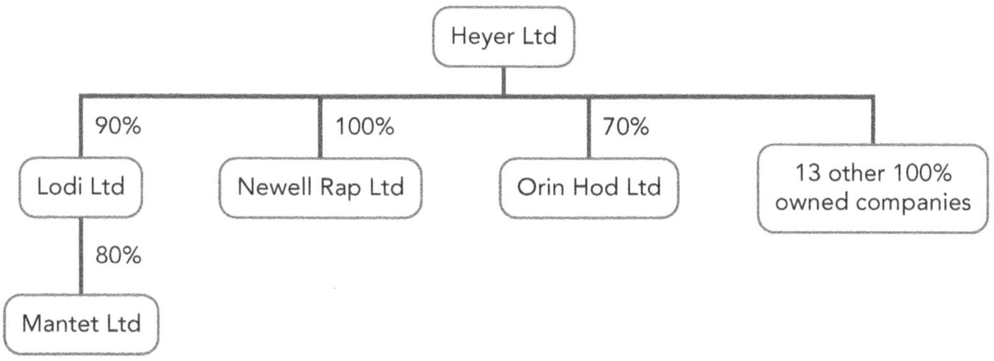

General information

- All of the companies are resident in the UK and prepare accounts to 31 March each year. Heyer Plc is a quoted trading company.
- The figures given below of taxable total profits (TTP) take account of all possible rollover relief claims.
- None of the companies has received any dividend income from non-group companies.

Specific information

Mantet Ltd

- Mantet Ltd has TTP of between £40,000 and £50,000 every year which include substantial chargeable gains.

Newell Rap Ltd

- Heyer Ltd acquired Newell Rap Ltd on 1 August 2024.
- Newell Rap Ltd has a capital loss brought forward as at April 2025 of £94,000. This loss arose on a sale of land on 1 May 2022.

Orin Hod Ltd

- The TTP of Orin Hod Ltd exceed £200,000 every year.
- In the year ending 31 March 2026 Orin Hod Ltd will make chargeable gains of £86,000.

Other 100% owned companies

- Each of these companies has TTP of more than £130,000 every year.
- Four of them will have substantial chargeable gains in the year ending 31 March 2026.
- Five of them will have capital losses in the year ending 31 March 2026.

Group restructuring

- It is intended that the trade and assets of five group companies (Newell Rap Ltd and four of the other 100% owned companies) will be sold to Lodi Ltd at some point in April 2026.
- The assets of the five companies, including the business premises, machinery and equipment will be sold to Lodi Ltd for their market value.
- The tax written down value of the main pool of each of the five companies immediately prior to the sale will be zero.

Exhibit 2: FL Partnership – notes from a telephone call with Farina and Lauda

Background

Farina and Lauda began trading as the FL Partnership on 1 May 2016. Accounts have always been prepared to 31 March each year. They are each entitled to 50% of the revenue profits and capital profits of the business.

On 1 March 2026, the whole of the FL Partnership business will be sold as a going concern to Heyer plc. The consideration for the sale will be a mixture of cash and shares. Capital gains tax relief on the transfer of a business to a company (incorporation relief) will be available in respect of the sale. The partnership's current financial adviser has told them that they should definitely claim incorporation relief.

Farina and Lauda will both pay income tax at the additional rate in the tax year 2025/26 and anticipate continuing to do so in future years. They are very wealthy individuals, who use their capital gains tax annual exempt amounts every year. Both of them are resident and domiciled in the UK.

The sale of the business on 1 March 2026

The assets of the FL Partnership business have been valued as set out below. All of the equipment qualified for capital allowances.

	Value	Cost
	£	£
Goodwill	1,300,000	Nil
Inventory and receivables	30,000	30,000
Equipment (no item to be sold for more than cost)	150,000	200,000
Total	1,480,000	

The total value of the consideration will be equal to the value of the assets sold. Farina and Lauda will **each** receive consideration of £740,000; £140,000 in cash and 200,000 shares in Heyer plc. Following the purchase of the FL Partnership, Heyer plc will have an issued share capital of 8,400,000 shares.

Future transactions

Lauda:

On 1 June 2027, Lauda will give 40,000 of her shares in Heyer plc to her son.

For the purposes of giving our advice, the value of a share in Heyer plc can be assumed to be:

	£
On 1 March 2026	3
On 1 June 2027	5

Exhibit 3: Email from your manager – work to be carried out

Please carry out the following work by producing notes for use in a forthcoming internal meeting:

(a) **Heyer Group planning**

The Heyer Group's objective is to minimise the amount of corporation tax payable by group companies in respect of the year ended 31 March 2026.

I have asked Cox, our tax assistant, to carry out this work and I have provided him with the details of the companies' budgeted results for 2026. There is no group relief available within the group.

Cox has not done this type of work before and he has had very little experience of capital gains groups, so I want you to prepare some guidance for him. The guidance should consist of explanations of:

(1) The circumstances which impact the rate of corporation tax paid by a company and its requirement to pay corporation tax by instalments, assuming that the profits threshold should be divided by 18.

(2) Which companies are members of a capital gains group;

(3) How Cox should determine the amount of chargeable gains and capital losses to transfer between the group companies in order to achieve the group's objective; and

(4) The relevance to the group's objective of the specific information provided in the schedule of information.

(11 marks)

(b) **Group restructuring**

Identify, with reasons, the implications of the proposed group restructuring in relation to chargeable gains, stamp duty land tax and capital allowances, and what will happen to any capital losses belonging to the five companies whose trade and assets are transferred.

(4 marks)

(c) **FL partnership**

(i) **Capital allowances**

A **detailed** explanation of the calculation of the capital allowances of the FL Partnership for its final trading period ending with the sale of its equipment to Heyer plc for £150,000 on 1 March 2026. **(5 marks)**

(ii) **Lauda**

A review of whether or not Lauda should disclaim incorporation relief.

The review should encompass the sale of the FL Partnership business, the gift of the shares to Lauda's son and the effect of incorporation relief on the base cost of the remaining shares owned by Lauda, as she intends to sell all of her shares in Heyer plc in the next few years.

It is important that you include a summary of your calculations and a statement of the key issues for me to discuss with Lauda. You should also include brief explanations of the amount of incorporation relief available, the availability of any additional or alternative reliefs, and the date(s) on which any capital gains tax will be payable. **(15 marks)**

(d) **Becoming tax advisers to Farina and Lauda**

It is anticipated that Farina and Lauda will require some highly sophisticated and specialised tax planning work in the future.

Prepare a summary of the information which would be required, together with any action(s) which should be taken by the firm before it agrees to become the tax advisers to Farina and Lauda. **(5 marks)**

Tax manager

4 Pippin (Mar/Jun 2017, amended) (98 mins)

You should assume that today's date is 1 June 2025.

Your manager has sent you the notes she prepared following meetings with Pippin and his partner, Florina. Pippin and Florina have been living together since 2003 but are not married. Both are established clients of your firm who are resident and domiciled in the UK.

Pippin would like advice in relation to the funds he will require during the first 20-month period of setting up a new business, advice in relation to a recent inheritance and advice on the sale of some shares.

Florina would like advice in relation to whether her company would be better to pay her a pension fund contribution rather than a dividend and in relation to whether her company should provide private fuel to her and Pippin.

The following exhibits provide information relevant to the question:

(1) Meeting notes re Pippin from your manager

(2) Meeting notes re Florina from your manager

(3) Extract from an email from your manager – work to be carried out.

This information should be used to answer the question **requirements** within your chosen **response option(s)**.

Required

You should assume that today's date is 1 June 2025.

Carry out the work requested in the email from your manager.

Note. The split of the mark allocation is shown in Exhibit 3 – Extract of an email from your manager. **(40 marks)**

Professional marks will be awarded for the demonstration of skill in communication, analysis & evaluation, scepticism and commercial acumen in your answer. **(10 marks)**

(Total = 50 marks)

Exhibit 1: Meeting notes re Pippin from your manager

Commencement of 'Pinova' business

Pippin intends to start a new unincorporated business, 'Pinova', on 1 August 2025. He has identified two alternative strategies: strategy A and strategy B.

The budgeted tax-adjusted profit/(loss) of the two strategies are set out below. These figures are before the adjustments necessary in respect of the equipment purchases and employment costs (see below).

	Strategy A		Strategy B	
	2025/26	2026/27 and future years	2025/26	2026/27 and future years
	£	£	£	£
Profit/ (loss)	13,000	60,000	(10,000)	130,000

Equipment purchases and employment costs

The above profit/loss figures need to be adjusted in respect of the following:

(1) Both strategies will require Pippin to purchase equipment in August 2025 for £8,000.

(2) Strategy B will require two employees from 1 April 2026. Pippin will pay each of them a gross salary of £2,500 per month. He will also pay them £0.50 per business mile for driving their own cars. He expects each of them to drive 250 business miles per month.

(3) Strategy A will not require any employees.

Pippin will claim the maximum capital allowances available to him. He will also claim opening years loss relief in respect of the trading loss arising under strategy B.

Cessation of previous business

Pippin's previous unincorporated business ceased trading on 31 December 2024. The taxable profits of the business for its final three tax years were:

	£
2022/23	82,000
2023/24	78,000
2024/25	14,000

Pippin had no other taxable income during these three years.

Receipt of £75,000

Pippin's aunt, Esme, died on 31 January 2025.

On 1 September 2019, Esme's father (Pippin's grandfather) died leaving the whole of his estate to Esme. However, on 1 January 2020 Pippin received £75,000 but cannot remember whether the money came from Esme, personally, or from his grandfather's estate, under a variation of Esme's interest in the will.

On 1 November 2019, Esme had transferred cash of £375,000 to a trust for the benefit of her children.

Shares in Akero Ltd

Pippin owns 16,000 shares in Akero Ltd which have a current market value of £4.50 per share. Pippin subscribed £16,000 for these shares on 4 January 2023. Pippin obtained income tax relief of £4,800 (£16,000 ×30%) under the enterprise investment scheme (EIS) in the tax year 2022/23. He also claimed EIS deferral relief in that year of £16,000 in relation to a chargeable gain on the sale of a painting.

Pippin is considering selling 5,000 of his Akero Ltd shares in order to fund his personal expenditure during the start-up phase of the Pinova business.

Exhibit 2: Meeting notes re Florina from your manager

Florina

Florina is a director of and shareholder in Flight Hip Ltd. She earns an annual salary of £50,270 and receives a dividend of £20,000 from the company every year. She received total taxable benefits of £25,000 from the company in the tax year 2024/25. Flight Hip Ltd is not a close company.

Florina's benefits include a company car together with free petrol for both business and private use. The car's benefit percentage by reference to its CO_2 emissions is 26%. Florina drives 19,000 miles per year of which 1,000 miles are in the performance of her employment duties. The total cost of all of the petrol used by Florina in the tax year 2024/25 was £4,000.

Florina's only other income consists of dividends of £500 received in June every year from Landing Properties Ltd. Landing Properties Ltd is an unquoted UK resident company, unrelated to Flight Hip Ltd.

Pippin

Although Pippin is not employed by Flight Hip Ltd, the company provides him with a car and free petrol. The car's benefit percentage by reference to its CO_2 emissions is 23%. Pippin drives 5,000 miles per year; the total cost of the petrol used by Pippin in the tax year 2024/25 was £800.

Exhibit 3: Extract from an email from your manager – work to be carried out

Please prepare a memorandum for Pippin's client files which addresses the following issues:

(a) **Additional funds required for the 20-month period from 1 August 2025 to 31 March 2027**

Pippin's taxable income will consist of the profits of the Pinova business and, for the tax year 2025/26 onwards, he expects to receive dividend income of £500 per year. His personal expenditure is £4,000 per month.

I want you to complete the table below to calculate the additional funds which Pippin would require during the first 20 months of the business under each of the two strategies (A and B) after putting aside sufficient funds to settle his tax liabilities for the tax years 2025/26 and 2026/27. You should then evaluate the two strategies by reference to the results of your calculations.

Pippin and I calculated his total **pre-tax** cash receipts; you do not need to check them. The only adjustment required to these pre-tax cash receipts is the cost of employing the two employees. Also, please assume current year rates and allowances apply to all years in your calculations.

	Strategy A	Strategy B
	£	£
Total pre-tax cash receipts for the 20-month period	61,000	109,500
Cost of employing the two employees	Nil	(____)
Pippin's total income tax and national insurance contribution liabilities for the tax years 2025/26 and 2026/27	________	________
Personal expenditure (£4,000 × 20)	(80,000)	(80,000)
Additional funds required	________	________

(21 marks)

(b) **Receipt of £75,000**

Explain, with supporting calculations, the inheritance tax implications for Pippin of the receipt of the £75,000. **(5 marks)**

(c) **Sale of shares in Akero Ltd**

Explain the tax liabilities which would result if Pippin were to sell 5,000 of his Akero Ltd shares in the tax year 2025/26. **(6 marks)**

(d) Also prepare a memorandum for Florina's client files which addresses the following issues:

(1) **Florina's remuneration from Flight Hip Ltd**

Calculate the total tax saving which could be achieved by Florina and Flight Hip Ltd if, in the tax year 2025/26, the company were to make a single lump sum payment of £20,000 into a personal pension fund for Florina instead of paying her a dividend of £20,000. These calculations should take account of the tax which Florina will pay when she eventually withdraws the £20,000 from the pension fund.

You should assume that:

(i) there will be no further contributions into the fund in future years

(ii) Florina will be a basic rate taxpayer when she makes a withdrawal from the fund

(iii) Flight Hip Ltd makes sufficient profits that it pays main rate corporation tax

(2) **Provision of free petrol**

By comparing the income tax due in respect of the petrol with the value of the petrol received, determine whether Florina and Pippin would be better off if:

(i) Florina were to reimburse Flight Hip Ltd for the cost of the petrol used by her for private purposes; and/or

(ii) Flight Hip Ltd were to stop providing Pippin with free petrol.

(8 marks)

Tax manager

5 Harrow Tan Ltd group (Sep/Dec 2017, amended) (98 mins)

You should assume that today's date is 1 September 2025.

Your manager has sent you a memorandum in relation to the Harrow Tan Ltd group, a client of your firm. Advice is required in relation to:

- The corporation tax consequences on the sale of shares in a subsidiary company
- Group relief
- Rollover relief
- Various VAT issues; and
- Some ethical iderations.

The following exhibits provide information relevant to the question:

(1) Memorandum from your manager – work to be carried out

(2) Schedule of group information – from Corella, the group finance director

This information should be used to answer the question **requirements** within your chosen **response option(s)**.

Required

You should assume that today's date is 1 September 2025.

Carry out the work requested in the memorandum from your manager.

Note. The split of the mark allocation is shown in Exhibit 1 – Memorandum from your manager.

(40 marks)

Professional marks will be awarded for the demonstration of skill in communication, analysis & evaluation, scepticism and commercial acumen in your answer. **(10 marks)**

(Total = 50 marks)

Exhibit 1: Memorandum from your manager – work to be carried out

Background

- We are advising Corella, the group finance director, on a number of matters. I've attached a schedule from Corella, which sets out much of the relevant information.
- Corella was only recently appointed the Harrow Tan Ltd group finance director. She has had very little experience of practical tax since qualifying as an accountant in 1994. I have carried out a brief review of Corella's schedule and concluded that it is mathematically correct but that we cannot rely on its tax technical content.
- All five group companies are UK resident trading companies which prepare accounts to 31 December each year.

Sale of shares in Rocha Ltd

Harrow Tan Ltd acquired the whole of the ordinary share capital of Rocha Ltd (100,000 shares) on 1 December 2024 for £8,900,000.

On 1 January 2025, Seckel Ltd (owned 80% by Harrow Tan Ltd) sold a commercial building situated in England to Rocha Ltd for £800,000, its market value on that date. The group claimed exemption from stamp duty land tax in respect of this transaction. Seckel Ltd had purchased the building on 1 May 2000 at a cost of £330,000.

However, the results of Rocha Ltd for the year ending 31 December 2025 are now expected to be significantly worse than originally budgeted and an agreement was signed on 31 July 2025 for Harrow Tan Ltd to sell 60,000 Rocha Ltd ordinary shares for £10,300,000. It is planned that the sale of these shares will take place on 1 October 2025, although the sale could be delayed by up to three months if necessary.

Tosca Ltd – promotion of new product

Tosca Ltd manufactures high quality glass bowls. It accounts for value added tax (VAT) using the annual accounting scheme.

Tosca Ltd has developed a new product, which is expected to increase the company's annual turnover from £1,200,000 to £2,000,000. The new product is to be marketed to the company's customers, all of whom are UK based retailers, via promotional evenings in various parts of the UK. They are also hoping to obtain contracts with a national hotel chain and have asked us to help. One of our clients is a different national hotel chain and an ex-client of ours provided services to a number of hotel chains. Accordingly, we have knowledge and experience in this area.

At the promotional evenings the retailers will be provided with a meal. They will also be given a sample of the new product costing approximately £90, and a pen costing £40.

Tosca Ltd intend to hire two new salespeople to help market the new product. Their proposed contractual arrangements given in part D of the schedule from Corella.

Please prepare notes for us to use in a meeting with Corella, which EXPLAIN the following matters:

(a) **Sale of shares in Rocha Ltd**

- The error(s) and omission(s) in part A of Corella's schedule together with any tax saving opportunities or other matters, including stamp duty land tax, which are not addressed in part A of her schedule. Please include a corrected calculation of the taxable gain on the sale on the assumption that it occurs on 1 October 2025.
- Take some time to think about this. From my brief review I think there may be three or four issues which need to be brought to Corella's attention.

Note. The following indexation factor should be used where applicable:

May 2000 to December 2017: 0.629

(13 marks)

(b) **Group relief – year ending 31 December 2025**

By reference to the information in part B of Corella's schedule, the maximum amount of Seckel Ltd's trading loss which can be surrendered to each of the other companies in the Harrow Tan Ltd group. **(6 marks)**

(c) **Rollover relief**

The rollover relief potentially available to the group and the accuracy of part C of Corella's schedule.

(7 marks)

(d) **Tosca Ltd – promotion of new product**

- The VAT implications of:
  - the expected increase in the turnover of Tosca Ltd; and
  - the entertainment and gifts at the promotional evenings
- Which of the proposed contractual arrangements with the salespeople indicate that they would be self-employed and state any changes which should be made to the other arrangements in order to maximise the likelihood of the salespeople being treated as self-employed.

(9 marks)

(e) The extent to which it is acceptable for us to use the knowledge we have gained in respect of our existing client and ex-client to assist Tosca Ltd. **(5 marks)**

Exhibit 2: Schedule of group information – from Corella, the group finance director

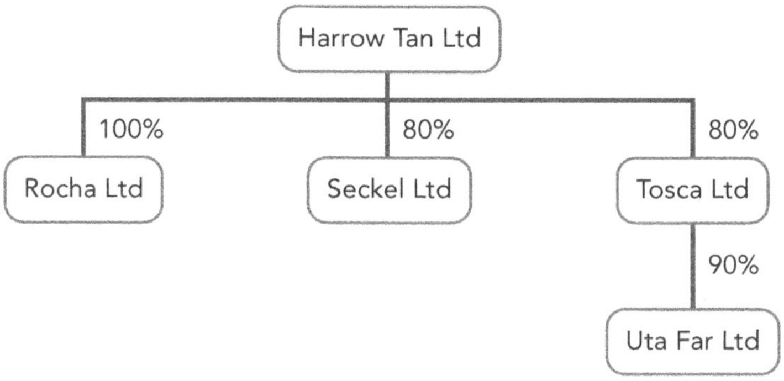

A: Taxable gain on the sale of shares in Rocha Ltd

	£
Sale proceeds	10,300,000
Less: Cost (£8,900,000 × 60%)	(5,340,000)
Chargeable gain	4,960,000
Rollover relief (analysed below)	(1,350,000)
Taxable gain	3,610,000

B: Budgeted results for the year ending 31 December 2025

	Harrow Tan Ltd	Rocha Ltd	Seckel Ltd	Tosca Ltd	Uta Far Ltd
	£	£	£	£	£
Trading profit/(loss)	40,000	60,000	(180,000)	70,000	600,000
Chargeable gains	Note 1	–	–	–	Note 2

Notes.

1 Disposal of shares in Rocha Ltd.

2 Uta Far Ltd sold a building used in its business on 1 May 2025 for £1,800,000. This resulted in a chargeable gain of £85,000.

C: Harrow Tan Ltd – Acquisitions in the year ending 31 December 2025 qualifying for rollover relief

	£
New factory, to be used in carrying on the company's business, consisting of:	
– Land	410,000
– Building	370,000
Total cost of factory	780,000
Machinery	430,000
Patents and trademarks	140,000
Total qualifying additions	1,350,000

D: Proposed contact with salespeople

Tosca Ltd is proposing to enter into the following contractual arrangements with two part-time salespeople:

- They will work on Tuesday and Wednesday mornings each week for a two-month period.
- They will be paid a fee of £300 for each new sales contract obtained. No other payments will be made.
- They will use their own cars.
- The company will lend each of them a laptop computer.

6 Snowdon (Mar/Jun 2018, amended) (98 mins)

You should assume that today's date is 1 June 2025.

Your manager has had a meeting with Snowdon, a potential new client. Snowdon's wife, Daisy, is the acting finance director of the Set Ltd group of companies which are also clients of your firm.

Snowdon would like advice in respect of a cottage he purchased from his sister, Coleen, and his unincorporated business, 'Siabod', which he started on 1 July 2012.

The usual finance director of the Set Ltd group of companies has become seriously ill and Daisy is standing in for her. Daisy would like some assistance with the corporation tax instalment payments to be paid from now until 31 December 2025.

The following exhibits provide information relevant to the question:

(1) Extracts from memorandum prepared by your manager following a meeting with Snowdon

(2) An inheritance tax computation prepared by Snowdon

(3) Background information on the Set Ltd group of companies

(4) An email from Daisy regarding the Set Ltd group of companies

(5) An email from your manager detailing the work you are required to do

This information should be used to answer the question **requirements** within your chosen **response option(s)**.

Required

You should assume that today's date is 1 June 2025.

Prepare the memorandum and email as requested in the email from your manager.

Note. The split of the mark allocation is shown in Exhibit 1 – Memorandum from your manager.
(40 marks)

Professional marks will be awarded for the demonstration of skill in communication, analysis & evaluation, scepticism and commercial acumen in your answer. **(10 marks)**

(Total = 50 marks)

Exhibit 1: Extracts from the memorandum prepared by your manager – dated 1 June 2025

Snowdon is resident and domiciled in the UK. He requires advice in respect of a cottage he purchased from his sister, Coleen, and his unincorporated business, 'Siabod', which he started on 1 July 2012.

Purchase of the cottage from Coleen

Snowdon's sister, Coleen, died on 1 June 2025.

Coleen had sold a holiday cottage to Snowdon on 1 May 2021 for £225,000. At that time, the cottage was worth £260,000. Coleen had purchased the cottage for £165,000. The cottage qualified for capital gains tax gift holdover relief and Snowdon and Coleen submitted a valid joint claim.

Coleen made a gift to a trust on 1 March 2017. This resulted in a gross chargeable transfer after all exemptions of £318,000.

Snowdon provided me with a computation he had prepared of the inheritance tax due as a result of Coleen's death in respect of the cottage. Snowdon is aware that he is not an expert when it comes to inheritance tax, such that this computation is unlikely to be totally accurate.

Siabod business

Budgeted figures relating to the unexpanded Siabod business for the year ending 31 March 2026 are:

	£
Turnover	255,000
Tax adjusted trading profit	85,000
Income tax on £85,000 using current rates	21,432
Class 4 national insurance contributions on £85,000 using current rates	4,088

The Siabod business is partially exempt for the purposes of value added tax (VAT). Snowdon's budgeted input tax for the unexpanded business for the year ending 31 March 2026 was £18,000. He would have been able to recover the whole of this amount because the business would have been below the *de minimis* limits.

Since the above figures were prepared, Snowdon has decided to expand the Siabod business and increase its budgeted turnover for the year ending 31 March 2026 from £255,000 to £435,000. In order to carry out this expansion, Snowdon will adopt either strategy A or strategy B. Whichever strategy is adopted, the partial exemption percentage of the business will continue to be 76% (recoverable).

Strategy A

Under this strategy Snowdon will recruit an additional employee with an annual salary of £48,000.

Strategy B

Under this strategy Snowdon will appoint a sub-contractor, Tor Ltd, which will carry out the work required for the expansion. Tor Ltd will charge fees of £90,000 plus VAT each year.

Budgeted costs of expanding the business

	Strategy A	Strategy B
	£	£
Salary of additional employee	48,000	N/A
Other expenditure relating to the expansion, net of VAT @20%:		
– Overheads	38,000	N/A
– Advertising	2,000	2,000
Fees payable to Tor Ltd, net of VAT at 20%	N/A	90,000

Additional information

- Prior to the expansion of the Siabod business, Snowdon's liability to employer's class 1 national insurance contributions for the year exceeded £5,000.
- Apart from the profits of the Siabod business, Snowdon's only income is £740 of bank interest each year.

Exhibit 2: Inheritance tax computation prepared by Snowdon – dated 1 June 2025

Inheritance tax due in respect of the cottage

	£
Value of the cottage as at 1 May 2021 (no annual exemption on death)	260,000
Less: taper relief (£260,000 x 40%) (between four and five years)	(104,000)
	156,000
Nil rate band	325,000
Less: gifts in the seven years prior to death	0
Available nil rate band	325,000
Inheritance tax (the gift is fully covered by the available nil rate band)	0

Exhibit 3: Background information on the Set Ltd group of companies

Set Ltd has three wholly owned subsidiaries, Ghost Ltd, Steam Ltd and Wagon Ltd, and also owns shares in a number of other companies. Set Ltd and all of its wholly owned subsidiaries are resident in the UK.

Assume that all of the UK resident companies in the Set Ltd group, including Ghost Ltd, pay main rate corporation tax in instalments every year and will continue to do so, regardless of any loss relief planning entered into.

Exhibit 4: Email from Daisy regarding the Set Ltd group of companies – dated 1 June 2025

Ghost Ltd – corporation tax payments

I'm working on the corporation tax instalment payments which Ghost Ltd will be required to pay in the period from now until 31 December 2025.

Set Ltd will acquire the whole of the ordinary share capital of Ghost Ltd on 1 June 2025. Ghost Ltd had always prepared accounts to 30 April but following its acquisition will change its year end to 31 December in line with all of the other companies in the Set Ltd group.

The finalised corporation tax liability of Ghost Ltd for the year ended 30 April 2025 was £597,500. I am now estimating the company's liability for the eight-month period ending 31 December 2025 so that I can determine the instalment payments required. As part of this work, I need to know if the company's corporation tax liability can be reduced in respect of the following:

- Steam Ltd will sell a building on 1 August 2025, which is expected to result in a loss.
- Wagon Ltd has a trading loss brought forward as at 1 January 2025 of £31,500. It is expected to make a further trading loss in the year ending 31 December 2025.

Please explain:

- How Ghost Ltd could make use of the losses of Steam Ltd and Wagon Ltd in the period ending 31 December 2025. Ghost Ltd has no unused losses brought forward at 1 June 2025.
- The payments of corporation tax which will need to be made by Ghost Ltd in the period starting today, 1 June 2025, and ending on 31 December 2025. For the purpose of this explanation, please assume that Ghost Ltd's corporation tax liability for the eight-month period ending 31 December 2025 is £460,000.

Exhibit 5: Email from your manager – dated 1 June 2025

Please prepare a memorandum for Snowdon's client file covering the following:

(a) **Purchase of the cottage from Coleen**

(i) Identification and explanation of the errors in the inheritance tax (IHT) computation prepared by Snowdon (Exhibit 2), and a calculation of the correct amount of IHT due.

I have already established that the cottage did not qualify for business property relief. **(7 marks)**

(ii) The capital gains tax gift holdover relief claimed by Coleen in respect of the cottage and Snowdon's base cost for the purposes of a future disposal by him (Exhibit 1). **(2 marks)**

(b) **Expansion of the Siabod business (Exhibit 1)**

(i) Calculations to show which of the two strategies is the most financially advantageous, ie the one which is expected to generate the most additional tax adjusted trading profit for the year ending 31 March 2026. **(9 marks)**

(ii) A calculation of the additional budgeted post-tax income for the tax year 2025/26 which is expected to be generated by the most financially advantageous strategy. **(8 marks)**

(c) **Procedures we should follow before we agree to become Snowdon's tax advisers**

A summary of the procedures we should follow before we agree to become Snowdon's tax advisers. **(5 marks)**

(d) Please can you also draft a reply to Daisy's email about Ghost Ltd's corporation tax (Exhibits 3 and 4)? **(9 marks)**

Thanks,

Tax manager

7 Wanda (Dec 2018, amended) (98 mins)

You should assume that today's date is 1 December 2025.

Your manager has had a meeting with Wanda and her mother-in-law Emma, both clients of your firm.

Wanda would like advice in relation to her post-tax inheritance from Lucy. In addition, Wanda intends to set up her own business and would like advice on voluntary registration for VAT, choice of business structure and the tax relief available in respect of a trading loss arising in the first year of trading.

Emma would like advice in relation to whether it would be better from a tax perspective to sell her shares in Potts plc now or on her return to the UK.

The following exhibits provide information relevant to the question:

(1) Extract from a memorandum prepared by your manager

(2) Email from your manager – work to be carried out

This information should be used to answer the question **requirements** within your chosen **response option(s).**

Required

You should assume that today's date is 1 December 2025.

Prepare the notes for use in a meeting with Wanda and Emma as requested in the email from your manager. **(40 marks)**

Professional marks will be awarded for the demonstration of skill in communication, analysis and evaluation, scepticism and commercial acumen in your answer. **(10 marks)**

(Total = 50 marks)

Exhibit 1: Extracts from the memorandum prepared by your manager – dated 1 December 2025

Background

Wanda intends to start a new business, KS, selling children's clothes. This business will be partly financed by an inheritance which Wanda will receive following the recent death of her mother. Wanda's husband, Roth, will also be involved in the business.

Wanda has not been employed since 31 December 2019 and has not received any taxable income since that date. Roth is employed and earns a gross salary of £95,000 per year. This salary is his only source of income. Wanda and Roth have not made any chargeable disposals for the purposes of capital gains tax and will not make any in the tax year 2026/27.

Wanda's inheritances and gift from her parents

On 1 February 2020, Wanda's father, Pavel, died. He left £160,000 to Wanda and the residue of his estate to his wife, Lucy (Wanda's mother). The residue of Pavel's estate was valued at £720,000 and included the family home. Pavel had not made any gifts during his life.

On 1 April 2020, Lucy gave Wanda £180,000 in cash. This was the only lifetime gift Lucy made.

On 1 November 2025, Lucy died. Wanda inherited the whole of Lucy's estate, which was valued at £950,000. The estate consisted of the family home (valued at £440,000), together with furniture, cash and quoted shares (valued in total at £510,000).

Wanda's new business – KS

Wanda intends to begin trading on 1 April 2026. The business will be operated either:

- by Wanda and Roth in partnership; or
- by a limited company owned 70% by Wanda and 30% by Roth.

The turnover of the business for the year ending 31 March 2027 is expected to be £48,000.

Budgeted profitability of KS

In its first year of trading the business will make either a small profit or, possibly, a loss (of no more than £20,000). However, once the business is fully operational, it is budgeted to make a tax adjusted trading profit of £100,000 per year. This figure is before deducting any salaries paid to Wanda and Roth.

The manner in which the profits will be extracted from the business depends on whether the business is operated as a partnership or as a limited company. The two alternatives are summarised below.

	Partnership		Company	
	Wanda	Roth	Wanda	Roth
Salary	£14,000	£0	£42,000	£32,000
Profit share percentage	60%	40%	N/A	N/A
Dividend	N/A	N/A	£14,000	£6,000

In addition to advising her on the tax cost of the alternative business structures, Wanda has asked us to advise her on the relief available in respect of the possible trading loss in the first year of trading.

Emma

Roth's mother Emma is 74 years old and married to Bill. Emma was resident in the UK from 6 April 2002 until she and Bill moved to Falgar on 1 February 2023. On her return to the UK on 1 May 2026, Emma will resume UK residency.

When carrying out this work, you should assume that Emma is a higher rate taxpayer.

Income tax refund

Wanda has received an unexpected refund of income tax from HM Revenue and Customs (HMRC) in respect of the tax year 2018/19.

Exhibit 2: Email from your manager – work to be carried out

Please prepare the following notes and calculations for use in a meeting with Wanda and Emma.

(a) **Wanda's post-tax inheritance from Lucy**

Calculate the amount which Wanda will inherit from Lucy after any inheritance tax has been paid. **(6 marks)**

(b) **Voluntary registration for value added tax (VAT)**

The sale of children's clothes is a zero rated supply for the purposes of VAT. With this is mind, explain:

- why the business would be permitted to register for VAT from 1 April 2026; and
- the advantages and disadvantages of doing so.

(4 marks)

(c) **Choice of business structure**

(i) **Income tax and corporation tax payable**

For a single tax year, calculate the income tax payable by Roth and any corporation tax payable:

- if the business is operated as a partnership; and
- if the business is operated as a company.

Prepare a summary of the total tax payable if Wanda's income tax liabilities are:

Business operated:

- as a partnership: £13,672
- as a company: £8,500

You should assume that:

- the business is fully operational and makes a tax adjusted trading profit of £100,000. This figure is before deducting any salaries paid to Wanda and Roth.
- profits are extracted from the business in accordance with the summary in my memorandum.
- Roth continues to earn his existing gross salary of £95,000 per year.

When carrying out this work, you should **ignore** any national insurance contribution liabilities and any relief available in respect of losses. **(12 marks)**

(ii) **Other matters**

Compare the tax relief available to Wanda and Roth in respect of a trading loss arising in the first year of trading, depending on whether the business is operated as a partnership or as a company. **(4 marks)**

(d) **Sale of shares in Potts plc**

Emma is going to sell her shares in Potts plc, an investment company, which she has owned as an investment since 1 December 2021. She could sell them now, in which case she would realise a chargeable gain of £330,000. Alternatively, if she waits until she is back in the UK, she would be able to increase the selling price by £60,000. She said:

I plan to sell the shares now, for the lower price, as I believe this will mean that no UK capital gains tax will be due. Please explain whether or not this is the best thing to do from a tax perspective. **(9 marks)**

(e) **Income tax refund**

Prepare a summary of the actions which we should take, and the matters of which Wanda should be aware, in relation to the income tax refund. **(5 marks)**

8 Maia (Mar/Jun 2019, amended) (98 mins)

You should assume that today's date is 1 June 2025.

Your manager has had a meeting with Maia, a client of your firm

Advice is required in relation to:

- Additional cash required by Josh
- Maia's plan to gift Josh an investment property to provide financial assistance
- Group relief available on setup of a new wholly-owned subsidiary.
- Implication of an unreported chargeable gain.

The following exhibits provide information relevant to the question:

(1) Extracts from the memorandum prepared by your manager following the meeting – dated 31 May 2025

(2) Email from Maia – dated 31 May 2025

(3) Extract from the email from your manager detailing the work she requires you to do – dated 1 June 2025

This information should be used to answer the question **requirements** within your chosen **response option(s).**

Required

You should assume that today's date is 1 December 2025.

Prepare the memorandum as requested in the email from your manager. **(40 marks)**

Professional marks will be awarded for the demonstration of skill in communication, analysis & evaluation, scepticism and commercial acumen in your answer. **(10 marks)**

(Total = 50 marks)

Exhibit 1: Extracts from the memorandum prepared by your manager – dated 31 May 2025

Maia

Maia is 63 years old and has significant personal wealth. She has taxable income of approximately £120,000 each year, much of which she is able to save. She uses her inheritance tax annual exemption every year, and sold a residential investment property realising a chargeable gain of £15,000 in May 2025. She is resident and domiciled in the UK.

Maia has agreed to provide financial assistance to her nephew, Josh.

Josh – financial position

Josh recently left university and, on 6 April 2025, he started working for NL Ltd, an unquoted company. He earns an annual gross salary of £25,200.

On 1 June 2025, NL Ltd issued 200 £1 ordinary shares to Josh. This share issue was not made as part of a tax-advantaged share scheme. Josh paid £300 for these shares, which had a market value of £2,100 at that time. The shares are not readily convertible assets and Josh is not permitted to sell them until 1 April 2029.

Josh currently receives dividend income of £420 each year. He is resident and domiciled in the UK.

Josh estimates that from 6 April 2025 he needs £2,500 per month to pay his rent and living expenses. Maia has asked us to calculate how much cash Josh will need for the tax years 2025/26 and 2026/27, over and above his post-tax income from all sources.

Providing financial assistance to Josh

Maia is planning to gift Josh an investment property on 1 July 2025 to provide financial assistance.

This investment property is currently worth £370,000.

Maia purchased the property for £130,000 on 1 July 2009. Since its acquisition, this property has been rented out for taxable net rental income of £1,100 per month. It is a residential building, which has been let to long-term tenants. Maia's friend has told her she can say it's furnished holiday accommodation to get tax benefits.

Following the gift, Josh will continue to rent out the property on the same basis from 1 July 2025 onwards.

Exhibit 2: Email from Maia – dated 31 May 2025

To: Tax manager

From: Maia

Date: 31 May 2025

Subject: Plad Ltd and new company, Quil Ltd

Hi

I would like some assistance about a new company which I would like to incorporate, Quil Ltd. I set out information for you about my plans below.

Plad Ltd

I have owned the whole of the ordinary share capital of Plad Ltd since 2007. Plad Ltd trades mainly in the UK and is a UK resident company. It purchases components from third parties to be assembled into finished products. It also has a permanent establishment in the country of Chekka. The profits realised in Chekka are subject to 14% Chekkan business tax. There is no double tax treaty between the UK and the country of Chekka.

The budgeted taxable profits of Plad Ltd for the year ending 30 June 2026 are set out below. Plad Ltd's profitability is very stable, so please assume that the figures for the following year will be the same.

	£
Trading profit in the UK	48,000
Trading profit in the country of Chekka (before deduction of 14% Chekkan tax)	7,000
Taxable total profits	55,000

Quil Ltd

Quil Ltd will be incorporated, registered for value added tax (VAT) and commence trading on 1 July 2025. It will trade in the UK and be a UK resident company.

From a commercial standpoint, my intention was to own Quil Ltd personally. However, if there is a sufficient tax advantage, I will consider establishing the company as a wholly-owned subsidiary of Plad Ltd.

The first two years of budgeted results of Quil Ltd are set out below. The trading profit/(loss) figures are before the deduction of capital allowances, but have otherwise been adjusted for the purposes of corporation tax. The chargeable gain will not qualify for rollover relief.

Year ending 30 June 2026 – trading loss	(£32,922)		
Year ending 30 June 2027 – trading profit	£995,672	chargeable gain	£16,000

On 1 July 2025, Quil Ltd will purchase the following capital assets:

Machinery and equipment	£160,000 (excluding VAT)
Building used for manufacturing and storage	£1,400,000 (excluding VAT)

The cost of the building includes £60,000 for land, £300,000 for construction of a factory and £1,040,000 in respect of thermal insulation and air cooling equipment in order to create the appropriate conditions for manufacturing. Once completed, the building will be brought into use on 1 October 2025.

Plad Ltd – unreported chargeable gain

I have just discovered that a chargeable gain of £21,600 realised by Plad Ltd in the year ended 30 June 2021 was omitted from its corporation tax return. However, because the gain arose in respect of the sale of land, it was reported for the purposes of stamp duty land tax. Accordingly, I assume we do not need to do anything and that HM Revenue and Customs (HMRC) will contact us about this at some point.

I'd appreciate your advice as to ownership of Quil Ltd and also the unreported gain in Plad Ltd.

Best wishes

Maia

Exhibit 3: Extract from the email from your manager – dated 1 June 2025

Please prepare a memorandum for the client files consisting of the work set out below.

(a) **Josh – additional cash requirement**

Calculate the total additional cash required by Josh, over and above his income from all sources, for the tax years 2025/26 and 2026/27, after deducting tax and national insurance contributions (NIC).

In order to prepare the calculations efficiently, you should think about how Josh's taxable income in 2026/27 will differ from that in 2025/26. There is no need to provide any narrative explanation of your calculations. **(8 marks)**

(b) **Providing financial assistance to Josh**

With regard to Maia's plan to gift Josh the investment property, explain:

- The increase in Josh's post-tax income for the 21-month period ending 5 April 2027.

There is no need to consider the capital value of the property as, in the short term, Josh will not realise any of this value.

- The capital gains tax liability FOR MAIA ONLY.
- The inheritance tax implications for Maia and Josh including consideration of the availability of business property relief.

(9 marks)

(c) **Plad Ltd and Quil Ltd**

In order to help Maia make her decision on the ownership of Quil Ltd, advise her of the tax advantage of Quil Ltd being a wholly-owned subsidiary of Plad Ltd, such that the two companies form a group relief group. You should carry out this work in three stages as set out below.

When carrying out this work, you should be aware of the following:

- in the year ending 30 June 2027, the whole of the annual investment allowance will be available to Quil Ltd, and Quil Ltd will claim the maximum capital allowances available;
- neither of the two companies will be required to pay corporation tax in quarterly instalments. This will be true regardless of who owns Quil Ltd.

(i) Explain, with supporting calculations, the maximum amount of group relief which Plad Ltd would need to receive for the year ending 30 June 2026 such that none of its double tax relief in respect of the Chekkan tax would be wasted and its UK corporation tax payable would be £nil. **(4 marks)**

(ii) Prepare calculations of the corporation tax liabilities of the two companies for the two years ending 30 June 2027. Your calculations should be on the basis that the trading loss of Quil Ltd will be used as soon as possible whilst restricting the amount of group relief in an accounting period to the maximum figure you calculated in part (i).

You SHOULD NOT provide any explanations of these calculations. **(11 marks)**

(iii) Conclude by explaining the tax advantage of Quil Ltd becoming a wholly-owned subsidiary of Plad Ltd, as opposed to being owned personally by Maia. **(3 marks)**

(d) **Plad Ltd – unreported chargeable gain**

Explain the implications for Plad Ltd, and our firm, of the failure to report the chargeable gain to HM Revenue and Customs (HMRC). You SHOULD NOT address money laundering or the possibility of penalties, as I have already spoken to Maia about these matters. **(5 marks)**

I look forward to reviewing your memorandum shortly.

Thanks

Tax Manager

9 Nelson (Sep/Dec 2019, amended) (98 mins)

You should assume that today's date is 1 December 2025.

Your manager has received a letter from Nelson, a potential new client, in relation to his unincorporated business and a subsequent email from him regarding a potential gift to his wife. Extracts from the letter and email, and from an email from your manager detailing the work he requires you to do, are set out below.

The following exhibits provide information relevant to the question:

(1) Extracts from the letter from Nelson – dated 30 November 2025

(2) Extract from subsequent email from Nelson

(3) Extract from the email from your manager – dated 1 December 2025

This information should be used to answer the question **requirements** within your chosen **response option(s).**

Required

You should assume that today's date is 1 December 2025.

Prepare the memorandum as requested in the email from your manager. **(40 marks)**

Professional marks will be awarded for the demonstration of skill in communication, analysis & evaluation, scepticism and commercial acumen in your answer. **(10 marks)**

(Total = 50 marks)

Exhibit 1: Extracts from the letter from Nelson – dated 30 November 2025

Background

I was employed from 1 May 2020 until I was made redundant on 28 February 2024. My gross annual salary was £80,000.

Just over a year later, on 1 June 2025, I began trading as an unincorporated business preparing accounts to 30 April each year. My tax adviser advised me to trade as an unincorporated business because it was expected that I would make a tax adjusted trading loss for my first tax year 2025/26. However, due to the speed with which the business has grown, the forecast for 2025/26 now shows a budgeted tax adjusted trading profit of £70,500.

Transfer of my business to NQA Ltd

In the future, I expect sales to be generated mainly from overseas customers, possibly via companies incorporated and trading outside the UK. In view of this, it has become clear to me that I need to be operating the business through a limited company.

Accordingly, I intend to incorporate my business by transferring its trade and assets to a new unquoted company, NQA Ltd, in exchange for ordinary shares. I will own the whole of the ordinary share capital of NQA Ltd and, for the time being, I will be its only director and employee. This incorporation will take place on 1 May 2026.

I will realise chargeable gains of £45,000 in respect of the goodwill of the business and £30,000 in respect of the Arch building (which I use as my business premises). I understand from our discussions that these gains will not be subject to capital gains tax due to the relief available when a business is transferred to a company in exchange for shares.

Other information

- Since 1 March 2024, I have had no source of income other than my unincorporated business.
- In the tax year 2025/26, I will not make any disposals for the purposes of capital gains tax other than the sale of my business to NQA Ltd.

Advice required

(1) I am trying to determine whether or not I should have been advised to begin trading through a limited company from 1 June 2025 rather than as an unincorporated business.

I would like to know if I will pay more tax as a result of the advice I was given. I would also like to understand the relevance of the expected trading loss in the first trading period together with any other reasons my existing tax adviser might have had for advising me to begin trading as an unincorporated business rather than through a limited company. I'd prefer you didn't contact my existing advisers as I can give you any information you might need relating to my previous tax returns.

(2) Ideally, I would prefer to retain personal ownership of the Arch building when I incorporate my business, rather than transfer it to NQA Ltd. However, this will depend on how it affects my capital gains tax position.

(3) Once NQA Ltd has begun trading, I would like to be able to borrow any excess funds in the company for my personal use. I would then repay the loan as and when I can afford to. I appreciate there may be an employment income benefit in respect of this.

(4) One of my customers has gone into liquidation, and I do not expect to be able to recover any part of the outstanding debt.

(i) Does this mean that the value added tax (VAT) which I have already paid to HM Revenue and Customs (HMRC) in respect of this sale is lost?

(ii) Am I correct in thinking that, if I had used the cash accounting scheme for VAT, I would not have had this particular problem, and that my cash flow generally would have benefited?

Exhibit 2: Extract from subsequent email from Nelson

I also wanted to ask you about the potential sale of a house I inherited from my father when he died on 1 June 2024. The house had a value of £390,000 for probate purposes but is now worth £450,000. My father purchased the house for £130,000 in 1986 and I intend to sell the house as quickly as possible.

I currently plan to gift £150,000 of the proceeds from the sale of the house to Cam, my wife. She moved to the UK in January 2020 and we married in June 2021. I gave her a half interest in my home in August 2021. The value of this gift was £600,000. Cam is resident in the UK but domiciled in the country of Riviera and has employment income of £20,000 per year.

Will there be any inheritance tax on my gift to Cam? Is there any tax planning we could do here?

Exhibit 3: Extract from the email from your manager – dated 1 December 2025

Please prepare a memorandum for the client file consisting of the work set out below.

(a) **Becoming tax advisers to Nelson**

Explain the information we require, the matters we should consider and the actions we should take before we agree to become Nelson's tax advisers. **(5 marks)**

(b) **Trading through a limited company rather than as an unincorporated business**

(i) **Total taxes payable**

The total taxes payable by Nelson for the tax year 2025/26 in respect of his budgeted tax adjusted trading profit will be £18,299. Prepare calculations to determine whether or not a lower amount would have been payable if Nelson had commenced trading through a limited company rather than as an unincorporated business.

You should assume:

- the company's accounting period ends on 31 March 2026;
- the company's MONTHLY trading profit for this accounting period is £7,050. This figure is before deducting the cost of Nelson's monthly salary;
- the company pays Nelson a gross salary of £1,300 per month and a dividend equal to its post-tax profits.

(8 marks)

(ii) **Reasons for advice given by existing tax adviser**

Explain why the expectation that Nelson's business would make a tax adjusted trading loss would have been an important consideration when deciding on whether he should begin trading as an unincorporated business or through a limited company.

State any other reasons why Nelson's existing tax adviser may have advised him to commence trading as an unincorporated business rather than through a limited company. **(4 marks)**

(c) **Other matters**

(i) Explain the capital gains tax (CGT) implications for Nelson of retaining personal ownership of the Arch building when he incorporates his business. You ARE NOT REQUIRED to consider CGT gift holdover relief. **(4 marks)**

(ii) Explain the tax implications for NQA Ltd of Nelson borrowing excess funds from the company and the subsequent repayment of those funds. You ARE NOT REQUIRED to explain any matters relating to employment income benefits in respect of this arrangement. **(5 marks)**

(iii) Provide explanations in response to the two questions raised by Nelson in respect of value added tax (VAT). **(4 marks)**

(d) **Gift to Cam**

(i) By reference to Cam's domicile status, explain why Nelson's proposed gift of £150,000 to Cam could result in an inheritance tax liability and how this potential liability might be avoided. **(5 marks)**

(ii) Prepare calculations in order to show the capital gains tax saving which would be achieved if Nelson were to give Cam a one-third interest in the London house prior to its sale (as opposed to cash of £150,000 following its sale). Assume the disposal of the house happens before 5 April 2026. **(5 marks)**

Tax Manager

10 Corey (Mar 2020, amended) (98 mins)

You should assume that today's date is 1 March 2026.

You are an ACCA student working for a firm of accountants. Your manager has had a meeting with Corey, a client of your firm, and requires your assistance to draft a memorandum to deal with the issues raised. A diagram summarising the relationships between the parties is set out in Exhibit 5.

Corey has recently returned to the UK after a period of living overseas in the country of Medora. In addition to some ethical considerations which have been raised by your manager, Corey requires advice in respect of:

- Clarification of his UK residence status;
- The capital gains treatment of some disposals which have occurred;
- The inheritance tax consequences of certain gifts which his mother is proposing to make;
- The deductibility, for tax purposes, of certain costs which are to be incurred by Quod Ltd, a new company which will be established; and
- The availability of tax losses within Quod Ltd and the extent to which they can be relieved.

The following **exhibits** summarise the meeting between Corey and your manager on each of the relevant issues, and outline what you need to do.

(1) Corey's personal situation

(2) Disposals made by Corey

(3) Proposed gifts by Emer (Corey's mother)

(4) Quod Ltd

(5) Manager's email – outlining what you are required to do

This information should be used to answer the question **requirements** within your chosen **response option(s).**

Required

You should assume that today's date is 1 March 2026.

Prepare the memorandum as requested in the email from your manager. **(40 marks)**

Professional marks will be awarded for the demonstration of skill in communication, analysis and evaluation, scepticism and commercial acumen in your answers. **(10 marks)**

(Total = 50 marks)

Exhibit 1: Corey's personal situation

Extracts from the memorandum prepared by your manager dated 1 March 2026

Background

Corey had always lived in the UK until, on 6 April 2022, he sold his home in the UK and moved to the country of Medora with his wife, Dana, and their daughter, aged 10. They always planned to return to the UK at some point, such that they continued to be domiciled in the UK. Corey began working for a company in Medora on 1 May 2022.

In March 2025, Corey's sister, Florence, became seriously ill. Consequently, Corey and his family returned to live in the UK on 6 April 2025.

Period from 6 April 2022 to 5 April 2025

Corey was not resident in the UK for tax purposes during this period. However, he visited the UK (staying in hotels) as follows:

Tax year	Days in the UK
2022/23	49
2023/24	105
2024/25	74

Since 6 April 2025

On 1 June 2025, Corey and Dana purchased a new home in the UK. On the same date, Dana started a new full-time job in the UK and became UK resident. Corey and Dana have retained their home in Medora because Corey has continued working there and does not work in the UK. It is envisaged that Corey will have been in the UK for 115 days in the tax year 2025/26.

Exhibit 2: Disposals made by Corey

Extracts from the memorandum prepared by your manager dated 1 March 2026

Disposals of assets in the tax year 2024/25

- On 1 December 2024, Corey sold a statue situated in the garden of his home in Medora. He had purchased the statue for £17,000 on 1 September 2022. The sale resulted in a capital loss of £7,400.
- On 1 February 2025, as a result of a commercial takeover, Corey received 4,000 shares in TW plc (a holding of less than 1%) and £12,000 in cash in exchange for 2,000 shares in SQ plc. One share in TW plc was worth £3.50 on that day. Corey had purchased his 2,000 shares in SQ plc (a holding of less than 1%) for £13,500 on 1 June 2017. SQ plc and TW plc are quoted companies.

Disposals of assets in the tax year 2025/26

- On 1 August 2025, Corey sold a house situated in Medora. This house was purchased on 1 July 2022 and has always been rented out. The sale realised a gain of £34,500.
- On 1 December 2025, Corey gave his sister, Florence, 700 of the 4,000 shares he owned in TW plc. One share in TW plc was worth £4.50 on that day.

Note. I have subsequently carried out some research on the system of taxation in Medora and can confirm that:

- There is no capital gains tax (CGT)
- There is no double tax treaty between the UK and Medora

Exhibit 3: Proposed gifts by Emer (Corey's mother)

Extracts from the memorandum prepared by your manager dated 1 March 2026

Paintings owned by Corey's mother

Corey has asked for advice on the inheritance tax (IHT) advantages of his mother, Emer, who is UK domiciled, making lifetime gifts to Corey of either, or both, of the following paintings.

	Current market value	Anticipated change in value
Watercolour	£41,000	Falling in value
Portrait	£37,000	Increasing in value

Exhibit 4: Quod Ltd

Extracts from the memorandum prepared by your manager dated 1 March 2026

Joint Venture

Corey owns 100% of the share capital of Porth Ltd, an unquoted trading company with annual profits of around £100,000. On 1 April 2026, Porth Ltd will invest in a new company, Quod Ltd. Quod Ltd will be resident in the UK for tax purposes and will begin to trade immediately. It will develop a range of products over the next few years.

The planned ownership of the ordinary share capital of Quod Ltd is as follows:

Porth Ltd	60%
Either Mr Berm or Mr Berm's company, BJB Ltd	30%
CX Ltd	10%

Porth Ltd, BJB Ltd, CX Ltd and Mr Berm are all UK resident for tax purposes.

Quod Ltd – financial information

Corey has calculated Quod Ltd's budgeted tax adjusted trading loss for the year ending 31 March 2027 to be £44,000.

When calculating the loss, Corey has deducted £1,000, being the annual amortisation charge included in the accounts, in respect of the Cloque brand (note 1). He was unsure how to treat this but a friend of his, with some knowledge of corporation tax, advised him that it was fully deductible.

The loss also includes a deduction for the whole of the costs attributable to a scientific research project amounting to £74,500 (note 2).

Notes.

1 **Purchase of the Cloque brand**

On 1 April 2026, Quod Ltd will acquire a brand (the Cloque brand) for £35,000 and begin to trade. The brand will have a 35-year life and will be written off for accounts purposes on a straight-line basis.

2 **Scientific research costs**

	£
Materials	21,000
Rent	17,400
Electricity and water	6,600
Staff costs	29,500
	74,500

- The rent is an appropriate allocation of the rent payable for Quod Ltd's premises for the year.
- All of the staff costs relate to employees of Quod Ltd with the exception of £7,000, which was paid to an external contractor provided by an unconnected company.
- I have already established that the research to be carried out by Quod Ltd will qualify for R&D relief.

Exhibit 5: Manager's email

To: Tax Senior

From: Tax Manager

Date: 1 March 2026

Subject: Corey

Hi

The relationship between the parties are set out below:

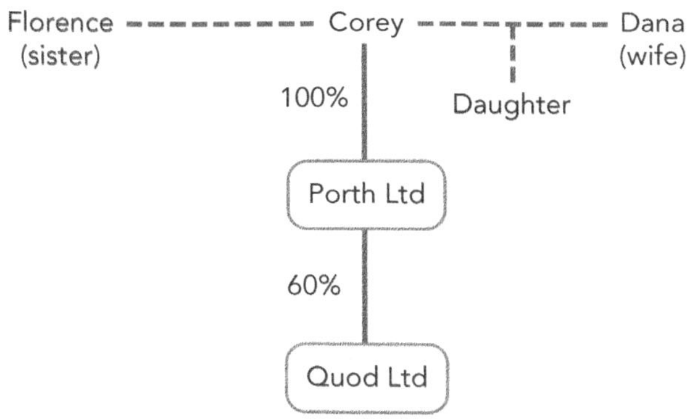

(a) **Corey's UK residence status for the tax year 2025/26 (Exhibit 1)**

For the purposes of this part, you are NOT required to consider the availability of split year treatment.

(i) Explain how Corey's UK residence status for the tax year 2025/26 will be determined and conclude on his likely residence status for that year. I have already confirmed that none of the automatic overseas or automatic UK test have been met for 2025/26 and you therefore DO NOT need to consider these further. **(5 marks)**

(ii) State how becoming UK resident would affect Corey's liability to UK income tax. **(1 mark)**

(b) **Corey's disposals of assets in the tax years 2024/25 and 2025/26 (Exhibits 1 and 2)**

For this part of the work, you should assume Corey is UK resident for the whole of the tax year 2025/26 and will receive taxable income in that year of £42,320, before the deduction of his personal allowance.

(i) Explain how each of Corey's disposals in the tax year 2024/25 will be treated for the purposes of capital gains tax (CGT). **(3 marks)**

(ii) Calculate Corey's CGT liability for the tax year 2025/26. **(8 marks)**

(c) **Lifetime gifts of paintings by Emer (Exhibit 3)**

Explain, with respect to the amount of inheritance tax (IHT) payable ONLY, whether it would be beneficial for Emer to make a lifetime gift of either or both of her paintings (as opposed to retaining them until her death).

There is no need to address the annual exemption, as Emer makes use of this every year.

You should assume there will be no nil rate band available regardless of when the transfer takes place.

(6 marks)

(d) **Quod Ltd (Exhibit 4)**

(i) Given that Corey is keen to maximise the company's trading loss for the year ending 31 March 2027, explain whether you agree with the advice given by his friend concerning the tax treatment of the proposed purchase of the Cloque brand (an intangible fixed asset) for £35,000. **(2 marks)**

(ii) Explain the tax relief which will be available to Quod Ltd in respect of the scientific research costs of £74,500 to be incurred in the year ending 31 March 2027. **(5 marks)**

(iii) Calculate the amended budgeted tax adjusted trading loss for Quod Ltd for the year ending 31 March 2027, taking into account the explanations requested above. **(2 marks)**

(iv) Explain how much of Quod Ltd's amended budgeted trading loss will be available for use by Porth Ltd. **(3 marks)**

(e) **Refund of income tax**

I have become aware that, a few months ago, Corey received a refund of income tax from H M Revenue and Customs (HMRC) in respect of the tax year 2021/22. He has not been able to determine why the refund was made.

In respect of the income tax refund, set out the actions which our firm should take and the matters which should be brought to Corey's attention. **(5 marks)**

Regards

Tax manager

11 Joe (Mar/Jun 2021) (98 mins)

You should assume that today's date is 1 June 2025.

You are an ACCA student working for a firm of accountants. Joe Sands, the finance director of VNL Ltd, has had a meeting with your manager to discuss the liquidation of the company and Joe's future plans in terms of starting his own unincorporated business. In addition, Joe has asked whether your firm will be able to advise his mother, Fiona, who is returning to the UK after living overseas for several years.

Advice is required in respect of the following issues:

- The consequences of VNL Ltd disposing of certain intangible assets and the timing of a dividend payment;
- For Joe's new business, consideration as to the cost of taking on a new employee and the ability to be able to recover value added tax (VAT) on certain initial costs; and
- The basis of taxation which will apply to Fiona on her return to the UK and her projected income tax liability.

There are also some ethical issues to be considered if the firm is to accept Fiona as a new client.

The following exhibits summarise the discussions between Joe and your manager on each of the relevant issues, and outline what you need to do.

(1) VNL Ltd

(2) Joe's future business plans

(3) Fiona (Joe's mother)

(4) Manager's email – work to be carried out

This information should be used to answer the question **requirements** within your **chosen response option(s)**.

Required

You should assume that today's date is 1 June 2025.

Respond to the instruction in the email from your manager.

Note. The split of the mark allocation is shown in Exhibit 4 – Manager's email. **(40 marks)**

Professional marks will be awarded for demonstration of skill in communication, analysis and evaluation, scepticism and commercial acumen in your answer. **(10 marks)**

(Total = 50 marks)

Exhibit 1: VNL Ltd

Summary of points discussed in a meeting on 1 June 2025 and subsequent follow-up telephone conversation

Background

Joe advised me that the company's shareholders have decided to liquidate the company. A liquidator is to be appointed on 1 August 2025. The company will dispose of certain intangible fixed assets and will make certain payments to its shareholders.

Sale of intangible fixed assets

On 1 September 2022, VNL Ltd purchased the trade and assets of a business from an unrelated company.

The assets included goodwill and a brand name, as detailed below. These assets will be sold on 31 July 2025.

	Goodwill	Brand name
	£	£
Sale proceeds	75,000	47,000
Cost	95,000	36,000
Amortisation since acquisition	19,000	5,760

Further advice – payments to the shareholders

An interim payment will be made to the shareholders followed by a final payment at the conclusion of the liquidation which will take place in February 2026. Joe has been asked to consider the possibility of making the interim payment prior to the appointment of the liquidator.

Additional information

There are some further details which you will require and I have obtained these from the client file for you. These are as follows:

- VNL Ltd is a trading company. It has always made significant trading profits and will be profitable in its final accounting period paying main rate corporation tax. It prepares accounts to 31 March each year.
- The amortisation of the goodwill was not a tax deductible expense for VNL Ltd.
- No election was made to write off the cost of the brand name at the 4% rate.
- The company's shareholders are all individuals, some of whom are employed by VNL Ltd, and include both basic and higher rate taxpayers.
- The shares in VNL Ltd were subscribed for prior to 17 March 2016, such that investors' relief will not be available in respect of any disposal.

Exhibit 2: Joe's future business plans

Points discussed in meeting on 1 June 2025

Background

Joe confirmed his intention to start trading as an unincorporated trader on 1 November 2025.

Anticipated profits

Joe anticipates that his business will make taxable trading profits of £24,500 in 2025/26 and £97,000 in 2026/27. He is considering taking on a part time employee from 6 April 2026 to help his new business and would like to know the after-tax cost.

New employee

If he takes on the new employee, he will pay them a salary of £15,000 for 2026/27 in addition to providing them with a company car. The car will only be purchased if the new employee is taken on. The business will pay £14,000 for the new car which has a list price of £16,000 and CO_2 emissions of 72g/km. In addition, the business will pay £2,300 towards the employee's business mileage.

Costs already incurred

Since 1 October 2024, Joe has been purchasing consultancy services every month in respect of the design and manufacture of the product the new business will be selling.

Business premises

A building for use as the business premises has been identified. It is a commercial property unit, which was constructed in 2006. Joe has agreed a price with the vendor of £190,000 plus value added tax (VAT). He intends to lease a third of the building to an unrelated business until his trading activities have grown sufficiently to require the use of the whole building.

Joe confirmed that his trading activity will be standard-rated for VAT purposes.

Exhibit 3: Fiona (Joe's mother)

Points discussed in meeting on 1 June 2025

Background

Joe provided the following background on his mother's situation.

Fiona is 74 years old and in poor health. She has lived in the country of Parella since 1991. She will move to the UK on 1 August 2025 and acquire a home there.

Fiona's domicile and residence status

Based on the facts Joe provided, I have already established that as a result of moving to the UK:

- Fiona will become UK resident on 1 August 2025 under the split year basis.
- Fiona will also be UK resident in the tax year 2026/27.
- Fiona is domiciled in Parella. However, once she becomes UK resident, Fiona will be deemed domiciled in the UK for the purposes of income tax and capital gains tax (CGT) because she was born in the UK with a UK domicile of origin.

Property and interest income

Fiona's anticipated income for the tax year 2026/27, the year after she moves to the UK:

	£
Property income	
– Properties situated in the UK	26,000
– Properties situated in Parella	31,000
Interest income	
– UK bank interest	1,700
– Parellian bank interest	1,200

The income arising in Parella is stated gross of Parellian tax. Fiona will remit all of the rental income in respect of the properties situated in Parella to the UK. The interest arising on the Parellian bank accounts will be retained in Parella.

The rate of income tax in Parella is 18% and there is no double tax treaty between the UK and Parella.

Exhibit 4: Manager's email – work to be carried out

To: Tax senior

From: Tax manager

Date: 1 June 2025

Subject: Meeting with Joe Sands (VNL Ltd)

Hi

I need you to prepare some notes in preparation for an internal team meeting to discuss the various points which Joe has raised. They should address the following issues:

(a) **Liquidation of VNL Ltd (Exhibit 1)**

(i) **Sale of intangible fixed assets**

Calculate the post-tax proceeds for VNL Ltd as a result of the sale of the intangible fixed assets. **(4 marks)**

(ii) **Timing of payments to shareholders**

Explain the tax rates, taking into account any reliefs which may be available, which the shareholders will pay on the amounts received from VNL Ltd, depending on when the payment is made. **(9 marks)**

(b) **Unincorporated business (Exhibit 2)**

(i) **New employee**

Calculate the after-tax cost for Joe of taking on the new employee for 2026/27.

You should assume the employment allowance is not available. **(6 marks)**

(ii) **Costs already incurred and the business premises**

Explain whether or not Joe will be able to recover the related input tax for value added tax (VAT) purposes in respect of the consultancy costs already incurred and the planned purchase of the business premises. **(6 marks)**

(c) **Becoming Fiona's tax advisers (Exhibit 3)**

Explain the actions which we should carry out before we become Fiona's tax advisers. I have already obtained proof of her address and her identity. **(5 marks)**

(d) **Taxation of overseas income (Exhibit 3)**

- Explain why the remittance basis will be available to Fiona in the tax year 2026/27 and whether or not she will be subject to the remittance basis charge.
- Calculate Fiona's income tax liability for the tax year 2026/27 based on her anticipated income figures.

(10 marks)

The notes which you prepare will subsequently be distributed to all team members within our firm, so please do present them in a way which will be suitable for circulation.

Tax manager

12 Jeg Ltd (Sept/Dec 2021) (98 mins)

You should assume that today's date is 1 September 2025.

You are an ACCA student working for a firm of accountants. Your manager has received a schedule of information and an email from your client Hale, who is the managing director of Jeg Ltd, a potential client of your firm. Your manager has asked for your assistance in preparing a memorandum for the client file which addresses the following issues:

- Information and actions required by the firm before becoming tax advisers to the Jeg Ltd group
- The availability of rollover relief on the sale of business premises
- The taxation of overseas profits
- VAT group issues, and
- Personal tax issues relating to Hale's financial position

The following exhibits provide information relevant to the question:

(1) Schedule from Hale dated 1 September 2025 regarding the Jeg Ltd group

(2) Extract from an email from Hale regarding his financial position

(3) Email extract from your manager - work to be carried out dated 1 September 2025

This information should be used to answer the question **requirements** within your chosen **response option(s).**

Required

You should assume that today's date is 1 September 2025.

Prepare the memorandum as requested in the email from your manager.

Note. The split of the mark allocation is shown in Exhibit 3 – Manager's email **(40 marks)**

Professional marks will be awarded for the demonstration of skill in communication, analysis & evaluation, scepticism and commercial acumen in your answer. **(10 marks)**

(Total = 50 marks)

Exhibit 1: Schedule from Hale

Background

On 1 August 2023, Jeg Ltd purchased the whole of the ordinary share capital of two companies: Kod Ltd and Lis Co.

On 1 July 2025, Jeg Ltd purchased the whole of the ordinary share capital of Mot Ltd.

All four companies in the Jeg Ltd group prepare accounts to 31 March each year and are budgeted to be profitable in the year ending 31 March 2026.

Further details of the companies are set out below, followed by a summary of recent significant transactions.

	Jeg Ltd	Kod Ltd	Lis Co	Mot Ltd
Country of residence	UK	UK	Silana	UK
Country of trading activity	UK	UK	Silana	Puran
Whether registered for VAT	Yes	Yes	No	No
Rate of overseas tax	N/A	N/A	11%	13%

Jeg Ltd – purchase of business

On 1 February 2025, Jeg Ltd purchased the trade and assets of a business. The only significant asset of the business was its production line, which consisted of three large items of fixed machinery. Jeg Ltd paid £290,000 for this machinery.

Kod Ltd

Kod Ltd is experiencing cash flow problems. On 30 June 2025, it sold its business premises to a unconnected party for £485,000, resulting in a chargeable gain on £247,000. This building was entirely used in Kod Ltd's trade throughout the period it was owned. Kod Ltd now trades from rented premises. On 1 August 2025, it used £120,000 of the sale proceeds to purchase eight delivery vans for use in its trade.

Lis Co

On 1 July 2025, Lis Co purchased a building situated in Silana for £170,000. This building was immediately brought into use in Lis Co's trade.

Lis Co manufactures industrial components, which it supplies to customers in Silana and in other countries. It is intended that Jeg Ltd will purchase components from Lis Co and import them for use in its own manufacturing trade.

In view of the low rate of business tax in Silana, I am considering pricing strategies which would maximise the profits of the group which are taxed there.

Mot Ltd

Mot Ltd carries on its trade in Puran where it has production and distribution facilities. It has not made any capital additions or disposals of significant since 2023.

Value added tax (VAT)

I am looking into the possibility of a group VAT registration.

Exhibit 2: Extract from an email from Hale regarding his financial position

Income from employment 2025/26

On 6 April 2025, I began working full time in the UK for Jeg Ltd. For the tax year 2025/26, my employment package will comprise the following:

- A gross annual salary of £87,800
- Employment income benefits in respect of a car and accommodation, amounting to £26,230
- 7,200 ordinary shares issued to me by Jeg Ltd on 1 May 2025 as an introductory 'thank you' for joining the company. I paid £14,400 for these shares, which had a market value of £23,200 at the time. Shares in Jeg Ltd are not readily convertible assets.

Exhibit 3: Email extract from your manager – work to be carried out

I expect the Jeg Ltd group to be an exciting new client for our firm. Hale has ambitious plans and, although we advise a number of corporate groups, this will give us our first experience of companies operating through permanent establishments situated overseas.

I can confirm:

- there is no double tax treaty between the UK and either the country of Silana or the country of Puran;
- there are no controlled foreign companies implications for you to consider.

Please prepare a memorandum for the client file consisting of the work set out below.

(a) **Becoming tax advisers to the Jeg Ltd group of companies**

Set out the information we require, and the actions we should take, before we agree to become tax advisers to the Jeg Ltd group of companies. **(5 marks)**

(b) **Relieving the chargeable gain on the sale of Kod Ltd's business premises (Exhibit 1)**

Explain the matters which should be brought to Hale's attention in relation to the availability of rollover relief in respect of the chargeable gain on the sale of Kod Ltd's business premises, and the way in which the relief would operate.

(9 marks)

(c) **Taxation of profits generated overseas (Exhibit 1)**

Lis Co

Explain the implications, in relation to UK corporation tax payable, of Lis Co charging Jeg Ltd inflated prices for its components in order to maximise the profits of the group which are taxed in Silana. Jeg Ltd is a small enterprise for the purposes of the transfer pricing regime.

Mot Ltd

Explain:

- the rate of corporation tax which will be suffered by Mot Ltd in the UK on the profits generated by its permanent establishment in Puran; and
- the matters to consider when deciding whether or not to make an election to exempt the profits of the permanent establishment in Puran from UK tax.

(9 marks)

(d) **Value added tax (VAT) (Exhibit 1)**

I have already established that Lis Co cannot be included within a group VAT registration with Jeg Ltd. With this in mind, explain:

- which of the other companies within the group could be included within a group VAT registration;
- any potential disadvantages, relevant to the Jeg Ltd group of companies, of registering for VAT as a group;
- the VAT implications for Jeg Ltd of purchasing components from Lis Co.

(8 marks)

(e) **Hale's financial position for the tax year 2025/26 (Exhibit 2)**

Hale cannot understand why, despite receiving a substantial amount of UK source income, his annual personal expenditure of £57,600 exceeds his available post-tax income.

Prepare calculations for the tax year 2025/26 in order to explain why Hale is in this financial position and summarise your findings.

When carrying out this work you should include Hale's dividend income of £18,300 in 2025/26 in respect of his portfolio of shares. **(9 marks)**

Personal tax

13 Kesme and Soba (ACCA specimen exam (FA21), amended to FA24) (49 mins)

You should assume that today's date is 1 December 2025.

Kesme and Soba, a married couple, require advice on:

- Kesme's taxable income, rent a room relief and share based remuneration, the remittance basis, and
- the assets which will be received by Soba under Kesme's will.

The following exhibit, available on the left hand side of the screen, provides information relevant to the question;

(1) Kesme and Soba

This information should be used to answer the question **requirements** within your chosen **response option(s).**

Required

You should assume that today's date is 1 December 2025.

(a) Explain the availability and operation of rent a room relief in relation to Kesme and calculate his taxable income for the tax year 2024/25 on the assumption that the relief is claimed. **(8 marks)**

(b) State, with reasons, whether or not the remittance basis is available to Kesme and Soba and, on the assumption that it is available to both of them, explain whether or not it is likely to be beneficial for each of them. **(6 marks)**

(c) Calculate the value of the residue of the estate that Soba would receive under Kesme's will if Kesme were to die today. **(4 marks)**

(d) Explain how the spouse exemption available in respect of transfers from Soba to Kesme would be different if Soba were domiciled in the UK. **(2 marks)**

Professional marks will be awarded for the demonstration of skill in analysis & evaluation and commercial acumen in your answer. **(5 marks)**

(Total = 25 marks)

Exhibit: Kesme and Soba

Kesme:

- Has been UK resident since the tax year 2021/22 but is non-UK domiciled
- Is married to Soba
- Has not made any lifetime gifts for the purposes of inheritance tax

Soba:

- Has been UK resident since the tax year 2011/12 but is non-UK domiciled

Kesme's income for the tax year 2024/25 includes:

- Salary (gross) and benefits from Noodl plc, his current employer, of £48,500
- Pension from a former employer of £24,100 (gross)

- Rental income in respect of a furnished room in the main residence he owns jointly with Soba; the joint rental income received was £17,650
- Allowable expenses paid in respect of the joint rental income of £1,600, none of which are finance costs

Share-based remuneration provided to Kesme by Noodl plc in the tax year 2024/25:

- 400 shares in Noodl plc were issued to Kesme for £2,500.
- Kesme was granted share options which were not tax advantaged to purchase 300 shares for £4 per share.
- Kesme exercised not tax advantaged share options and purchased 250 shares for £3 per share. Kesme had paid 50 pence for each of these options.
- A share in Noodl plc can be assumed to be worth £12 throughout the tax year 2024/25.
- Noodl plc offers its staff share-based remuneration but does not operate any tax advantaged share schemes.

Income to be received in future years in respect of investments in the country of Penne:

- Kesme will receive £1,400 per year.
- Soba will receive £19,500 per year.
- Neither Kesme nor Soba plan to remit any of this income into the UK.
- There is no income tax in the country of Penne.

Kesme's estate and his will:

- Kesme's gross chargeable estate will have a value of £1,280,000.
- This value includes a plot of land situated in the UK worth £370,000.
- Kesme has left the plot of land to his daughter and the residue of his estate to his wife, Soba.

14 Jessica (Mar/Jun 2018, amended) (49 mins)

You should assume that today's date is 1 June 2025.

Your client, Jessica, has requested advice in relation to:

- the tax liability arising on a redundancy payment;
- the options available to relieve her share of a partnership trading loss; and
- the maximum contribution she can make to a personal pension scheme.

The following exhibit, available on the left hand side of the screen, provides information relevant to the question:

(1) Jessica

This information should be used to answer the question **requirements** within your chosen **response option(s).**

Required

You should assume that today's date is 1 June 2025.

(a) Explain the income tax and NIC treatment of each element of the redundancy package received from Berens Ltd on 31 March 2025. Calculate the amount(s) liable to income tax on Jessica. **(5 marks)**

(b) Answer the following questions assuming that Jessica's share of the partnership's loss gives her a trade loss of £48,000 in 2025/26:

(i) Advise Jessica of the options available to her to relieve her share of the Langley Partnership loss for 2025/26, on the assumption that she does not wish to carry any of her share of the loss forward. **(3 marks)**

(ii) Determine, by reference to the amount of income tax saved in each case, which of the available loss relief options (as identified in (i) above) will result in the highest overall income tax saving for Jessica. **(7 marks)**

(c) Explain, with supporting calculations, the maximum amount of the contributions Jessica can pay into her pension scheme in each of the tax years 2025/26 and 2026/27 without incurring an annual allowance charge. **(5 marks)**

Professional marks will be awarded for the demonstration of skill in analysis and evaluation and commercial acumen in your answer. **(5 marks)**

(Total = 25 marks)

Exhibit: Jessica

Jessica:

- Is resident and domiciled in the UK.
- Was employed by Berens Ltd up to 31 March 2025, when she was made redundant.
- Will become a partner in the Langley Partnership on 1 July 2025.
- Has never made any disposals for capital gains tax (CGT) purposes.

Jessica – income from Berens Ltd:

- Jessica received an annual salary from Berens Ltd of £147,000 each year from the tax year 2022/23.
- From 6 April 2024, Jessica was provided with a new company laptop computer, which cost Berens Ltd £850. Jessica had significant private use of this laptop computer.

Jessica – other income:

- Prior to the tax year 2024/25 Jessica had no other source of income.
- Starting from the tax year 2024/25, Jessica receives rental income of £6,000 each tax year.

Jessica – redundancy package from Berens Ltd:

- The package, received on 31 March 2025, included a statutory redundancy payment of £18,000, one month's payment in lieu of notice and a non-contractual *ex-gratia* payment of £32,000.
- As part of the package, Berens Ltd also allowed Jessica to keep the laptop computer, which had a market value of £540 on 31 March 2025.

The Langley Partnership:

- Prior to 1 July 2025, there were two partners in the partnership – Issa and Finn.
- From 1 July 2025, the profit sharing ratio will be: Issa 20%, Finn 40%, and Jessica 40%.
- The budgeted tax-adjusted trading (loss)/profit of the partnership is:
  - Year ending 31 March 2026 – (£160,000)
  - Year ending 31 March 2027 – £305,000.

Jessica – personal pension plan contributions:

- Jessica joined a registered personal pension scheme on 1 May 2025.
- She has not previously been in any pension scheme.
- She wishes to make the maximum possible contributions which will qualify for tax relief in each of the tax years 2025/26 and 2026/27.

15 Demeter (Dec 2018, amended) (49 mins)

You should assume that today's date is 1 December 2025.

Demeter has recently taken up a new employment and is seeking advice on the following issues:

- the tax treatment of certain components of his remuneration package; and
- the relief(s) available to reduce the chargeable gain on the sale of his house.

The following exhibit, available on the left hand side of the screen, provides information relevant to the question;

(1) Demeter

This information should be used to answer the question **requirements** within your chosen **response option(s).**

Required

You should assume that today's date is 1 December 2025.

(a) Explain the extent to which the receipt of the £20,000 lump sum inducement payment, and the relocation package in relation to Demeter's move to London, will give rise to taxable employment income for him. **(5 marks)**

(b) Identify, and calculate, with brief explanations, the relief(s) available to Demeter to reduce the chargeable gain of £94,000 on the sale of his house in Manchester on 31 October 2025. **(6 marks)**

(c) Explain, with supporting calculations, the tax consequences for Demeter of participating in:

Note. Ignore national insurance contributions (NIC).

(i) Poseidon Ltd's approved occupational pension scheme in the tax year 2026/27. **(5 marks)**

(ii) Poseidon Ltd's non tax-advantaged share option scheme, in respect of the grant of the options on 30 November 2025 and the exercise of the options and subsequent sale of the shares on 6 April 2031. **(4 marks)**

Professional marks will be awarded for the demonstration of skill in analysis and evaluation and commercial acumen in your answer. **(5 marks)**

(Total = 25 marks)

Exhibit: Demeter

Demeter:

- Is UK resident and domiciled.
- Commenced employment with Poseidon Ltd on 1 December 2025.
- Will have no source of income, other than from Poseidon Ltd, in all relevant future tax years.
- Will be an additional rate taxpayer in all relevant future tax years.
- Has relocated to London, from Manchester, a city more than 150 miles north of London, to take up this employment.

Remuneration package from Poseidon Ltd:

- Demeter will receive an annual salary of £220,000.
- On 30 November 2025, Poseidon Ltd made a one-off lump sum payment of £20,000 to Demeter as an inducement to take up employment with the company.
- Poseidon Ltd paid Demeter £5,000 towards his costs of relocating to London. The company is also paying him £1,500 each month for four months from 1 December 2025 towards renting accommodation in London until he purchases a new house during April 2026.
- On 30 November 2025, Demeter was granted share options in Poseidon Ltd's non-tax advantaged share option scheme.

- From 6 April 2026, Demeter will participate in Poseidon Ltd's approved occupational pension scheme.

Relocation to London:

- Demeter incurred costs in relation to his relocation to London of £6,000. This amount includes estate agent fees of £2,800 in connection with the sale of his house in Manchester on 31 October 2025.
- Demeter signed a four-month lease for a flat in London from 1 December 2025 at a monthly rental of £1,700.

House in Manchester:

- Demeter purchased the house on 1 February 2013 and lived in it as his main residence.
- Demeter let the top floor of the house (comprising 30% of the total house) to tenants from 1 February 2015 to 31 October 2025. The tenants did not share Demeter's living accommodation or take meals with him.
- Demeter continued to occupy the remainder of the house as his main residence until 31 October 2025, when the entire house was sold.
- The sale gave rise to a gain, before any reliefs, of £94,000.
- Demeter did not own any other house throughout the period from 1 February 2013 to 31 October 2025.

Demeter – pension contributions:

- Demeter has made tax-allowable contributions of £60,000 (gross) to a personal pension plan for the last three tax years and will continue to do so in future tax years.
- From the tax year 2026/27, Poseidon Ltd will contribute an amount equal to 10% of Demeter's annual salary to its approved occupational pension scheme.
- Demeter will make no contributions to Poseidon Ltd's occupational pension scheme.

Poseidon Ltd's share option scheme:

- On 30 November 2025, Poseidon Ltd granted Demeter options over 3,000 shares in its non tax-advantaged share option scheme at a 5% discount on the market value of the shares on that date.
- The market value of Poseidon Ltd shares on 1 December 2025 was £4.20 per share.
- Demeter will exercise the options on 6 April 2031, and immediately sell the shares.
- Poseidon Ltd believes that the market value of its shares on 6 April 2031 will be £6.00 per share.

16 Pedro (Mar 2020, amended) (49 mins)

You should assume that today's date is 1 March 2026.

Pedro requires advice on:

- the reason he has had to pay inheritance tax in respect of a holiday cottage following the death of his aunt, Marina;
- an explanation of the calculation of taxable property income; and
- the income tax implications of a significant contribution into his personal pension scheme.

The following exhibit, available on the left hand side of the screen, provides information relevant to the question:

(1) Pedro

This information should be used to answer the question **requirements** within your chosen **response option(s).**

Required

You should assume that today's date is 1 March 2026.

(a) Explain the inheritance tax implications of the gift of the cottage to Pedro at the time the gift was made, and as a result of Marina's death. **(5 marks)**

(b) Explain the calculation of taxable property income for Pedro and the tax relief available in respect of the future mortgage to be taken out by Pedro. **(5 marks)**

(c) Calculate the reduction in Pedro's income tax liability for the tax year 2025/26 as a result of making the planned contribution of £85,000 (gross) into his personal pension scheme on 31 March 2026. Your answer should include an explanation of the amount of the personal allowance available to Pedro in this case. **(10 marks)**

Professional marks will be awarded for the demonstration of skill in analysis and evaluation and commercial acumen in your answer. **(5 marks)**

(Total = 25 marks)

Exhibit: Pedro

Pedro:

- Was given a holiday cottage in the UK by his aunt, Marina, on 4 March 2015.
- Paid inheritance tax in respect of this gift of the holiday cottage, following Marina's death on 8 June 2025.
- Inherited a portfolio of UK unfurnished residential properties, valued at £670,000 on Marina's death.

Gift of the holiday cottage in the UK by Marina:

- Marina and Pedro agreed that she could stay in the house for two months each year, rent-free, which she did every year until her death.
- For the remainder of each year, Marina lived in her main home.

Pedro – property income:

- The rental receipts (net of expenses of £1,700) from the unfurnished holiday cottage in the tax year 2025/26 will be £14,500.
- Pedro is considering taking out an interest only mortgage on the cottage to build an extension and purchase furniture in 2026/27.
- In the tax year 2025/26, Pedro will also receive net rental income of £22,000 from the unfurnished residential properties which he inherited from Marina.

Employment income:

- Pedro has been employed by Loule Ltd since 6 April 2024.
- Pedro receives an annual gross salary of £85,000 from Loule Ltd.
- Loule Ltd has contributed £28,000 in each of the tax years 2024/25 and 2025/26 to its occupational pension scheme on behalf of Pedro.

Personal pension scheme:

- Pedro had never been a member of a pension scheme prior to taking up employment with Loule Ltd.
- Pedro wishes to start contributing to a personal pension scheme in the tax year 2025/26.
- Pedro intends to make his first contribution into the new personal pension scheme, of £85,000 (gross), on 31 March 2026.
- The annual allowance available to Pedro was not restricted in any previous tax year.
- Pedro's income tax liability for the tax year 2025/26, before taking into account the planned contribution into his personal pension scheme, is £40,332.

17 Caden and Amahle (Sep/Dec 2021) (49 mins)

You should assume that today's date is 1 September 2025.

Caden requires advice on:

- the capital gains tax implications of a proposed sale of antique chairs
- payment of the potential inheritance tax liability in respect of two lifetime gifts, and
- the application of the personal service company (IR35) legislation.
- His wife, Amahle, requires advice on the income tax implications of receiving overseas income.

The following exhibit provides information relevant to the question:

(1) Caden and Amahle

This information should be used to answer the question **requirements** within your chosen **response option(s).**

Required

You should assume that today's date is 1 September 2025.

(a) Answer the following questions.

(i) Explain, with supporting calculations, the capital loss which will arise on the proposed sale of the antique chairs to Nathi and how this loss can be relieved. **(4 marks)**

(ii) Advise on the availability and effect of the instalment options for payment of Nathi's inheritance tax liability in respect of each of the investment property and the antique chairs, on the assumption that Caden will die on 20 March 2030.

Note. No calculations are required for part (a)(ii). **(3 marks)**

(b) Calculate Caden's taxable income for the tax year 2025/26 on the basis that the personal services company (IR35) legislation applies to the budgeted fee income receivable by Mandini Ltd in the year ending 31 March 2026. **(5 marks)**

(c) For the tax year 2025/26, advise Amahle why the interest receivable in respect of her bank account in the country of Komor will be subject to UK income tax and explain, with supporting calculations, why this will not actually result in any UK tax payable. **(8 marks)**

Professional marks will be awarded for the demonstration of skill in analysis & evaluation, scepticism and commercial acumen in your answer. **(5 marks)**

(Total = 25 marks)

Exhibit: Caden and Amahle

Caden

- Is resident and domiciled in the UK.
- Will sell four antique chairs on 6 October 2025.
- Is the sole shareholder, director and employee of Mandini Ltd.

Acquisition of antique chairs

- Caden was gifted a set of six antique chairs by his mother, Feba, on 3 March 2019.
- The chairs had a market value of £152,000 on that date.
- Feba had purchased the chairs for £106,000 on 8 August 2010.

Sale of antique chairs

- Caden sold two of the chairs to an unconnected person for £42,000 on 10 September 2019. The four remaining chairs were valued at £93,000 on that date.
- Caden is proposing to sell the four remaining chairs to his son, Nathi, for £35,000, on 6 October 2025. These four chairs are expected to be valued at £99,000 on that date.

- Nathi's friend tells him that if he does this he'll be able to realise a capital loss which he can use to save tax on other gains.

Caden – previous lifetime gift

- Caden's only previous lifetime gift was of an investment property to Nathi on 2 July 2025.
- This gift resulted in a gross chargeable transfer of £380,000.

Mandini Ltd

- Is a personal services company for the purposes of the IR35 legislation.
- Has budgeted fee income, wholly from relevant engagements, of £65,000 in the year ending 31 March 2026. The client is a small organisation for the purposes of the IR35 legislation.
- Pays Caden a gross monthly salary of £1,500.
- Will pay Caden a dividend of £35,000 on 28 February 2026.
- Neither Caden nor Mandini Ltd has any other sources of income.

Amahle

- Is resident and domiciled in the UK.
- Earns employment income of £45,000 (gross) every year.
- Receives interest income in respect of a bank deposit account in Komor.
- Makes a contribution to a personal pension scheme of £3,000 (net) every year.

Amahle – bank account in Komor

- On 1 January 2025, Amahle deposited £150,000 in a bank account in Komor.
- This account pays interest at the rate of 5% (gross) each year.
- Amahle will not remit any of this interest income to the UK.

The tax regime in Komor

- Tax is withheld at the rate of 18% on all interest income arising in Komor.
- The UK does not have a double taxation treaty with Komor.

Capital tax

18 Luis (Mar/Jun 2022) (49 mins)

You should assume that today's date is 1 June 2025.

Luis has requested advice in relation to the following:

- the potential inheritance tax (IHT) payable in respect of a planned gift of an investment property;
- the tax implications of the sale of qualifying enterprise investment scheme (EIS) shares; and
- the income tax implications of using the sales proceeds to repay a debt.

The following **exhibit**, available on the left-hand side of the screen, provides information relevant to the question:

(1) Luis

This information should be used to answer the question **requirements** within your chosen **response option(s)**.

Required

You should assume that today's date is 1 June 2025.

(a) Explain the circumstances under which the maximum liability to inheritance tax (IHT) will arise in respect of Luis' planned gift of Ivy Cottage to Silvia and calculate the amount which would be payable by Silvia in this situation. **(5 marks)**

(b) (i) Explain the immediate income tax and capital gains tax implications of Luis' sale of his Flores Ltd shares. **(5 marks)**

(ii) State the relief(s) available for the capital loss arising on this sale, including the rate of tax saved in respect of each relief, and advise Luis of the most tax-advantageous relief available to him. **(4 marks)**

(c) (i) Explain the income tax treatment for Luis of the receipt of the bank interest and payment of the mortgage loan interest. **(3 marks)**

(ii) Calculate the after-tax net interest saving for a full tax year if he decides to repay the mortgage loan. **(3 marks)**

Professional marks will be awarded for the demonstration of skill in analysis & evaluation, commercial acumen and scepticism in your answer. **(5 marks)**

(Total = 25 marks)

Exhibit: Luis

- Is resident and domiciled in the UK.
- Has a son, Mario, and a daughter, Silvia.
- Has never been married or had a civil partner.
- Owns a portfolio of residential investment properties.
- Has previously been a higher rate taxpayer in all relevant tax years, with the exception of the tax year 2023/24, when he was an additional rate taxpayer.
- Prior to the tax year 2025/26, his income in every tax year entirely comprised non-savings income.

Planned gift of Ivy Cottage to Silvia:

- Luis will gift Ivy Cottage, a residential investment property, to Silvia on 31 July 2025.
- Ivy Cottage will be worth £245,000 on that date, and is expected to appreciate in value over the next few years.
- Luis has made one previous gift, of £250,000 in cash to Mario on 1 January 2022.

Sale of Yew House:

- On 1 May 2023, Luis sold Yew House, a residential investment property, for proceeds of £366,000.
- This sale gave rise to a chargeable gain of £71,000.

Acquisition of shares in Flores Ltd:

- On 1 June 2023, Luis subscribed £120,000 for 50,000 newly issued ordinary shares in Flores Ltd, a UK resident trading company.
- These shares were qualifying enterprise investment scheme (EIS) shares.
- Luis obtained EIS relief of £36,000 (£120,000 × 30%) against his income tax liability for the tax year 2023/24.
- Luis elected to defer the maximum amount of the gain on the sale of Yew House as a result of the acquisition of these shares.

Sale of shares in Flores Ltd:

- On 1 April 2025, Luis sold all of his shares in Flores Ltd to an unconnected person for £85,000, their market value on that date.
- Luis will claim the most tax-advantageous relief for any loss which arises in respect of this sale.

Luis – interest receivable and payable:

- On 6 April 2025, Luis deposited the whole of the proceeds from the sale of the Flores Ltd shares in a bank deposit account, which will pay annual interest of £850.
- Luis is considering withdrawing all the deposited funds and using the money to repay the mortgage loan outstanding on one of his residential investment properties (not Ivy Cottage).
- Interest of £1,275 per annum is currently charged on this mortgage loan.
- Luis will be a higher rate taxpayer in all tax years for the foreseeable future.

19 Noah and Dan (Mar/Jun 2017, amended) (49 mins)

You should assume that today's date is 15 June 2025.

Your client, Dan, requires advice on the following issues:

- The inheritance tax implications arising as a result of the recent death of his father, Noah
- Dan's own UK residence status
- The potential chargeable gain arising on his proposed disposals of UK land.

The following exhibits, available on the left hand side of the screen, provide information relevant to the question;

(1) Noah

(2) Dan

This information should be used to answer the question **requirements** within your chosen **response option(s).**

Required

You should assume that today's date is 15 June 2025.

(a) (i) State, giving reasons, whether or not the house in Skarta will be included in Noah's chargeable estate on death for the purposes of UK inheritance tax. **(3 marks)**

(ii) Assuming that the house in Skarta is subject to inheritance tax in the UK, calculate the value of Dan's inheritance from Noah after all taxes and liabilities have been paid. **(6 marks)**

(b) (i) On the assumption that Dan does not satisfy either of the automatic tests for determining his UK residence status, explain why Dan will **NOT** be resident in the UK for tax purposes in the tax year 2025/26. **(5 marks)**

(ii) Calculate the chargeable gains arising on the disposal of Dan's UK land on 1 August 2025 and 1 October 2025, and state when the tax will be due. **(6 marks)**

Professional marks will be awarded for the demonstration of skill in analysis and evaluation and commercial acumen in your answer. **(5 marks)**

(Total = 25 marks)

Exhibit 1: Noah

Noah:

- Was resident in the UK from 1 April 2006 until his death on 31 May 2025, following a short illness
- Had a domicile of origin in the country of Skarta and did not acquire a domicile of choice in the UK
- Has one child, Dan

Noah – information for inheritance tax:

- Noah had not made any lifetime gifts.
- Noah left all the assets in his estate upon his death to Dan.

Noah – valuation of assets owned at death on 31 May 2025:

	£
Main residence located in the country of Skarta	242,000
Chattels and cash in the UK	460,000

Inheritance tax and liabilities in the country of Skarta:

- Under the tax system in Skarta, the inheritance tax payable will be £56,080.
- Legal and administration fees of £12,400 will be payable in Skarta in respect of Noah's house.
- There is no double tax treaty between the UK and Skarta.

Exhibit 2: Dan

Dan:

- Is domiciled in the country of Skarta
- Is unmarried, and has no children
- First became resident in the UK on 1 July 2019
- Left the UK on 1 January 2024 to go travelling
- Returned to the UK for the first time on 15 May 2025, when his father was taken ill
- Intends to work part time in the UK throughout the month of July 2025 only
- Will remain in the UK until 5 August 2025, when he intends to move permanently to Skarta

Dan – disposal of UK house:

- Dan purchased a house in the UK on 1 October 2019 for £286,000, where he lived until 1 January 2024.
- He has not lived in the house since this date.
- He allowed his father, Noah, to live in the house, rent-free, until his father's death.
- He has agreed to sell the house on 1 August 2025 for £361,000.

Dan – disposal of shop:

- Dan purchased a shop as an investment on 1 November 2018 for £130,000.
- The shop has been let out to a sole trader since it was acquired.
- He has agreed to sell the shop for £165,000 on 1 October 2025.
- The shop was valued at £150,000 on 5 April 2019.

20 Max (Mar/Jun 2018, amended) (49 mins)

You should assume that today's date is 1 June 2025.

Max ceased trading two years ago, and is now about to move overseas. He would like advice on:

- the capital gains tax (CGT) implications of the disposal of two assets previously used in his unincorporated business, and
- the inheritance tax (IHT) implications of gifting one of them.

The following exhibit, available on the left hand side of the screen, provides information relevant to the question;

(1) Max

This information should be used to answer the question **requirements** within your chosen **response option(s).**

Required

You should assume that today's date is 1 June 2025.

(a) In respect of the proposed gift of the office premises to Fara on 30 June 2025:

(i) Advise Max whether or not capital gains tax (CGT) gift holdover relief will be available, and if so, to what extent. **(3 marks)**

(ii) Advise Max of the maximum potential inheritance tax (IHT) liability, and the circumstances in which this would arise. **(5 marks)**

(b) Explain the effect of Max's period of living overseas on his UK residence status for all relevant tax years, and advise him of the CGT consequences of the sale of the warehouse (1) in June 2025, or alternatively (2) in June 2026.

Note. No calculations are required for this part. **(4 marks)**

(c) Explain whether or not business asset disposal relief will be available on the sale of the warehouse, and calculate Max's after-tax proceeds in order to recommend whether he should sell the warehouse in June 2025 or in June 2026. **(8 marks)**

Professional marks will be awarded for the demonstration of skill in analysis and evaluation, scepticism and commercial acumen in your answer. **(5 marks)**

(Total = 25 marks)

Exhibit: Max

Max:

- Has always been UK resident and domiciled.
- Is widowed and has one daughter, Fara.
- Is, and will continue to be, a higher-rate taxpayer.
- Has made one previous lifetime gift to Fara on 6 May 2022, which resulted in a gross chargeable transfer of £194,000.

Max – unincorporated business:

- Max operated as a sole trader for many years, but ceased trading on 31 May 2023.
- Max still owns office premises and a warehouse which had been used exclusively in his business until 31 May 2023.
- Max now wishes to dispose of these buildings prior to moving overseas.

Proposed gift of the office premises:

- Max is proposing to gift the office premises to Fara on 30 June 2025.
- Max acquired the premises on 1 April 2016.
- Since 1 June 2023, the premises have been let to an unconnected company.
- The market value of the premises in June 2025 is £168,000, which exceeds the original cost.

Max – move overseas:

- Max has decided to move overseas for a period of at least six years commencing on 1 November 2025.
- Max does not intend to return to the UK at all during this period.
- Max is not entitled to use the split year treatment for determination of his residence status in any tax year.

Proposed sale of the warehouse:

- The warehouse was acquired on 1 August 2017 for a cost of £50,000.
- Max had the warehouse valued on 5 April 2019 when it was worth £70,000.
- Max has received an offer of £84,000 for the immediate sale of the warehouse in June 2025.
- An alternative buyer has offered £90,000 for the warehouse, but will not be able to complete the purchase until June 2026.

21 Liber and Vesta (Dec 2018, amended) (49 mins)

You should assume that today's date is 1 December 2025.

Liber has requested advice on the timing of the sale of the shares which he acquired in a recent company takeover. His sister, Vesta, requires advice on the tax consequences of making a lifetime gift, rather than leaving an asset in her estate upon her death.

The following exhibit, available on the left hand side of the screen, provides information relevant to the question;

(1) Liber and Vesta

This information should be used to answer the question **requirements** within your chosen **response option(s).**

Required

You should assume that today's date is 1 December 2025.

(a) (i) Explain, with supporting calculations, the capital gains tax implications for Liber of the takeover of Vulcan Ltd by Mercury plc on 1 June 2025, and a subsequent sale of his Mercury plc shares on 1 January 2026. **(8 marks)**

(ii) Explain, with supporting calculations, why it would be beneficial for Liber to sell his Mercury plc shares on 1 May 2026, instead of on 1 January 2026. **(4 marks)**

(b) Advise Vesta whether or not there are any capital gains tax or inheritance tax advantages, for herself, or for Janus, if she were to gift the investment property to Janus on 31 December 2025, rather than leaving it to him in her estate on death. **(8 marks)**

Professional marks will be awarded for the demonstration of skill in analysis and evaluation and commercial acumen in your answer. **(5 marks)**

(Total = 25 marks)

Exhibit: Liber and Vesta

Liber:

- Is UK resident and domiciled.
- Has taxable income of £30,200 each year.

Liber – acquisition of ordinary shares in Mercury plc:

- Liber purchased 800 ordinary shares (a 40% holding) in Vulcan Ltd for £14,000 on 1 July 2011.
- Mercury plc acquired 100% of the ordinary share capital of Vulcan Ltd on 1 June 2025.
- In exchange for each ordinary share in Vulcan Ltd Liber received the following:
  - Four ordinary shares in Mercury plc valued at £20 per share immediately after the takeover; and
  - £15 cash
- Mercury plc has 200,000 issued ordinary shares.
- Liber has never been a director or employee of either Vulcan Ltd or Mercury plc.
- The takeover was for *bona fide* commercial reasons and not for the avoidance of tax.

Liber – proposed transaction in Mercury plc shares:

- Liber now wishes to sell all of his shares in Mercury plc.
- He has received an offer from an unconnected person to purchase these shares on 1 January 2026 at a price of £28 per share.
- Liber would prefer to sell the shares to his nephew, Janus. However, this would delay the sale as his nephew will not have the necessary funds to purchase the shares until 1 May 2026.
- Janus has said he will also pay £28 per share.

Vesta:

- Is 66 years old and has never married or had a civil partner.
- Is in ill-health and is expected to die at some time within the tax year 2026/27.
- Has made no disposals for capital gains tax purposes in the tax year 2025/26 to date and will not make any in the tax year 2026/27.
- Has made one previous lifetime gift, of £350,000 cash, to her son, Janus, on 1 June 2025.

Vesta – investment property:

- Vesta owns a residential investment property, which has never been used as her private residence.
- The current market value of the property is less than the price Vesta paid for it, and its value is expected to fall further throughout the tax year 2026/27.

- Vesta is considering gifting the investment property to Janus in her lifetime, rather than leaving it to him in her estate on death.
- Janus is the sole beneficiary of Vesta's estate.

22 Yacon Ltd and Daikon (Mar/Jun 2021) (49 mins)

You should assume that today's date is 1 December 2025.

Daikon, the managing director of Yacon Ltd, has requested advice on;

- the tax implications of Yacon Ltd setting up a tax-advantaged share incentive scheme for its employees;
- the capital gains tax relief(s) available on the sale of his house; and
- the potential inheritance tax liability arising on the gift of an apartment.

The following **exhibit** provides information relevant to the question:

(1) Yacon Ltd and Daikon

This information should be used to answer the question **requirements** within your chosen **response option(s)**.

Required

You should assume that today's date is 1 December 2025.

(a) Explain whether (1) a company share option scheme (CSOP) and (2) a share incentive plan (SIP) will satisfy Yacon Ltd's criteria for a tax advantaged share incentive scheme, and the income tax implications for the employees of acquiring the shares in each case. **(8 marks)**

(b) Calculate, with brief explanations, the private residence relief (PRR), and letting relief, which are available to reduce the chargeable gain on Daikon's sale of his house. **(7 marks)**

(c) Explain the inheritance tax implications of Jicama's gift of the apartment to Daikon on 5 June 2023, if Jicama were to die in December 2028. **(5 marks)**

Professional marks will be awarded for the demonstration of skill in analysis and evaluation and commercial acumen in your answer. **(5 marks)**

(Total = 25 marks)

Exhibit: Yacon Ltd and Daikon

Yacon Ltd:

- Is a UK resident, unquoted trading company which is not part of a group.
- Is considering setting up either a company share option plan (CSOP), or a share incentive plan (SIP), both of which would be offered to selected employees.

Yacon Ltd – criteria for its tax-advantaged share incentive scheme:

- Employees will be selected to join the scheme dependent on their period of employment with the company.
- If the scheme is a CSOP, each employee will be offered options to purchase shares worth up to £3,000 each year.
- Employees will exercise the options five years after being granted them.
- If the scheme is a SIP, each employee will be given free shares worth up to £3,000 each year.
- Employees will remove the shares from the plan after five years.

Daikon:

- Was gifted an apartment by his aunt, Jicama, on 5 June 2023.
- Has never lived in this apartment.
- Will sell the house he currently lives in, and move into this apartment on 31 December 2025.

Daikon – sale of his current house:

- Daikon purchased this house on 1 July 2017, when he was employed overseas.
- Daikon did not own any other property between 1 July 2017 and 4 June 2023.
- The sale of the house on 31 December 2025 will give rise to a chargeable gain of £145,000, before any reliefs.

Daikon – occupation of his current house:

- Daikon moved into the house on 1 January 2018, on his return to the UK.
- Daikon has occupied the house since 1 January 2018, apart from the period from 1 July 2019 to 31 December 2020, when he was, once again, employed overseas.
- Daikon resumed exclusive occupation of the house on 1 January 2021.
- Since 1 April 2021, Daikon has let the basement of the house (which comprises 25% of the property) for residential use, retaining exclusive occupation of the remaining 75% for himself.

Gift of the apartment by Jicama:

- When Jicama gifted the apartment to Daikon on 5 June 2023, it was on condition of her continuing to live in the property for the foreseeable future.
- On 12 March 2025, Jicama began living with her sister, and she removed the condition she had previously imposed on the gift from that date.

Owner managed businesses

23 Spike (ACCA specimen exam (FA21), amended to FA24)

(49 mins)

You should assume that today's date is 1 December 2025.

Spike requires advice on

- the loss relief available and the value added tax (VAT) position following the cessation of his business and
- on the tax implications of a relocation payment provided by his new employer.

Information relevant to the question can be found in the following exhibit, available on the left hand side of the screen:

(1) Spike

This information should be used to answer the question **requirements** within your chosen **response option(s).**

Required

You should assume that today's date is 1 December 2025.

(a) (i) Calculate the trading loss for the tax year 2024/25, and the terminal loss, on the cessation of Spike's unincorporated business. **(2 marks)**

(ii) Explain the reliefs available in respect of the trade loss in 2024/25 and the terminal loss and quantify the potential tax savings for each of them. **(9 marks)**

(b) State the VAT implications of the cessation of the business and the sale of the business assets. **(7 marks)**

(c) Explain the income tax implications for Spike of the relocation payment. **(2 marks)**

Professional marks will be awarded for the demonstration of skill in analysis & evaluation, scepticism and commercial acumen in your answer. **(5 marks)**

Note. You should assume that the tax rates and allowances for the tax year 2024/25 apply to all tax years.

Ignore national insurance contributions throughout this question.

(Total = 25 marks)

Exhibit: Spike

Spike:

- Ceased to trade on 31 December 2024 and sold the assets used in his unincorporated business
- Sold his house, 'Sea View', on 1 March 2025 for £125,000 more than he had paid for it
- Began working for Set Ltd on 1 May 2025
- Has no income or chargeable gains other than the amounts referred to in the information below

Spike's unincorporated business:

- The sale of the business resulted in net capital gains of £78,000.
- The tax adjusted profits/(loss) of the business have been:

		£
Year ended 31 March 2021	Profit	52,500
Year ended March 2022	Profit	68,000
Year ended 31 March 2023	Profit	54,000
Year ended 31 March 2024	Profit	22,850
Nine months ending 31 December 2024	Loss	(21,800)

- Spike's business has always had taxable supplies, being 70% of total supplies.

Sale of the business:

- The majority of the business assets were sold to unrelated purchasers during December 2024.
- This included a workshop which Spike had bought newly constructed in the year ended 31 March 2021. He had bought the workshop for £300,000 plus VAT and had used the workshop throughout his period of ownership in his trade. The workshop was sold in December 2024 for £360,000 and the resulting gain is included in the net capital gains of £78,000 stated earlier. Spike has not opted to tax the workshop.
- Spike retained some of his business assets for his own use.

Remuneration from Set Ltd:

- Spike is being paid a salary of £65,000 per year.
- On 1 July 2025, Set Ltd will pay Spike a relocation payment of £33,500.

The relocation payment of £33,500:

- Spike sold 'Sea View', and purchased a new house, in order to live near the premises of Set Ltd.
- £22,000 of the payment is to compensate Spike for having to sell his house at short notice at a low price.
- £11,500 of the payment is in respect of the costs incurred by Spike in relation to moving house.

24 Enid (Sep 2018, amended) (49 mins)

You should assume that today's date is 1 September 2025.

Enid requires advice on the following issues:

- capital gains tax (CGT) and value added tax (VAT) implications of transferring her unincorporated sole trader business to a newly incorporated company, Niche Ltd
- the tax implications of alternative ways of extracting profits from the new company

The following exhibit, available on the left hand side of the screen, provides information relevant to the question;

(1) Enid

This information should be used to answer the question **requirements** within your chosen **response option(s).**

Required

You should assume that today's date is 1 September 2025.

(a) Explain how Enid can obtain relief for the trading losses of £51,000 brought forward in her unincorporated business at 6 April 2025. **(4 marks)**

(b) Explain why the transfer of Enid's business to Niche Ltd qualifies for incorporation relief, and, on the assumption that Enid does not elect to disapply this relief, calculate the balance on her loan account with Niche Ltd after deducting the cash to be withdrawn to pay any capital gains tax (CGT) due. **(7 marks)**

(c) Advise Enid of the impact on the total amount of tax payable by both herself and Niche Ltd if, instead of a dividend of £15,000, she (1) receives additional salary of £15,000, or alternatively (2) withdraws £15,000 from her loan account in the tax year 2026/27.

Note. You should assume that there will be sufficient funds in Enid's loan account to permit this withdrawal. **(6 marks)**

(d) Advise Enid of her administrative obligations under the value added tax (VAT) legislation, arising from the transfer of her business to Niche Ltd, and whether or not she is able to transfer the VAT registration from her unincorporated business to Niche Ltd.

Note. You should assume that the transfer of a going concern rules will apply for VAT purposes, but are NOT required to discuss these rules. **(3 marks)**

Professional marks will be awarded for the demonstration of skill in analysis and evaluation, scepticism and commercial acumen in your answer. **(5 marks)**

(Total = 25 marks)

Exhibit: Enid

Enid:

- Has been in business as an unincorporated sole trader for many years.
- Receives dividends from a portfolio of investments of £500 each year.
- Has no other source of income.
- Is a higher rate taxpayer for all relevant tax years.
- Will transfer all the assets and liabilities of her business to Niche Ltd on 1 October 2025.
- Will make no other disposals for CGT purposes in the tax year 2025/26.
- Will be the only director and shareholder of Niche Ltd.

Enid's unincorporated business:

- At 6 April 2025 Enid had trading losses brought forward of £51,000.
- During 2025/26, Enid's business will have a taxable trading profit of £42,000, prior to the transfer to Niche Ltd.
- Is registered for the purposes of value added tax (VAT).

The assets and liabilities to be transferred to Niche Ltd:

	Cost	*Value at 1 October 2025*
	£	£
Goodwill	0	83,000
Workshop (purchased in 2001)	55,000	122,000
Inventory	7,000	5,000
Liabilities	n/a	(10,000)

Consideration to be paid by Niche Ltd:

- 1,000 £1 ordinary shares in respect of 85% of the total value of the consideration for the business.
- The remainder of the consideration will be left on loan account payable by Niche Ltd to Enid.
- Enid will withdraw cash from the loan account to pay any CGT liability arising on the transfer of the business.

Niche Ltd:

- Will pay Enid a salary of £75,000 per year, and dividends of £15,000 on 31 March each year.
- Will have taxable total profits of approximately £200,000 per annum.
- Will not be regarded as a personal service company under the provisions of the IR35 legislation.

25 Yacqui (Sep/Dec 2022) (49 mins)

You should assume that today's date is 1 September 2025.

Yaqui has requested advice on the following:

- the income tax and capital gains tax (CGT) implications of selling two assets following the cessation of an unincorporated business; and
- the value added tax (VAT) consequences of either selling or renting out a warehouse.

The following **exhibit**, available on the left-hand side of the screen, provides information relevant to the question:

(1) Yaqui

This information should be used to answer the question **requirements** within your chosen **response option(s).**

Required

You should assume that today's date is 1 September 2025.

(a) Explain the income tax adjustments required to the trading profit for the three-month period ending 30 September 2025 in respect of the disposal of the specialist fixed machine and the planned disposal of the warehouse. Calculate the increase/(decrease) in Yaqui's tax payable due to these changes in trading profit due to the disposal of the assets. **(5 marks)**

(b) (i) Explain the capital gains tax implications for Yaqui of selling the specialist fixed machine on 10 July 2025. Your answer should include an explanation of the tax treatment of the chargeable gain of £11,000 which was deferred on the acquisition of this machine.

Note. Ignore VAT for this part of the question. **(3 marks)**

(ii) Explain whether or not business asset disposal relief (BADR) would be available to Yaqui if he sells the warehouse on 30 September 2025 as planned and calculate the chargeable gain which would arise. **(6 marks)**

(c) Explain the VAT capital goods scheme consequences for Yaqui if:

(i) he sells the warehouse as planned on 30 September 2025; or, alternatively **(2 marks)**

(ii) he starts to rent out the warehouse to unconnected tenants from 1 October 2025.

Note. For guidance, part (i) is worth two marks and part (ii) is worth four marks.

(4 marks)

Professional marks will be awarded for the demonstration of skill in analysis & evaluation and commercial acumen in your answer. **(5 marks)**

(Total = 25 marks)

Exhibit: Yaqui

Yaqui:

- Is a higher rate taxpayer for all relevant tax years.
- Is registered for value added tax (VAT) purposes.
- Will cease trading as YP Trading on 30 September 2025.
- Will not be required to deregister for the purposes of VAT on the cessation of YP Trading as he will continue to run an existing, second, unincorporated business.

YP Trading:

- Accounts have been prepared on an accruals basis to 30 June each year up to 30 June 2025, and the final accounts will be prepared for the three-month period to 30 September 2025. He has elected to use the accruals basis to calculate his taxable trading income
- The business makes wholly standard rated supplies.

YP Trading – capital assets:

- On 1 July 2025, these comprised a specialist fixed machine and a warehouse.
- On 1 July 2025, the brought forward written down value on the capital allowances main pool was £nil.
- Yaqui has always claimed all available capital allowances.

Acquisition and sale of the specialist fixed machine:

- Yaqui acquired the machine on 31 March 2015 for £65,000.
- Rollover relief was claimed on this purchase to defer a chargeable gain of £11,000.
- Yaqui sold the machine on 10 July 2025 for £23,000.

Acquisition of the warehouse:

- Yaqui purchased the newly constructed warehouse from the builder on 1 October 2023 and started to use it in his business on 1 November 2023.
- The warehouse qualifies for structures and buildings allowances (SBA).
- The warehouse will continue to be wholly used in the YP Trading business until 30 September 2025.
- The warehouse cost £263,000 (exclusive of VAT) including £48,000 for the land.
- Yaqui has not opted to tax this building for VAT purposes and will not do so in the future.
- The warehouse is subject to the capital goods scheme for the purposes of VAT.

Sale of the warehouse:

- Yaqui is planning to sell the warehouse on 30 September 2025.
- The sale proceeds would be £296,000 (exclusive of VAT), which would include £55,000 for the land.

26 Rod (Mar/Jun 2019, amended) (49 mins)

You should assume that today's date is 1 June 2025.

Rod has requested advice in relation to:

- the capital gains tax implications of selling shares he obtained through his employer's enterprise management incentive (EMI) scheme, and
- the potential income tax relief available in respect of his share of a trading loss of a partnership which he has recently joined.

The following exhibit, available on the left hand side of the screen, provides information relevant to the question;

(1) Rod

This information should be used to answer the question **requirements** within your chosen **response option(s).**

Required

You should assume that today's date is 1 June 2025.

(a) Calculate Rod's after-tax proceeds from the sale of his shares in Lumba plc and explain your calculation of the base cost for the shares. **(6 marks)**

(b) (i) Calculate Rod's share of the tax-adjusted trading loss in the Thora Partnership for the tax years 2024/25 and 2025/26.

Note. You should assume that Rod's share of the profits since he joined the partnership until 31 March 2025 will equal his trading profits for the tax year 2024/25. **(5 marks)**

(ii) State how Rod is able to relieve the trading loss(es) calculated in (b)(i) above as early as possible, and explain, with supporting calculations, the total amount of income tax saved if Rod follows this strategy.

Note. You should assume the tax rates and allowances for the tax year 2024/25 apply to all tax years. **(9 marks)**

Professional marks will be awarded for the demonstration of skill in analysis and evaluation and commercial acumen in your answer. **(5 marks)**

(Total = 25 marks)

Exhibit: Rod

Rod:

- Is resident and domiciled in the UK.
- Was employed for many years by Lumba plc, before taking early retirement on 30 June 2024.
- Joined the Thora Partnership on 1 December 2024.
- Made no disposals for capital gains tax in the tax year 2024/25, other than the sale of his shares in Lumba plc (as detailed below).

Sale of Lumba plc shares:

- In May 2020, Lumba plc granted Rod options to purchase 20,000 shares under its EMI scheme.
- The market value of a share at the date of the grant was £2.60 and the option price was £2.30 per share.
- Rod exercised all of the options on 31 May 2024, when the market value was 3.90 per share.
- Rod sold all the shares on 1 December 2024, when the market value was £4.00 per share.
- The gain is eligible for business asset disposal relief.

The Thora Partnership:

- Has been carried on for many years by two partners, Abe and Bob.
- Prepares accounts to 31 March annually.
- Admitted Rod into the partnership on 1 December 2024.
- Is expected to make a tax-adjusted trading loss of £47,000 in the year ending 31 March 2025 and £10,000 in the year ending 31 March 2026.

The Thora Partnership – profit/loss sharing arrangements:

- The partnership's profit/loss sharing arrangements from 1 December 2024 are as follows:

	Abe	Bob	Rod
Annual salary	£20,000	£20,000	£0
Profit/loss sharing ratio	1	1	1

Rod's income in the tax years 2021/22 to 2024/25:

Tax year	*Employment income*	*Dividends*
	£	£
2021/22	82,000	0
2022/23	90,000	16,000
2023/24	86,000	12,000
2024/25	26,000	8,000

27 Rosa (Sep/Dec 2019, amended) (49 mins)

You should assume that today's date is 1 December 2025.

Your client, Rosa, has requested advice in relation to:

- the consequences of her daughter, Siena, becoming either an employee or a partner in her unincorporated business
- the options available to her to relieve a trading loss incurred by the business
- the value added tax (VAT) implications of selling a retail unit.

The following exhibit, available on the left hand side of the screen, provides information relevant to the question:

(1) Rosa

This information should be used to answer the question **requirements** within your chosen **response option(s).**

Required

You should assume that today's date is 1 December 2025.

(a) Advise Rosa of the difference in the total amount of income tax and national insurance contributions (NICs) payable by her and Siena for the tax year 2026/27, if Siena is taken on as (i) a partner, or (ii) an employee by RS Trading on 1 April 2026. **(9 marks)**

(b) Assuming Siena is employed by RS Trading from 1 April 2026, identify and explain the relief(s) available to Rosa to relieve her trading loss of the year ending 31 March 2027, and calculate the maximum tax saving available to her as a result of claiming such relief(s) in the tax year 2025/26.

Note. You should NOT consider the possibility of Rosa carrying all, or any part, of the loss forward for relief for part (b). **(7 marks)**

(c) Explain the value added tax (VAT) implications of the disposal of the retail unit on 6 April 2026 and calculate the final VAT adjustment under the capital goods scheme. **(4 marks)**

Professional marks will be awarded for the demonstration of skill in analysis and evaluation and commercial acumen in your answer **(5 marks)**

(Total = 25 marks)

Exhibit: Rosa

Rosa:

- Is 62 years old and is widowed.
- Has one daughter, Siena.
- Owns an unincorporated business, RS Trading, which she has run for many years.
- Currently has no employees in her business.
- Will bring her daughter, Siena, into the business either as an employee or a partner, on 1 April 2026.
- Has a budgeted income tax liability of £22,232, and a budgeted capital gains tax liability of £22,080 for the tax year 2025/26.

Siena:

- Will have no source of taxable income in the tax year 2026/27, other than from RS Trading.

RS Trading:

- Has an accounting date of 31 March each year.
- Has a budgeted tax adjusted trading profit of £27,000 for the year ending 31 March 2026.
- Has a budgeted trading loss of £62,000, before any payment to Siena, for the year ending 31 March 2027.
- Is registered for VAT and makes only standard rated supplies.

RS Trading – future plans:

- Siena will become either an employee or a partner in RS Trading on 1 April 2026.
- If Siena becomes an employee, she will receive an annual salary of £22,000 which is a commercial rate for the duties she will perform.
- Alternatively, if Siena becomes a partner, the profit sharing arrangements from 1 April 2026 will be:

	Rosa	Siena
Annual salary	£0	£12,000
Profit sharing ratio	80%	20%

Rosa – investment properties:

- Rosa will receive net rental income of £60,000 from a portfolio of residential properties and a retail unit in the tax year 2025/26.
- Rosa sold all the residential properties on 30 November 2025, realising total chargeable gains of £92,000.

Disposal of the retail unit:

- Rosa will sell the retail unit, which is currently being rented to tenants up to 5 April 2026, for its market value of £280,000 on 6 April 2026.
- Rosa had bought the retail unit when it was newly constructed, on 1 May 2019, for £290,000 plus VAT at 20%.

- Rosa used the retail unit in her business until 30 April 2023, since when she has let it to unconnected tenants.
- The retail unit is subject to the capital goods scheme for VAT.
- Rosa has not opted to tax the retail unit for VAT purposes.
- Rosa's VAT year end is 31 March.

28 Tomas and Ines (Mar 2020, amended) (49 mins)

You should assume that today's date is 1 May 2025.

Tomas and his wife, Ines, require advice in connection with the following:

- the tax implications of commencing to trade;
- voluntary registration for value added tax (VAT) purposes and the implications of purchasing services from overseas; and
- the tax implications of selling shares in respect of which enterprise investment scheme (EIS) relief has been obtained

The following exhibit, available on the left-hand side of the screen, provides information relevant to the question;

(1) Tomas and Ines

This information should be used to answer the question **requirements** within your chosen **response option(s)**.

Required

You should assume that today's date is 1 May 2025.

(a) On the assumption that Tomas prepares his first set of accounts to 31 March 2026, explain, with supporting calculations, the difference in the total amount of tax payable by him for the tax year 2025/26 as a result of the profit on the sales of sporting memorabilia being treated as trading income, rather than chargeable gains. **(5 marks)**

(b) (i) Explain TWO matters which Tomas should consider in deciding whether or not it will be financially beneficial to voluntarily register for value added tax (VAT). **(4 marks)**

(ii) Assuming Tomas DOES voluntarily register for VAT, explain the implications of purchasing advice from the overseas supplier, rather than using one based in the UK. **(3 marks)**

(c) Explain the tax implications for Ines of her intended sale of the Tavira Ltd shares on 1 June 2025, and calculate her after-tax proceeds from this sale. **(8 marks)**

Professional marks will be awarded for the demonstration of skill in analysis and evaluation and commercial acumen in your answer **(5 marks)**

(Total = 25 marks)

Exhibit: Tomas and Ines

Tomas:

- Is UK resident and domiciled.
- Uses his capital gains tax (CGT) annual exempt amount every year.
- Receives dividends of £1,000 every year.

Tomas – sale of sporting memorabilia:

- Tomas started selling items of sporting memorabilia from his collection during the tax year 2024/25.
- HM Revenue and Customs (HMRC) agreed that these sales should be subject to CGT in the tax year 2024/25.

- In April 2025, Tomas started purchasing and selling more items of sporting memorabilia, such that HMRC have said that he will be regarded as trading with effect from 6 April 2025.
- Tomas will not be required to register for value added tax (VAT) for the foreseeable future.
- Tomas will, however, consider registering voluntarily for VAT if it is financially beneficial for him to do so.
- Tomas will obtain advice on how to develop his business through the use of social media, and has been recommended a company based overseas (in a country where the rate of VAT is 9%) to complete this work.

Tomas – expected trading results from the sale of sporting memorabilia:

- Tomas estimates that his total income less expenditure for the 12 months ending 31 March 2026 will be £14,000.
- Each item of memorabilia is purchased and sold for no more than £1,000.
- All of the costs he incurs are deductible for tax purposes.

Ines:

- Is UK resident and domiciled.
- Is a higher rate taxpayer.
- Has made/will make no disposals for CGT purposes, other than as described below.

Ines – sale of painting:

- Ines sold a painting on 4 July 2022 for proceeds of £196,000.
- The sale gave rise to a gain of £86,000.

Ines – acquisition of shares in Tavira Ltd:

- Ines subscribed £72,000 for 20,000 shares in Tavira Ltd on 8 October 2022.
- These shares are qualifying enterprise investment scheme (EIS) shares.
- Ines elected to defer the maximum possible amount of the gain on the sale of the painting against the acquisition of these shares.
- Ines obtained EIS relief of £18,600 against her income tax liability for the tax year 2022/23.
- Ines intends to sell all of the shares in Tavira Ltd for £95,000 on 1 June 2025.
- If undertaken, this sale would qualify for business asset disposal relief.

29 Sabin and Patan Ltd (Sep/Dec 2021, amended) (49 mins)

You should assume that today's date is 1 September 2025.

Sabin requires advice on:

- the tax implications of ceasing his loss-making unincorporated business and
- selling his business assets.

Patan Ltd is seeking advice in respect of:

- the corporation tax relief available for capital expenditure, and
- for expenditure related to research and development activities.

The following exhibit provides information relevant to the question:

(1) Sabin and Patan Ltd

This information should be used to answer the question **requirements** within your chosen **response option(s).**

Required

You should assume that today's date is 1 September 2025.

(a) Calculate, with supporting explanations, the income tax saving for Sabin if he claims terminal loss relief ONLY for the trading losses arising in his final two trading periods. **(6 marks)**

(b) Explain the capital gains tax (CGT) implications for Sabin arising from the sale of the business premises and specialist machine to Patan Ltd, and calculate the amount available to Sabin from the sale of these assets, after paying any CGT liability arising. **(5 marks)**

(c) Explain the tax deductions and reliefs available to Patan Ltd in the year ending 31 March 2026 in respect of:

- the acquisition of the new factory, and;
- the expenditure on research and development.

(9 marks)

Professional marks will be awarded for the demonstration of skill in analysis & evaluation and commercial acumen in your answer. **(5 marks)**

(Total = 25 marks)

Exhibit: Sabin and Patan Ltd

Sabin

- Ceased trading on 31 December 2024.
- Sold his business premises and a specialist machine to Patan Ltd, an unconnected company, on 1 April 2025.
- Has income from his business (see below), and from part-time employment (£6,000 gross per year).
- Uses his annual exempt amount for capital gains tax purposes every year.

Sabin's unincorporated business

- Sabin commenced in business as a sole trader on 1 July 2013 and has always calculated his taxable trading income on an accruals basis.
- Tax-adjusted trading profits/(losses) of the business were as follows:

2021/22	2022/23	2023/24	2024/25
£44,000	£32,000	£21,000	£(34,800)

Sabin's terminal loss is £32,800.

Sabin – sale of business premises and specialist machinery to Patan Ltd on 1 April 2025

	Date of acquisition	Cost	Sale proceeds (cash)
		£	£
Business premises	1 July 2013	86,000	114,000
Specialist machine	1 May 2018	49,000	41,000

- The business premises had been wholly occupied by Sabin's business throughout his period of ownership.
- Sabin had claimed capital allowances on the specialist machine.

Patan Ltd

- Was incorporated and commenced trading on 1 April 2025.
- Expects to make a tax-adjusted trading loss in the year ending 31 March 2026.
- Has no other source of income or gains in this accounting period.

- Qualifies for R&D relief.

Patan Ltd – capital acquisitions and disposals

- Patan Ltd purchased a newly-constructed factory building from a developer on 1 April 2025.
- Patan Ltd paid £242,000 for the factory, which included £106,000 for the land, £30,000 for planning permission and £20,000 of fees and stamp taxes.
- The factory was brought into use on 1 May 2025.

Patan Ltd – expenditure on research and development activities

- One of Patan Ltd's employees is wholly engaged in qualifying research and development activities at an annual cost to the company of £40,000.
- Patan Ltd also engages external subcontractors, provided by unconnected companies. The total cost of these will be £22,000 in the year ending 31 March 2026.
- Patan Ltd purchased specialist research equipment for £20,000 and £1,000 on computer software.

Taxation of companies

30 Maria and Granada Ltd (Mar/Jun 2016, amended) (49 mins)

You should assume that today's date is 1 June 2025.

Your firm has been asked to provide advice to Granada Ltd and one of its shareholders, Maria. These taxpayers require advice on the following issues:

- Maria wants advice on the tax consequences of selling some of her shares back to Granada Ltd.
- Granada Ltd wants advice on the corporation tax and value added tax (VAT) implications of the recent acquisition of an unincorporated business.

The following exhibit, available on the left hand side of the screen, provides information relevant to the question:

(1) Maria and Granada Ltd

This information should be used to answer the question **requirements** within your chosen **response option(s).**

Required

You should assume that today's date is 1 June 2025.

(a) (i) Explain, with the aid of calculations, why the capital treatment **WILL NOT** apply if Maria sells 2,700 of her shares back to Granada Ltd, but **WILL** apply if, alternatively, she sells back 3,200 shares. **(4 marks)**

(ii) Calculate Maria's after-tax proceeds per share if she sells:

- 2,700 shares back to Granada Ltd; and, alternatively
- 3,200 shares back to Granada Ltd.

(4 marks)

(b) (i) Describe the corporation tax treatment of the acquisition of the patent by Granada Ltd if no charge for amortisation was required in its statement of profit or loss. **(3 marks)**

(ii) Discuss how Granada Ltd could obtain relief for the trading loss expected to be incurred by the trade acquired from Starling Partners, if it does not wish to carry any of the loss back. **(5 marks)**

(c) Explain the VAT implications for Granada Ltd in respect of the acquisition of the business of Starling Partners, and the additional information needed in relation to the building to fully clarify the VAT position. **(4 marks)**

Professional marks will be awarded for the demonstration of skill in analysis and evaluation, scepticism and commercial acumen in your answer **(5 marks)**

(Total = 25 marks)

Exhibit: Maria and Granada Ltd

Maria:

- Is resident and domiciled in the UK.
- Is a higher rate taxpayer and will remain so in the future.
- Will have dividend income of £3,000 in the tax year 2025/26.
- Will realise chargeable gains of £15,000 in the tax year 2025/26, excluding any gains that may arise on the disposal of her Granada Ltd shares.

Shares in Granada Ltd:

- Maria subscribed for 10,000 £1 ordinary shares in Granada Ltd at par in June 2012.
- Maria is one of four equal shareholders and directors of Granada Ltd.
- Maria intends to sell either 2,700 or 3,200 shares back to the company on 31 March 2026 at their current market value of £12.80 per share.
- All of the conditions for capital treatment are satisfied except for, potentially, the condition relating to the reduction in the level of shareholding.

Granada Ltd:

- Is a UK resident trading company which manufactures knitwear.
- Prepares accounts to 31 December each year.
- Is registered for VAT.
- Acquired the trade and assets of an unincorporated business, Starling Partners, on 1 January 2025.

Starling Partners:

- Had been trading as a partnership for many years as a wholesaler of handbags within the UK.
- Starling Partners' main assets comprise a freehold commercial building and a patent for a process used in making handbags, which were valued on acquisition by Granada Ltd at £105,000 and £40,000 respectively.
- Is registered for VAT.
- The transfer of its trade and assets to Granada Ltd qualified as a transfer of a going concern (TOGC) for VAT purposes.
- Due to overseas competition, the trading activities of the business are likely to be treated by HM Revenue & Customs (HMRC) as small or negligible in the year ended 31 December 2025.
- The business is forecast to make a trading loss of £130,000 in the year ended 31 December 2025.

Granada Ltd – results and proposed expansion:

- The knitwear business is expected to continue making a taxable trading profit of around £100,000 each year.
- Granada Ltd has no non-trading income but realised a chargeable gain of £10,000 on 28 February 2025.
- Granada Ltd is considering expanding the wholesale handbag trade acquired from Starling Partners into the export market from 1 January 2026.
- Granada Ltd anticipates that this expansion will result in the wholesale handbag trade returning a profit of £15,000 in the year ended 31 December 2026.

31 Acryl Ltd and Cresco Ltd (Sep/Dec 2016, amended) (49 mins)

You should assume that today's date is 1 September 2025.

Acryl Ltd and Cresco Ltd are two unrelated companies. Acryl Ltd requires advice on the implications of being placed into liquidation, particularly the timing of distributions to its shareholders.

Cresco Ltd requires advice on:

- the relief for losses on the cessation of trade
- its obligations in relation to value added tax (VAT)

The following exhibits, available on the left-hand side of the screen, provide information relevant to the question.

(1) Acryl Ltd

(2) Cresco Ltd

This information should be used to answer the question **requirements** within your chosen **response option(s).**

Required

You should assume that today's date is 1 September 2025.

(a) Acryl Ltd:

   (i) State the corporation tax consequences arising from the commencement of Acryl Ltd's winding up on 1 January 2026. **(2 marks)**

   (ii) Explain the tax implications for both Mambo Ltd and Alan if the distribution to be made by Acryl Ltd occurs either on 31 December 2025, or alternatively on 31 March 2026, and conclude as to which date would be preferable. **(7 marks)**

(b) Cresco Ltd:

   (i) Set out, together with supporting explanations, how Cresco Ltd will claim relief for the trading losses incurred and identify the amount of trading losses which will remain unrelieved after all available loss reliefs have been claimed. **(8 marks)**

   (ii) Advise Cresco Ltd of the VAT implications of the cessation of its trade. **(3 marks)**

Professional marks will be awarded for the demonstration of skill in analysis and evaluation and commercial acumen in your answer. **(5 marks)**

(Total = 25 marks)

Exhibit 1: Acryl Ltd

Acryl Ltd:

- Is a UK resident trading company.
- Has always used a 30 June accounting reference date.
- Has substantial distributable profits.
- 70% of the company's share capital is owned by Mambo Ltd.
- The remaining 30% of the share capital is owned by Mambo Ltd's managing director, Alan.
- Mambo Ltd and Alan both subscribed for their shares at par value on 1 March 2017.

Mambo Ltd:

- Is a UK resident trading company.

Alan:

- Will be an additional rate taxpayer in the tax year 2025/26.
- Will be eligible for business asset disposal relief on the disposal of his shares in Acryl Ltd.

Liquidation of Acryl Ltd:

- Winding up will commence on 1 January 2026 with the appointment of a liquidator.
- It is anticipated that the winding up will be completed on 31 March 2026, when the company will cease trading

Alternative timing of distributions being considered by Acryl Ltd:

- Acryl Ltd is prepared to distribute the available profits to its shareholders on 31 December 2025.
- Alternatively, Acryl Ltd will delay the distribution until the completion of the winding up of the company on 31 March 2026.

Exhibit 2: Cresco Ltd

Cresco Ltd:

- Is a UK resident trading company.
- Commenced trading on 1 April 2023.
- Is registered for the purposes of VAT.
- Has made significant trading losses in recent months such that the company will need to cease trading on 31 October 2027.

Cresco Ltd – trading losses:

- Recent and anticipated results are as follows:

	Y/e 31 March 2024	*Y/e 31 March 2025*	*Y/e 31 March 2026*	*Y/e 31 March 2027*	*P/e 31 October 2027*
	£	£	£	£	£
Trading (loss)/profit	(5,000)	21,000	8,000	(24,000)	(40,000)
Bank interest receivable	1,000	3,000	3,000	Nil	Nil

- Cresco Ltd always claims relief for trading losses as early as possible.

32 Achiote Ltd, Borage Ltd and Caraway Inc (Mar/Jun 2017, amended) (49 mins)

You should assume that today's date is 1 June 2025.

The finance director of Achiote Ltd would like your advice on:

- the tax implications of the acquisition of two intangible fixed assets;
- various transactions involving an overseas subsidiary, and
- opting to tax a commercial building.

The following exhibit, available on the left hand side of the screen, provides information relevant to the question:

(1) Achiote Ltd, Borage Ltd and Caraway Inc

This information should be used to answer the question **requirements** within your chosen **response option(s).**

Required

You should assume that today's date is 1 June 2025.

(a) Explain, with supporting calculations where appropriate, the corporation tax treatment in the year ended 31 March 2025, of the goodwill and the patent acquired by Borage Ltd. **(4 marks)**

(b) Explain the implications of the rate of interest charged by Achiote Ltd on the loan to Caraway Inc by reference to the transfer pricing legislation, and any action which should be taken by Achiote Ltd. **(5 marks)**

(c) Advise Achiote Ltd of the chargeable gains implications arising from (1) the sale of the item of equipment to Caraway Inc; and (2) its proposed sale of the shares in Caraway Inc. **(5 marks)**

(d) (i) On the assumption that Rye Ltd makes only taxable supplies, state **TWO** legitimate reasons why it might not charge VAT on its sales to Achiote Ltd. **(2 marks)**

(ii) Explain whether or not it would be financially beneficial for Achiote Ltd to opt to tax the commercial building, and the implications for Rye Ltd if it chooses to do so. **(4 marks)**

Professional marks will be awarded for the demonstration of skill in analysis and evaluation and commercial acumen in your answer **(5 marks)**

(Total = 25 marks)

Exhibit: Achiote Ltd, Borage Ltd and Caraway Inc

Achiote Ltd:

- Owns 100% of the ordinary shares in Borage Ltd and 80% of the ordinary shares in Caraway Inc.
- Achiote Ltd and Borage Ltd are resident in the UK. Caraway Inc is resident in the country of Nuxabar.
- All three companies are trading companies and prepare accounts to 31 March annually.

Borage Ltd – purchase of intangible fixed assets:

- Borage Ltd purchased the goodwill of an unincorporated business for £62,000 on 1 September 2024.
- Borage Ltd will amortise this goodwill in its accounts on a straight-line basis over a five-year period.
- Borage Ltd also purchased a patent from Achiote Ltd for £45,000 on 1 January 2025.
- Achiote Ltd had purchased the patent for £38,000 on 1 January 2022.
- The patent was being amortised in Achiote Ltd's accounts on a straight-line basis over a ten-year period.
- Borage Ltd will continue to amortise the patent over the remainder of its ten-year life.

Achiote Ltd – loan to Caraway Inc:

- Achiote Ltd made a loan of £100,000 to Caraway Inc on 1 April 2025.
- The rate of interest on the loan is 6% per annum, which is 2% below the rate applicable to an equivalent loan from an unrelated party.
- There is no double tax treaty between the UK and Nuxabar.

Achiote Ltd – sale of equipment to, and proposed sale of shares in, Caraway Inc:

- Achiote Ltd acquired its 80% shareholding in Caraway Inc on 1 January 2025 for £258,000.
- Achiote Ltd is now proposing to sell an 8% shareholding in Caraway Inc to an unconnected company on 1 October 2025 for £66,000.
- An item of equipment owned by Achiote Ltd and used in its trade was sold to Caraway Inc on 1 March 2025 for its market value of £21,000.
- The item of equipment had cost Achiote Ltd £32,000 in May 2022 and the super-deduction had been claimed.

Achiote Ltd – purchase and rental of a commercial building:

- Achiote Ltd has recently purchased a two-year-old commercial building from an unconnected vendor.
- The building will be rented to an unconnected company, Rye Ltd.
- Rye Ltd is a small local company, which supplies goods to Achiote Ltd but does not charge value added tax (VAT) on these sales.

33 Kitz Ltd (Sep/Dec 2019, amended) (49 mins)

You should assume that today's date is 1 December 2025.

The finance director of Kitz Ltd has requested advice on:

- the tax implications of selling shares in a subsidiary company,
- making a loan to another subsidiary company, and
- selling an intangible fixed asset.

The following exhibit, available on the left-hand side of the screen, provides information relevant to the question;

(1) Kitz Ltd

This information should be used to answer the question **requirements** within your chosen **response option(s).**

Required

You should assume that today's date is 1 December 2025.

(a) Explain the chargeable gains implications for Kitz Ltd arising from the sale of its shares in Mayr Ltd on 1 July 2025.

Note. No calculations are required for part (a). **(6 marks)**

(b) Explain, with brief supporting calculations, the corporation tax implications for both Kitz Ltd and Feld Ltd in respect of the interest charged on the loan by Kitz Ltd to Feld Ltd for the year ending 31 March 2027. **(7 marks)**

(c) (i) Explain the corporation tax implications for Kitz Ltd of the sale of the patent to Durn Ltd on 3 May 2026, assuming Kitz Ltd does not make a claim for intangible fixed asset rollover relief. **(3 marks)**

(ii) Explain why rollover relief for intangible fixed assets will be available in respect of the sale of the patent to Durn Ltd, and, on the assumption the maximum rollover relief is claimed, calculate the impact of the claim on Kitz Ltd's corporation tax liability for the year ending 31 March 2027. **(4 marks)**

Professional marks will be awarded for the demonstration of skill in analysis and evaluation and commercial acumen. **(5 marks)**

(Total = 25 marks)

Exhibit: Kitz Ltd

Kitz Ltd:

- Kitz Ltd owns 100% of the ordinary shares in Feld Ltd.
- Kitz Ltd and Feld Ltd are UK resident trading companies which both pay main rate corporation tax.
- Both companies use a 31 March accounting reference date.
- Neither company is a small or medium-sized enterprise (SME) for the purpose of transfer pricing.

Kitz Ltd – sale of 7,500 ordinary shares (a 75% holding) in Mayr Ltd on 1 July 2025:

- Mayr Ltd is a UK resident trading company.
- The shares, which represent the whole of Kitz Ltd's shareholding, were sold to an unconnected purchaser for £790,000.
- Kitz Ltd had acquired these shares on 1 March 2015 for £455,000.
- Kitz Ltd had sold a warehouse to Mayr Ltd on 8 April 2020 for its market value on that date of £165,000.
- Kitz Ltd had purchased the warehouse on 12 May 2015 for £129,000.

- Mayr Ltd still owned the warehouse on 1 July 2025.

Kitz Ltd – loan to Feld Ltd:

- Kitz Ltd will make a loan of £450,000 to Feld Ltd on 1 April 2026.
- Feld Ltd will use the loan to purchase goodwill and office premises for use in its business, and 70% of the ordinary share capital of Durn Ltd.
- The cost of these acquisitions is as follows:

	£
Goodwill	68,000
Office premises	137,000
70% shareholding in Durn Ltd	245,000

- Kitz Ltd will charge interest at the rate of 7% per year on this loan.
- Feld Ltd has been offered a loan of £450,000 from a bank at an interest rate of 10% per annum.
- In the year ending 31 March 2027, Feld Ltd will have a trading profit of £587,000 and interest receivable of £48,100.

Kitz Ltd – proposed sale of a patent:

- Kitz Ltd will sell a patent to Durn Ltd on 3 May 2026 for £72,000.
- Kitz Ltd purchased the patent for £60,000 on 3 May 2021.
- The tax written down value of the patent on 3 May 2026 will be £30,000.
- Kitz Ltd has always used the patent in its business.

34 Fox Ltd (Mar/Jun 2022) (49 mins)

You should assume that today's date is 1 June 2025.

The finance director of Fox Ltd has requested advice on:

- the chargeable gains implications of the assignment (sale) of an existing lease;
- the subsequent acquisition of a freehold factory; and
- the availability of group relief in respect of a trading loss.

The following **exhibit**, available on the left-hand side of the screen, provides information relevant to the question:

(1) Fox Ltd

This information should be used to answer the question **requirements** within your chosen **response option(s)**.

Required

You should assume that today's date is 1 June 2025.

(a) (i) Calculate the chargeable gain arising on the assignment of the lease on 1 October 2024 and explain the tax treatment of the deferred gain in respect of the sale of the office building.

Notes.

1 The following lease percentages should be used where necessary:

26 years: 82.496

40 years: 95.457

2 You should ignore indexation allowance and any potential claim for rollover relief in respect of the disposal of the lease. **(4 marks)**

(ii) In relation to the chargeable gain calculated in (a)(i), explain, with supporting calculations:

- the extent to which rollover relief will currently be available within the Fox Ltd group; and
- the minimum amount which Fox Ltd will need to spend on the new freehold factory, such that the full amount of the eligible gain in (a)(i) can be deferred using rollover relief.

(7 marks)

(b) Explain the group relief claims available to the Fox Ltd Group in respect of Salas Ltd's trading loss of the year ending 30 June 2025. **(9 marks)**

Professional marks will be awarded for the demonstration of skill in analysis & evaluation and commercial acumen in your answer. **(5 marks)**

(Total = 25 marks)

Exhibit: Fox Ltd

Fox Ltd Group at 1 June 2025:

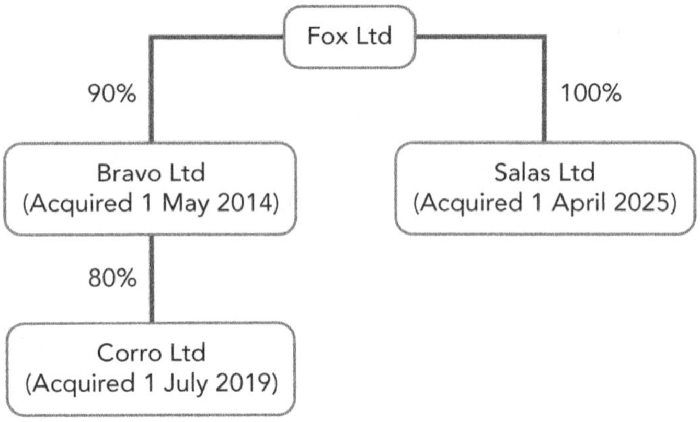

- All four companies are UK resident trading companies with a 30 June year end.

Fox Ltd – assignment of a lease and acquisition of a new freehold:

- On 1 October 2024, Fox Ltd assigned a 26-year lease on a factory to an unconnected company for £180,000.
- The lease had been acquired by Fox Ltd on 1 October 2010 for £102,000 when it had 40 years remaining.
- The leased factory was used by Fox Ltd for trading purposes throughout its period of ownership.
- Fox Ltd sold an office building on 8 March 2009 which resulted in a chargeable gain of £43,000.
- Fox Ltd claimed rollover relief in order to defer this chargeable gain following the acquisition of the lease of the factory.
- Fox Ltd plans to purchase a new freehold factory building in July 2025.

Corro Ltd:

- Acquired a warehouse on 1 July 2024 from an unconnected company for £168,000.
- Uses 70% of the building itself for trading purposes; the remaining 30% is rented out.

Salas Ltd:

- Was incorporated on 1 July 2023.
- Was wholly owned by an individual prior to joining the Fox Ltd group.
- Incurred a trading loss in the year ended 30 June 2024.
- Has no other sources of income in any accounting period.

- There are no plans to change the nature or conduct of Salas Ltd's trade.

Forecast results:

- Salas Ltd is expected to incur a tax-adjusted trading loss of £225,000 in the year ending 30 June 2025.
- Fox Ltd, Bravo Ltd and Corro Ltd will each have taxable total profits in the year ending 30 June 2025 sufficient that they pay main rate corporation tax. These companies have always been profitable in the past and will continue to be profitable in the foreseeable future.

35 Samphire Ltd and Kelp Ltd (Mar/Jun 2021) (49 mins)

You should assume that today's date is 1 March 2026.

Nori, an individual, owns 75% of the ordinary shares in Samphire Ltd and the whole of the ordinary share capital of Kelp Ltd. Advice is required on;

- the cost for Samphire Ltd of gifting a computer, or, alternatively, making a loan to Nori; and
- the tax implications of Kelp Ltd replacing a factory and acquiring a new warehouse.

The following **exhibit** provides information relevant to the question:

(1) Samphire Ltd and Kelp Ltd.

This information should be used to answer the question **requirements** within your chosen **response option(s).**

Required

You should assume that today's date is 1 March 2026.

(a) Explain, with supporting calculations, the total additional taxes payable by Samphire Ltd:

(i) If Samphire Ltd gifts the computer to Nori (Alternative 1); **(4 marks)**

(ii) If Samphire Ltd makes a loan of £1,500 to Nori, and then writes off the loan on 6 April 2028 (Alternative 2).

Note. Ignore value added tax (VAT). **(6 marks)**

(b) (i) Calculate the chargeable gain for Kelp Ltd on the sale of the lease on Factory 1. **(3 marks)**

(ii) Explain, with supporting calculations, the amount of the chargeable gain calculated in (b)(i) which will remain liable to corporation tax (if any), if Kelp Ltd claims the maximum amount of rollover relief available. **(7 marks)**

Professional skills marks will be awarded for demonstration of skill in analysis and evaluation and commercial acumen in your answer. **(5 marks)**

Note. The following lease percentages should be used, where necessary:

40 years: 95.457

48 years: 99.289

The following indexation factors should be used where necessary:

August 2014 to December 2017: 0.082

November 2017 to December 2017: 0.008

(Total = 25 marks)

Exhibit: Samphire Ltd and Kelp Ltd

Nori:

- Has been a director of Samphire Ltd for many years.

Samphire Ltd:

- Is a UK resident close trading company, which prepares accounts to 31 March annually and has sufficient profits that it pays main rate corporation tax.
- Will either gift a computer to Nori on 6 April 2026, or make a loan to Nori on the same date, to allow him to purchase a computer.

Alternative 1 – Samphire Ltd gifts the computer to Nori:

- The computer was purchased by Samphire Ltd in March 2023 for £2,600 and has a current market value of £1,500.
- Samphire Ltd has purchased no other plant and machinery for several years, and the written down value of its main pool at 6 April 2026 will be £nil.
- The sale proceeds for the purpose of capital allowances with be £nil.
- Nori's private use of the computer has been insignificant throughout Samphire Ltd's period of ownership.

Alternative 2 – Samphire Ltd makes a loan to Nori:

- On 6 April 2026 Samphire Ltd will make an interest-free loan of £1,500 to Nori.
- Samphire Ltd will write off the loan on 6 April 2028.

Kelp Ltd – disposal of lease on Factory 1:

- Kelp Ltd is a UK resident trading company.
- Kelp Ltd was assigned a 48-year lease on a factory building ('Factory 1') on 1 November 2017, for which it paid a premium of £165,000.
- Kelp Ltd used Factory 1 in its trade until 30 April 2025, since when it has been rented to tenants who are not connected with the company.
- On 1 November 2025 Kelp Ltd sold the lease with 40 years remaining for £206,000.

Kelp Ltd – acquisition of Factory 2:

- Kelp Ltd acquired a factory building ('Factory 2') from Samphire Ltd on 1 May 2025, and immediately started to use it in its trade.
- Samphire Ltd had acquired Factory 2 for £96,000 on 5 August 2014.
- Kelp Ltd paid £ 140,000 for Factory 2, which was its market value on 1 May 2025.

Kelp Ltd – acquisition of warehouse:

- Kelp Ltd will acquire a warehouse from an unconnected company for £78,000 on 1 April 2026.
- Kelp Ltd will occupy 70% of this warehouse for its own trade, and will rent out the remaining 30%.

Answers

Section A questions

1 Forti Ltd group

Course Book references

Corporation tax computation, gains and administration are covered in Chapter 16. Close companies are covered in Chapter 21. Groups and consortia are the subject of Chapter 19. Corporate advice is the subject of Chapter 25. The value added tax annual accounting scheme is covered in Chapter 23. Inheritance tax is covered in Chapters 11 and 12 with ethics in Chapter 1.

Top tips

Try to see this question in lots of smaller parts to make it less daunting. If you are asked to correct a computation, don't assume that **all** the figures are incorrect. You were specifically told that some were correct, but there was an adjustment which was correct as well. You could attempt the ethical part first to make sure you gain those easier marks.

Easy marks

There were some easy marks in part (a) for computing taxable total profits and the corporation tax liability, even if you were not sure why some of the corrections to the original schedule needed to be made. The adjustment for transfer pricing should have been well known in part (b)(ii). The annual accounting scheme in part (c) was brought forward knowledge from Taxation (TX – UK). The calculation of IHT due should have also provided some easier marks. Even if your explanation of the circumstances for maximum IHT were wrong you would have been awarded follow-on marks. Finally, the ethical requirement should also have provided some easier marks.

ACCA Examining team's comments

Part (a) was well done by many candidates. In relation to the tax adjusted trading income, many candidates thought, incorrectly, that the cost of entertaining overseas customers was allowable. In addition, there was a general, correct, view that the management bonus should be disallowed but very candidates knew that it was because it had not been paid within nine months of the end of the accounting period. The majority of candidates picked up the point in relation to group relief and arrangements in force in respect of Marussia Ltd. However, candidates did not do so well in relation to the position of Eagle Ltd, which could not be a consortium company as it was a 75% subsidiary of Ligier Ltd. The majority of candidates handled the degrouping charge and the annual exempt amount correctly. When calculating the corporation tax liability, most candidates recognised that Eagle Ltd was not an associated company but very few identified the fact that Brawn Ltd was not a close investment holding company, such that the main rate of corporation tax did not apply automatically.

Part (b)(i) required candidates to set out the matters that need to be considered in order to determine whether or not a company is a close company. This was intended to be a relatively straightforward requirement, which then required some thought if a very good mark were to be obtained. However, the majority of candidates simply did not know the rules, such that the performance in this part of the question was poor. On the whole, candidates focussed on the owners of the company and knew the rules had something to do with five shareholders and any number of directors. However, the key to the rules is who controls the company as opposed to who owns it. Some candidates tried to make up for their lack of knowledge by writing about the implications of a company being close. As always, regardless of its technical accuracy, such irrelevant information did not score any marks.

Part (b)(ii) concerned transfer pricing. Many candidates were able to score two out of the three marks but very few addressed the availability or otherwise of the exemption for small and medium-sized enterprises.

Part (c) of the question required candidates to state the conditions and operation of the VAT annual accounting scheme. Candidates' performance in this part of the question was very good. A small minority of candidates confused the annual accounting scheme with group registration, perhaps because there was a group in the question, but the majority produced brief succinct answers that scored well.

There are no Examining team's comments in relation to parts (d) and (e) as these requirements come from an earlier ATX–UK specimen exam and, as such, no comments are available

Marking guide

		Marks	
(a)	**Notes**		
	Tax adjusted trading income – other matters	2	
	Research and development	2	
	Chargeable gains	2	
	Losses transferred from Marussia Ltd	1.5	
	Losses transferred from Eagle Ltd	2	
	Calculation	5	
			12
(b)	(i) Definition of close company	2.5	
	Associates	1.5	
	Application	2	
			5
	(ii) Reasons why transfer pricing rules apply	2.5	
	Adjustment required	1	
			3
(c)	Conditions	3	
	Operation of the scheme	3	
			5
(d)	Emma's death	2	
	Ownership of shares	5	
	Calculation		
	Fall in value	3.5	
	Inheritance tax liability	2.5	
			10
(e)	Implications for Emma	3	
	Fundamental principles	1	
	Cease to act	2.5	
			5

Professional skills marks

Scepticism

- Effective challenge and critical assessment of information within the assistant's schedule (a)
- Effective challenge of Emma's suggestion not to report her gains
- Identification of missing or additional information, which may alter the decision reached – for example whether Emma's shares are still held by her son at her death, to determine whether BPR applies in (d)

Marking guide	Marks

Analysis and Evaluation

- Appropriate use of information in the scenario to determine a suitable revised corporation tax computation in (a)
- Ability to evaluate information objectively to explain each error and recommend how each error should be corrected in (a)
- Appropriate use of information in the scenario to support discussion and draw appropriate conclusions as to the circumstances of maximum IHT in (d)
- Demonstration of ability to consider relevant factors applicable as to whether BPR will be available in (d)
- Identification of further information as to the directors of Forti Ltd to enable an appropriate decision about its close company status to be made
- Adoption of a logical approach to prepare suitable calculations of the maximum IHT in (d)

Communication

- General format and structure of notes (eg use of headings/sub-headings, easy to refer to)
- Style, language and clarity (tone of notes, presentation of calculations, appropriate use of tools, easy to follow and more than a negligible amount of content)
- Effectiveness of communication (answer is relevant, specific rather than general and focussed on the requirement)
- Adherence to specific instructions made in the scenario (eg answering each specific task listed and not checking the items you're told are correct in (a))

Commercial Acumen

- Practical considerations for our firm if Emma fails to disclose her gains in (e)
- Recognition of alternative VAT payment options under the annual accounting scheme in (c)

Maximum	10
Total	50

(a) **Brawn Ltd – Corporation tax computation for the year ended 31 March 2025**

	Notes	£
Tax adjusted trading income per original schedule		240,800
Less: Costs relating to company share option plan	1	(6,000)
Add:		
– Accrued management bonuses	2	7,000
– Research and development expenditure 20% × (£21,000 + £17,550)	3	7,710
Tax adjusted trading income		249,510
Add:		
– Sale of Marussia Ltd:		
– Chargeable gain £(81,700 + 21,500 + 6,000)	4, 5	109,200
Total taxable profits before loss relief		358,710
Less:		
– Losses transferred from:		
– Marussia Ltd £60,000 × 3/12	6	(15,000)
– Eagle Ltd	7	(0)
Taxable total profits		343,710
Corporation tax @ 25%		85,928
Less RDEC		(7,710)
Corporation tax payable		78,218

Notes.

1 The cost of establishing a company share option plan is an allowable deduction when computing tax adjusted trading income.

2 The management bonuses are not an allowable cost as they have not been paid within nine months of the end of the accounting period.

3 Brawn Ltd can claim a R&D expenditure credit (RDEC) in respect of the research and development expenditure. The credit is 20% of the qualifying R&D. In relation to payments for subcontracted labour, the amount qualifying for the RDEC is only 65% of the amount paid. Accordingly, the total RDEC is £7,710 (20% × (£21,000 + (£27,000 × 65%)). This is added to the company's taxable trading profits and then deducted from the company's corporation tax liability.

4 The degrouping charge must be added to the sales proceeds on the sale of Marussia Ltd so it increases the chargeable gain arising.

5 The capital gains tax annual exempt amount of £3,000 is not available to companies.

6 For the purposes of group relief, Marussia Ltd is regarded as having left the group once there were arrangements in force for it to leave the group. The signing of the contract on 1 November 2024 amounts to such arrangements. This means that Marussia Ltd is only a member of the group relief group for the three months from 1 August 2024 until 31 October 2024 and the loss must therefore be apportioned on a time basis.

7 Eagle Ltd is not a consortium company because it is in a group relief group with Ligier Ltd. Accordingly, it is not possible for any of Eagle Ltd's trading losses to be transferred to Brawn Ltd.

> **Tutorial note.** The costs of entertaining customers (whether UK or overseas) are disallowable in computing the trading profit. The distinction between UK and overseas customers is only relevant for value added tax purposes.

(b) (i) **Close companies**

Forti Ltd will be a close company if it is controlled by:

(1) Any number of directors who are shareholders; or

(2) Its five largest shareholders.

A company is controlled by those shareholders who own more than half of the company's share capital.

When determining whether or not a company is close within this definition, each shareholder is regarded as owning any shares owned by their associates as well as the shares owned personally. A person's associates include their direct relatives, business partners and the trustees of certain trusts set up by the shareholder or their direct relatives.

Control of Forti Ltd can be exercised by seven shareholders holding 58.3% (7/12) of the shares.

Accordingly, unless Forti Ltd is controlled by shareholder directors, it will only be close if some of its shareholders are associated with each other.

> **Tutorial note.** There are further complexities when determining whether or not a company is close but the points set out above were sufficient to score full marks.

(ii) **Transfer pricing (Note 6 to the schedule)**

The transfer pricing rules will apply to the sale of components by Brawn Ltd to Gordini Co because these two companies are both controlled by Forti Ltd. The exemption for small and medium-sized enterprises is unlikely to be available, regardless of the size of the Forti Ltd group, as there is no double tax treaty between the UK and the country of Arrowsia.

Under the transfer pricing rules, if Brawn Ltd has sold components to Gordini Co for less than an arm's length price, it is required to increase its taxable profits by the excess of the arm's length price over the price charged.

(c) **Value added tax (VAT) annual accounting scheme**

Conditions

(1) The company's VAT reporting and payments must be up to date, such that its VAT debt is not increasing.

(2) Taxable supplies (excluding VAT) must not be expected to exceed £1,350,000 in the following 12 months.

(3) The company must notify HM Revenue & Customs (HMRC) if it expects its taxable supplies for a year to exceed £1,600,000. The company must leave the scheme if its taxable supplies for a year exceed £1,600,000.

(4) The scheme is not available where registration is in the name of a group.

> **Tutorial note.** Companies which are normally in a repayment situation can account for VAT annually if they wish, but this would not be advisable from a cash flow point of view as they would only receive one repayment for the whole year.

Operation of the scheme

(1) The company will be required to make nine monthly payments starting at the end of the fourth month of the year.

(2) Each payment is equal to 10% of the company's liability for the previous year as adjusted for any additional information provided to HMRC.

(3) Alternatively, a company can choose to make three larger interim payments equal to 25% of its liability for the previous year.

(4) The company must submit its VAT return within two months of the end of the year together with any final balancing payment.

(d) **Gift of shares in Vyc Ltd**

Circumstances resulting in the maximum inheritance tax (IHT) liability

The maximum IHT liability will occur where both condition (i) and condition (ii), set out below, are satisfied.

(i) Emma dies by 30 September 2028, ie within seven years of 1 October 2021, the date on which she made the cash gift to her daughter. Once seven years have elapsed, the gift on 1 October 2021 will no longer be accumulated in determining the nil rate band available in respect of the gift of the shares in Vyc Ltd.

> **Tutorial note.** If Emma dies within seven years of 1 October 2021, ie by 30 September 2028, she will have died within three years of the gift of the shares to Edward. Accordingly, taper relief will not be available.

(ii) At the time of Emma's death, business property relief (BPR) IS NOT available. The gift of the shares in Vyc Ltd will qualify for 100% BPR at the time of the gift because:

- Vyc Ltd is an unquoted trading company, such that the shares are relevant business property; and
- Emma has owned the shares for at least two years.

However, BPR will not be available on Emma's death if:

- the shares are no longer qualifying business property; or
- Edward has disposed of the shares prior to Emma's death, unless:
  - Edward has replaced the shares with qualifying business property; or
  - Edward has died before Emma, whilst still owning the shares (or qualifying replacement business property).

Maximum possible IHT liability

	£	£
Transfer of value (W)		340,000
Annual exemptions:		
– 2026/27		(3,000)
– 2025/26		(3,000)
		334,000
Nil rate band	325,000	
Less: chargeable transfer in the previous seven years	(280,000)	
		(45,000)
Taxable amount		289,000
IHT payable (£289,000 × 40%)		115,600

Working

Transfer of value by reference to related property

	£
Value of shares held prior to the gift: (35,000 × £19 (54% (35% + 19%))	665,000
Value of shares held after the gift: (25,000 × £13 (44% (25% + 19%))	(325,000)
	340,000

Assumption: The transfer of value has been calculated by reference to related property as these give the higher valuations than if the related property were ignored.

Tutorial note. The value of Emma's shares is determined by reference to the shares held by her and her husband under the related property rules. In ATX–UK it is sufficient to make a statement that the related property valuation is assumed to give a higher valuation than under the normal rules. Calculation of the valuation under the normal rules is not required.

Candidates who prepared calculations both with and without reference to related property to determine which resulted in the higher valuation (rather than stating an assumption) received equal credit.

(e) Emma will need to report the gains she makes on the disposal of her investment properties. Even if rollover relief were fully available resulting in no charge to CGT (which is unlikely unless the investment properties Emma plans to sell and acquire all qualified as furnished holiday accommodation), Emma must still report her gains and make claims for rollover relief. Emma may be liable to interest and penalties (based on potential lost revenue) if she does not report her chargeable gains to HM Revenue & Customs (HMRC).

The evasion or attempted evasion of tax by Emma may also be the subject of criminal charges under both tax law and money laundering legislation. We may need to submit a report under the money laundering rules. Our firm must not be associated with a client who has deliberately evaded tax as this is against the ACCA fundamental principles of integrity and professional behaviour.

We should not continue to act for Emma if she does not agree to disclose the chargeable gains to HMRC. Is she does not agree to disclosure, we are still under a professional duty to ensure that she understands the seriousness of offences against HMRC. If we do cease to act for Emma, we must inform HMRC of this cessation but not the reasons for it. We should advise Emma that the notification that we are no longer acting for her may alert HMRC that tax irregularities have taken place and urge on Emma the desirability of making a full disclosure.

2 Hahn Ltd group

Course Book references

Groups are dealt with in Chapter 19. Transfer pricing is dealt with in Chapter 22. Payment of corporation tax and chargeable gains for companies are covered in Chapter 16. Group registration for value added tax is covered in Chapter 23. Ethics are dealt with in Chapter 1. Corporate planning is the subject of Chapter 25. The death estate, including the reduced rate of inheritance tax, is covered in Chapter 11. Capital tax advice is covered in Chapter 13.

Top tips

It is important to deal with the specific points asked in the question rather than provide a general explanation of topics examined. For example, in part (b) it was important to discuss the interaction between group registration, the annual accounting scheme and the partial exemption rules.

Easy marks

There were easy marks in part (a)(ii) for computation of corporation tax and the schedule of payments. In part (c), the ethical issues arising from an unexpected refund of tax should have been well known

ACCA examining team's comments

Part (a), which was in two parts, related to a group of UK resident companies. The first of these parts required candidates to calculate the amount to be reinvested in qualifying assets in order to leave no gain on the disposal of a building chargeable to corporation tax. Most candidates made a reasonable attempt at this, but a very significant proportion also included detailed explanations to accompany their calculations, despite these clearly not being required. The fact that this question part was worth only three marks should have led candidates to realise that a lengthy discussion was not required. Accordingly, these candidates wasted time, which could have beneficially been spent elsewhere. Candidates would be advised to double check what is required by each question before making a start. The main technical error was a failure to realise that the total investment needed must equal the sale proceeds of the building, not the chargeable gain. The second part of part (a) required candidates to relieve a trading loss within a group so as to minimise the amount of corporation tax payable by the group companies in instalments. Clearly, the majority of candidates were not aware of how this could be achieved, and therefore did not state a strategy for relieving the loss. The loss was therefore relieved in a somewhat random manner within the group. There were a good number of easy marks in this part for calculating the amount of corporation tax payable by each company, which most candidates achieved, but a few didn't appear to have read this part of the requirements and so failed to produce the necessary schedule. The answers to the requirement to state the due dates for payment of the instalments, where necessary, elicited a significant number of incorrect answers in relation to the starting date as many candidates thought that this was after the end of the accounting period, rather than within it. Practical issues such as due dates for payment of tax by both companies and individuals are essential knowledge within many tax planning scenarios in Advanced Taxation (ATX–UK). Overall, group aspects of corporation tax remain a key topic in Advanced Taxation (ATX–UK) and candidates should endeavour to practise a wide range of questions on these to ensure that they are confident in dealing with different aspects of this area.

Part (b) of this question related to the consideration of specific matters relating to the group of companies when deciding which companies should be included in a group registration for value added tax (VAT) purposes. Despite the requirement stating that candidates were to refer only to the specific matters within the memorandum provided, a significant number wrote in detail about the general advantages and disadvantages of registering as a group, which was not relevant, and so wasted time. However, many candidates did identify the specific issues – one of the companies being partially exempt, and another using the annual accounting scheme and the cash accounting scheme – but then discussed what this meant for the relevant companies themselves, rather than the implications of including that company within a group registration. Unfortunately though, having identified the issues, they didn't go on to score as many marks as they could have done by answering the precise requirement.

Part (c) of this question concerned an unexpected refund of tax from HM Revenue & Customs (HMRC), and the actions to be undertaken by the firm in respect of this. This is a frequently tested area of ethics, and on the whole, candidates' performance was good, with clear explanations of the advice to be given to the client, and the consequences of the client not following this advice. Candidates generally appeared to have practised this type of question, and a good number scored full marks.

The final part of this question required candidates to identify errors in an inheritance tax computation on a death estate, and to calculate the amount to be received by the sole beneficiary of the estate, after the correct inheritance tax had been paid. Performance on this part of the question was mixed, with a disappointing number of candidates believing that the capital gains tax exemption for chattels with a value below £6,000 also applies to inheritance tax, and that inheritance tax annual exemptions are available against assets in the death estate. These are fundamental errors which candidates in Advanced Taxation (ATX–UK) should not be making. Candidates should ensure that they are able to identify and apply correctly the different exemptions available for capital gains tax and inheritance tax as these are tested on a very regular basis. In order to calculate the correct amount of inheritance tax to be paid after correcting the errors found, the majority of candidates rewrote the entire death estate. This succeeded in gaining the relevant marks, but was probably fairly time consuming, and candidates are encouraged to try to adopt a more efficient approach, focusing on the effect of correcting the error on the value of the chargeable estate as this would save time.

[**BPP note**: The residence nil rate band was not relevant when this question was originally set so the ACCA examining team made no comments on this aspect but it is likely that some candidates would have missed this error in a similar way to the other errors.] Questions in Advanced Taxation (ATX–UK) frequently ask for a calculation of after-tax proceeds – here, the amount receivable by the sole beneficiary of the estate. Candidates need to think more carefully about the starting point for this type of calculation. Here, it wasn't the value of the chargeable estate, as this includes a deduction for the nil rate band. Candidates needed to identify the actual value which would be received prior to making this deduction. Failure to identify the correct starting point is a common error.

Marking guide			**Marks**	
(a)	(i)	Calculation	3.5	
				3
	(ii)	Transfer pricing	3.5	
		Rationale for loss planning	2	
		Threshold for payment by instalments	2.5	
		Members of group relief group	1	
		Allocation of loss between group companies	4	
		Corporation tax liabilities	6	
		Payment schedule	4	
				19
(b)	Companies to be included		2	
	Sales between members of the VAT group		1	
	VAT schemes		2	
	Frit Ltd		1	
				5
(c)	The need to repay the tax		3	
	Ceasing to act		3	
				5
(d)	Identification of errors		5.5	
	Calculations			
	– Inheritance tax liability		2.5	
	– Inheritance received by Jonny		1.5	
				8

Marking guide | **Marks**

Professional skill marks

Scepticism

- Effective challenge of evidence and assumptions supplied with respect to Sophie's inheritance tax calculation.

Analysis and Evaluation

- Appropriate use of information in the scenario to determine suitable calculations for corporation tax payable in (a)
- Adoption of a logical approach to prepare suitable calculations for the inheritance tax liability and post-tax inheritance in (d)
- Appropriate use of information in the scenario to support discussion and draw appropriate conclusions as to how Frit Ltd's trading loss should be allocated around the group.

Communication

- General format and structure of memorandum/notes (eg use of headings/sub-headings, easy to refer to)
- Style, language and clarity (tone of memorandum/notes, presentation of calculations, appropriate use of tools, easy to follow and more than a negligible amount of content)
- Effectiveness of communication (answer is relevant, specific rather than general and focussed on the requirement)
- Adherence to specific instructions made in the scenario (eg to assume the whole of Frit Ltd's gain is relieved by rollover relief, to only consider specific information in the memorandum regarding VAT registration and the statements about what is correct in the IHT computation)

Commercial Acumen

- Recognising the need to confirm whether the VAT refund is an error before proceeding with the procedures for a mistake
- Effective use of calculations to provide a post-tax inheritance figure for Sophie
- Recognition of possible consequences of Frit Ltd being included in a VAT group with regard to it being partially exempt
- Recognition of the groups stated priorities with regards to offsetting Frit Ltd's trading loss

Maximum	10
Total	50

Memorandum

Client: Hahn Ltd group

Subject: Group loss planning and other matters

Prepared by: Tax senior

Date: 1 September 2025

(a) (i) **Chargeable gain of Frit Ltd**

The additional qualifying assets which would need to be purchased in order for the chargeable gain realised by Frit Ltd to be fully relieved by its capital losses brought forward is calculated as follows:

	£'000
Sales proceeds of asset sold	125
Proceeds retained to equal capital losses brought forward	(31)
Proceeds to be spent	94
Qualifying assets already purchased by group companies (14 + 10)	(24)
Additional amount to be spent	70

> **Tutorial note.** The amount of the chargeable gain which cannot be rolled over will be the amount of sales proceeds not reinvested. Accordingly, an amount of £31,000 should not be reinvested, such that only £34,000 of the gain will be rolled over and the remaining £31,000 of the gain will be relieved by the capital losses brought forward.
>
> The additional assets can be purchased by any member of the capital gains group. The group consists of all of the companies apart from Joli Ltd (not a 75% subsidiary of Hahn Ltd) and Ruth Ltd (not a 75% subsidiary of Lise Ltd). Therefore, the £6,000 spent on purchases of assets by Ruth Ltd does not represent a qualifying reinvestment for the purposes of rollover relief.

(ii) **Relieving the trading loss of Frit Ltd**

Intercompany trading

A transfer pricing adjustment will be required in respect of the sales at undervalue from Hahn Ltd to Stra Ltd. This is because Hahn Ltd controls Stra Ltd, and the group is large for the purposes of the transfer pricing rules. Accordingly, the trading profit of Hahn Ltd must be increased by £10,000 (£104,000 – £94,000), the excess of the arm's length price over the price charged for the intra-group sales. As Stra Ltd is also within the charge to UK corporation tax, its trading profits can be reduced by the same amount.

Rationale for the allocation of the trading loss

In order to maximise the benefit to the group's cash flow position, Frit Ltd's trading loss should be surrendered to those companies paying corporation tax by quarterly instalments.

- First to any company whose profits can be reduced to the payment by instalments threshold, such that instalments will no longer be required;
- Then to any other company with profits in excess of the payment by instalments threshold, such that their instalments will be reduced; and
- Finally, to any other company.

The payment by instalments threshold for the Hahn Ltd group companies (excluding Chad Ltd) for the year ending 31 March 2026 is £300,000. This is the threshold of £1,500,000 divided by five (the number of associated companies as at 31 March 2025 being Hahn Ltd, Frit Ltd, Lise Ltd, Ruth Ltd and Stra Ltd).

The threshold for Chad Ltd for the year ending 31 March 2026 is £187,500. This is the threshold of £1,500,000 divided by eight (the number of associated companies in the Zeno Ltd group as at 31 March 2025, being Zeno Ltd and its associates).

> **Tutorial note.** The instalments threshold is divided by the number of associated companies as at the end of the **previous** accounting period.

ANSWERS

Allocation of the loss

	Notes	£'000
Frit Ltd – trading loss		540
Surrender to:		
– Lise Ltd (375 – 300)	1	(75)
– Chad Ltd	2	(315)
– Hahn Ltd – the balance	3, 4	150

Notes.

1 The taxable total profits of Lise Ltd should be reduced to no more than £300,000 so that the company will not have to pay corporation tax by instalments.

2 Chad Ltd will have been a member of the group relief group for only seven months of the accounting period. Accordingly, the maximum loss which can be surrendered by Frit Ltd to Chad Ltd is £315,000, ie the lower of:

- Frit Ltd – loss for the corresponding seven-month period of £315,000 (£540,000 × 7/12); and
- Chad Ltd – profit for the corresponding seven-month period of £393,750 (£675,000 × 7/12).

This is not sufficient to reduce the taxable total profits of Chad Ltd to £187,500 but it will reduce the company's corporation tax liability and therefore the instalments due.

3 The trading profit of Stra Ltd of £28,000 (£38,000 – £10,000) can be reduced to zero by a claim to use its trading loss brought forward and there is no excess loss to be group relieved.

4 Joli Ltd and Ruth Ltd are not effective 75% subsidiaries of Hahn Ltd and are therefore not in the group relief group.

> **Tutorial note.** It might also have been considered that the balance of the loss of £150,000 could be surrendered to Lise Ltd rather than Hahn Ltd because the corporation tax liability of both companies is due on 1 January 2027 rather than by quarterly instalments. However, the Hahn Ltd group will benefit from more of the tax saving by surrendering this loss to Hahn Ltd since Lise Ltd is only 80% owned by Hahn Ltd.

Corporation tax liabilities for the year ending 31 March 2026

	Hahn Ltd	Chad Ltd	Lise Ltd	Ruth Ltd
	£'000	£'000	£'000	£'000
Taxable total profit	180	675	375	320
Transfer pricing adjustment	10			
Group relief	(150)	(315)	(75)	Nil
	40	360	300	320
Corporation tax at 25%	10.0	90.0	75.0	80.0
Less marginal relief (£41,667 – £40,000) × 3/200	(0.02)			
	9.98			
Due in instalments		90.0		80.0
Due on 1 January 2027	9.98		75.0	

Frit Ltd and Stra Ltd will have no taxable total profits and therefore will not have a corporation tax liability.

Lower and upper limit for Hahn Ltd, Lise Ltd and Ruth Ltd (Hahn Ltd, Chad Ltd, Frit Ltd, Lise Ltd, Ruth Ltd and Stra Ltd are associates during the year)

£50,000/6 = £8,333

£250,000/6 = £41,667

Lower and upper limit for Chad Ltd (same associated as above but also associated to Zeno Ltd and its six wholly-owned subsidiaries)

£50,000/13= £3,846

£250,000/13 = £19,230

Payment schedule

Date	Payment	Working
	£'000	£'000
14 October 2025	42.5	(¼ × (90.0 + 80.0))
14 January 2026	42.5	
14 April 2026	42.5	
14 July 2026	42.5	
1 January 2027	84.98	(9.98 + 75.0)

(b) **Group registration for the purposes of value added tax (VAT)**

A group registration could be made in respect of all of the companies in the Hahn Ltd group with the exception of Joli Ltd (because this company is not controlled by Hahn Ltd). However, it is not necessary to include all of the qualifying companies within the group registration.

Sales from one company in the VAT group to another would be disregarded for the purposes of VAT. Therefore, there would be no requirement to charge VAT on the sales made by Hahn Ltd to Stra Ltd.

The annual accounting scheme is not available where companies are registered as a group. The cash accounting scheme would be available but only if the group's taxable turnover was less than £1,350,000. These matters should be considered before deciding whether or not Stra Ltd should be included in the group registration.

The inclusion of Frit Ltd in the group registration would result in the group being partially exempt. This could increase the total input tax recovered by the group, for example, if the results of the group as a whole satisfy the partial exemption *de minimis* limits. Alternatively, the calculation of the recoverable input tax for the group as a whole could result in a reduction in the total input tax recovered. Accordingly, further consideration is required before deciding whether or not Frit Ltd should be included in the group registration.

(c) **Chad Ltd – refund of VAT**

We should investigate the VAT reporting of Chad Ltd in order to determine whether or not there is a valid reason for the refund.

If we are unable to identify a valid reason, we would have to conclude that the refund was made as a result of error on the part of HM Revenue & Customs (HMRC), in which case it should be repaid immediately. We should inform Chad Ltd that failing to return the money in these circumstances may well be a civil and/or a criminal offence.

We should also advise Chad Ltd to inform HMRC of their error as soon as possible in order to minimise any interest and penalties which may otherwise become payable.

If Chad Ltd is unwilling to return the money, we would have to consider ceasing to act as advisers to the company. We would then have to notify the tax authorities that we no longer act for Chad Ltd, although we would not provide them with any reason for our action. We should also consider whether or not it is necessary to make a report under the money laundering rules.

(d) **Sophie's inheritance from her mother**

Errors identified

(1) Chattels (for example, furniture, paintings and jewellery) with a value of less than £6,000 are not exempt for the purposes of inheritance tax (although they are exempt for the purposes of capital gains tax).

(2) The annual exemption is not available in respect of transfers on death.

(3) The residence nil rate band will apply because Sophie's mother left her main residence to Sophie. The residence nil rate band is the lower of £175,000 and the value of the house of £530,000 ie £175,000.

(4) The reduced rate of inheritance tax of 36% will apply. This is because:

(i) The chargeable estate, before deduction of the charitable donation but after deduction of the nil rate band (not the residence nil rate band), is £689,000 (£619,000 (£591,000 + £25,000 + £3,000) + £70,000)

(ii) The gift to the charity of £70,000 is more than 10% of this amount

Value of inheritance receivable by Sophie

	£
Chargeable estate per draft computation	892,000
No exemption for chattels valued at less than £6,000	25,000
No annual exemption	3,000
	920,000
Less:	
– Residence nil rate band	(175,000)
– Nil rate band	(301,000)
	444,000
Inheritance tax at 36%	159,840
Assets inherited by Sophie (£530,000 + £400,000 + £40,000 + £20,000 – £70,000)	920,000
Less inheritance tax payable	(159,840)
Inheritance receivable by Sophie	760,160

3 Heyer Plc group

Course Book references

Corporation tax administration is covered in Chapter 16. Groups are covered in Chapter 19. Stamp taxes are dealt with in Chapter 24. Corporate tax planning is the subject of Chapter 25. Ethics are covered in Chapter 1. Capital allowances are dealt with in Chapter 14. Capital gains tax principles will be found in Chapter 7 and reliefs in Chapter 8. Capital tax advice is the subject of Chapter 13.

Top tips

Make sure you work logically through this question ensuring you make the time to address each sub requirement. It's important to take time at the start of the question noting the various group relationships and noticing that the transfers in (b) are to Lodi Ltd – a group company rather than an unconnected company. Did you remember to include a summary of your calculations and a statement of the key issues in part (c)(ii)? These were awarded four valuable marks.

Easy marks

Part (d) should have been the source of some easy ethics marks provided you attempted it. In part (a) there were also basic marks looking at rates of corporation tax, when companies pay tax in instalments and chargeable gains group planning. In addition to giving the explanations explicitly requested, which involved stating your knowledge, you should also have addressed the request to apply your knowledge specifically to the facts from the question. In part (c) there were some easy marks for basic computations.

ACCA examining team's comments

Part (a) of this question has been amended since it was originally set due to syllabus changes regarding the differing rates of corporation tax. As such the ACCA examining team's comments have not been reproduced.

Part (b) concerned the proposal to transfer the trades and assets of five of the group companies to another of the group companies and was also challenging. The challenge here was to address all of the issues set out in the manager's email in the time available. Only four points needed to be made but there was only one mark for each point. Having said that this was a challenging question, many candidates made a good job of it. In particular, they kept their answers brief and tried to address all of the issues raised. Weaker candidates focussed on only one or two of the manager's issues which restricted the number of marks which could be obtained. The one common technical error concerned the capital allowances treatment. The point here is that the assets would be automatically transferred at tax written down value because the companies are all under 75% common control both before and after the transfer of the trades.

There are no ACCA examining team's comments in relation to parts (c) and (d) as these requirements come from an earlier ATX–UK specimen exam and, as such, no comments are available.

Marking guide

		Marks	
(a)	Rates of corporation tax and requirement to pay in instalments	4.5	
	Definition of capital gains group	2	
	Amount to transfer	4	
	Specific information		
	– Mantet Ltd	2	
	– Newell Rap Ltd	2	
	– Orin Hod Ltd	1	
	– Other 100% companies	0.5	
			11
(b)	One mark for each relevant point (maximum of 4 marks)	4	
			4
(c) (i)	Allowances available	1.5	
	Calculation of balancing adjustment	2	
	Consideration of transfer at tax written down value	1.5	
			5

Marking guide		Marks
(ii) Capital gains tax on sale of business	1.5	
With incorporation relief		
– Incorporation relief	1.5	
– Capital gains tax and due date	1	
– Capital gains tax on gift of shares	2	
– Capital gains tax and due date	1	
Without incorporation relief		
– Capital gains tax on sale of business	1	
– Capital gains tax on gift of shares	1.5	
Explanations	4	
Summary and key issues	4	
		15
(d) Information required	1	
Contact existing tax adviser	1	
Fundamental principles	1	
Competence	1	
Conflict of interest	2	
		5

Professional skills marks

Scepticism

- Effective challenge of validity of advice provided by partnership's financial adviser in part (c)

Analysis and Evaluation

- Appropriate use of information in the scenario to support discussion and draw appropriate conclusions about group planning in part (a)
- Demonstration of ability to consider all relevant taxes specified in the requirements (eg gains, SDLT, capital allowances and capital losses in part (b))
- Adoption of logical approach to prepare suitable calculations summarising Farina's position in part (c)
- Appropriate use of information in the scenario to determine suitable calculations in part (c)
- Ability to evaluate information objectively to make a recommendation as to whether Farina should disclaim incorporation relief in part (c)

Communication

- General format and structure of notes (eg use of headings/sub-headings, easy to refer to)
- Style, language and clarity (tone of notes, presentation of calculations, appropriate use of tools, easy to follow and more than a negligible amount of content)
- Effectiveness of communication (answer is relevant, specific rather than general and focussed on the requirement)
- Adherence to specific instructions made in the scenario (eg covering the points specifically asked for in parts (a) and (c))

Commercial Acumen

- Recognition of difference in tax position with incorporation relief/disclaiming incorporation relief in part (d)
- Recognition of the importance of timing in relation to when Farina pays the CGT in part (c)

Maximum	10
Total	50

(a) **Heyer Group planning**

(1) **Group planning**

Rate of corporation tax paid

The rate of corporation tax paid will depend on each company's level of augmented profits (which are the same as TTP as no non-group dividends are received) relative to the lower and upper limits. The limits are divided by the number of associated companies in the period which are 18.

Lower limit = £50,000/18 = £2,777

Upper limit = £250,000/18 = £13,888

As all the group companies have projected TTP of over £13,888 before any capital losses are considered they will be paying tax at the main rate of 25% during the year. However, if capital losses can be offset to bring a company's augmented profits below £13,888 the company will access the higher marginal rate savings.

Requirement to pay corporation tax by instalments

In respect of the year ending 31 March 2026, a company in the Heyer Plc group will be required to pay corporation tax in instalments if its taxable total profits (TTP) exceed £83,333 (£1,500,000/18) and either:

(i) It had TTP of more than £83,333 in the year ended 31 March 2025; or

(ii) Its TTP for the year ended 31 March 2026 are more than £555,556 (£10,000,000/18).

(2) **The Heyer Plc capital gains group**

The Heyer Plc capital gains group consists of Heyer Plc, its 75% subsidiaries and their 75% subsidiaries. In addition, Heyer Plc must have an effective interest of more than 50% in any company which it does not own directly. Accordingly, all of the group companies are in a single capital gains group with the exception of Orin Hod Ltd.

(3) **Amount of chargeable gains and capital losses to transfer between group companies**

You should aim to:

(i) Minimise the rate of corporation tax payable by the group, capital losses should be allocated to companies to bring their TTP to below £13,888 when corporation tax will be saved at the highest marginal rate of 26.5%.

(ii) Once a company's TTP has been reduced to £2,777 no further losses should be allocated as these will only save 19%.

(iii) Instead, other companies within the group with TTP exceeding £13,888 should be considered. Where net gains are taxed in these companies at main rate of 25%, bringing their TTP down into the marginal rate band of tax can achieve higher savings.

(iv) The whole or part of any current period chargeable gain and/or capital loss can be transferred between companies in a capital gains group.

(a) Gains and losses should be transferred in order to match them against each other.

(b) Gains should be transferred from a company which has TTP of over £13,888 if possible to bring their TTP to between £2,777 – £13,888. This will reduce the average rate of corporation tax being paid to below main rate.

(4) **Relevance of the specific information**

Mantet Ltd

Mantet Ltd had TTP for the year ended 31 March 2026 of between £40,000 – £50,000. Accordingly, capital losses should be used to offset any gains to bring TTP to below £13,888 thus saving the highest marginal rate of tax.

Newell Rap Ltd

Newell Rap Ltd's capital losses are pre-entry capital losses because they were realised before Newell Rap Ltd was acquired by Heyer Plc. These losses cannot be used to relieve gains on assets realised by other members of the Heyer Plc capital gains group.

Orin Hod Ltd

Orin Hod Ltd's TTP exceed £83,333 for the purposes of instalment payments and will pay main rate corporation tax. However, it is not a member of the Heyer Plc capital gains group because it is not a 75% subsidiary of Heyer Plc. Accordingly, it is not possible to reduce its TTP by, for example, transferring its chargeable gains to other companies.

Other 100% owned companies

All of these companies are required to pay main rate corporation tax in instalments.

Current period chargeable gains and capital losses realised by these companies should be transferred to other companies in the Heyer Plc capital gains group in accordance with the guidance set out above.

(b) **Group restructuring**

Chargeable gains

Chargeable assets, including the business premises, will be transferred at no gain, no loss automatically, because all of the companies are 75% subsidiaries of Heyer Plc. Accordingly, no chargeable gains will arise. Any chargeable gains arising on the eventual sale of these assets to a third party by Lodi Ltd will be adjusted (increased) by any structures and buildings allowances (SBAs) claimed either by the transferor company or by Lodi Ltd.

Stamp duty land tax (SDLT)

No SDLT will be due in respect of the sale of the business premises because Heyer Plc owns at least 75% of the ordinary share capital of all of the companies.

Capital allowances

Machinery and equipment will be automatically transferred at tax written down value, rather than market value, because Heyer Plc controls at least 75% of each of the companies. Accordingly, no balancing charges will arise.

Lodi Ltd will continue to claim SBAs based on the original qualifying cost of any relevant buildings transferred to it.

Capital losses

The unused capital losses of Newell Rap Ltd, and any other company whose trade and assets will be transferred, will not be transferred to Lodi Ltd, but current period capital losses can be transferred to companies in the same capital gains group, as set out above.

(c) (i) **Capital allowances of the FL Partnership for its final trading period**

There will be no annual investment allowance, first year allowances or writing down allowances in the period in which the partnership business ceases. Instead, there will be a balancing adjustment which will be either a balancing allowance or a balancing charge.

The balancing adjustment will be calculated as follows:

	£
Tax written down value brought forward at the start of the period	X
Add additions in the period	X
Less disposals during the period at the lower of cost and sales proceeds	(X)
	X
Less proceeds on the sale of the equipment on 1 March 2026	(150,000)
Balancing allowance/(balancing charge)	X/(X)

It is not possible for an election to be made to transfer the equipment to Heyer plc at its tax written down value because Farina and Lauda will not be connected with Heyer plc. This is because they will not control the company.

(ii) **Lauda**

The sale of the business will result in a chargeable gain in respect of the goodwill. The gain, equal to the market value of the goodwill of £1,300,000, will be split equally between Farina and Lauda. Lauda's chargeable gain will therefore be £650,000. As all of the equipment qualified for capital allowances, no capital losses will arise on its disposal.

With incorporation relief

Sale of business on 1 March 2026

	£
Chargeable gain on the sale of the goodwill	650,000
Less incorporation relief £650,000 × (£600,000/£740,000) (note 1)	(527,027)
Chargeable gain after incorporation relief	122,973
Capital gains tax @ 10% (note 2)	12,297

The tax will be payable on 31 January 2027.

Shares in JH plc – Lauda's base cost

	£
Market value of shares received 200,000 × £3	600,000
Less incorporation relief	(527,027)
Base cost	72,973

Gift of 40,000 shares on 1 June 2027 (note 3)

	£
Deemed proceeds (market value) 40,000 × £5	200,000
Less cost £72,973 × (40,000/200,000)	(14,595)
Chargeable gain	185,405
Capital gains tax @ 20% (note 4)	37,081

The tax will be payable on 31 January 2029.

Notes.

1 The relief is restricted by reference to the value of the shares divided by the value of the total consideration received. Lauda will receive a total of £740,000, consisting of cash of £140,000 and shares worth 200,000 × £3 = £600,000.

2 Capital gains tax will be charged at 10% because business asset disposal relief will be available. This relief is available because the business is to be sold as a going concern and has been owned for at least two years. It is assumed that Lauda has not exceeded the lifetime limit of £1,000,000 and will claim this relief. The restriction for goodwill does not apply because Heyer plc is not a close company.

3 Gift holdover relief will not be available in respect of this gift because the shares are quoted and Lauda will hold 200,000/8,400,000 = 2.38% of the shares which is less than 5% of the company so it is not Lauda's personal company.

4 Capital gains tax will be charged at 20% because Lauda pays income tax at the additional rate and so has used up her basic rate band. Business asset disposal relief (BADR) will not be available because Lauda will hold less than 5% of Heyer plc.

Tutorial note. In order for BADR to be available in respect of the gift of the shares, Lauda would also need to be an officer or employee of Heyer plc. Investors' relief cannot be available because Heyer plc is a quoted (listed) company.

Without incorporation relief

Sale of business on 1 March 2026

	£
Chargeable gain on the sale of the goodwill	650,000
Capital gains tax @ 10% (note 2 above)	65,000

The tax will be payable on 31 January 2027.

Shares in JH plc – Lauda's base cost

	£
Market value of shares received 200,000 × £3	600,000

Gift of 40,000 shares on 1 June 2027 (note 3 above)

	£
Deemed proceeds (market value) 40,000 × £5	200,000
Less cost £600,000 × (40,000/200,000)	(120,000)
Chargeable gain	80,000
Capital gains tax @ 20% (note 4 above)	16,000

The tax will be payable on 31 January 2029.

Summary

	With incorporation relief	Without incorporation relief
	£	£
Capital gains tax on sale of business	12,297	65,000
Capital gains tax on gift of shares 1 June 2027	37,081	16,000
	49,378	81,000

Effect of incorporation relief on base cost of shares

	With incorporation relief	Without incorporation relief
	£	£
Base cost	72,973	600,000
Less used on gift of shares 1 June 2027	(14,595)	(120,000)
	58,378	480,000
Increase in gain on eventual disposal of shares		
if incorporation relief applies £(480,000 – 58,378)		421,622
Increase in capital gains tax £421,622 @ 20%		84,324

Key issues

If Lauda were to disclaim incorporation relief, she would have a higher initial capital gains tax liability.

However, disclaiming incorporation relief will result in a higher base cost in the shares such that, on a sale of the shares in the future, there will be tax savings which will exceed the increased initial liability.

The current financial adviser has only considered the reduction of Farina's initial CGT liability on incorporation. They have not considered the total tax liability including that on the eventual sale of her remaining shares which will be lower if incorporation relief is disclaimed.

Tutorial note. Note the following:

(1) Incorporation relief reduces the capital gains tax payable on the sale of the business and the gift of the shares by £31,622 (£81,000 – £49,378). When this amount is deducted from the additional tax due because of the reduced base cost, we arrive at an overall increase in the capital gains tax liability of £52,702 (£84,324 – £31,622).

This overall increase in the capital gains tax liability is simply the tax on the deferred gain of £527,027 at 20% in the future rather than at 10%, due to the availability of BADR, now: £527,027 × 10% (20% – 10%) = £52,703 (and a rounding difference of £1).

(2) Capital gains tax gift holdover relief in respect of gifts of business assets will not be available on the sale of the business to Heyer plc, because Farina and Lauda are not gifting the business to the company. They are selling the business for market value, which is received in the form of cash and shares.

(d) **Becoming tax advisers to Farina and Lauda**

Information required in respect of Farina and Lauda:

- Evidence of their identities; and
- Their addresses.

Action to be taken by the firm

(1) The firm should contact their existing tax advisers. This is to ensure that there has been no action by either Farina or Lauda which would, on ethical grounds, preclude the acceptance of the appointment.

(2) The firm should consider whether becoming tax advisers to Farina and Lauda would create any threats to compliance with the fundamental principles of professional ethics. Unless the threats can be reduced to an acceptable level via the implementation of safeguards.

With this in mind, the firm must ensure that it has sufficient competence to carry out the sophisticated tax planning required by Farina and Lauda.

In addition, given that we advise Heyer Plc to whom they will be selling their partnership, it is possible that providing advice to Farina and Lauda could give rise to a conflict of interest. Furthermore, there is a potential conflict of interest created by us advising both Farina and Lauda, as a course of action (for example, the timing of the sale) which is beneficial for one of them may not be beneficial for the other. The firm should obtain permission from Heyer Plc and both Farina and Lauda to act for them and should consider making a different member of the firm responsible for each of them.

4 Pippin

Course Book references

Employment income (including taxable benefits) is the subject of Chapter 4. Trade profits, capital allowances and national insurance contributions for the self-employed are covered in Chapter 14. Inheritance tax on potentially exempt transfers is covered in Chapter 11 and variations of wills in Chapter 12. The enterprise investment scheme (EIS) is dealt with in Chapter 3 with EIS deferral relief being dealt with in Chapter 8. Capital tax advice is dealt with in Chapter 13 and Owner Managed Business planning is the subject of Chapter 18. Taxation of dividends is covered in Chapter 2 and pensions in Chapter 3.

Top tips

In part (a) of the question make sure you follow the structure as set out in the question – the ACCA examining team have tried to word the question to help you have a process to follow. Make sure you leave sufficient time to look at the remaining parts of the question as you must complete the whole question. Structure will be important to help the marker follow your answer – in part (a) ensure your supporting calculations are clearly referenced for example by stating which tax year they relate to and in parts (b) and (c) ensure you use sub-headings to make clear the different scenarios you are discussing. Make sure you present your answer to (d) as a separate client file memorandum and try to ensure you provide Florina with advice on the most advantageous course of action.

You should note that the 50-mark case study question in your exam would contain a five-mark ethics requirement, and thus this question does not fully replicate the style of your exam.

Easy marks

There should have been easy marks available in terms of calculating income tax and national insurance due for each tax year and each strategy in part (a) of the question. Explaining the IHT consequences of a direct gift from Esme should also have provided some core marks. The tax consequences of investing in EIS shares and then selling them should also be core marks which should have provided you with the opportunity to show your knowledge of this important part of the syllabus.

ACCA examining team's comments

Part (a) concerned a plan to start a new unincorporated business. Candidates were asked to prepare a table of figures in order to determine the individual's cash position for two alternative business strategies after two years of trading. One of the strategies required the individual to take on two employees. The technical content of this part of the question was reasonably straightforward and required candidates to:

- Recognise the availability of the annual investment allowance
- Determine the relief available in respect of a trading loss in the first tax year of trading
- Deal with the tax implications for the employer of paying a mileage allowance to the employees
- Calculate the employer's class 1 contributions in respect of the employees
- Calculate the income tax and class 4 liabilities of the individual

Accordingly, in order to do well, candidates needed to concentrate on the detail, be brisk in their approach and avoid any unnecessary narrative. Many candidates were able to do this and there were some very high quality answers to this part of the question. Weaker candidates were less willing to commit themselves to the numbers and instead wrote about the tax implications in more general terms. Some candidates also let themselves down by failing to consider the individual's national insurance contributions position, such that they did not attempt quite a few of the marks on offer. There were few technical problems with this part of the question. The one common error was the implications of the mileage allowance, with most candidates knowing there was a rule regarding the excess over 45p per mile but many thinking it related to the tax deductibility of the payments made as opposed to the class 1 contributions due.

Part (b) concerned inheritance tax and was done reasonably well. Candidates were very comfortable with the basic mechanics of the tax including death within seven years of a potentially exempt transfer (PET), the nil rate band and the availability of taper relief. Weaker candidates did not always relate the facts of the question to the requirement, such that they ignored the chargeable lifetime transfer which was made prior to, but in the same tax year as, the PET. This meant that they wrote in general terms about the availability of the annual exemption and the nil rate band rather than applying the rules to the specific facts of the question.

Part (c) required candidates to explain the tax liabilities on the sale of shares in respect of which income tax relief under the enterprise investment scheme and EIS deferral relief had been claimed. As is so often the case, in order to score well, candidates needed to stop and think. In particular, they needed to identify the three separate implications of the sale of the shares. It was important to do this first because candidates then knew how much needed to be explained in the relatively short amount of time available.

The three implications which needed to be explained were:

- The gain which was deferred when the shares would become chargeable
- An element of the income tax relief obtained when the shares were acquired would be withdrawn
- There would be a chargeable gain on the sale of the shares themselves

Weaker candidates identified one of these points and wrote about it at length rather than identifying all of the points which needed to be made.

Part (d) tested extraction of profits by an individual from a company which is another frequently tested topic. Candidates essentially had to compare the tax implications, for both the individual and the company, of two alternative ways of extracting profits from the company. An appropriate first step in such a question is to determine the current income tax position of the individual in terms of their marginal rate of tax, to ascertain whether a marginal approach can be taken. Despite the fact that this approach has been used in several past exam questions, very few candidates adopted this approach here, which was very surprising. The majority of candidates wasted a considerable amount of time calculating the individual's total income tax liability under both options, involving lengthy, detailed computations. Although, on occasion, detailed computations may be needed, candidates would be advised to ensure that they are able to identify when a marginal approach is appropriate, and able to calculate the relevant tax liabilities using this method.

The decision of whether or not it is beneficial to reimburse fuel provided by the company for private travel in a company car, is a very practical one. Taxable benefits are covered in depth in TX–UK, and candidates should expect to see further testing of this knowledge in ATX–UK, albeit in more practical scenarios. Many candidates produced very muddled answer here, in particular confusing application of the fuel benefit, which is relevant where the individual has a company car, with the tax-free statutory mileage allowance, which is used where an individual uses their own car for business journeys. Although this technical knowledge is not new in ATX–UK, candidates should ensure they have practise past ATX–UK exam questions so they are familiar with the ATX–UK exam approach.

Marking guide

		Marks	
(a)	Completion of table	1.5	
	Strategy A		
	– 2025/26	3.5	
	– 2026/27	5	
	Strategy B		
	– Cost of employees	5.5	
	– 2025/26	3.5	
	– 2026/27	2.5	
	Evaluation	2	
			21
(b)	PET and death within seven years	3.5	
	Deed of variation	2	
			5
(c)	Gain on shares sold	2	
	Deferred gain	2	
	Capital gains tax liability	1.5	
	Income tax	1.5	
			6
(d)	Dividend or pension		
	– Dividend	1.5	
	– Pension contributions	4	
	Free petrol		
	– Florina	2	
	– Pippin	2.5	
			8

Professional skill marks

Scepticism

- Identification of missing or additional information, which may alter the decision reached eg needing to know whether the £75,000 comes from Esme or from Pippin's grandfather

Analysis and Evaluation

- Appropriate use of calculations in (a) to support evaluation of the two strategies and draw appropriate conclusions
- Appropriate use of calculations in (d) to support evaluation of the options with regard to provision of free petrol
- Appropriate use calculations to show the net tax saving of the pension contribution rather than dividend in part (d)
- Demonstration of ability to consider all relevant taxes specified in the requirements (eg both income tax and NIC (class 4) in part (a))
- Adoption of a logical approach to prepare suitable calculations in part (a) and (d)

Communication

- General format and structure (eg use of headings/sub-headings, easy to refer to)
- Style, language and clarity (tone, presentation of calculations, appropriate use of tools, easy to follow and more than a negligible amount of content)
- Effectiveness of communication (answer is relevant, specific rather than general and focussed on the requirement)
- Adherence to specific instructions made in the scenario (eg not checking pre-tax cash receipts and only making adjustments re employees in (a))

Commercial Acumen

- Recognising that Pippin's car will be a taxable benefit on Florina
- Recognition of opportunities for opening year trade loss relief allowing a 42% tax saving
- Recognition of possible consequences of selling the Akero shares before or after 4 January 2026 and the impact on Pippin's tax position — 10

Total — 50

Memorandum

Client: Pippin

Subject: Pinova business

Prepared by Tax senior

Date: 1 June 2025

(a) **Additional funds required for the 20-month period from 1 August 2025 to 31 March 2027**

	Strategy A	Strategy B
	£	£
Total pre-tax cash receipts for the 20-month period	61,000	109,500
Cost of employing the two employees:		
– (£60,000 + £3,000 + £810)	0	(63,810)
Total income tax and national insurance contribution liabilities for the tax years 2025/26 and 2026/27		
– (£0 + £13,889)	(13,889)	
– (£16,489 – £7,560)		(8,929)
	47,111	36,761
Personal expenditure	(80,000)	(80,000)
Additional funds required	32,889	43,239

Strategy A

2025/26

	£
Budgeted profit	13,000
Less: Capital allowances 100% AIA	(8,000)
Tax adjusted trading profit	5,000
Income tax:	
Covered by the personal allowance	0
Class 4 national insurance contributions (NIC):	
Below the lower profits limit	0
Total tax and NIC	0

2026/27

	Non-savings income	Dividend income	Total
	£	£	£
Trading income	60,000		
Dividends		500	
Net income	60,000	500	60,500
Less personal allowance	(12,570)		
Taxable income	47,430	500	47,930

Income tax:

Trading income

	£	£
£37,700 × 20%	7,540	
£9,730 × 40%	3,892	
		11,432
Dividend income – nil rate band		0
Class 4 NIC		
– (£50,270 – £12,570) × 6%	2,262	
– (£60,000 – £50,270) × 2%	195	
		2,457
Total tax and NIC		13,889

ANSWERS

Strategy B

2025/26

	£
Budgeted loss	(10,000)
Less: Capital allowances 100% AIA	(8,000)
Tax adjusted trading loss	(18,000)

Claiming opening years loss relief will result in a repayment of income tax and class 4 NIC of £7,560 (£18,000 × 42%) in respect of 2022/23. This is because in that tax year Pippin has at least £18,000 of trading income in the higher rate band for income tax and above the upper limit for Class 4 NIC.

2026/27

	£	£
Budgeted profit		130,000
Less:		
– Cost of employees		
– Salaries (£2,500 × 12 × 2)		(60,000)
– Mileage allowance (£0.50 × 250 × 12 × 2)		(3,000)
Class 1 NIC:		
Salary (£2,500 × 12)	30,000	
Mileage payments ((£0.50 – £0.45) × 250 × 12)	150	
	30,150	
(£30,150 – £9,100) × 13.8% × 2	5,810	
Less: Employment allowance	(5,000)	
		(810)
Tax adjusted trading profit		66,190
Income tax and NIC on profit of £60,000 (per strategy A)		13,889
Income tax and class 4 NIC on excess over £60,000 (£66,190 – £60,000) × 42%		2,600
Total tax and NIC		16,489

Evaluation of the two strategies

Strategy A requires less additional funding than strategy B over the 20-month period.

However, the annual profit under strategy A will only be £60,000, with post-tax receipts of approximately £46,111 (£60,000 – £13,889). This income alone will not be sufficient to generate the £48,000 (£4,000 × 12) required by Pippin every year for his personal expenditure.

The annual post-tax profit under Strategy B will be £49,701 (£130,000 – £63,810 – £16,489), such that there should be sufficient post-tax cash receipts for Pippin's needs.

(b) **Receipt of £75,000**

The tax implications for Pippin depend on whether the £75,000 was a direct gift from Esme or the result of Esme having made a tax-effective deed of variation of her father's will.

Gift from Esme

The gift would have been a potentially exempt transfer. Esme's death within seven years of the gift would result in an inheritance tax liability for Pippin as follows:

	£
Transfer	75,000
Inheritance tax at 40% (Note)	30,000
Less: Taper relief (5 to 6 years) (£30,000 × 60%)	(18,000)
	12,000

> **Tutorial note.** Esme's annual exemptions and her nil rate band were used by the gift on 1 November 2019.

Deed of variation

A variation whereby £75,000 of Esme's inheritance was transferred to Pippin would not be treated as a gift from Esme to Pippin. Instead, the money would be regarded as having passed to Pippin via his grandfather's will. Accordingly, in these circumstances, there would be no inheritance tax implications for Pippin as a result of the death of Esme.

(c) **Sale of shares in Akero Ltd**

Capital gains tax

Chargeable gain on the sale of the shares

Pippin will realise a chargeable gain of £17,500 ((£4.50 – £1) × 5,000) if the shares are sold prior to 4 January 2026 at their current market value.

However, if the shares are sold on or after 4 January 2026, the chargeable gain arising on the sale will be exempt.

Chargeable gain deferred in respect of the painting

Regardless of when the shares are sold, the chargeable gain which was deferred on their acquisition will become chargeable. The chargeable gain deferred was £16,000, or £1 per share, such that, on the sale of 5,000 shares, a gain of £5,000 will become chargeable.

Capital gains tax liability

Any chargeable gains realised by Pippin in the tax year 2025/26 will be reduced by his annual exempt amount of £3,000. Any gains not covered by the annual exempt amount will be taxed at 10%, as Pippin has no taxable income.

Income tax

If the shares are sold prior to 4 January 2026 at their current market value, there will be a withdrawal of £1,500 (5,000 × £1 × 30%) of the income tax relief originally obtained by Pippin. This is because the shares will have been sold for more than their cost.

(d) To: Florina's client files

From: Tax senior

Date: 1 June 2025

Subject: Remuneration and provision of free petrol

Florina's remuneration from Flight Hip Ltd

Payment of dividend of £20,000

	£
Income tax: £20,000 × 33.75% (N1)	6,750
Tax cost (equal to the tax saving if the dividend is not paid)	6,750

ANSWERS

Payment of pension contributions of £20,000

	£	£
Corporation tax saving (£20,000 × 25%)		5,000
Income tax:		
– On the employer pension contributions	0	
– On future pension income (£20,000 × 75% × 20%) (N2)	3,000	
		(3,000)
Net tax saving		2,000

The total tax saving would be £8,750 (£6,750 + £2,000).

Provision of free petrol

	Florina	Pippin
	£	£
Income tax payable by Florina on the fuel benefit:		
Car used by Florina (£27,800 × 26% × 40%)	2,891	
Car used by Pippin (£27,800 × 23% × 40%) (N3)		2,558
Cost of private petrol:		
Florina (£4,000 × 18,000/19,000)	(3,789)	
Pippin		(800)
Financial benefit/cost of the free petrol:		
Florina – income tax is less than cost	(898)	
Pippin – income tax is more than cost		1,758

It would be financially beneficial for Pippin to stop receiving free petrol from Flight Hip Ltd, as Florina's tax liability in respect of the benefit exceeds the cost of the petrol.

Tutorial note. Note the following:

(1) The dividend from Landing Properties Ltd will use up £500 of the dividend nil rate band.

(2) When Florina withdraws £20,000 from the pension, 25% will be tax-free and the remaining 75% will be subject to income tax.

(3) It has been assumed that the provision of the car and free petrol to Pippin will give rise to a taxable benefit for Florina because Pippin is not an employee of Flight Hip Ltd but is a member of Florina's household. The definition of member of a household is that Pippin would have to be a member of Florina's family, or one of her domestic staff, or her guest. Since Florina and Pippin are not married, Pippin would only be a member of Florina's family if he was her dependent and this is questionable on the facts given in the scenario since Pippin has taxable trading income, even though it is lower than Florina's level of income.

Videos can be viewed online by accessing your ebook version on VitalSource.

5 Harrow Tan Ltd group

Course Book references

Chargeable gains for companies, including the substantial shareholding exemption and relief for replacement of business assets, are covered in Chapter 16. Stamp duty land tax is dealt with in Chapter 24. Groups of companies are covered in Chapter 19. Corporate tax advice is covered in Chapter 25. Value added tax (VAT) special schemes and the rules for entertainment, gifts and samples are dealt with in Chapter 23. Tests of employment versus self-employment are dealt with in Chapter 4. Ethics are covered in Chapter 1.

Top tips

Make sure you read the question carefully and only answer what you are asked. In this question, students had been prepared to answer about the planning aspects of corporation tax groups and payment of corporation tax by instalments which had been tested in a previous sitting and therefore brought in this aspect which was irrelevant.

Easy marks

Groups in part (c) and the VAT aspects in part (d) were brought forward knowledge from Taxation (TX–UK) and so should have yielded easy marks. It is important to make sure you revise TX–UK topics and not just concentrate on those topics only examinable in Advanced Taxation (ATX–UK). There were some easy marks for identifying the factors which would indicate self-employment in part (d). The ethical issues in part (e) should have been well known.

ACCA examining team's comments

This question concerned a variety of corporation tax issues facing different members of a group of companies. It was quite a challenging question, but some good answers were provided by candidates who read the question carefully, and followed the detailed guidance. The use of subheadings, taken from the issues in the manager's email, provides a useful structure in this type of question, which all candidates should consider adopting.

The first part of the question, which was worth 13 marks, related to the sale of shares in one of the group companies. For 13 marks, a candidate should expect to have to identify several different issues, and in this case, the ACCA examining team indicated that there were three or four issues to be considered here. Many candidates managed to identify one or two, but relatively few were able to produce a comprehensive answer to this part. Candidates who had practised past exam questions in this subject area would have been able to identify and discuss the key issues of substantial shareholding exemption, degrouping charge, and withdrawal of the stamp duty land tax exemption, and consequently scored well. These are key elements of knowledge in ATX–UK and are tested frequently in a variety of different ways.

The second part of the question concerned group relief available for the trading loss of one of the group companies. It was pleasing to see that many candidates were able to accurately define a group for group relief purposes, and to apply this to the group in the scenario. The question required candidates to state the maximum loss which could be surrendered to each of the group companies. However, a significant number of candidates appeared to misread this, and introduced a planning element, discussing in some detail, the optimum relief available to the group, taking into consideration whether or not each company would pay corporation tax in instalments. Candidates are strongly advised to spend a little time reading the detail of the requirements very carefully, to ensure that they focus their efforts in the right direction. Time spent in this way should help to ensure that candidates focus their answer on what is required, and do not go off at a tangent, providing irrelevant information or computations, which waste time.

The third part of the question related to the availability of rollover relief within the group, and, again, it was pleasing that most candidates were able to correctly define a group for this purpose and apply this to the group in the scenario. However, knowledge of the assets which qualify for rollover relief was rather more vague, with many candidates failing to recognise that a share disposal does not qualify. Whereas many candidates were aware that the gain eligible to be rolled over might be restricted, very few could accurately explain the restriction. Candidates sitting ATX–UK will frequently be tested on the capital gains reliefs available for both companies and individuals, and would be well advised to ensure that they spend some time learning the details of these.

The next part of the question concerned VAT implications of using the annual accounting scheme and of incurring expenditure on promotional activities, the ethical implications of using previous knowledge to help a client and the tax status of new salespeople. The majority of candidates were familiar with the terms of the annual accounting scheme. However, many answers relating to the expenditure on entertainment, gifts, and samples, related to the corporation tax implications of these not being allowable, with no reference at all to VAT. Although some candidates did appreciate the VAT implications with regard to input VAT on each of these, very few identified the correct output VAT implications.

The next part concerning the employment status of two part-time salespeople was done extremely well. The majority of candidates were able to identify which of the specific contractual arrangements given in the question concerning the work to be done by the salespeople indicated self-employment and any changes required to the other arrangements in order to maximise the likelihood of the salespeople being treated as self-employed. Many candidates gave the impression of being very confident with this topic, and happy to write at length about the different arrangements, giving the impression that they may well have exceeded the four marks' worth of time which should have been allocated to this part. Candidates should always take note of the number of marks available for each question part and resist the temptation to elaborate unnecessarily on areas with which they are very comfortable.

The final part covered the ethical issue of confidentiality in relation to using knowledge and experience gained from dealing with both current and ex-clients to assist a new client. This part was done very well by the vast majority of candidates, with many scoring full marks. It was pleasing to see that most candidates related well to the specific client and the facts given in the scenario.

Marking guide

		Marks	
(a)	Substantial shareholding exemption	3.5	
	Degrouping charge		
	– Explanation	4	
	– Calculation	1	
	Rollover relief	1	
	Calculation of taxable gain	2	
	Stamp duty land tax	2.5	
			13
(b)	Harrow Tan Ltd	2	
	Rocha Ltd	2	
	Tosca Ltd	1	
	Uta Far Ltd	3	
			6
(c)	Chargeable gains group	3	
	Implications	3	
	Part C of the schedule	2	
			7

Marking guide	Marks	
(d) Increase in turnover	3.5	
Entertainment and gifts	3	
Salespeople (1 mark for each relevant point, up to 4 marks)	4	
		9
(e) 1 mark for each relevant point, up to 5 marks	5	
		5

Professional skill marks

Scepticism

- Effective challenge and critical assessment of Corella's schedule
- Identification of missing or additional information, which may alter the decision reached as to group rollover relief availability

Analysis and Evaluation

- Appropriate use of information in the scenario to determine suitable calculations for the gain on the disposal of the Rocha Ltd shares, the degrouping charge and the stamp duty land tax
- Demonstration of reasoned judgement when considering group matters - both group relief and gains groups

Communication

- General format and structure of meeting notes (eg use of headings/sub-headings, easy to refer to)
- Style, language and clarity (tone of meeting notes, presentation of calculations, appropriate use of tools, easy to follow and more than a negligible amount of content)
- Effectiveness of communication (answer is relevant, specific rather than general and focussed on the requirement)
- Adherence to specific instructions made in the scenario (eg identifying three or four issues in Corella's schedule and addressing each task requested)

Commercial Acumen

- Recognising the degrouping charge and retrospective stamp duty land tax charge due to Rocha Ltd shares being sold
- Recognition of administrative and cashflow consequences of leaving the annual accounting scheme
- Recognition of changes to be made to salespeople's contracts to make them self-employed
- Recognition of the importance of timing with regard to the disposal of the Rocha Ltd shares impacting on the availability of the substantial shareholding exemption

Maximum	10
Total	50

Meeting notes

Client: Harrow Tan Ltd group

Subject: Various group matters

Prepared by: Tax senior

Date: 1 September 2025

(a) **Sale of shares in Rocha Ltd**

Substantial shareholding exemption

The gain on the sale of the shares in Rocha Ltd will not be subject to tax if the conditions of the substantial shareholding exemption (SSE) are satisfied.

The conditions are:

- Rocha Ltd must be a trading company – this condition is satisfied.
- At least 10% of the ordinary share capital must have been held for 12 months during the six years prior to the sale.

Accordingly, in order for the SSE to be available, the sale would need to be delayed until 1 December 2025.

Taxable gain

If the sale takes place on 1 October 2025 the SSE **will not** be available, and the taxable gain will be calculated as follows:

	Notes	£
Gain per company (per Schedule A)		3,610,000
Add:		
– Degrouping charge	1	262,430
– Rollover relief	2	1,350,000
Taxable gain		5,222,430

This taxable gain would result in a substantial corporation tax liability. Accordingly, it is important that the SSE conditions are satisfied.

Notes.

1 **Degrouping charge**

A degrouping charge will arise in respect of the building which was sold to Rocha Ltd by Seckel Ltd.

This is because:

- Rocha Ltd and Seckel Ltd are members of the Harrow Tan Ltd chargeable gains group (they are both 75% subsidiaries of Harrow Tan Ltd).
- The building would have been transferred automatically at no gain, no loss.
- Rocha Ltd will leave the Harrow Tan Ltd chargeable gains group when it ceases to be a 75% subsidiary on the sale of the shares. This will occur within six years of the acquisition of the building.
- Rocha Ltd will still own the building when it leaves the group.

The degrouping charge will be calculated as follows:

	£
Market value on 1 January 2025	800,000
Less:	
– Cost	(330,000)
– Indexation allowance May 2000 to December 2017 (£330,000 × 0.629)	(207,570)
Degrouping charge	262,430

2 **Rollover relief**

- Company shares are not qualifying assets for the purposes of rollover relief.
- Accordingly, it will not be possible to roll over any of the gain on the sale of the shares.

Stamp duty land tax

Stamp duty land tax (SDLT) will not have been payable by Rocha Ltd in respect of the purchase of the building from Seckel Ltd because both companies were 75% subsidiaries of Harrow Tan Ltd at that time.

However, because Rocha Ltd will cease to be a 75% subsidiary of Harrow Tan Ltd within three years of purchasing the building, it will have to pay SDLT of £29,500.

	£
£150,000 × 0%	0
£100,000 × 2%	2,000
£550,000 × 5%	27,500
	29,500

(b) **Group relief – year ending 31 December 2025**

Harrow Tan Ltd

A company can claim available group losses up to a maximum of its taxable total profits (TTP).

For Harrow Tan Ltd, this will be £40,000 plus the chargeable gain on the sale of the shares in Rocha Ltd (if the SSE is not available).

Rocha Ltd

For the purposes of group relief, Rocha Ltd left the group on 31 July 2025, when the agreement was signed to sell 60,000 of the company's shares.

The maximum surrender to Rocha Ltd will therefore be £35,000 (£60,000 × 7/12), as this is less than the loss available for this period.

Tosca Ltd

The maximum surrender to Tosca Ltd will be its TTP for the year of £70,000.

Uta Far Ltd

The effective interest of Harrow Tan Ltd in Uta Far Ltd is less than 75% (80% × 90% = 72%). Accordingly, Uta Far Ltd is not in a group relief group with Seckel Ltd and cannot receive any losses.

However, it is possible to transfer some or all of Uta Far Ltd's chargeable gain on the sale of the building to another group company, such that it could then be relieved by group relief from Seckel Ltd.

(c) **Rollover relief**

Relief potentially available to the group

For the purposes of rollover relief, a chargeable gains group is treated as a single entity. The Harrow Tan Ltd chargeable gains group consists of:

- Harrow Tan Ltd
- its 75% subsidiaries
- and their 75% subsidiaries
- Harrow Tan Ltd must have an effective interest of more than 50% in any non-directly held companies.

Harrow Tan Ltd's interest in Uta Far Ltd is 72% (80% × 90%), such that all five companies are in the Harrow Tan Ltd capital gains group.

The implications of this are:

(1) Rollover relief is available in respect of the gain on the building sold by Uta Far Ltd on 1 May 2025.

The whole of the gain can be rolled over if there are qualifying additions in the qualifying period of at least £1,800,000. Any amount of the sales proceeds which has not been used to acquire qualifying business assets cannot be relieved and will be subject to corporation tax up to a maximum of the gain of £85,000.

(2) There may be other qualifying additions.

(i) Qualifying business assets can be acquired by any company in the same chargeable gains group as the company which has sold a qualifying business asset.

(ii) The qualifying period is the four-year period starting one year prior to the date on which the disposal of a qualifying business asset occurred.

Part C of Corella's schedule

The land and building qualify for rollover relief.

Further information is needed in respect of the machinery; it must be fixed, rather than movable, if it is to qualify for rollover relief.

Patents and trademarks are intangible assets which are not qualifying additions for the purposes of chargeable gains rollover relief.

(d) **Tosca Ltd – promotion of new product**

Increase in turnover

Tosca Ltd should notify HM Revenue & Customs that it expects its turnover to exceed the annual accounting turnover limit of £1,600,000. The company may then be required to leave the scheme. Once its turnover for an accounting year does exceed this limit, it will be required to leave the scheme.

Once the company is no longer in the annual accounting scheme, it will have to submit four VAT returns a year rather than one. Its VAT payments will then fluctuate because they will be calculated by reference to its outputs and inputs in the quarter rather than being based on its VAT liability for the previous year.

Entertainment and gifts

Tosca Ltd will not be able to recover the input tax in respect of the cost of the meal because this is entertaining its UK customers.

It will not be necessary to account for output tax on the gifts of the pens, provided the total cost of any gifts made to the same person does not exceed £50 in a year. The related input tax will be recoverable in full.

It will also not be necessary to account for output tax on the gifts of the new product, even though its value exceeds £50, because it is a sample of the company's own products. Again, the related input tax will be recoverable in full.

Salespeople

Proposed contractual arrangements indicating self-employed status

(1) The salespeople will be paid a fee by reference to the work they do. This will enable them to earn more by working more efficiently and effectively.

(2) The salespeople will not be paid sick pay or holiday pay; such payments would be indicative of employed status.

(3) The salespeople will be required to use their own cars.

Suggested changes in order to maximise the likelihood of the salesmen being treated as self-employed

(1) It would be helpful if the salespeople were able to work on the days they choose rather than being required to work on specific days.

(2) The salespeople should be required to provide their own laptop computer rather than borrowing one from Tosca Ltd.

> **Tutorial note.** The period for which the salespeople will work is not a relevant factor in determining their status. However, the longer they are appointed for, the more likely it is that the factors indicating employment (for example, the degree of control over the worker) will be present.

(e) **New contracts for the business**

(1) ACCA's Code of Ethics and Conduct includes confidentiality as one of the fundamental principles of ethics on which we should base our professional behaviour.

(2) Where we have acquired confidential information as a result of our professional and business relationships, we are obliged to refrain from using it to our own advantage or to the advantage of third parties.

(3) This principle of confidentiality applies to both ex-clients and continuing clients.

(4) As a result of this, we should not use any confidential information relating to our existing clients or ex-clients to assist Tosca Ltd.

(5) We are permitted to use the experience and expertise we have gained from advising our clients.

6 Snowdon

Course Book references

Inheritance tax on lifetime gifts is covered in Chapter 11. Computation of chargeable gains is dealt with in Chapter 7 and gift holdover relief in Chapter 8. Capital tax planning is the subject of Chapter 13. Income tax computation is covered in Chapter 2. National insurance for employees is dealt with in Chapter 4 and for the self-employed in Chapter 14. Partial exemption for value added tax is covered in Chapter 23. Ethics is dealt with in Chapter 1. Groups are dealt with in Chapter 19 and corporation tax administration in Chapter 16.

Top tips

In part (a) remember that a transfer of value is the loss to the transferor's estate. You also need to look back seven years from the date of the transfer (not the date of death) to see if there are any chargeable lifetime transfers to cumulate. Corporation tax administration is brought-forward knowledge from Taxation (TX–UK) but is often examined in Advanced Taxation (ATX–UK) so you must know the rules in detail.

Easy marks

There should be some easy marks in part (a) for dealing with a basic capital gains tax computation and the effect of gift holdover relief. The ethical matters in part (c) are often examined and should be familiar to you.

ACCA examining team's comments

This question required appropriate advice on a variety of personal tax matters, including inheritance tax, capital gains tax, income tax and value added tax (VAT) issues, together with consideration of the procedures to be considered before taking on a new client. It also contained corporation tax issues for a group of companies. It was quite a challenging question, requiring a structured logical approach in order to produce a good answer. A good number of candidates did achieve this, but a significant number appeared to struggle with the detailed calculations required. The use of subheadings, taken from the issues in the manager's email, provides a useful structure in this type of question, which future candidates should consider adopting.

The first part of the question, which was worth 9 marks, required candidates to identify, explain, and correct errors made by the potential new client in their calculation of an inheritance tax liability on a lifetime gift, and calculate the implications for the recipient of having made a valid gift holdover relief claim in relation to this asset. This type of 'correction of errors' question has been used several times in the past in Section A questions, and it was pleasing to see many candidates try to both explain the errors, and provide a revised calculation, as required. Consequently, these candidates scored well. Weaker candidates tended to rely too much on just producing the revised calculations, without adequate explanations of the reasons for the revisions, which were required in order to score a high mark on this question part. This is a challenging question type, but one which candidates should expect to appear regularly in the Advanced Taxation (ATX–UK) exam. Many candidates' knowledge of capital gains tax gift holdover relief was rather vague and very few dealt correctly with the fact that this was actually a sale at undervalue ie some proceeds had been received and therefore the deferred gain would be restricted. Candidates need to be familiar with the precise consequences of claiming capital gains tax reliefs such as this.

The second part of the question concerned the appraisal of two alternative strategies being considered by the potential client in relation to expanding their unincorporated business. This part was worth 17 marks and was wholly computational involving mainly income tax, and a few marks of VAT. It contained a considerable amount of detail relating to each of the strategies, and of the VAT implications, including possible partial exemption. Questions involving a series of detailed computations, such as this one, require careful reading, thinking and planning before starting to write, in order to produce a logical, easy to follow set of calculations. Lengthy computations such as this are challenging questions, with a number of different 'issues' embedded within them, such as the consideration of the impact of VAT, and in particular partial exemption, as there was here. Time spent in planning at the start ensures that candidates don't waste time with unnecessary calculations, which, in some cases were quite lengthy, but were irrelevant, so gained no marks. Also, candidates are able to recognise the point in the computation when specific aspects – such as partial exemption for VAT – need to be considered. It was clear where candidates had done such preparation; their computations were logically presented, and easy to mark. It cannot be stressed enough how vital it is to spend a few minutes reading, thinking and planning before starting to write an answer to these longer question parts.

The third part of the question required a summary of the procedures to be followed before agreeing to become tax advisers for the potential new client. This appeared to be a question for which most candidates were well prepared, and most scored well. Those that didn't tended to be too general in their comments, such as talking about the need to ensure adherence to ACCA's fundamental ethical principles, without identifying which of these principles is/are particularly relevant in this scenario. It is always important in an ethics requirement to relate your answer specifically to the (potential) client, and the scenario in the question.

The final part of the question concerned a corporate group with a newly acquired, wholly owned subsidiary company, and its ability to receive a capital loss or trading loss from other group companies, and, separately, the corporation tax instalments which will fall due in the next seven months.

In relation to the losses, many answers were disappointingly vague, in particular not stating whether the candidate was considering the capital loss or the trading loss in their discussion, or implying that the rules were the same for both, which is not the case. Dates were given in the question, so candidates were expected to refer to these in their answers.

The identification of the amounts and due dates for payment of the company's corporation tax instalments was, surprisingly, not well done. Virtually no candidate recognised that the final instalment for payment of a company's corporation tax liability was going to be the balance of the final corporation tax liability for the year, ie the final liability less the three instalments paid previously, which is extremely unlikely to be the same as one quarter of the final liability, as the previous instalments have been based on estimates. A good number of candidates correctly calculated the amount of the first instalment for the subsequent short accounting period, but in both cases, application of knowledge of the due dates was weak. These must be accurately stated in order to score the marks.

Marking guide

			Marks	
(a)	(i)	Identification of errors		
		– Value of the gift	1.5	
		– Annual exemptions	1.5	
		– Taper relief	2	
		– Nil rate band	1	
		Calculation of inheritance tax	2.5	
		Marks Available	8.5	
		Maximum		7
	(ii)	Base cost for the purpose of capital gains tax	2	
				2
(b)	(i)	Additional tax adjusted trading profit – strategy A		
		– Additional turnover	.5	
		– Salary, class 1 NIC and overheads	2	
		– Recoverable input tax	3	
		Additional tax adjusted trading profit – strategy B		
		– Additional turnover and fee paid to Tor Ltd	1	
		– Recoverable input tax	3	
		Maximum		9
	(ii)	Taxable income	3	
		Income tax and class 4 NIC on trading income	2.5	
		Income tax on interest income	1	
		Remainder of calculation	3	
		Marks Available	9.5	
		Maximum		8
(c)	Identity		1	
	Fundamental principles		3	
	Contact existing tax advisers		1	
	Money laundering		1	
	Marks Available		6	
	Maximum			5

ANSWERS

Marking guide

		Marks	
(d)	Steam Ltd capital loss	2	
	Wagon Ltd trading losses		
	Loss brought forward	2	
	Current period loss	3	
	Payments of corporation tax		
	In respect of the year ended 30 April 2025	2.5	
	In respect of the eight-month period ended 31 December 2025	2	
	Marks Available	11.5	
	Maximum		9

Professional skills marks

Scepticism

- Effective challenge and critical assessment of the errors in Snowdon's IHT calculation.

Analysis and Evaluation

- Appropriate use of information in the scenario to determine suitable calculations as to which strategy is most financially beneficial in relation to the expansion of the Siabod business.
- Appropriate use of information in the scenario and calculations performed to draw appropriate conclusions as to which expansion strategy is most financially advantageous.
- Appropriate use of information to determine the additional post-tax income to be generated from the most financially advantageous strategy.
- Demonstration of ability to consider all relevant taxes specified in the requirements (eg both income tax and NIC in the calculation of additional post-tax income).
- Demonstration of ability to consider relevant factors applicable to the Set Ltd group relief and gains group and use of the losses by the group members.

Communication

- General format and structure of memorandum/e-mail (eg use of headings/sub-headings, easy to refer to)
- Style, language and clarity (tone of memorandum/e-mail, presentation of calculations, appropriate use of tools, easy to follow and more than a negligible amount of content)
- Effectiveness of communication (answer is relevant, specific rather than general and focussed on the requirement)
- Adherence to specific instructions made in the scenario (eg not to consider whether the cottage qualified for business property relief and to answer each query raised by the manager)

Commercial Acumen

- Demonstrating awareness that a change in Siabod's input VAT suffered will impact on the VAT recoverable under the partial exemption scheme leading to input VAT becoming irrecoverable through Strategy B.
- Recognition of opportunities for group tax planning regarding the use of losses in the Set Ltd group
- Recommendations are practical and plausible in the context of the situation
- Recognition of the final quarterly instalment being due for the year ended 30 April 2025

Maximum	10
Total	50

(a) **Memorandum**

Client: Snowdon

Subject: Personal tax matters

Prepared by: Tax senior

Date: 1 June 2025

(i) **Purchase of the cottage from Coleen**

Errors in Snowdon's computation

(1) The value of the gift for the purpose of inheritance tax (IHT) is the fall in value of Coleen's estate, ie £35,000 (£260,000 – £225,000) being the value of the cottage less the amount paid by Snowdon.

(2) The cottage was a lifetime gift and not a gift on death. Accordingly, the annual exemption for both the year of the gift and the previous year are available: a total of £6,000 (2 × £3,000).

(3) The 40% rate of taper relief is correct. However, the relief should be 40% of the inheritance tax due as opposed to 40% of the gift.

(4) The nil rate band of £325,000 should be reduced by chargeable transfers in the seven years prior to 1 May 2021. Accordingly, it will be reduced by the chargeable lifetime transfer made by Coleen on 1 March 2017.

Inheritance tax due in respect of the gift of the cottage

	£
Value of the gift	35,000
Less: annual exemptions (£3,000 × 2)	(6,000)
	29,000
Nil rate band	325,000
Less: chargeable transfer in the seven years prior to 1 May 2021	(318,000)
Available nil rate band	7,000
Inheritance tax ((£29,000 – £7,000) × 40%)	8,800
Less: taper relief (£8,800 × 40%) (between 4 and 5 years)	(3,520)
	5,280

(ii) **Base cost of the cottage for the purposes of a future disposal**

	£	£
Value of the cottage as at 1 May 2021		260,000
Less: gift holdover relief		
Proceeds (market value)	260,000	
Less: cost	(165,000)	
	95,000	
Less: cash gain £(225,000 – 165,000)	(60,000)	
Gift holdover relief		(35,000)
Base cost of cottage		225,000

ANSWERS

(b) (i) **Expansion of the Siabod business**

Strategy A

	£
Additional turnover (£435,000 – £255,000)	180,000
Salary	48,000
Employer's class 1 NIC ((£48,000 – £9,100) × 13.8%)	5,368
Overheads and advertising (£38,000 + £2,000)	40,000
Irrecoverable VAT (W1)	0
	93,368
Additional tax adjusted trading profit (£180,000 – £93,368)	86,632

Strategy B

	£
Additional turnover (as for strategy A)	180,000
Fee paid to Tor Ltd	90,000
Advertising	2,000
Irrecoverable VAT (W2)	8,736
	100,736
Additional tax adjusted trading profit (£180,000 – £100,736)	79,264

The most financially advantageous strategy would be strategy A.

Workings

1 ***Strategy A – recoverable input tax***

	£
Total input tax (£18,000 + ((£38,000 + £2,000) × 20%))	26,000
Attributable to taxable supplies (£26,000 × 76%)	(19,760)
Attributable to exempt supplies	6,240

The VAT attributable to exempt supplies can be recovered in full as it is below the annual de minimis limit of £7,500 (£625 × 12) and is less than half of the total input tax.

2 ***Strategy B – recoverable input tax***

	£
Total input tax (£18,000 + ((£90,000 + £2,000) × 20%))	36,400
Attributable to taxable supplies (£36,400 × 76%)	(27,664)
Attributable to exempt supplies	8,736

The VAT attributable to exempt supplies cannot be recovered as it exceeds the annual de *minimis* limit of £7,500 (£625 × 12).

(ii) **Additional post-tax income in respect of strategy A**

	Non-savings income	Savings income	Total
	£	£	£
Tax adjusted trading profit prior to expansion	85,000		
Tax adjusted trading profit in respect of expansion (above)	86,632		
Interest income		740	
Net income	171,632	740	172,372
Less personal allowance	(0)	(0)	
Taxable income	171,632	740	172,372

Income tax	
Non-savings income	
– £37,700 × 20%	7,540
– £87,440 (125,140 – 37,700) × 40%	34,976
– £46,492 (171,632 – 125,140) × 45%	20,921
Savings income	
– £740 × 45%	333
Class 4 NIC	
– £37,700 (50,270 – 12,570) × 6%	2,262
– £121,362 (171,632 – 50,270) × 2%	2,427
Total income tax and NIC	68,459
Less:	
– income tax and Class 4 NIC on profit of £85,000 £(21,432 + 2,957)	(24,389)
– income tax on interest income prior to expansion of business £(740 – 500) = £240 × 40%	(96)
Additional income tax and Class 4 NIC in respect of expansion	43,974
Additional post-tax income £(86,632 – 43,974)	42,658

ANSWERS

Alternative computation of additional post-tax income in respect of strategy A

	£
Additional income tax	
– £12,570 × 40%	5,028
– £40,140 (125,140 – 85,000) × 40%	16,056
– £46,492 (171,632 – 125,140) × 45%	20,921
– £500 × 45%	225
– £240 (740 – 500) × 5 (45 – 40)%	12
Additional Class 4 NIC	
– £86,632 × 2%	1,733
Additional income tax and Class 4 NIC in respect of expansion	43,975
Additional post-tax income £(86,632 – 43,975)	42,657

> **Tutorial note.** Prior to expanding the business, Snowdon was a higher rate taxpayer and was therefore entitled to a savings income nil rate band of £500. Following the expansion of the business, he will be an additional rate taxpayer and will not be entitled to this allowance.
>
> The alternative computation gives an answer £1 different to the first due to rounding differences. The ACCA have confirmed that small differences due to rounding will not be penalised.

(c) **Procedures we should follow before we agree to become Snowdon's tax advisers**

- We must obtain evidence of Snowdon's identity (for example, his passport) and his address.
- We must have regard to the fundamental principles of professional ethics. This requires us to consider whether becoming tax advisers to Snowdon would create any threats to compliance with these principles.
  - Integrity: we must consider the appropriateness of Snowdon's attitude to complying with the law and the disclosure of information to HM Revenue & Customs (HMRC).
  - Professional competence: we must ensure that we have the skills and competence necessary to be able to deal with the matters which may arise in connection with Snowdon's affairs.

  If any such threats are identified, we should not accept the appointment unless the threats can be reduced to an acceptable level via the implementation of safeguards.
- We should contact Snowdon's existing tax adviser(s) in order to ensure that there has been no action by Snowdon which would preclude the acceptance of the appointment on ethical grounds.
- We must carry out a review in order to satisfy ourselves that Snowdon is not carrying on any activities which may be regarded as money laundering.

(d) To: Daisy

From: Tax senior

Date: 1 June 2025

Subject: Ghost Ltd - corporation tax payments

Thank you for your query about Ghost Ltd's corporation tax payments. I set out answers to your queries below:

Ghost Ltd – corporation tax payments

Steam Ltd capital loss

Ghost Ltd and Steam Ltd are members of a chargeable gains group because Set Ltd owns at least 75% of the ordinary share capital of both companies.

Accordingly, the capital loss in respect of the disposal of the building by Steam Ltd could be transferred to Ghost Ltd. However, the loss could only be offset against chargeable gains (ie not trading profit or other income) realised by Ghost Ltd after it became a member of the Set Ltd chargeable gains group on 1 June 2025.

Wagon Ltd trading losses

Ghost Ltd and Wagon Ltd are members of a group relief group because Set Ltd owns at least 75% of the ordinary share capital of both companies. Trading losses made whilst the companies are members of the group can be transferred from one company to the other.

Ghost Ltd became a member of the Set Ltd group relief group on 1 June 2025. Its eight-month accounting period ending on 31 December 2025 will have seven months in common with the 12-month accounting period of Wagon Ltd ending on 31 December 2025. Accordingly, the maximum trading loss which can be transferred from Wagon Ltd to Ghost Ltd is the lower of:

- 7/12 of the trading loss of Wagon Ltd for the year ending 31 December 2025; and
- 7/8 of the taxable trading profit of Ghost Ltd for the eight-month period ending 31 December 2025.

Wagon Ltd can also transfer part of its trading loss brought forward to Ghost Ltd. The maximum brought forward trading loss that can be transferred from Wagon Ltd to Ghost Ltd is the lower of:

- 7/12 of the brought forward trading loss of Wagon Ltd ie 7/12 × £31,500 = £18,375; and
- 7/8 of the taxable trading profit, less the current period group relief, of Ghost Ltd for the eight-month period ending 31 December 2025.

Payments of corporation tax

In respect of the year ended 30 April 2025

14 August 2025	The final payment for this accounting period will be due. The amount due is £597,500 (the total liability for the accounting period), less all the instalment payments already made in respect of the period.

In respect of the eight-month period ended 31 December 2025

14 November 2025	The first payment for this accounting period will be due. The amount due will be 3/8 of the estimated corporation tax liability for the eight-month period, ie £172,500 (3/8 × £460,000).

I trust this provides you with the information you need but please do let me know if you have any further questions.

Regards

Tax senior

7 Wanda

Course Book references

Inheritance tax (IHT) computation is covered in Chapter 11. Capital tax planning, including computation of post-tax inheritance, is the subject of Chapter 13. Value added tax (VAT) is the subject of Chapter 23. Income tax computation is covered in Chapter 2. Unincorporated business losses and partnerships are covered in Chapter 15. Corporation tax computation is covered in Chapter 16 and corporation tax losses in Chapter 17. Overseas aspects of personal tax are covered in Chapter 9. Ethics is dealt with in Chapter 1.

Top tips

In part (a) when working out the post-tax inheritance, you need to go back to the amount of the estate, not just the part which is taxable at 40%. In part (c)(i) don't forget that operating a business through a company has both income tax and corporation tax aspects. Also note that you were told to ignore national insurance contributions. Overseas tax issues are frequently tested in ATX and if you didn't spot the temporary non-residence rules then you need to spend more time consolidating these topics. They are frequently examined and you need to be able to spot these issues as you read the question.

Easy marks

There were some easy marks in part (a) for basic IHT computations which should have been familiar from your TX – UK studies. The VAT registration aspects in part (b) should also be well-known, but make sure you distinguish clearly between advantages and disadvantages.

ACCA examining team's comments

Part (a) required calculations to determine an amount of post-tax inheritance available. In the question scenario, the husband had died some years earlier, not fully utilising his nil rate bands. When the wife died both she and her deceased husband's nil rate bands required consideration. Many candidates answered this part well, with a significant number of candidates achieving full marks. However a number of candidates failed to recognise the availability of the deceased husband's unused nil rate bands in the wife's subsequent death estate.

Another area where some candidates failed to earn marks was in the final calculation of the post- tax inheritance which required consideration of the assets inherited less the IHT due on the estate. This final element of the question required an understanding of a very real world client question regarding their post-tax inheritance.

Part (b) asked for an explanation of the advantages and disadvantages of voluntary VAT registration. There were lots of good answers to this part of the question. Those candidates who did not do so well would have benefitted from taking a moment before writing to identify the points they wished to make. This should have prevented the tendency to repeat the same points and allow for more mark-worthy points to be made.

Part (c)(i) required a summary of total tax payable if the proposed business were operated as a partnership or as a company. There were some excellent answers to this part of the question, dealing with each of the relevant tax liabilities in a clear and logical manner. Those candidates who did not do so well often failed to recognise both the income tax and corporation tax liabilities when operating via a company. They also often failed to produce a final summary, comparing the total tax liabilities under each scenario. These candidates would have benefitted from spending time to ensure they were clear on the requirement and planning their answer, before they began to write.

Part (c)(ii) examined possible trading loss reliefs available for each of two partners within a partnership compared to the trading loss reliefs available for a company. Some high-scoring candidates were able to apply their knowledge to the particular facts of the question, recognising that each partner would have different loss relief options. Low-scoring candidates tended to list loss relief rules whether they related to the scenario or not.

Part (d) tested a knowledge and application of temporary non-UK residence rules. The client was unsure whether to sell a UK asset now whilst temporary non-UK resident or wait until they returned to the UK and sell it for substantially more proceeds. Many candidates correctly recognised that selling the asset at either time would result in a taxable gain, chargeable in the tax year of return to the UK. However, many candidates then incorrectly advised that since higher proceeds would result in a higher tax bill, the client should sell for a lower proceeds to reduce their tax bill. This is very unsound, uncommercial advice. The commercial point is that the advice should be based on maximising 'post tax proceeds' for the client. Candidates are expected to apply the detailed tax rules but also apply sound commercial judgement to their client advice.

Part (e) concerned the actions to be taken where a client had received an unexpected refund of income tax. Most candidates demonstrated a good understanding of the actions to be taken and scored high marks. Candidates scoring lower marks tended to repeat the same limited points. Again candidates would be well advised to stop and think about the points they wish to address before they start writing. By doing this, they should save themselves time in the long run and earn more marks.

Marking guide			Marks	
(a)		Residence nil rate band	1.5	
		Nil rate band		
		– Lucy	2	
		– Pavel	1.5	
		Post-tax inheritance	1.5	
		Marks Available	6.5	
		Maximum		6
(b)		One mark for each point – maximum four marks	4	
				4
(c)	(i)	**Partnership**		
		Roth		
		– income tax		
		– income	3	
		– personal allowance and income tax liability	2	
		Company		
		Roth		
		– income tax		
		– income	2	
		– personal allowance and income tax liability	3	
		Corporation tax	2	
		Summary	1	
		Marks Available	13	
		Maximum		12
	(ii)	**Relief for trading loss**		
		Business operated as a partnership	3	
		Business operated as a company	1	
		Comparison	1	
		Marks Available	5	
		Maximum		4

ANSWERS

Marking guide		Marks
(d) Temporary non-UK resident	3	
Capital gains tax liability		
– Sale before returning to the UK	2	
– Sale after returning to the UK	1.5	
Payment date	1	
Advice	2.5	
Marks Available	10	
Maximum		9
(e) The need to repay the tax	4	
Ceasing to act	3	
Marks Available	7	
Maximum		5

Professional skills marks

Communication

- General format and structure of meeting notes (eg use of headings / sub-headings to make meeting notes easy to refer to)
- Style, language and clarity (tone of meeting notes, presentation of calculations, appropriate use of the tools, easy to follow and more than a negligible amount of content)
- Effectiveness of communication (answer is relevant, specific rather than general and focussed to the requirement)
- Adherence to specific instructions / information provided in the scenario (eg ignoring any national insurance contribution liabilities and any relief available in respect of losses, preparing a summary of the total tax liabilities under each scenario)

Analysis and evaluation

- Appropriate use of information to determine post-inheritance tax proceeds of the inheritance from Lucy
- Appropriate use of information and adoption of a logical approach when establishing the total tax payable whether the proposed business were operated as a partnership or as a company
- Demonstration of ability to consider relevant factors with regard to whether the business will be permitted to register for VAT
- Demonstration of ability to consider both the income tax and corporation tax liabilities when operating via a company
- Recognition of the relevance of Emma's residence status to the tax liability on the sale of the shares in Potts Ltd.

Scepticism

- Critical assessment of Emma's assertion that no capital gains tax will be payable if she sells the shares now

Commercial acumen

- Demonstration of an understanding of the need to make use of Pavel's unused nil rate bands in Wanda's subsequent death estate
- Demonstrating an awareness of organisational and external factors in relation to the advantages and disadvantages of voluntarily registering for VAT
- Practical considerations relating to the context to illustrate points being made relating to trading loss relief options

Maximum	10
Total	50

Notes for use in a client meeting

Client: Wanda and Emma

Subject: Various matters

Prepared by: Tax senior

Date: 1 December 2025

(a) **Wanda's post-tax inheritance from Lucy**

	£	£
Chargeable estate		
(£440,000 + £510,000)		950,000
Residence nil rate band available		
Lucy	175,000	
Pavel's unused amount transferred to Lucy	175,000	
		350,000
Nil rate band available		
Lucy		325,000
Pavel's unused amount transferred to Lucy:		
– Nil rate band	325,000	
– Less: legacy to Wanda	(160,000)	
		165,000
		490,000
Less: gift to Wanda on 1 April 2020 (£180,000 – £3,000 – £3,000)		(174,000)
		316,000
Inheritance tax		
((£950,000 – £350,000 – £316,000) × 40%)		113,600
Post-tax inheritance		
(£950,000 – £113,600)		836,400

(b) **Voluntary registration for value added tax (VAT)**

Voluntary registration will be permitted because the business will be making taxable (zero rated) supplies.

Advantages of voluntary registration

- It would remove the need to monitor the turnover of the business with regard to the compulsory registration limit and avoid the possibility of any penalty for late registration.
- It would enable the business to recover any input tax incurred.

ANSWERS

Disadvantages of voluntary registration

- There will be additional administration due to the need to record and report the VAT position of the business.
- There will be the possibility of interest and/or penalties if inaccurate figures are reported or reporting deadlines are not adhered to.

Tutorial note. Credit was also available for other relevant points.

(c) (i) **Income tax and corporation tax payable**

Business operated as a partnership

Roth – income tax

	Non-savings income
	£
Salary from existing employment	95,000
Partnership profit share ((£100,000 – £14,000) × 40%)	34,400
	129,400
Personal allowance	(0)
Taxable income	129,400
£37,700 × 20%	7,540
£(125,140 – 37,700) 87,440 × 40%	34,976
£(129,400 – 125,140) 4,260 × 45%	1,917
Income tax liability	44,433

Business operated as a company

Roth – income tax

	Non-savings income	Dividend income
	£	£
Salary from existing employment	95,000	
Salary from new company	32,000	
Dividend from new company		6,000
Less: personal allowance	(0)	(0)
Taxable income	127,000	6,000

	Non-savings income	Dividend income
	£	£
Non-savings income		
£37,700 × 20%	7,540	
£(125,140 – 37,700) = 87,440 × 40%	34,976	
£(127,000 – 125,140) = 1,860 × 45%	837	
Dividend income		
£500 × 0%	0	
£(6,000 – 500) = 5,500 × 39.35%	2,164	
	45,517	
Corporation tax		
((£100,000 – £42,000 – £32,000) × 19%) (AP < £50,000 so small rate)		4,940

Summary

	Partnership	Company
	£	£
Income tax:		
– Wanda (email from manager)	13,672	8,500
– Roth (as above)	45,517	45,209
Corporation tax (as above)	N/A	4,940
	59,189	58,649

(ii) **Other matters**

Tax relief available in respect of a trading loss arising in the first year of trading

Business operated as a partnership

- Wanda's only option would be to carry her share of the loss forward for relief against future profits of the same trade.
- Roth would be able to offset his share of the loss against his total income of the tax year of the loss, 2026/27, or the preceding year, 2025/26, or, under the opening year rules, 2023/24. Regardless of the year of offset, he will obtain a tax saving now, rather than in the future, equal to 40% of his share of the loss.

Business operated as a company

The loss would be automatically carried forward and a claim could be made to set it, wholly or partly, against total profits in the next accounting period. This would effectively be against trading profits, on the assumption that the business has no other source of income and does not realise any chargeable gains.

Summary

If the business is operated as a partnership, relief will be available immediately, rather than in the future, for a proportion of any trading loss.

(d) **Sale of shares in Potts plc**

For the purposes of UK CGT, Emma is a temporary non-UK resident whilst she is living in Falgar. This is because:

- she was UK resident for at least four of the seven tax years immediately prior to 2022/23 (the tax year of departure); and
- on her return to the UK, she will have been absent for less than five years.

Accordingly, if Emma sells the shares now, the chargeable gain of £330,000 will still be subject to UK CGT, albeit in 2026/27 (the tax year in which she returns to the UK) as opposed to 2025/26, the tax year of sale. This rule applies because Emma owned the shares on 1 February 2023 (the date she left the UK) and will have disposed of them whilst living in Falgar.

If Emma waits until she has returned to the UK, the chargeable gain will increase by £60,000 to £390,000. It will be subject to CGT in 2026/27, the tax year of disposal.

Accordingly, the chargeable gain will be subject to CGT in the tax year 2026/27 regardless of the date of sale and therefore UK CGT, at the rate of 20%, will be due on 31 January 2028.

In order to maximise her post-tax proceeds, Emma should sell the shares after she has returned to the UK. By doing so, she will realise additional post-tax proceeds of £48,000 (£60,000 × 80% (100% – 20%)).

(e) **Income tax refund**

We should assist Wanda in investigating whether or not there was a valid reason for the refund of income tax.

If we are unable to identify a valid reason, we would have to conclude that the refund was made as a result of an error on the part of HM Revenue and Customs (HMRC). In these circumstances we should inform Wanda:

- that the amount should be repaid immediately;
- that failing to return the money may well be a civil and/or a criminal offence;
- that HMRC should be informed of their error as soon as possible in order to minimise any interest and penalties which may otherwise become payable.

If Wanda is unwilling to return the money, we would have to consider ceasing to act as her tax advisers. We would then have to notify the tax authorities that we no longer act for her, although we would not provide them with any reason for our action. We should also consider whether or not it is necessary to make a report under the money laundering rules.

Videos can be viewed online by accessing your ebook version on VitalSource.

8 Maia

Course Book references

Employment income and Class 1 NICs are covered in Chapter 4. The computation of income tax is the subject of Chapter 2. Capital gains computation is dealt with in Chapter 7 and CGT reliefs are covered in Chapter 8. Inheritance tax computation (including Business Property Relief) is dealt with in Chapter 11. Corporation tax computations are covered in Chapter 16. Losses for a single company are dealt with in Chapter 17 and group relief in Chapter 19. Overseas aspects are covered in Chapter 22. Ethics are covered in Chapter 1.

Top tips

In part (a), follow the ACCA examining team's hint that you don't need to do a full computation for the second tax year, just identify how it differs from the first tax year. Also you don't have to provide any narrative explanations of your computations. In part (b) make sure you think about each of the three things your manager has asked you about. In part (c), remember that a company must use its losses against its own profits first before considering carry forward group relief.

Easy marks

There were some easy marks in part (a) for basic income tax computations. Part (d) on ethics was a standard scenario with which you should have been familiar.

ACCA examining team's comments

The first part of the question required calculations to determine how much additional cash would be required by the nephew over a two-year period, by comparing his cash income to his cash outgoings. In order to calculate his outgoings, candidates needed to calculate his income tax and national insurance contributions. It was pleasing to see that many candidates answered this part well, with a significant number of candidates achieving almost full marks.

However, many candidates lost valuable time producing two full income tax computations for the two tax years instead of looking at the change that had occurred between the two years and simply calculating how this would affect income tax payable.

Despite the fact that this part of the question specifically asked candidates not to provide any narrative explanation of the calculations, many candidates spent time providing explanations for which although correct, there were no marks awarded.

The second part of the question was split into three sub-parts, considering a gift to her nephew to provide income. [Note the Examiner's comments have been edited for this part as the question has been edited from its original form due to syllabus updates. Only relevant Examiner's comments have been given.]

The strategy to provide financial assistance was for the aunt to gift an investment property to the nephew. The requirement asked for the capital gains tax consequence for the aunt and the inheritance tax consequences for both the aunt and the nephew of such a gift.

Many candidates were able to identify that business property relief might be available when calculating inheritance tax but appeared to lack knowledge of the conditions required for this relief.

The third part of the question asked candidates to explain, with supporting calculations, the maximum amount of group relief which could be transferred between two group companies, whilst preserving double tax relief in the recipient company. A number of candidates were able to produce the calculations but did not offer any explanation, thereby not achieving full marks. As previously mentioned, future candidates should focus on the 'command' words in the requirement to ensure they are answering all parts of the requirement.

The next element in this part of the question required candidates to calculate the corporation tax liabilities of two group companies assuming the available trading loss was used as soon as possible. Most candidates answered well in respect of the capital allowances part of this question but performed less well at group relieving the loss, where many candidates appeared to lack a clear understanding of the technical rules. To succeed in the ATX–UK exam, both a detailed knowledge of the technical areas of the syllabus is required as well as the ability to apply that knowledge to a given scenario. [Note that the structures and buildings allowance element of this question has been added since originally set.]

Many candidates were able to conclude correctly on the advantage of a particular group holding structure.

The final part of the question concerned the ethical issues arising from an unreported chargeable gain. It was pleasing to see most candidates answering well on this issue. However the requirement specifically asked candidates not to address money laundering or penalties and yet many candidates went on to discuss these matters, which again, was not an effective use of their valuable time and earned them no marks. Once again these candidates would have benefitted from spending time ensuring they fully understood the requirement and planning their answer, before beginning to write.

Marking guide

		Marks	
(a)	Tax year 2025/26		
	– Employment income	1.5	
	– PA and tax liability	2	
	– National insurance contributions	1.5	
	Tax year 2026/27	1.5	
	Additional cash required	2	
	Marks Available	8.5	
	Maximum		8
(b)	Income tax	2	
	Capital gains tax		
	– Taxable gain	1	
	– Building is not furnished holiday accommodation (FHA)	0.5	
	– CGT implications	2	
	Inheritance tax implications	4	
	Marks Available	9.5	
	Maximum		9
(c)	(i) Tax-efficient group relief	4	
			4
	(ii) Plad Ltd corporation tax liabilities		
	– Year ending 30 June 2026	1	
	– Year ending 30 June 2027	3.5	
	Quil Ltd corporation tax liabilities		
	– Capital allowances	4	
	– SBAs	2	
	– Two years ending 30 June 2027	3.5	
	Marks Available	14	
	Maximum		11
	(iii) Conclusion	3	
			3
(d)	Plad Ltd	2.5	
	Our firm	4	
	Maximum		5

Professional skills marks

Scepticism

- Effective challenge of information provided by Maia's friend with regards to furnished holiday accommodation in (b)

Analysis and Evaluation

- Appropriate use of information in the scenario to calculate Josh's additional cash requirement in part (a)
- Appropriate use of information in the scenario to realise that Maia has already used her AEA and is a higher rate taxpayer when considering CGT rates in (b)

Marking guide | **Marks**

- Identification that earlier gifts made by Maia could have used some of her available nil rate band and the need to check this in part (b)
- Demonstration of ability to consider all relevant taxes specified in the requirements (eg both income tax and NIC in part (a) and income tax, CGT and IHT in part (b))
- Adoption of a logical approach to prepare suitable calculations on group relief in part (c)
- Adoption of a logical approach to capital allowance calculations in part (c)

Communication

- General format and structure of memorandum (eg use of headings/sub-headings, easy to refer to)
- Style, language and clarity (tone of memorandum, presentation of calculations, appropriate use of tools, easy to follow and more than a negligible amount of content)
- Effectiveness of communication (answer is relevant, specific rather than general and focussed on the requirement)
- Adherence to specific instructions made in the scenario (eg no narrative explanation and marginal approach to 26/27 income tax in part (a), specific requirements in (b), no explanations to calculations in (c)(ii), no money laundering in (d))

Commercial Acumen

- Concluding as to ownership of Quil Ltd in (c)
- Recognition of the importance of timing in that Plad Ltd and Quil Ltd being in a group relief group will allow earlier offset of losses giving a cashflow advantage and marginal tax savings in (c)

Maximum	10
Total	50

Memorandum

Client: Maia

Subject: Provision of financial assistance for Josh

Prepared by: Tax senior

Date: 1 June 2025

(a) **Josh – additional cash requirement**

Income tax liabilities

2025/26

	Non-savings income	Dividend income
	£	£
Salary	25,200	
Shares in NL Ltd £(2,100 – 300)	1,800	
Employment income	27,000	
Dividends		420
Less personal allowance	(12,570)	
Taxable income	14,430	420

	Non-savings income	Dividend income
	£	£
Non-savings income		
£14,430 × 20%	2,886	
Dividend income		
£420 × 0%	0	
	2,886	

2026/27

	£
As for 2025/26	2,886
Less: tax on NL Ltd shares £1,800 × 20%	(360)
	2,526

Class 1 national insurance contributions (NICs) 2025/26 and 2026/27

	£
£(25,200 – 12,570) × 8%	1,010

Additional cash required

	£	£
Cash required £2,500 × 24		60,000
Salary £25,200 × 2	50,400	
Dividend income £420 × 2	840	
	51,240	
Less:		
– income tax 2025/26	(2,886)	
– income tax 2026/27	(2,526)	
– NICs 2025/26 and 2026/27 £1,010 × 2	(2,020)	
Anticipated income		(43,808)
Additional cash required		16,192

(b) **Providing financial assistance to Josh**

Gift of investment property

Increase in Josh's post-tax income

Josh would receive net rental income of £13,200 (£1,100 × 12) in a full tax year, such that he would continue to be a basic rate taxpayer. Accordingly, his additional post-tax income in the 21-month period from 1 July 2025 to 5 April 2027 would be £18,480 (£1,100 × 21 × 80%).

Capital gains tax (CGT) liabilities for Maia

Maia's gift of the building would be treated as a sale at market value for the purposes of calculating the chargeable gain. This gives rise to a gain of £240,000 (£370,000 – £130,000).

As the building is rented to long term tenant it will not qualify as furnished holiday accommodation. We need to explain to Maia that her friend's advice is incorrect as a long term tenant will mean the property will not qualify. Therefore:

- The building would not be a business asset, such that neither gift holdover relief nor business asset disposal relief would be available.
- Maia is a higher rate taxpayer and will have already used her annual exempt amount for 2025/26 on her May 2025 residential property sale. Accordingly, her CGT liability on the gift of the building will be £57,600 (£240,000 × 24%).
- As a disposal of residential property Maia would need to make a payment on account of the capital gains tax due within 60 days of the disposal.

Inheritance tax (IHT) implications for Maia and Josh

As the building is not furnished holiday accommodation:

- The gift would be a potentially exempt transfer, such that there would be no inheritance tax due unless Maia were to die within seven years of the gift.
- If Maia were to die within seven years of the gift, the excess of the market value of the property at the time of the gift (ie £370,000) over Maia's available nil rate band would be subject to IHT at 40%. This tax would be payable by Josh.
- Maia's available nil rate band would be the nil rate band for the year of death (assumed to be £325,000) less her chargeable transfers in the seven years prior to 1 July 2025.
- Taper relief would be available if Maia were to survive the gift by more than three years. This would reduce the IHT by 20% for each additional full year for which she survived the gift.

(c) (i) **Group relief**

Maximum group relief

- The whole of Plad Ltd's UK trading profit of £48,000 should be covered by group relief. However, in order not to waste double tax relief (DTR), an amount of Plad Ltd's Chekkan profits should remain subject to corporation tax.
- The amount of Chekkan profits which should remain subject to corporation tax is £5,158 (£7,000 × 14%/19%), being the amount on which the UK corporation tax (£5,158 × 19% = £980) equals the whole of the Chekkan tax paid by Plad Ltd (£7,000 × 14% = £980). Note that there will be two associated companies and so the lower limit for determining the rate of corporation tax will be £25,000 (£50,000/2). Consequently with TTP (and augmented profits) of £5,158 19% corporation tax will apply).
- In this situation, the Chekkan tax suffered will be fully relieved as DTR (being the lower of the UK tax on the Chekkan income and the Chekkan tax suffered).
- Accordingly, the group relief should be the UK profits of £48,000 plus the balance of the Chekkan profits of £1,842 (£7,000 – £5,158), ie £49,842. With group relief of this amount, Plad Ltd's UK corporation tax liability will be fully covered by DTR, such that there will be no UK corporation tax payable.

	£	£
Taxable total profits before group relief		55,000
Group relief		(49,842)
Taxable total profits		5,158
Corporation tax at 19%		980
Double tax relief – the lower of:		
– UK tax on overseas profits (£5,158 × 19%)	980	
– Overseas tax (£7,000 × 14%)	980	
		(980)
Corporation tax liability		0

Tutorial note. The above calculation demonstrates that where the group relief is £49,842, as calculated above, none of the DTR will be wasted and the corporation tax liability will be zero.

(ii) **Corporation tax liabilities**

Plad Ltd

Year ending 30 June 2026

The corporation tax liability of Plad Ltd for the first year will be £0, as explained above.

Year ending 30 June 2027

The corporation tax liability of Plad Ltd for the second year will also be £0.

	£
Taxable total profit pre group relief	55,000
Less: group relief (W2)	(49,842)
Taxable total profit	5,158
Corporation tax at 19% (AP=TTP < £25,000)	980
Less: DTR – the lower of:	
– UK tax on the Chekkan profits of £1,330 (£7,000 × 19%)	
– Chekkan tax of £980	(980)
Corporation tax liability	0

Quil Ltd

	Year ending 30 June	
	2026	2027
	£	£
Trading profit/(loss) before capital allowances	(32,922)	995,672
Capital allowances (W1)		
(£1,180,000 + £6,750)	(1,186,750)	
(£1,200 + £9,000)		(10,200)
Trading loss	(1,219,672)	
Trading profit	0	985,472
Chargeable gain		16,000
Total profits	0	1,001,472
Loss brought forward (W2)		(1,001,472)
Taxable total profit	0	0
Corporation tax liability at 19%	0	0

Workings

1 ***Capital allowances***

	FYA	Main pool	Special rate pool	Allowances
	£	£	£	£
Year ending 30 June 2026				
Additions qualifying for AIA				
– Machinery and equipment	160,000			
– Thermal insulation	1,040,000			
AIA (to thermal insulation in priority to machinery)	(1,000,000)			1,000,000
Balance of machinery: Full expense relief	(160,000)			160,000
Balance of insulation: 50% SRA (50% × £40,000)	(20,000)			20,000
Transfer balance to SRP	(20,000)		20,000	
TWDV carried forward		0	20,000	1,180,000
Year ending 30 June 2027				
WDA at 18%/6%			(1,200)	1,200
TWDV carried forward		0	18,800	

The building will be eligible for a Structures and Buildings Allowance (SBA) based on the cost of construction of the factory excluding the land, ie £300,000.

Y/e 30 June 2026

SBA = 3% × £300,000 × 9/12

= £6,750

Y/e 30 June 2027

SBA = 3% × £300,000

= £9,000

2 ***Quil Ltd - loss memorandum***

	Year ending 30 June	
	2025	2026
	£	£
Trading loss brought forward	0	1,169,830
Trading loss for the current year	1,219,672	
Offset against total profits of Quil Ltd	–	(1,001,472)
Surrender to Plad Ltd	(49,842)	(49,842)
Trading loss carried forward	1,169,830	118,516

(iii) **Conclusion**

(1) Where the two companies are in a group relief group (as opposed to being owned personally by Claire) trading losses of £99,684 (£49,842 + £49,842) would be relieved by group relief in the two-year period rather than being carried forward.

(2) At the least, this is advantageous from the point of view of cash flow, as it delays total tax payments of £18,940 (£99,684 × 19%). Given that Plad Ltd's TTP pre group relief is £55,000, which means that the company has AP of over the £25,000 lower limit, this will also allow £30,000 of the loss in each year to save at the marginal rate of 26.5% with the balance each year then saving 19% tax.

(3) In addition, if group relief were not available, such that Quil Ltd had to carry forward unused losses, there is no certainty that the losses would ever be relieved.

> **Tutorial note.** Quil Ltd is required to use its losses brought forward against its own taxable total profits before it can surrender losses to Plad Ltd as carry forward group relief.

(d) **Plad Ltd – unreported chargeable gain**

Plad Ltd

- The company has a responsibility to report this omission to HM Revenue and Customs (HMRC) and to pay the outstanding corporation tax. It will be committing tax evasion, a criminal offence, if it fails to do so.
- HMRC will charge Plad Ltd interest on any tax which becomes payable.

Our firm

- We should investigate how this error arose and consider whether or not there are likely to be further errors.
- We will not retain a client which is engaged in deliberate tax evasion, as this poses a threat to the fundamental principles of integrity and professional behaviour. Accordingly, we could not continue to act for Plad Ltd unless the chargeable gain is disclosed to HMRC.
- If we were to cease to act for Plad Ltd, we would notify HMRC, although we would not provide them with any reason for our action.

9 Nelson

Course Book references

Ethics is covered in Chapter 1. Choice of business structure, use of trade losses, incorporation and close companies are covered in Chapter 18 OMB tax planning. The cash accounting scheme is covered in Chapter 23. Inheritance tax exemptions are covered in Chapter 11 and variations in Chapter 12. Chargeable gains computation is covered in Chapter 7 and capital tax planning in Chapter 13.

Top tips

Make sure you break this memorandum down into each smaller part and allocate your time spent accordingly. Also make sure you follow any specific advice given in the question. For example in this question you are given the total tax payable by Nelson if he trades as an unincorporated business- don't waste time checking those calculations! Also, in the section on other matters you are specifically told not to consider CGT gift holdover relief and matters relating to employment income- make sure you follow these instructions. Even if you write a technically correct point on these topics the marking guide won't allow you any credit. It's also part of a communication skill to follow specific instructions given in the question.

The most difficult part of this question will be calculating the total tax payable if Nelson trades through a limited company. You could consider leaving this until later in the question so as not to over run on time and you'll need to make sure you lay out your calculations clearly to make it easier for the marker to award you marks.

Easy marks

The ethical requirement about becoming Nelson's tax advisor should have been the source of easy marks in this question. Ethics is always tested on every ATX paper and this topic is frequently examined. In addition, the VAT part of this question should also have provided easier marks provided you ensured you had time to attempt it.

ACCA examining team's comments

This question concerned a potential new client looking for financial assistance in relation to his unincorporated business, which he was considering incorporating. The question covered the areas of ethics, income tax, corporation tax, national insurance, capital gains tax, close companies, VAT, IHT and CGT.

The first part of the question required an explanation of matters to be considered and actions required before taking on a new client. It was pleasing to see many candidates scoring well on this question part. However a significant number of candidates failed to mention consideration of the fundamental principles of professional ethics. Ethics will be examined on every ATX–UK paper and candidates would be well advised to take the time to understand the ethical requirements of the ACCA.

The second part of the question was split into two further requirements. The first requirement was a comparison of tax payable if trading through a limited company compared to trading as an unincorporated trader. However the tax payable if trading as an unincorporated trader was given in the question and did not need to be recalculated. Despite this, a number of candidates recalculated this tax payable figure, wasting their valuable time and earning no marks. These candidates would have benefitted from spending time to ensure they were clear on the requirement and planning their answer, before they began to write. By doing this, they should save themselves time in the long run and earn more marks.

The question stated that after incorporation, the owner would take a mixture of dividend and salary from the company. Most candidates were able to calculate the corporation tax payable if the business were incorporated and recognised that employer's national insurance would be both payable and tax deductible for corporation tax purposes if the owner took a salary from the company. Many candidates then successfully went on to calculate the income tax payable by the owner of the company, given the mixture of dividends and salary withdrawn from the company. However most candidates failed to recognise that the owner would also have to pay employees' national insurance if he took a salary from the company.

The second requirement of this part of the question was an explanation of why the business owner may have been advised to trade as an unincorporated business rather than through a company when trading losses were anticipated in the first couple of years of the business. Many candidates wasted time and earned no marks by simply describing all the losses rules of companies and unincorporated businesses whereas what was needed was for the candidates to apply their knowledge to the specific facts of the question. This business anticipated losses in 'opening years' and the relevant loss relief to discuss was opening years loss relief for unincorporated businesses which is not available for companies.

The third part of the question concerned three other matters relevant to the business. The first matter was the capital gains tax implication of retaining ownership of a business asset when incorporating all other business assets. Many candidates correctly identified that this would mean that incorporation relief would not be available but some then went on to calculate capital gains tax on the asset which was being retained instead of the capital asset being transferred to the company.

The second matter concerned the tax implications of the owner borrowing funds from the company and subsequently repaying them. Many candidates recognised that this was a close company issue and would involve a payment from the company to HMRC, which would be repayable when the loan was repaid. However the requirement specifically asked candidates not to address employment income benefits in respect of the arrangement and yet many candidates went on to discuss these matters, again wasting their valuable time and earning no marks. Once again these candidates would have benefitted from spending time to ensure they were clear on the requirement and planning their answer, before they began to write. By doing this, they should save themselves time in the long run and earn more marks overall.

The third matter required an explanation of whether VAT on a bad debt could be recovered and whether this would not be a problem with the cash accounting scheme for VAT. Many candidates were very clear on the rules in this area and scored well. However once again, some candidates wasted time and earned no extra marks by explaining everything they knew about the cash accounting scheme instead of the specific aspect required by the question.

Many candidates were failing to produce answers that were sufficiently specific to the scenario, tending towards general statements of knowledge in the particular area. To score well at ATX–UK, candidates must 'apply' their knowledge. Writing out lots of rules in the hope that one of the rules might apply is not a good use of candidates' time.

The final part of the question related to the IHT implications of a UK domiciled spouse gifting cash from the sale of a property to their non-UK domiciled spouse, and the CGT saving from gifting a share of the property prior to the sale, rather than the cash following the sale. Although many candidates were not aware of the precise restriction on the spouse exemption in respect of a non-UK domiciled spouse, it was pleasing to see that the majority realised that the full spouse exemption was not likely to be available, so were able to score marks from recognising that there would only be a liability to IHT if the donor spouse died within seven years, and that a non-UK domiciled spouse is able to change their domicile on election.

In calculating the CGT saving as a result of transferring a share in the house to a spouse prior to sale, the majority of candidates adopted a full 'before and after' calculation in this case, calculating the total tax payable by husband if he sold the house before gifting to his wife a share of the proceeds, with total payable by the husband and wife together if he gave her a share of the house prior to sale. This latter strategy enabled the couple to take advantage of the wife's annual exempt amount (AEA), and lower rate of CGT. This was an entirely reasonable approach to take in this scenario, as the calculation of the liability was quite straightforward. The main errors were, firstly, not recognising that, as this was a sale of a private residence, the higher rate of CGT will apply, and secondly, focusing only on the reduction in the CGT payable by the husband, without taking into account that there would also be a small liability for the wife in the latter strategy. A minority of candidates used a marginal approach to directly identify the amount of tax which would be saved. This proved to be very efficient if done correctly, but was quite tricky, and several candidates just provided a lot of numbers, without adequate labelling, which made it difficult to award marks in some cases.

Marking guide			Marks	
(a)		Information required	1	
		Matters to consider	4	
		Actions to take	1	
		Marks Available	6	
		Maximum		5
(b)	(i)	Trading as a limited company		
		– Corporation tax	3.5	
		– Income tax	3.5	
		– Employee's class 1 national insurance contributions	1	
				8
	(ii)	Relief for expected trading loss	4	
		Other reasons	2	
		Marks Available	6	
		Maximum		4
(c)	(i)	Incorporation relief not available	2	
		Capital gains tax	2	
				4
	(ii)	Reason why NQA Ltd will be a close company	1	
		Tax payment required	3	
		Repayment of tax	1	
				5
	(iii)	Recovery of output tax	3	
		Cash accounting scheme and cash flow	2	
		Marks Available	5	
		Maximum		4
(d)	(i)	Potential liability	3	
		Advice	3	
		Marks Available	6	
		Maximum		5
	(ii)	Nelson owns the whole of the house	2	
		Transfer of one-third of the house to Cam	2	
		Saving	1	
				5

Professional skills marks

Scepticism

- Use of ethical principles to challenge Nelson's request not to contact his old adviser.

Analysis and evaluation

- Appropriate use of facts in the scenario to determine that NQA Ltd will be a close company in part (c)
- Appropriate use of calculations to draw appropriate conclusions as to whether a lower amount would have been payable if Nelson had commenced trading through a limited company rather than as an unincorporated business in (b).

- Appropriate use of calculations to ascertain the CGT saving in (d)
- Appropriate use of information to recognise that two annual exemptions would be available and that a lower tax rate would apply if part of the gain is taxed on Cam in (d)
- Demonstration of ability to consider all relevant taxes specified in the requirements (eg recognising the need to consider corporation tax and employer's NIC to calculate Nelson's dividend, to then be able to consider his income tax and employee's NIC in part (b))
- Adoption of a logical approach to prepare suitable calculations in part (b) and (d)

Communication

- General format and structure of memorandum (eg use of headings/sub-headings, easy to refer to)
- Style, language and clarity (tone of memorandum, presentation of calculations, appropriate use of tools, easy to follow and more than a negligible amount of content)
- Effectiveness of communication (answer is relevant, specific rather than general and focussed on the requirement)
- Adherence to specific instructions made in the scenario (eg following stated assumptions in (b) and not considering CGT gift holdover relief, not considering employment income in (c))

Commercial acumen

- Effective use of IHT tax planning in (d)
- Recognition of non-tax factors as to Nelson being advised to commence as an unincorporated business rather than a company
- Recognition of possible consequences of using the cash accounting scheme on cashflow in part (c) 10

Total 50

Memorandum

For: The files

Subject Nelson – Incorporation of business and other matters

Prepared by: Tax senior

Date: 1 December 2025

(a) **Becoming tax advisers to Nelson**

Information required:

- Proof of Nelson's identity and his address.

Matters to consider:

- We must give consideration to the fundamental principles of professional ethics, for example, integrity and professional competence and due care. This requires us to consider whether becoming tax advisers to Nelson would create any threats to compliance with these principles.

  If any such threats are identified, we should not accept the appointment unless the threats can be reduced to an acceptable level via the implementation of safeguards.

  Nelson is planning to sell mainly to overseas customers in the future, possibly via companies that are resident overseas. We should consider the likelihood of these plans being realised and whether or not we would have the necessary technical expertise to provide Nelson with the best advice.

- We must assure ourselves that Nelson is not involved in any form of money laundering.

Actions to take:

- We need permission from Nelson to contact his existing tax advisers in order to ensure that there is nothing in the past which would preclude us from accepting the appointment on ethical grounds. Nelson's suggestion that we don't need to contact his previous advisers is incorrect.

If Nelson refuses to give permission, we should seriously consider refusing to act for him.

(b) (i) **Trading through a limited company rather than as an unincorporated business**

Total taxes payable if Nelson had commenced trading through a limited company

Taxes payable by the company for the accounting period ending 31 March 2026

	£	£	£
Trading profit (£7,050 × 10)		70,500	
Salary for Nelson (£1,300 × 10)		(13,000)	
Employer's class 1 national insurance contributions (NIC) (£5,417 (£13,000 – (£9,100 × 10/12)) × 13.8%)		(748)	748
Taxable total profits		56,752	
Corporation tax (£56,752 × 25%)	14,188		
Less marginal relief (£250,000 – £56,752) × 3/200	(2,899)		
	11,289	(11,289)	11,289
Available for dividend		45,463	
Total taxes payable			12,037

Taxes payable by Nelson for the tax year 2025/26

	£
Salary	13,000
Dividend income	45,463
	58,463
Less: personal allowance	(12,570)
	45,893

ANSWERS

Income tax for the tax year 2025/26

	£	£
Non-savings income		
– £430 (£13,000 – £12,570) × 20%		86
Dividend income		
– £500 × 0%	0	
– £36,770 (£37,700 – £500 – £430) × 8.75%	3,217	
– £8,193 (£45,893 – 37,700) × 33.75%	2,765	
		5,982
Employee's class 1 NIC		
£2,525 (£13,000 – (£12,570 × 10/12)) × 8%		202
Total taxes payable		6,270
Total taxes payable (£12,037 + £6,270)		18,307

The total tax payable for the tax year 2025/26 would have been £8 (£18,307 – £18,299) more if Nelson had commenced trading through a limited company rather than as an unincorporated business.

> **Tutorial note.** The employment allowance which provides relief of up to £5,000 from employer's class 1 NIC would not be available to the company because Nelson would be the company's only employee.

(ii) **Reasons for advice given by existing tax adviser**

Trading loss

Where a self-employed individual makes a trading loss in any of the first four tax years of trading, the loss can be offset against the individual's total income of the three tax years prior to the year of loss starting with the earliest year. Accordingly, Nelson could have offset the loss against his employment income for 2022/23 and 2023/24. This would have resulted in a repayment of income tax at 40% and 20%.

If Nelson were to also make a loss in 2026/27 this extended loss carried back would continue to be available.

If Nelson had begun trading through a limited company, there would have been no immediate relief for a trading loss. It would have been carried forward for relief against the future total profits of the company.

Other possible reasons

- Trading via a company would have increased the complexity of Nelson's financial affairs.
- Trading via a company would have meant that Nelson's ability to access the profits of the business would not have been as straightforward as it has been.

> **Tutorial note.** Nelson would not have been able to relieve a trading loss against total income of the year of loss or the preceding year because he had no income in the tax year 2024/25 and, if his business had made a loss, he would have had no income in the tax year 2025/26.

(c) (i) **Nelson retaining personal ownership of the Arch building**

If Nelson retains personal ownership of the business premises, incorporation relief (the relief which is available where a business is transferred to a company in exchange for shares) will no longer be available. This is because he will not be transferring all of the assets of the business (excluding cash) to NQA Ltd.

As a result, the chargeable gain arising in respect of the goodwill will be subject to capital gains tax (CGT). The annual exempt amount of £3,000 will be deducted from the gain and the balance of £42,000 will be taxed at 20% (on the assumption that Nelson will be a higher rate taxpayer in the tax year 2026/27). Accordingly, there will be a CGT liability of £8,400, which will be due on 31 January 2028.

> **Tutorial note.** Business asset disposal relief is not available in respect of a chargeable gain on goodwill as a result of incorporating a company in this way. Even if it were, it would not be available to Nelson because he will not have owned the business for 12 months at the time of disposal.

(ii) **Nelson borrowing money from NQA Ltd**

Nelson will control NQA Ltd because he will own all of the company's issued share capital. As a result, because NQA Ltd will be controlled by five or fewer shareholders, it will be a close company.

Where a close company (NQA Ltd) makes a loan to a shareholder (Nelson), it is required to make a payment equal to 33.75% of the loan to HM Revenue and Customs (HMRC) within nine months and one day of the end of the accounting period.

There is no need to make this payment to HMRC if Nelson repays the loan prior to the date on which the tax is due to be paid.

HMRC will repay the tax to NQA Ltd when the loan is repaid by Nelson

(iii) **Value added tax (VAT)**

The VAT paid to HMRC in respect of the irrecoverable debt is not lost. It can be recovered, provided:

- the debt has been written off by Nelson; and
- six months have elapsed since the date on which the payment was due.

Use of the cash accounting scheme would have avoided this problem, as Nelson would not have had to account for output tax until he had received payment from the customer. This would also result in a cash flow advantage to Nelson where a customer does not pay promptly.

On the downside, Nelson would not be able to recover input tax until he has paid for the relevant goods or services. Accordingly, whether or not the cash accounting scheme would benefit Nelson's cash flow position depends on the timing of payments to creditors and receipts from debtors.

(d) (i) **Gift to Cam**

Inheritance tax

Cam is non-UK domiciled, such that the spouse exemption, which applies to gifts between spouses, is limited to a lifetime maximum of £325,000. This limit has already been exceeded due to the gift made by Nelson to Cam on 1 August 2021, which was valued at £600,000.

Accordingly, Nelson's gift of £150,000 to Cam would be a potentially exempt transfer, which could give rise to an inheritance tax liability if Nelson were to die within seven years of the gift.

This potential liability could be avoided in either of the following ways:

- The terms of Nelson's father's will could be altered via a deed of variation, such that one-third of the London house is left directly to Cam. This would avoid the need for Nelson to make a potentially exempt transfer to Cam.

The deed would have to be signed by Nelson and Cam and be executed within two years of Nelson's father's death. It should state that it is intended to be effective for both inheritance tax and capital gains tax purposes.

- Cam could elect to be treated as UK domiciled for the purposes of inheritance tax. This would mean that all gifts from Nelson would be exempt under the spouse exemption with no upper limit.

The downside would be that any non-UK assets owned by Cam would cease to be outside UK inheritance tax and so would become taxable.

(ii)

	Nelson	Cam
	£	£
Sale of the house by Nelson as planned		
Chargeable gain (£450,000 – £390,000)	60,000	
Less: annual exempt amount (N1)	(3,000)	
	57,000	
CGT at 24% (Nelson is HRTP)	13,680	
Gift of one-third of the house to Cam		
Chargeable gain 2/3:1/3 (N2)	40,000	20,000
Less: annual exempt amount	(3,000)	(3,000)
	37,000	17,000
CGT at 24%/18%	8,880	3,060

CGT saving of £1,740 (£13,680 – (8,880 + 3,060)).

Tutorial note. Note the following:

(1) The house will be sold in 2025/26 whereas Nelson's business will be incorporated in 2026/27. Therefore, assuming Nelson makes no other disposals the annual exempt amount for 2025/26 will be available to set against the gain on the sale of the house.

(2) The gift of one-third of the house to Cam would take place at no gain, no loss because Nelson and Cam are married. As a result, the gain of £60,000 would be split between them in the ratio 2/3:1/3.

10 Corey

Course Book references

Overseas aspects of personal tax are covered in Chapter 9. CGT basics and takeovers are covered in Chapter 7 and 8 and IHT is covered in Chapters 11 and 12. The specifics of whether to gift in someone's lifetime or on their death is also covered in Chapter 13. Corporation tax basics are covered in Chapter 16 with group aspects in Chapter 19. Ethics is covered in Chapter 1.

Top tips

Make sure you follow the guidance given in the question for part (a)- you're specifically told that Corey does not meet the automatic overseas nor automatic UK tests and not to consider them further. So you need to go straight into the sufficient ties test.

In part (b) you must spot the trigger for you to consider the temporary non-residence rules when we have an individual who becomes non-resident and then returns to the UK. This is a topic which is frequently tested, and you need to be able to spot it when reading and planning. Make sure that even if you're worried your gains calculations aren't quite right that you do still pull together all your gains and calculate the CGT- you will receive follow on marks.

In part (c) you are told that one painting is increasing in value while the other is decreasing. It will be really important that you make reference to this in your answer and will be a way you can demonstrate commercial acumen.

In (d) you must ensure that you answer each of the four sub-requirements. When you see a friend give advice in a question you should always consider whether you need to be sceptical of their advice. When you think about Porth Ltd being able to use Quod Ltd's loss remember to think about whether it makes a difference if the 30% holding is through Mr Berm or Mr Berm's company.

Finally, make sure you allow enough time to attempt (e) which is actually the more straightforward part of this question. You mustn't allow yourself to get bogged down early in the question and then run out of time.

Easy marks

The ethical part of this question (e) about an unexpected tax refund is frequently examined and should have been the source of easy marks in this question. In addition, considering lifetime versus death gifts in part (c) is another topic which is often tested and should have provided some more straightforward marks to students. Also, given the availability of follow-on marks, the CGT calculations in (b) should have provided some more basic marks.

ACCA examining team's comments

This question related to an individual who has returned to the UK after spending several years abroad, who required advice on his residence status, the capital gains tax implications of a series of disposals made both during his absence and on this return, the inheritance tax implications of his mother making lifetime gifts, or leaving assets in her estate, some corporate issues and finally the ethical considerations for the firm of the client having received an unexpected income tax refund.

Candidates should note that the requirements for this question were clearly set out, using a series of subheadings, and the use of these subheadings in their answer, provides a useful structure in this type of question, which all candidates should consider adopting.

The first part of the question, which was worth 6 marks, required an explanation of how the individual's UK residence status will be determined for the tax year 2025/26, following his return to the UK.

A reasonable number of candidates produced good, comprehensive answers to this part, demonstrating thorough learning and good application skills. However, candidates should note the following points:

- Unless they are given in the scenario, or specifically excluded in the requirement (as in this question), candidates should start the process of determining someone's residence status by considering the automatic overseas and UK residence tests.
- When considering the number of UK ties someone has, knowledge must be precise. Clearly most candidates made use of the information in the tax tables, but didn't fully understand it. The tables say that someone who is in the UK for 91-120 days, who has been previously resident, needs only two ties to be UK resident in the current tax year. However, this omits the information that it relates only to the previous three tax years, when, in this case the individual has been non-resident.
- When discussing the number of ties an individual satisfies, a good approach is to consider each in turn, and state whether or not it applies. This will ensure you maximise your mark in this type of question.
- The requirement asked for a conclusion. This is usually worth one mark, and just requires the candidate to conclude sensibly from what they have written, but a minority of candidates did not do this.
- Again, in the final part of this requirement many candidates did not score full marks due to lack of precision. Asked how becoming UK resident would affect the individual's liability to income tax, just stating 'he would be liable to UK income tax' is not enough. Candidates must make it clear this applies to overseas income, as well as UK income.

The second part of this question, which was worth 11 marks, required explanations and calculations in respect of a number of disposals which the individual had made, both in the tax year prior to his return to live in the UK, and the following year. It was disappointing to see how few candidates recognised that he would have been regarded as temporarily non-UK resident for capital gains tax (CGT) purposes during his absence from the UK. This topic is frequently tested, and is often not flagged, leaving it as a test of candidates' knowledge and skill to be able to identify when it applies. The key here is question practice.

One of the disposals concerned a takeover of a company in exchange for shares in another company plus cash. It appeared that a large number of candidates were not prepared for this question, as answers were generally poorer than on recent occasions when this has been examined, with the majority of candidates not apportioning the cost, or calculating a gain on the cash element. The disposal of the shares and recognition of the chargeability of the overseas house in the current tax year were handled better, but, surprisingly, relatively few candidates applied different rates of CGT to the house and shares, and some even appeared to be using income tax rates. These are fundamental points and should have been relatively easier marks to get. Again, the importance of knowledge of the basics of each tax cannot be overemphasised.

The third part of the question related to an often-tested IHT decision – whether to make lifetime gifts or leave assets in the estate on death. The assets in question this time were two paintings, one of which was expected to increase in value, and one of which was expected to fall in value. Most candidates scored quite well on this question part, with the main problem often being a vagueness about fall in value relief. In a good number of cases, candidates mentioned this, but with no explanation of what it is or how it works, or in a context which led us to believe that the candidate did not understand the relief. It is important with all reliefs – for CGT as well as IHT – that candidates understand when, why and how they are available. It is often not enough just to write the words in an explanatory question, without any further explanation.

The fourth part of the question was worth 12 marks and comprised four tasks. In the first two tasks relating to the explanation of the tax treatment of research and development and the acquisition of an intangible asset, many candidates displayed a surprising lack of technical knowledge, despite both being frequently tested areas. Fortunately, many were able to gain follow through marks in their calculation of the effect of these on the company's budgeted trading loss for the period. It was good to see that a majority of candidates recognised that the loss making company would be a consortium company such that proportionate loss relief would be available to the parent company.

The final part of this question concerned the ethics of a client receiving an unexpected refund from HM Revenue and Customs (HMRC). As expected, most candidates produced very good answers to this part, with a significant number scoring full marks.

Marking guide				Marks
(a)	(i)	UK ties		
		– Number of ties required	1	
		– Consideration of each tie (1 mark each)	4	
		– Conclusion	1	
		Marks Available	6	
		Maximum		5
	(ii)	Liability to UK income tax	1	
		Double tax relief	1	
		Marks Available	2	
		Maximum		1
(b)	(i)	Explanations		
		– Disposals in 2024/25	4	
		Marks Available	4	
		Maximum		3
	(ii)	Calculations		
		– Sale of house	.5	
		– Sale and gift of shares	4	
		– Capital gains tax	3.5	
				8
(c)		Potentially exempt transfers and taper relief	2.5	
		Valuation and exemptions	3	
		Conclusion	1	
		Marks Available	6.5	
		Maximum		6
(d)	(i)	Amortisation of brand	3	
		Marks Available	3	
		Maximum		2
	(ii)	Research costs		
		– Notes	3	
		– Calculation	2	
				5
	(iii)	Calculation of available loss	2	
				2
	(iv)	Consortium relief	4	
		Marks Available	4	
		Maximum		3

Marking guide		Marks
(e) If caused by HMRC error, inform HMRC and refund	2	
Offence, penalties/ interest, money laundering	2	
Corey unwilling to return the money	2	
Marks Available	6	
Maximum		5

Professional skills marks

Communication

- General format and structure of memorandum (eg use of headings/sub-headings, easy to refer to)
- Style, language and clarity (tone of memorandum, presentation of calculations, appropriate use of tools, easy to follow and more than a negligible amount of content)
- Effectiveness of communication (answer is relevant, specific rather than general and focused to the requirement)
- Adherence to specific instructions made in the scenario (eg ignoring the availability of the annual exemption/ nil rate band in part (c) or provision of explanatory comment in support of calculations performed in part (d))

Analysis and evaluation

- Appropriate use of the facts in the scenario when seeking to apply sufficient ties test to Corey's situation in part (a)
- Relevant reference to the facts in the scenario when analysing Corey's capital gains position for the tax year 2024/25 in part (b)
- Appropriate use of the information and adoption of a logical approach when establishing the cost of the TW plc shares disposed of in part (b)
- Reasonable calculation of amended trading loss in part (d) supported by previous analysis and argument
- Reasonable consideration of the impact of consortium relief rules in part (d)

Scepticism

- Critical assessment of Corey's residency position in part (a) and any potential information that should be clarified before finalising the position
- Critical assessment of friend's advice in part (d)

Commercial acumen

- Demonstration of an understanding of the need to make the most efficient use of the annual exempt amount when providing the calculations in part (b)
- Distinction made between the two different asset profiles (one increasing in value and one decreasing in value) when providing recommendations in respect of part (c)
- Recognition of viable alternative treatment of the Cloque brand in part (d)

Maximum	10
Total	50

Memorandum

For: The files

Client: Corey

Subject: Personal and company tax matters

Prepared by: Tax senior

Date: 1 March 2026

(a) (i) Corey's residency will be determined by reference to the statutory residency test, which requires we apply a number of prescribed tests to determine whether is a UK resident for the relevant tax year.

As you have already confirmed, Corey's status cannot be determined automatically, and therefore it will be determined by the number of ties he has with the UK. He was not UK resident in any of the three tax years prior to 2025/26, and he will have been in the UK for between 91 and 120 days in the tax year 2025/26. He will therefore be UK resident if he satisfies three or more UK ties.

The ties to be considered are:

	Satisfied?
In the UK for more than 90 days in either or both of the tax years 2023/24 and 2024/25	Yes
Spouse/civil partner or children under 18 who are resident in the UK	Yes
Working in the UK for 40 days or more	No
Accommodation available in the UK for a continuous period of more than 90 days	Yes

Corey will satisfy three of the UK ties, such that he will be UK resident in the tax year 2025/26.

(ii) As a UK resident, Corey will be subject to UK income tax on his overseas income in addition to his UK income. He will however be able to obtain relief in the UK for any tax suffered in Medora. This relief is the lower of, the tax paid in the UK on his overseas income, and the tax paid on that same income in Medora.

(b) (i) **Disposals in the tax year 2024/25**

For the purposes of UK capital gains tax (CGT), Corey will be regarded as only temporarily non-UK resident whilst living in Medora. This is because:

- he was absent from the UK for less than five years; and
- having always lived in the UK prior to moving to Medora, he was UK resident for at least four of the seven tax years immediately prior to the tax year of departure.

As a temporary non-UK resident, Corey will be subject to UK CGT on any assets sold whilst he was living overseas, which he owned at the date of his departure from the UK. Any such gains or losses are subject to CGT in the tax year in which Corey returned to the UK, in this case 2025/26.

- The statue was both bought and sold while Corey was living in Medora. Accordingly, the capital loss on the sale is not available for relief in the UK.
- The gain resulting from the takeover of SQ plc will be subject to tax in 2025/26, and not in tho year of the takeover.

(ii) **CGT liability for the tax year 2025/26**

	Other gains	Residential property
	£	£
Chargeable gains:		
– Shares in SQ plc (W1)	5,769	
– House in Medora		34,500
– Shares in TW plc (W3)	1,878	
Less: annual exempt amount		(3,000)
Taxable gains	7,647	31,500
Basic rate band	37,700	
Taxable income (£42,320 – £12,570)	(29,750)	
Basic rate band remaining	7,950	
CGT		
Other gains: 7,647 x.10%	765	
Residential property: (Tutorial note)		
– £303 × 18%	55	
– £31,197 × 24%	7,487	
CGT liability	8,307	

Workings

1 ***Disposal of 2,000 shares in SQ plc on 1 February 2025***

	£
Proceeds in cash	12,000
Less: cost (W2)	(6,231)
Chargeable gain	5,769

2 ***Allocation of cost of shares in SQ plc following takeover by TW plc***

	Consideration		Cost
	£		£
Shares in TW plc (4,000 × £3.50)	14,000	£13,500 × £14,000/£26,000	7,269
Cash	12,000	£13,500 × £12,000/£26,000	6,231
Total	26,000		13,500

3 ***Gift of 700 shares in TW plc on 1 December 2024***

	£
Proceeds at market value (700 × £4.50)	3,150
Less: cost (700/4,000 × £7,269 (W2))	(1,272)
Chargeable gain	1,878

(c) The advantages of making a lifetime gift are:

- As the gifts would be potentially exempt transfers (PETs), no inheritance tax (IHT) will be charged if Emer survives the gift by a minimum of seven years.
- If Emer dies before the expiration of seven years but after at least three years have elapsed, any IHT due will be reduced by taper relief. The relief is 20% of the tax if she survives the gift by three years with a further 20% relief for each additional year.
- The value of a lifetime gift is determined at the time of the gift rather than at the date of death. Accordingly, one of the benefits of making a lifetime gift of the portrait is that, if the gift becomes chargeable, IHT will be charged on the value at the time of the gift rather than the value as at the date of death (which is expected to be higher).

  The watercolour is expected to fall in value. However, if its value at the time of death is lower than it was at the time of the gift, fall in value relief would be available (provided Corey still owns the painting or has sold it at arms' length). As a result, the value of the painting at the time of death would be used to calculate any IHT due, resulting in a lower tax charge.

  However, the fall in value relief would only affect the IHT due on the watercolour itself. When calculating the IHT on subsequent gifts and on the death estate, the value of the watercolour at the time of the gift, ie the higher amount, would be used.

In view of the above, it is likely that both paintings should be the subject of a lifetime gift.

(d) (i) **Tax treatment of the purchase of the Cloque brand**

- Corey's friend is correct that the amount of £1,000 charged to the profit and loss account in respect of this expenditure would be allowable for the purposes of calculating taxable trading profit.
- Alternatively, Quod Ltd can make a claim to receive tax relief at a rate of 4% on a straight-line basis. This claim would mean that relief of £1,400 (£35,000 × 4%) is available each year, which would clearly be beneficial compared to the actual amortisation charged.

(ii) **Tax relief available in respect of the scientific research costs**

As Quod Ltd will be carrying out R&D in the period, certain categories of revenue expenditure which are directly related to research and development activities will qualify for the R&D expenditure credit (RDEC). The credit is 20% of the qualifying R&D and it is first added to the company's taxable trading profits and then offset against the company's corporation tax liability. As Quod Ltd has no corporation tax liability for the period, it may be possible to have the RDEC paid to the company or it can be carried forward and offset against the corporation tax liability of future periods.

The rental costs do not qualify for the RDEC.

Only 65% of amounts paid to external contractors qualifies for the RDEC.

RDEC available

	£	£
Total research costs	74,500	
Less:		
– Rent	(17,400)	
– Staff costs (£7,000 × 35% (100% – 65%))	(2,450)	
Amount qualifying for RDEC	54,650	
RDEC (20% × 54,650)		10,930

(iii) **Amended adjusted trading loss for the year ending 31 March 2027**

	£
Budgeted tax adjusted trading loss	(44,000)
RDEC (20% × 54,650)	10,930
Amortisation of Cloque brand (£1,400 (£35,000 × 4%) – £1,000)	(400)
Amended tax adjusted trading loss	(33,470)

(iv) **Amount of trading loss available for use by Porth Ltd**

- Porth Ltd will not be able to use the trading loss of Quod Ltd unless Quod Ltd is a consortium company. Quod Ltd will be a consortium company if at least 75% of its ordinary share capital is owned by companies, each of which own at least 5% but less than 75%.
- Accordingly, for consortium relief to be available, BJB Ltd must own the 30% holding rather than Mr Berm.
- The maximum amount which could be surrendered to Porth Ltd as consortium relief is £20,082 (£33,470 × 60%), reflecting Porth Ltd's holding of 60% of the ordinary share capital of Quod Ltd.

(e) **Refund of income tax**

- We should review Corey's tax return for 2021/22 in order to determine whether there is a valid reason for the refund.
- If we conclude that the refund was made as a result of an error on the part of HM Revenue and Customs (HMRC), we should tell Corey to repay the money immediately. We should inform him that failing to return the money in these circumstances may well be a civil and/or a criminal offence.
- HMRC should be informed of their error as soon as possible, as this will minimise any interest and penalties which may otherwise become payable. We should inform HMRC if our letter of engagement authorises us to do so. Alternatively, we should advise Corey to do so.
- If Corey is unwilling to return the money, we would have to consider ceasing to act as his tax adviser. We would then have to notify HMRC that we no longer act for him, although we would not provide them with any reason for our action.
- Finally, we should consider whether it is necessary to make a report under the money laundering rules.

11 Joe

Course Book references

Corporation tax on liquidations is covered in Chapter 20 with tax on intangibles in Chapter 16. Basis period rules are revised in Chapter 14 with choice of year end date in Chapter 18. Deductibility of pre-trading expenses is covered in the essential reading to Chapter 14 with VAT recovery in Chapter 23. Ethics is covered in Chapter 1. Overseas aspects are in Chapter 9.

Top tips

Don't forget in (a)(i) that you've been asked for post-tax proceeds on the sale of the intangible fixed assets. Even if your tax figures are wrong there will be method marks for deducting your tax figure from the proceeds (not gains). In (a)(ii) it's important to note that it's a 7-mark requirement for the timing of payments to the shareholders – there must be more to say than simply it's taxed as x if it's pre-liquidation and as y if it's post liquidation. You're told the shareholders are a mix of taxpayers – so use this in your answer.

In part (c) make sure you don't suggest obtaining Fiona's address and proof of identity – your manager has already done that so no marks will be available. Make sure you leave time to attempt (d). There will be method marks for you calculating Fiona's income tax liability even if you make a mistake – you're told she can use the remittance basis so use it and don't forget that there'll be double tax relief on any overseas income taxed in the UK.

Easy marks

There should be some easy marks in (a)(ii) explaining how the distributions to the shareholders will be taxed. Just make sure you write enough to try to score 7 marks. The ethics in part (c) is frequently tested in ATX–UK and should have been a source of easy marks.

ACCA examining team's comments

Part (a) concerned the liquidation of a company which had always been profitable in the past.

Part (a)(i)

The company planned to sell two intangible assets just before the liquidator was appointed and part (a)(i) required a calculation of the post-tax proceeds of these disposals for the company.

It is important to always check the 'command' word being used in a question. In this part, it is to 'calculate'. Long explanations are therefore not required here and will not earn marks. Candidates should aim for clear labelling of figures and perhaps brief explanations of what is being done, but without wasting time on lots of narrative content.

It is also important to note that the question asks for 'post-tax proceeds'. To arrive at this figure there are distinct steps in the calculation which need to be followed. Given the facts in this scenario, it is first necessary to calculate any taxable profit or loss, then calculate any corporation tax paid or saved at 25%, and then finally calculate the proceeds less any tax paid, or plus any tax saved.

The tax treatment generally follows the accounting treatment for the sale of intangible assets which is why trading profits and losses as opposed to capital gains or losses are being calculated.

The first intangible asset sold was goodwill and candidates were told that the amortisation of this goodwill had not been a tax deductible expense for the company. As a result, the full unamortised cost of £95,000 should be used in calculating the loss on sale ie £75,000 – £95,000 = £20,000 loss.

The second intangible asset sold was the brand which had been amortised. As this is an intangible asset held by a company, it should be assumed that this amortisation is tax deductible, unless told otherwise. As such, the amortised cost should be used to work out the taxable profit on the sale of the brand ie £47,000 less (£36,000 – £5,760) = £16,760. A number of candidates incorrectly calculated the amortisation of the brand at 4%, but the question specifically states that no election to write it off at this fixed rate had been made.

Thus far only the taxable profits and losses on the disposal of these assets has been calculated. A number of candidates stopped at this point but it was important to appreciate that the requirement involved calculation of the 'post-tax proceeds' arising from these disposals.

The next stage is to therefore calculate the tax saved, or paid, at 25% on the relevant loss or profit.

Finally, this needs to be brought together to calculate the 'post tax proceeds' arising from these transactions. The starting point for this is to go back to the actual proceeds ie £75,000 + £47,000 = £122,000. Then to deduct any tax paid, or add any tax saved, to the total proceeds. A common mistake made in questions of this nature is to take the profit or loss on disposal and to adjust this for the tax figure. But it should be remembered that, when looking at post tax proceeds from the disposal of an asset, the cost itself is no longer relevant and although this does feature in the profit or loss on which the tax is based, it is the proceeds which are important, as adjusted for the tax paid or saved.

Part (a)(ii)

Part (a)(ii) of this question required an explanation of the tax rates which shareholders will pay on amounts received from the company, depending on the timing of the payment. Within the first exhibit, it was stated that there would be a final payment to shareholders at the conclusion of the liquidation but consideration was being given to making an interim payment, prior to the appointment of the liquidator.

The command word used here was 'explain'; it is important to identify this and to focus on what the requirement is actually requiring an explanation of ie 'tax rates'.

Many candidates were very good at dealing with the pre-liquidation payment, correctly identifying that it would be treated as a dividend and detailing the potential tax rates. The scenario had specifically stated that the shareholders would be a mix of basic and higher rate taxpayers. Some candidates merely referred to the dividend treatment but did not go on to discuss in sufficient detail the specific tax rates which would apply to these types of shareholders; therefore, they did not score the marks available for this. In this context, it is important that candidates do ensure they are happy with the precise detail of a question requirement before beginning their answer. It's always worth going back to double check exactly what it is they have been asked to do, perhaps by highlighting key words in the question so that they stand out when working on the response.

Many candidates were able to identify that any final payment by a liquidator would be treated as a capital payment, but not all went on to discuss the rates of capital gains tax which the shareholders would then pay. Not only were the standard rates of capital gains tax of 10% and 20% relevant here, but also the single rate of 10% for both basic and higher rate taxpayers if business asset disposal relief were to apply.

This part of the question was about Joe who was setting up in business as an unincorporated trader.

Part (b)(i)

This part of the question has been changed since originally set due to syllabus changes. As such the Examiner's comments are no longer relevant.

Part (b)(ii)

This part of the question involved an explanation of whether or not Joe could recover the input VAT on consultancy services and business premises.

A knowledge of the detailed rules and time limits for recovery of pre-registration VAT was required; namely six months prior to VAT registration for services, and four years prior to VAT registration for goods. A number of candidates demonstrated that they were aware that time limits existed but were not sufficiently precise as to exactly what these were. A detailed, rather than purely superficial, knowledge of the tax rules is required in order to score well in this exam.

Many candidates were confused regarding the input VAT recovery on the business premises; this is a challenging area of the syllabus. Joe intended to use two thirds of the premises for his trade and to rent out the remaining one third. This meant that he could recover two thirds of the input VAT on the original cost, but given that leasing is an exempt supply for VAT purposes, would not be able to recover the remaining one third. In order to change this position, and to be able to recover the full amount including that relating to the part which was let out, Joe would need to opt to tax the building.

Part (c)

Part (c) of the question tested knowledge of the actions to be taken before becoming Fiona's tax advisers.

This was a standard ethics requirement and many candidates were able to score well on this part of the question. However, when answering any ethics question dealing with aspects such as these, the need to address any threats to compliance with the fundamental principles such as integrity, professional competence and due care, should be borne in mind. If any such threats are identified, the point should be made that they can they be reduced to an acceptable level with the implementation of appropriate safeguards.

A small but significant number of candidates suggested that Fiona's address and proof of identity should be obtained, despite being specifically told in the question that this had already happened. Before starting on an answer, it is always worth rechecking the requirement and information contained within the scenario in order to avoid wasting time on points that cannot earn marks.

Part (d)

There were two subparts to part (d).

The first asked for an explanation of why Fiona would be eligible for the remittance basis and whether or not she would be subject to the remittance basis charge.

The remittance basis is available where an individual is UK resident but not UK domiciled. Fiona's status for the tax year 2026/27 was that of resident and deemed domicile. In this case, the remittance basis is only available if unremitted overseas income and gains in any tax year is less than £2,000; in this situation it applies automatically and there is no remittance basis charge.

Some candidates appeared to know the rules but were unclear on the amount of 'unremitted' overseas income when applied to Fiona's specific circumstances. The question specifically stated that her overseas bank interest income of £1,200 would not be remitted to the UK whereas that from her overseas rental properties would be. As such, with an amount of overseas unremitted income of less than £2,000, the remittance basis automatically applies to Fiona for the relevant tax year.

The second subpart of this requirement asked for a calculation of Fiona's income tax liability for the tax year 2026/27. It's worth emphasising here once again that, if asked for a calculation, there is no need to spend time providing detailed explanations of all of the relevant numbers. As long as they are all clearly labelled, and brief explanations of any workings are given if necessary, the focus should be on doing the calculations themselves in order to earn the marks.

Many candidates were able to produce an income tax computation in response to this part of the question and showed an awareness of the fundamentals of double tax relief. Strictly, in order to calculate the UK tax suffered on the overseas income for double tax relief purposes, a calculation of the income tax liability with the overseas income included should be performed and this should then be compared with a calculation of the liability with the foreign income excluded. The difference in these two tax liabilities represents the UK tax on the overseas income, which is then compared with the foreign tax suffered. This method is demonstrated in the model answer.

Marking guide

			Marks	
(a)	(i)	Loss on sale of goodwill	1	
		Profit on sale of brand	1	
		Post tax proceeds	2	
				4
	(ii)	Prior to appointment	4	
		After appointment	6	
		Marks Available	10	
		Maximum		9
(b)	(i)	Salary, car, fuel, NIC	1.5	
		IT and Class 4 NIC saved	2	
		After-tax cost	1	
		(W) Reduction in trade profits	2	
		Marks Available	6.5	
		Maximum		6

ANSWERS

Marking guide		Marks
(ii) Value added tax		
– Consultancy services	2	
– Premises	4	
		6
(c) Fundamental principles	3	
Other matters	3	
Marks Available	6	
Maximum		5
(d) Remittance basis	4	
Calculation of income tax liability		
– Liability before double tax relief	3.5	
– Double tax relief	3.5	
Marks Available	11	
Maximum		10

Professional skills marks

Communication

- General format and structure of meeting notes (eg use of headings/sub-headings to make meeting notes easy to refer to)
- Style, language and clarity (tone of meeting notes, presentation of calculations, appropriate use of the tools, easy to follow and more than a negligible amount of content)
- Effectiveness of communication (answer is relevant, specific rather than general, focused to the requirement)
- Adherence to specific instructions/information provided in the scenario (eg not writing off the brand at 4%)

Analysis and evaluation

- Appropriate use of information to determine post-tax proceeds in part (a)
- Appropriate use of information when calculating cost of taking on a new employee in part (b)(i)
- Appropriate use of information when establishing the UK liability on the overseas income for DTR purposes in part (d)
- Consideration of relevant factors when deciding whether or not the remittance basis charge applies to Fiona in part (d)

Scepticism

- Critical assessment of the potential for business asset disposal relief in part (a)(ii) and its application to the shareholders of VNL Ltd
- Recognition of the uncertainties in relation to the option to tax in part (b)(ii)

Commercial acumen

- Recognition of the importance of timing of VAT registration in order to maximise recovery of VAT on the consultancy costs in part (b)(ii)
- Effective use of information to determine the applicability of the capital goods scheme to Joe's situation in part (b)(ii)
- Recognition of the impact of the remittance basis on the subsequent computation in part (d)

Maximum	10
Total	50

Question 1 should be mainly prepared in the word processor response option as it will be a formal document. You can start by copying and pasting the detailed requirement which can be found in Exhibit 4, your manager's email. You can then head it up as notes and start to structure your answer.

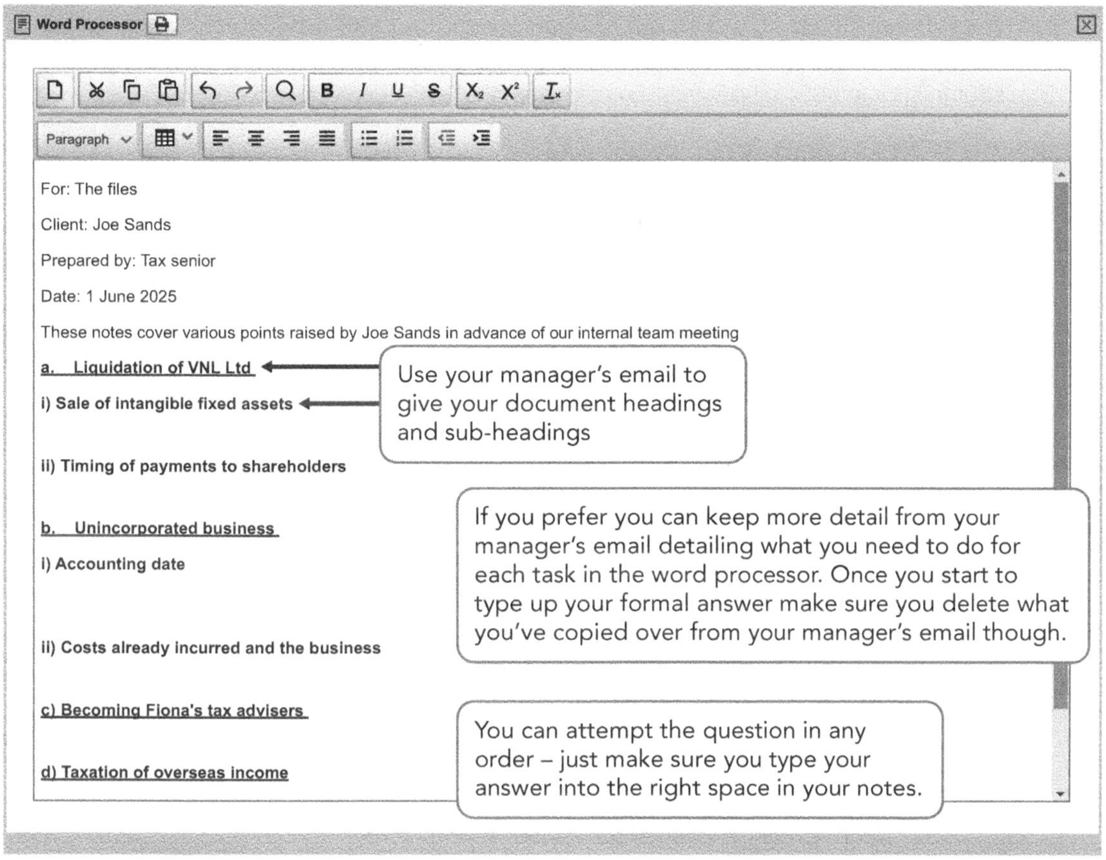

Notes for meeting

Notes for meeting

For: The files

Client: VNL Ltd – liquidation, Joe – establishment of new business

Prepared by: Tax senior

Date: 1 June 2025

(a) (i) **Liquidation of VNL Ltd**

Sale of intangible fixed assets

	Goodwill	Brand	
	£	£	£
Sales proceeds on 31 July 2025	75,000	47,000	122,000
Cost	(95,000)		
Tax written down value (£36,000 – £5,760)		(30,240)	
(Loss)/profit	(20,000)	16,760	
Corporation tax at 25% on profit			(4,190)
Loss relieved against total profits at 25%			5,000
Post tax proceeds			122,810

Tutorial note. The loss on the sale of the goodwill is a non-trading debit. This loss can be offset against the total income and gains of the current accounting period.

Here's an example of what the answer could look like:

The numbers in the spreadsheet are laid out slightly differently to the answer given above but either approach is acceptable – provided the marker can follow what you're saying you should be awarded marks.

Word Processor

Paragraph

For: The files

Client: Joe Sands

Prepared by: Tax senior

Date: 1 June 2025

These notes cover various points raised by Joe Sands in advance of our internal team meeting

a. Liquidation of VNL Ltd

i) Sale of intangible fixed assets

The sale of the intangible fixed assets will generate VNL Ltd £122,810 of post-tax proceeds. See Appendix 1 in the spreadsheet for these calculations.

ii) Timing of payments to shareholders

Make sure you reference any calculations in an Appendix which will be in the spreadsheet response option.

Spreadsheet

Edit Format

100%

M13

	A	B	C	D	E	F	G
1	**Appendix 1 - Sale of intangible fixed assets**						
2							
3	Sale of goodwill						
4		Proceeds	£75,000				
5		Cost	(£95,000)				
6		Non trade loss	(£20,000)	=SUM(C4:C5)			
7	Sale of brand						
8		Proceeds	£47,000				
9		TWDV	(£30,240)				
10		Trade profit	£16,760				
11							
12	Non trade loss on the sale of the goodwill can be offset against the total income and gains of the current period						
13							
14	Therefore, net impact on TTP		(£3,240)	=SUM(C6+C10)			
15	So, extra corporation tax at 25% as TTP has reduced.						
16	Extra CT @ 25%		£810	=-0.25*C14			
17							
18	Post-tax proceeds is, therefore:		£122,810	=C4+C8+C16			
19							
20							
21							

Make sure you format the cells – use 'format', 'cells' and then select 'number' and 'currency'. Alternatively, use .00 and select 'custom' and then 'number' if you don't want a "£" before each number. Either approach is acceptable.

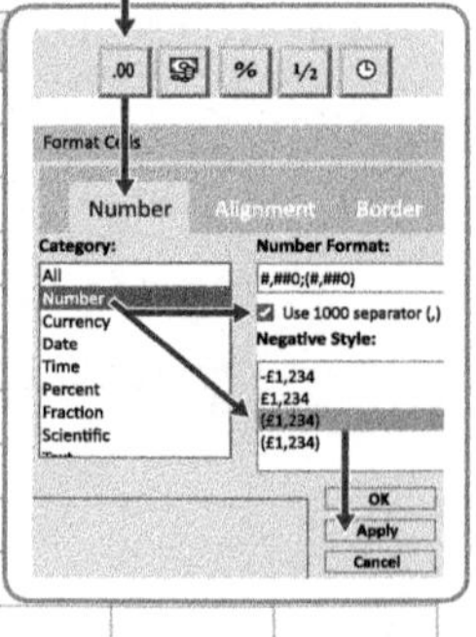

You can still type explanatory sentences into the spreadsheet if you need to explain your calculations.

(ii) **Timing of payments to shareholders**

Prior to the appointment of the liquidator

A payment made to the shareholders prior to the appointment of the liquidator will be subject to income tax as a dividend in a normal way.

The first £500 of an individual's dividend income in a tax year from all shareholdings is taxed at 0%. The excess over £500 will be taxed as a shareholder's top slice of income.

Any amount which falls into a shareholder's basic rate band will be subject to income tax at 8.75%. The balance of the dividend will be subject to income tax at 33.75%.

After the appointment of the liquidator

Once the liquidator has been appointed, amounts paid to shareholders will represent proceeds in respect of a part disposal of their shares for the purposes of capital gains tax (CGT).

Any amount of the chargeable gain which is not covered by the shareholder's annual exempt amount of £3,000 will be subject to CGT.

Where the disposal of the shares qualifies for business asset disposal relief, the whole of any chargeable gain (within the lifetime limit of £1,000,000) will be subject to CGT at 10% irrespective of whether the shareholders are basic rate or higher rate taxpayers.

As VNL Ltd is a trading company, business asset disposal relief will be available where:

- the shareholder had owned at least 5% of the company's ordinary share capital and been an officer or employee of the company for a period of at least two years prior to the cessation of VNL Ltd's trade, and
- the shares are disposed of within three years of the cessation of VNL Ltd's trade.

We would therefore need to establish if any individual shareholders satisfy these conditions.

Where business asset disposal relief is not available, the chargeable gain will be taxed after calculating tax on income, by reference to the income tax bands.

Any amount of the chargeable gain which falls into a shareholder's basic rate band will be subject to CGT at 10%. The balance of the chargeable gain will be subject to CGT at 20%.

Here's an example of an answer to (a)(ii) written using the word processor response option. As these are notes for an internal team meeting within your firm it is acceptable to use tax jargon and abbreviations. However, do ensure you type full sentences.

Word Processor

Date: 1 June 2025

These notes cover various points raised by Joe Sands in advance of our internal team meeting.

a. Liquidation of VNL Ltd

i) Sale of intangible fixed assets

The sale of the intangible fixed assets will generate VNL Ltd £122,810 of post-tax proceeds. See Appendix 1 in the spreadsheet for these calculations.

ii) Timing of payments to shareholders

Prior to appointment of the liquidator

Any payments made to shareholders before the liquidator is appointed will be taxed as a normal dividend.

So, given VNL Ltd has all indvidual shareholders, the first £500 would be taxed at 0% due to the dividend nil rate band with the balance being taxed as the top slice of the shareholder's income - so, at 8.75% for a basic rate taxpayer or 33.75% for a higher rate taxpayer.

After appointment of liquidator

Once a liquidator has been appointed any amounts paid up to shareholders will be treated as proceeds in respect of a disposal of their shares in VNL Ltd.

They will therefore take proceeds (the amount they receive) less their cost and their annual exempt amount of £6,000 and the balance will be the taxable gain.

If the particular shareholder qualifies for business asset disposal relief (BADR) they will pay CGT at 10% on their taxable gain. Otherwise, they will pay CGT at 10% if they have any basic rate band of tax remaining after their income tax or at 20% if they are already higher rate taxpayers.

BADR will apply where a shareholder:

- has owned at least 5% of the VNL Ltd shares and been an employee for at least 2 years prior to VNL Ltd ceasing to trade; and
- the shares are being sold within 3 yrs of VNL Ltd ceasing to trade.

We will need to determine whether any sharholders qualify for BADR.

You will not be penalised for a small typo as long as the marker can understand what you are trying to say.

(b) (i) **New employee**

After tax cost

	£	£
Salary		15,000
Purchase of car		14,000
Fuel for car		2,300
Class 1 secondary on salary (W1)		814
Class 1a on car benefit (W1)		420
IT and Class 4 NIC saved on tax reduction in trade profits (W1)	19,374 @ 42%	(8,137)
After-tax cost		24,397

Workings

1 ***Reduction in trade profit***

	£
Salary	15,000
Fuel for car	2,300
CAs on car @ 6% on £14,000	840
Class 1 secondary £(15,000 – 9,100) × 13.8%	814
Class 1A on car benefit (W2) £3,040 × 13.8%	420
	19,374

2 ***Car benefit***

£16,000 × 19% = £3,040

CO_2 emission %: 16% + ((72 – 55)/5) = 19%

(ii) **Costs already incurred and the business premises**

Recovery of input tax for the purposes of value added tax (VAT)

- **Consultancy services**

  Joe will be able to recover input VAT in respect of services provided to him for business purposes in the six months prior to registering for VAT.

  Accordingly, because Joe first incurred these costs more than six months ago, he should consider registering for VAT as soon as possible in order to recover as much of the input tax relating to the consultancy services he can.

- **Premises**

  The amount of input tax which Joe can recover will depend on whether or not he opts to tax the building for the purposes of VAT.

  - If he opts to tax the building, he will be able to recover all of the input tax.
  - Otherwise, he will only be able to recover two-thirds of it.

  This is because the granting of the lease will be an exempt supply unless an option to tax is made in respect of the building.

  The building will not be subject to the capital goods scheme because its VAT exclusive cost will be less than £250,000.

(c) **Becoming Fiona's tax advisers:**

The actions we should carry out before we become Fiona's tax advisers:

- We must give consideration to the fundamental principles of professional ethics, for example, integrity and professional competence and due care. This requires us to consider whether becoming tax advisers to Fiona would create any threats to compliance with these principles.

If any such threats are identified, we should not accept the appointment unless the threats can be reduced to an acceptable level via the implementation of safeguards.

Fiona's move to the UK will significantly affect her tax affairs, and we must be sure that we are able to deal with the technical aspects of these matters.

- We must assure ourselves that Fiona is not involved in any form of money laundering.
- We should obtain permission from Fiona to contact her existing tax advisers in order to ensure that there is nothing in the past which would preclude us from accepting the appointment on ethical grounds.
- We should issue a letter of engagement setting out the terms of our agreement with Fiona and our agreed responsibilities.

(d) **Taxation of overseas income**

Availability of the remittance basis

- The remittance basis is available where an individual is UK resident but not UK domiciled.
- Where an individual is UK resident and deemed domiciled in the UK, the remittance basis is only available if unremitted overseas income and gains in a tax year is less than £2,000. In these circumstances, the remittance basis applies automatically.
- Accordingly, for the tax year 2026/27, the amount of Fiona's taxable overseas income will be automatically calculated on the remittance basis. This is because her only unremitted overseas income will be her Parellian bank of £1,200.
- Fiona will not be subject to the remittance basis charge because she will qualify for the remittance basis automatically.

		Working
	£	£
Property income		
– Properties in the UK	26,000	26,000
– Properties in Parella	31,000	N/A
Interest income		
– UK bank interest	1,700	1,700
– Parellian bank interest (unremitted)		
Total income	58,700	27,700
Less: Personal allowance	(12,570)	(12,570)
Taxable income	46,130	15,130
Property income		
– £37,700/£13,430 × 20%	7,540	2,686
– £6,730 × 40%	2,692	–
Interest income		
– £500/£1,000 × 0%	0	0
– £1,200 × 40%/£700 × 20%	480	140
	10,712	2,826
Double tax relief, the lower of:		
– UK tax on overseas income		
– £10,712 – £2,826 (W) = £7,886		
Parellian tax suffered		
– £31,000 × 18% = £5,580	(5,580)	
	5,132	

> **Tutorial note.** The personal allowance will be given because the remittance basis is available automatically.

12 Jeg Ltd

Course Book references

Ethics is covered in Chapter 1. Capital gains reliefs and corporate groups are covered in Chapters 8 and 19 respectively. Overseas issues for companies are covered in Chapter 22 with VAT in Chapter 23. The income tax computation is covered in Chapter 2 with NICs in Chapter 4.

Top tips

Make sure you use Exhibit 2 to clearly copy across into the word processor response option the tasks your manager has asked you to include in the memorandum. Make sure you keep moving through the requirements- Part (e) is worth 9 marks and has some detailed calculations so you need to allow sufficient time to attempt it.

In part (b) note that you are asked two things- make sure you pick up the second part of the requirement about the way in which rollover relief would operate.

In part (c) ensure you check the wording of the second bullet point about Mot Ltd- you're asked for matters to consider when deciding whether or not to make the election to exempt the profits of overseas PEs from UK tax- so provide a balanced argument giving both the pros and cons of the election.

In part (d) make sure you follow the specific requirements given- you do not need to consider Lis Co and you are only asked for disadvantages for the Jeg Ltd group of a group VAT registration- not advantages.

In part (e) make sure you think about whether Hale suffers more than simply income tax on his income and incorporate that into your calculations.

Easy marks

There should be easy marks available for the ethics about us agreeing to become tax advisers in part (a). Easy marks should also be available in part (b) explaining rollover relief and how it operates. VAT groups in part (d) are often tested in ATX–UK and should also have provided easy marks. Finally, in part (e) there should be easy marks available for the income tax calculation and NICs too (if you realised NIC needed to be included). Remember to have confidence that you will be awarded method marks for using your own figures to calculate Hale's financial position- so keep going.

ACCA examining team's comments

Part (a) concerned the information required, and the actions to be taken, before accepting a group of companies as a client.

This was a standard ethics topic, which frequently gets tested, and many candidates were able to score well on this part of the question.

Two main issues were identified in weaker answers:

- Candidates suggested information which would have been relevant for an individual or a sole trader client, but not for a company. Candidates must be clear in terms of the status of the client they are advising when thinking about any ethical issues which may be involved.
- There was a tendency for some candidates to write out all they knew about the ethical principles, without relating their knowledge to the facts of the question. Although consideration of any threats to compliance with the fundamental principles of professional ethics will often be an integral part of an ethics question, these should be considered in the context of the particular scenario and in the light of the relevant facts which have been given. On this occasion, the company did not have any other clients who were operating overseas through permanent establishments. In view of this, it would be particularly important to ensure that the firm had the necessary professional competence in order to take on such an assignment.

Part (b) of this question required an explanation of the availability of rollover relief, and its application in respect of a qualifying asset sold by one company within the capital gains group.

It is important for candidates to always check the 'command' word(s) being used in a question, and to ensure that they note – possibly by the use of highlighting or copying and pasting – where more than one activity is required.

There were two parts to this requirement. The first part concerned the availability of rollover relief, and the second involved discussion of the way in which it would operate. Both parts needed to be addressed; it is easy to overlook the second part when immersed in the task of providing an answer to the first, so candidates should get into the habit of going back and re-reading each question requirement to ensure that it has been fully addressed.

A good starting point in any question which relates to reliefs within groups is to identify, with reasons, the qualifying group members for the purpose of the relief(s) being considered. Even on occasions where this may seem obvious, it should not be taken for granted that a marker knows that a candidate is aware of the underlying rules. Identification of the relevant group can often provide straightforward marks and should always be stated.

When going on to consider rollover relief it is necessary to identify the qualifying business asset(s) which has been sold – this was given in this case – and the qualifying business asset(s) which has been acquired. There were two fundamental aspects one needed to establish here: the types of assets involved (land and buildings and fixed plant and machinery) and the required time period for reinvestment (up to one year before and three years after the date of disposal of the qualifying asset).

The first exhibit provides quite a lot of information in relation to each of the group companies, and their recently acquired capital assets. Highlighting may therefore assist in order to pull out the relevant information on each of them. Time should be taken to carefully read the specific details provided about each company and each asset, noting the significance of information such as the non-UK-resident status of one of the companies (Lis Co), whether the machinery acquired is fixed or moveable (Jeg Ltd, Kod Ltd), whether an asset is wholly used in a company's trade (Kod Ltd) etc. The dates of sale and acquisition are also of importance in this context. Time should be spent reviewing and assimilating all of this detail in order to ensure that its relevance is understood when thinking about the answer.

Candidates who considered the whole scenario and adopted a logical, well thought out approach scored well here. Those who scored less well tended to restrict their answers to various general comments about rollover relief, without considering their relevance to this particular scenario, or taking the time to develop and expand in sufficient detail on the points being made.

In relation to the second part of this question, that which dealt with the application of rollover relief, two specific aspects needed to be considered:

- Firstly, whether or not all the proceeds from the disposal of the original asset had been reinvested in one or more qualifying assets. If so, the full amount of the gain arising would be eligible to be deferred. This is however not the case here, such that the relief needs to be restricted and a gain will remain chargeable equal to the proceeds retained.
- Secondly, the way in which the relief will be obtained. This involves consideration of whether the replacement asset is a depreciating asset or a non-depreciating one. Where it is a non-depreciating (ie has an expected life of more than 60 years on acquisition), the gain is rolled over and deducted from the cost of the new asset. This applies to assets such as land and buildings. Where the replacement asset is a depreciating one, (which includes fixed plant and machinery and leases with 60 years or less less to run), the gain is deferred until the earliest of three dates – the date of sale of the replacement asset, the date when the replacement ceases to be used in the business, and ten years from the date of its acquisition. There was on this occasion only one qualifying replacement asset – the fixed machinery purchased by Jeg Ltd. This meant that that an explanation of the deferral associated with the acquisition of a depreciating asset was required.

Candidates generally demonstrated a sound knowledge when dealing with this part of the question, but some struggled more when it came to applying their knowledge to the facts of the question and, in so doing, also failed to demonstrate the necessary professional skills. The ability to tailor and apply knowledge to specific scenarios is a key part of this exam and candidates are advised to build plenty of question practice into their revision programmes in order to become more adept and experienced at this.

Part (c) of this question involved a transfer pricing issue in relation to one group company (Lis Co), and the setting-up of an overseas permanent establishment (PE) in relation to another (Mot Ltd).

Careful reading of the entire requirement relating to Lis Co resulted in many candidates producing very comprehensive answers, which scored well. The reference to transfer pricing right at the end of the requirement provided a clear instruction as to what the first part involved. However, it was important for candidates to recognise why, on this occasion, a transfer pricing adjustment was actually going to be required. Jeg Ltd, a UK resident company, was intending to buy components from its overseas' subsidiary at a price above the arm's length price; this would therefore have the impact of artificially reducing its taxable profits. We were told that Jeg Ltd was a small company; this might potentially have exempted it from the transfer pricing regime had it not been for the fact that Lis Co was resident in a non-qualifying territory (ie there was no double taxation agreement in place with the UK).

Most candidates seemed to be comfortable with this situation and recognised that an adjustment would be required for tax purposes. However, a fair number did not go on to develop this idea in sufficient detail by explaining the impact of such an adjustment for the UK company. This should have been relatively straightforward – the company's profits would increase as a result of the adjustment, which would then give rise to a corresponding increase in its corporation tax liability. It is vital that candidates do take the time to read and fully understand the requirement – going back and rereading it if necessary - in order to ensure that they haven't missed out on anything when preparing their answers.

The second part of this requirement related to another group company, Mot Ltd, which was setting up an overseas PE. The question specifically asked for an explanation of the rate of tax suffered in the UK on the profits which were generated overseas. The majority of candidates appeared to be very comfortable with the general UK tax treatment of an overseas PE, recognising that its profits would be taxed as part of the profits of Mot Ltd, as it was a UK resident company. However, many did not go on to specifically relate this knowledge to the rate of tax being suffered on these profits in the UK on this occasion. This required recognition of the double taxation rules, such that the tax payable in the UK at 19% – 25% (dependent on augmented profits) would be reduced by the tax paid overseas at 13%.

Candidates were then required to explain the matters to consider when deciding whether or not to make an election to exempt the profits of the overseas PE from UK taxation. The wording of this requirement, 'whether or not', should have indicated to candidates that what was required was a consideration of both the advantages and the disadvantages of the election. Many candidates focussed exclusively on the disadvantages, overlooking the key advantage of the profits not being taxable in the UK and therefore saving UK tax. This may have seemed too obvious a point to mention but it did need to be stated since it was relevant to the final decision.

Part (d) of this question required an explanation of companies eligible to form part of a VAT group registration, and the VAT implications of purchasing goods from an overseas subsidiary.

Many answers to this part were rather vague. For all elections, across all taxes, it is necessary to have a sound understanding of the precise rules and conditions. On this occasion, a significant number of candidates were unable to accurately state and apply the rules for group VAT registration. In particular, many referred to the need for companies to be UK resident; this is incorrect for VAT purposes where, in order to meet the qualifying conditions, the company only needs to be established in the UK, or have a fixed place of business there.

A further point which was evident based on performance in this part was, once again, the need for candidates to read the requirement very carefully and ensure that effort is focused in terms of addressing the specific question, rather than wasting time on issues which would not earn marks.

There were two examples of this here.

- A significant minority included Lis Co in their discussion of companies which could potentially join the VAT group even though the requirement specifically excludes Lis Co from being eligible for group membership.
- The requirement only asked for the possible disadvantages of group registration. A fair number of candidates listed all of the consequences, including the advantages. Credit could not be awarded in respect of these points and time was therefore unnecessarily wasted.

Imports and exports remain an important topic within the VAT syllabus, and candidates must ensure that they are able to apply the correct rules, particularly following changes as a result of the UK leaving the European Union.

In many cases, candidates would have benefited from more precise explanations in response to this part. On importing components, many tended to be fairly vague by saying that the UK company would suffer UK VAT, but were not sufficiently clear in terms of how or when this would arise (on importation). In some cases, reference was made to the 'reverse charge' principle which was not relevant here.

Part (e) required a calculation of an individual's income tax and NIC liabilities in order to explain and summarise their poor cashflow position. The client could not understand why his expenses (which were given) exceeded his post-tax income (which needed to be calculated).

The requirement features three key command words or phrases; candidates were asked to 'prepare calculations' in order to 'explain' the client's financial position, and then to 'summarise' their findings.

Initially, a calculation of the client's post-tax income was required. There are four things to bear in mind when addressing this part of the requirement:

(1) The question asked for calculations, so time should not have been spent providing detailed explanations. Numbers should have been labelled and brief explanations of any workings provided but, in order to earn the marks available, the key focus here should have been on performance of the calculations themselves.

(2) Post-tax income means gross cash income less all relevant tax deductions. Note that the requirement did not refer to 'post-income tax' income specifically, nor did it contain an instruction to ignore national insurance contributions (NIC), so these also needed to be considered given that they were relevant to the client's position in his capacity as an employee.

(3) Calculation of post-tax income will require a computation of the individual's income tax liability for the tax year; this is therefore a good place to start.

(4) It should be noted that the tax calculated should then have been deducted from the individual's gross cash income of the tax year, not their taxable income (which is after deduction of the personal allowance). This will include both salary and dividend income, but will exclude non-cash items such as taxable benefits. Care needed to be taken in the calculation of this figure.

It was encouraging to see that most candidates recognised that the need to factor in NICs. This is something that candidates always need to be on the look-out for when considering the position of employed or self-employed taxpayers, since it is not something they will necessarily be specifically directed to. As mentioned above, a careful reading of the requirement is therefore important in this respect, just to confirm that NICs were not on this occasion being excluded, as is sometimes the case.

The final part, which required a summary of findings, involved going back to the original problem – a comparison of the client's post-tax income with his expenses for the year – and making sensible and relevant comments on the figures. An actual comparison, based on the figures already calculated, of the difference between the expenses and the post-tax income would have been useful here in order to illustrate the point and to summarise the underlying issue. However many candidates' answers didn't include such summaries, thereby missing out on the marks available for addressing this part of the requirement.

Marking guide		Marks
(a) Information required	3	
Actions to take	4	
Marks Available	7	
Maximum		5
(b) Assets sold	2	
Capital gains group	2	
Assets purchased	3	
Operation of relief	6.5	
Marks Available	13.5	
Maximum		9
(c) Transfer pricing	3.5	
UK rate of tax	2.5	
Election to exempt profits	4	
Marks Available	10	
Maximum		9
(d) Group VAT registration		
– Members of the group	3	
– Possible disadvantages	3	
Purchase of components from Lis Co	3	
Marks Available	9	
Maximum		8
(e) Taxable income	3.5	
Income tax and class 1 NIC liability	3.5	
Post-tax income and summary of findings	3.5	
Marks Available	10.5	
Maximum		9

Professional skills marks

Scepticism

- Recognition that the level of Mot Ltd's augmented profits will impact the UK corporation tax rate and that future permanent establishments (PEs) would be affected by an overseas branch election and the need to consider this in part (c)
- Recognition that the cashflow difficulties in Kod Ltd could mean it should not be included in the VAT group in part (d)
- Recognition that our lack of experience of overseas PEs could impact our professional competence in part (a)

Analysis and Evaluation

- Appropriate use of information in the scenario to support discussion and draw appropriate conclusions as to Hale's cash income after tax in part (e)
- Demonstration of ability to consider all relevant taxes (eg both income tax and NIC in part (e))

Communication

- General format and structure of memorandum (eg use of headings/sub-headings, easy to refer to)
- Style, language and clarity (tone of memorandum, presentation of calculations, appropriate use of tools, easy to follow and more than a negligible amount of content)

Marking guide | **Marks**

- Effectiveness of communication (answer is relevant, specific rather than general and focussed on the requirement)
- Adherence to specific instructions made in the scenario (eg addressing each task requested by our manager and not considering Lis Co with regard to VAT in part (d))

Commercial Acumen

- Recognising administrative problems with companies joining a VAT group and collating information
- Recognition of the calculation of cash income after tax in part (e)
- Understanding the significance of the high non-cash benefits impacting Hale's cash after tax in part (e)
- Recognition of the possibility to transfer the rollover relief in part (b) from depreciating to non-depreciating assets if later qualifying reinvestments made to further defer the gain

Maximum	10
Total	50

To set up an answer:

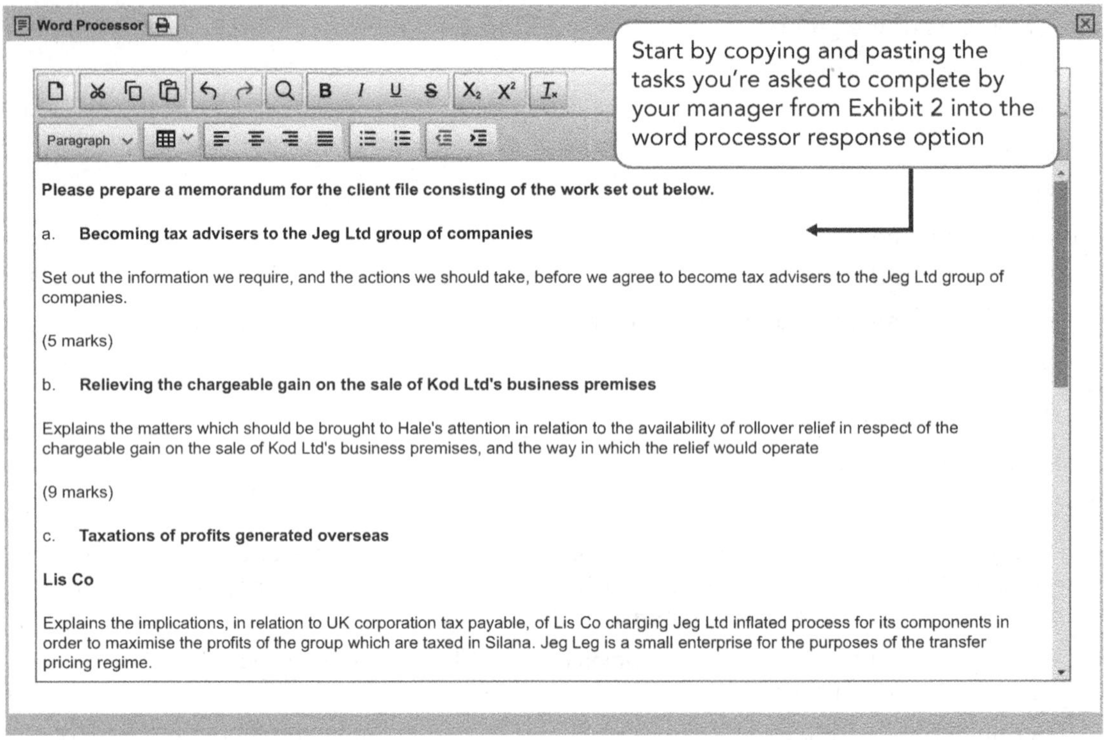

Please prepare a memorandum for the client file consisting of the work set out below.

a. **Becoming tax advisers to the Jeg Ltd group of companies**

Set out the information we require, and the actions we should take, before we agree to become tax advisers to the Jeg Ltd group of companies.

(5 marks)

b. **Relieving the chargeable gain on the sale of Kod Ltd's business premises**

Explains the matters which should be brought to Hale's attention in relation to the availability of rollover relief in respect of the chargeable gain on the sale of Kod Ltd's business premises, and the way in which the relief would operate

(9 marks)

c. **Taxations of profits generated overseas**

Lis Co

Explains the implications, in relation to UK corporation tax payable, of Lis Co charging Jeg Ltd inflated process for its components in order to maximise the profits of the group which are taxed in Silana. Jeg Leg is a small enterprise for the purposes of the transfer pricing regime.

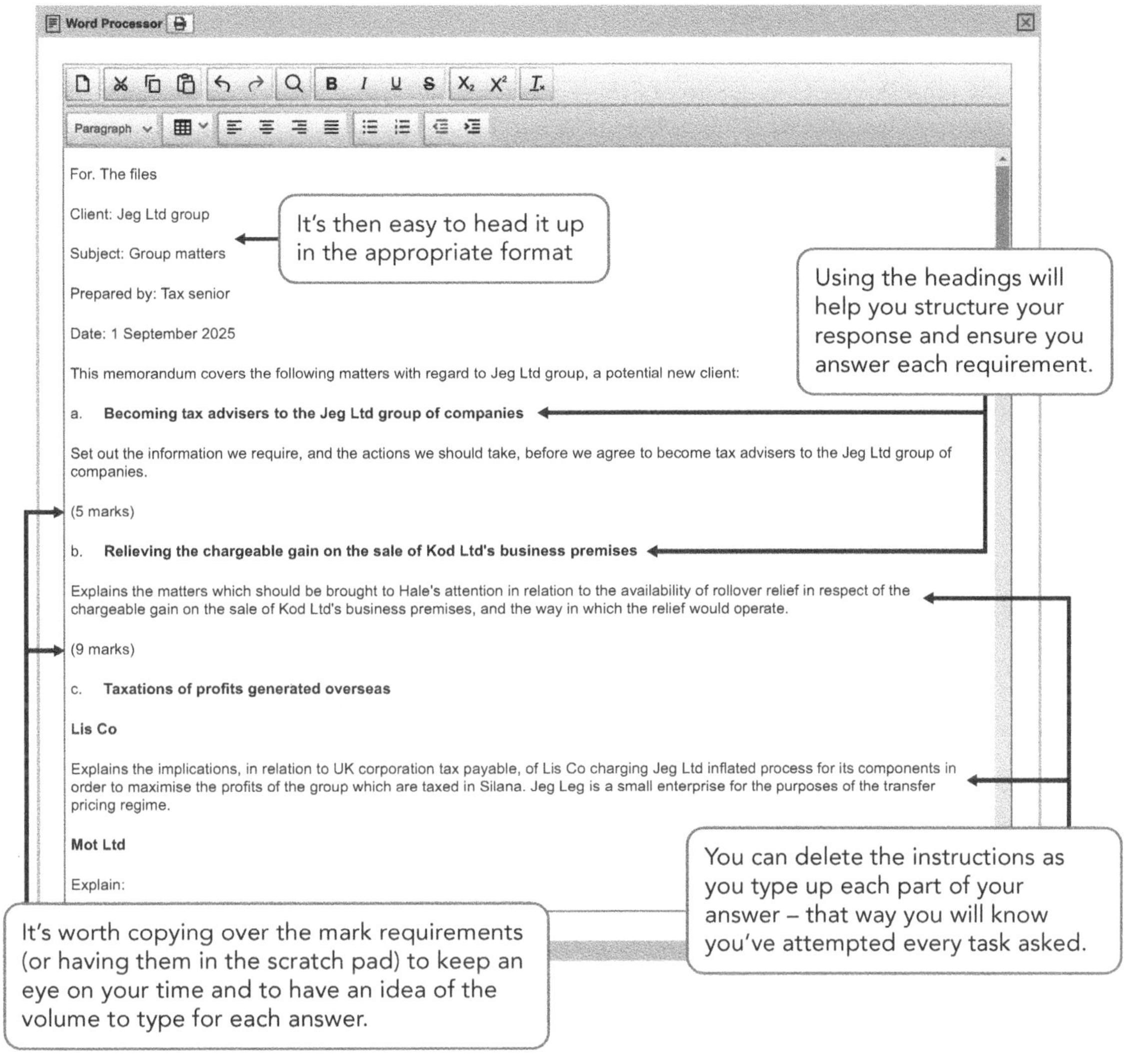

You're then ready to start typing up your answer into the appropriate space in your word processor response option:

Jeg Ltd group and Hale

Memorandum

For: The files

Client: Jeg Ltd group and Hale

Subject: Group matters

Prepared by: Tax senior

Date: 1 September 2025

(a) **Becoming tax advisers to the Jeg Ltd group of companies**

Information required:

- Proof of incorporation and primary business address and registered office of each company in the group.
- The group structure, directors and shareholders of the companies.
- The identities of those persons instructing the firm on behalf of the companies and those persons who are authorised to do so.

Actions to take:

- We must give consideration to the fundamental principles of professional ethics as set out in ACCA's *Professional Code of Ethics and Conduct*. This requires us to consider whether becoming tax advisers to the Jeg Ltd group would create any threats to compliance with these principles.

  In order to comply with the principle of professional competence and due care, we have an obligation to ensure that our clients receive competent, professional advice. As we have no experience of UK resident companies trading through permanent establishments situated overseas, we must obtain a thorough understanding of the relevant technical issues before we provide advice on these matters to the Jeg Ltd group of companies.
- We must assure ourselves that the companies are not involved in any form of money laundering.
- We should obtain permission to contact the group's existing tax advisers in order to ensure that there is nothing in the past which would preclude us from accepting the appointment on ethical grounds.

(b) **Relieving the chargeable gain on the sale of Kod Ltd's business premises**

Availability of rollover relief

- For rollover relief to be available:
  - qualifying assets, ie land and buildings and/or fixed plant and machinery, must be purchased;
  - in the four-year period commencing 1 July 2024 (one year prior to the sale of the premises);
  - by Kod Ltd or any company which was a member of the Jeg Ltd capital gains group at the time the replacement asset was purchased; and
  - the replacement assets must be either owned by a UK resident company for use in its trade or owned by a non-UK resident company and used to carry on a trade in the UK.

The Jeg Ltd capital gains group

- The Jeg Ltd capital gains group comprises Jeg Ltd and all of its subsidiaries, Kod Ltd, Lis Co and Mot Ltd. This is because Jeg Ltd owns at least 75% of the ordinary share capital of each of its subsidiaries.

Review of assets acquired

- The vans purchased by Kod Ltd are not qualifying assets because they are moveable as opposed to being fixed.
- The items of machinery purchased by Jeg Ltd will, however, qualify for rollover relief because they are fixed.
- Although Lis Co is a member of the Jeg Ltd capital gains group, the building, which it purchased on 1 July 2025, is not a qualifying asset for the purposes of rollover relief. This is because Lis Co is not a UK resident company and the building is not being used to carry on a trade in the UK.

Operation of rollover relief

- If the items of machinery purchased by Jeg Ltd are the only qualifying assets purchased during the qualifying period, it will not be possible to roll over the whole of the chargeable gain on the sale of Kod Ltd's business premises. The amount of proceeds not invested in qualifying assets of £195,000 (£485,000 – £290,000) will be charged to corporation tax.
- The remainder of the chargeable gain on the sale of the business premises of £52,000 (£247,000 – £195,000) could be deferred until the earliest of the following events in relation to the machinery purchased by Jeg Ltd:
  - the sale of the machinery;
  - the machinery no longer being used for the purposes of the trade;
  - ten years after the date of purchase of the machinery (ie 31 January 2035).

If non-depreciating assets are purchased before the crystallisation of the deferred gain, the deferred gain need not be charged and can instead be rolled over against the base cost of the non-depreciating assets.

(c) **Taxation of profits generated overseas**

Lis Co

- If components were sold by Lis Co to Jeg Ltd at an inflated price, a transfer pricing adjustment would be required.
- This is because the transaction would be between Jeg Ltd and a company which it controls and Lis Co would be resident in a non-qualifying territory, ie a territory which does not have a double tax agreement with the UK, such that the regime applies despite Jeg Ltd being a small company.
- Accordingly, the trading profit of Jeg Ltd, the company which would be gaining an advantage as a result of the inflated price, would have to be increased by the excess of the inflated price over the arm's length price. This increase would, in turn, increase the company's corporation tax payable.

Mot Ltd

Rate of corporation tax in the UK on the profits of the business

- UK resident companies are subject to UK corporation tax on their worldwide income.
- The business in Puran would be a permanent establishment (PE) of Mot Ltd as opposed to being a separate legal entity. Accordingly, the profits of the business will be subject to UK corporation tax as part of the profits of Mot Ltd.
- The rate of corporation tax suffered in the UK on the profits generated in Puran would be determined by the level of Mot Ltd's augmented profits and would be between 19% – 25%. Double tax relief would be available to offset the 13% tax suffered in Puran.

Election to exempt the profits of the PE from UK tax

- The advantage of making such an election would be that the profits made in Puran would not be subject to UK corporation tax.

  This would save UK corporation tax (net of the Puran tax as explained above).
- However, it should be recognised that it would no longer be possible to claim capital allowances in the UK in respect of assets purchased for use in the trade carried on in Puran.
- In addition, there would be no relief in the UK in the event of any losses being incurred in the trade in Puran in the future.
- Once made, the election is irrevocable and would apply to all future overseas PEs of Mot Ltd.

  Accordingly, there would be no relief in the UK for any losses incurred in any new overseas PEs operated by Mot Ltd.

(d) **Value added tax (VAT)**

Group VAT registration

- A company can be a member of the Jeg Ltd group VAT registration if:
  - it is controlled by Jeg Ltd (ie Jeg Ltd owns more than 50% of the company's ordinary share capital); and
  - it is established in the UK (eg its headquarters are in the UK) or it has a fixed establishment in the UK (eg it has a genuine trading presence in the UK).

  Accordingly, Kod Ltd could be included within a group VAT registration, whereas Mot Ltd could not unless it satisfies the second condition above.
- Possible disadvantages
  - The members of a group VAT registration are jointly and severally liable for the group's VAT liability.

    Accordingly, the inclusion in the group of Kod Ltd must be considered particularly carefully due to its financial problems.
- It will be necessary to obtain and collate information from the subsidiary companies in order to prepare a single VAT return, which may cause administrative difficulties.

Purchase of components from Lis Co

- Jeg Ltd will be able to use postponed VAT accounting. This means that input VAT at the standard rate on the goods imported will be accounted for on the next VAT return after the goods are imported.
- On this same VAT return Jeg Ltd will be able to reclaim the input VAT on the imported components thus giving a nil cash effect.
- Alternatively, Jeg Ltd could further delay accounting for the VAT by use of either the duty deferment scheme or by use of a bonded warehouse.

(e) **Hale's financial position for the tax year 2025/26**

Cash income after tax

	£
Salary	87,800
Dividend income	18,300
Total cash income	106,100
Income tax liability (W)	48,495
Class 1 national insurance contributions (NIC) liability (W)	3,767
Total tax	52,262
Cash income after tax (£106,100 – £52,262)	53,838

Summary of the situation

Hale's annual personal expenditure exceeds his cash income after tax by £3,762 (£57,600 – £53,838)

The tax payable by Hale in the tax year 2025/26 will be approximately half (£52,262/£106,100 = 49.3%) of the income he receives in cash. This is due to the significant non-cash benefits which he receives.

Tutorial note. Credit was also available to candidates who identified that on the assumption that Hale will not receive further shares in Jeg Ltd, his tax bill for the tax year 2026/27 will be reduced by £3,520 ((£8,800 x 40%).

Working

Income tax and class 1 NIC liability

	£
Salary	87,800
Benefits	26,230
Shares in Jeg Ltd (£23,200 – £14,400)	8,800
Employment income	122,830
Dividend income	18,300
Total income	141,130
Less: personal allowance	(0)
Taxable income	141,130
Employment income	
– £37,700 × 20%	7,540
– £85,130 (£122,830 – £37,700) × 40%	34,052
Dividend income	
– £500 × 0%	0
– £1,810 (£124,140 – £122,830 – £500) × 33.75%	611
– £15,990 (£18,300 – £500 – £1,810) × 39.35%	6,292
Income tax liability	48,495
£37,700 (£50,270 – £12,570) × 8%	3,016
£37,530 (£87,800 – £50,270) × 2%	751
Class 1 NIC liability	3,767

Tutorial note. The shares in Jeg Ltd are not readily convertible assets, such that they will not result in a liability to class 1 NIC.

ANSWERS

Here's how you could have answered this part using the CBE software:

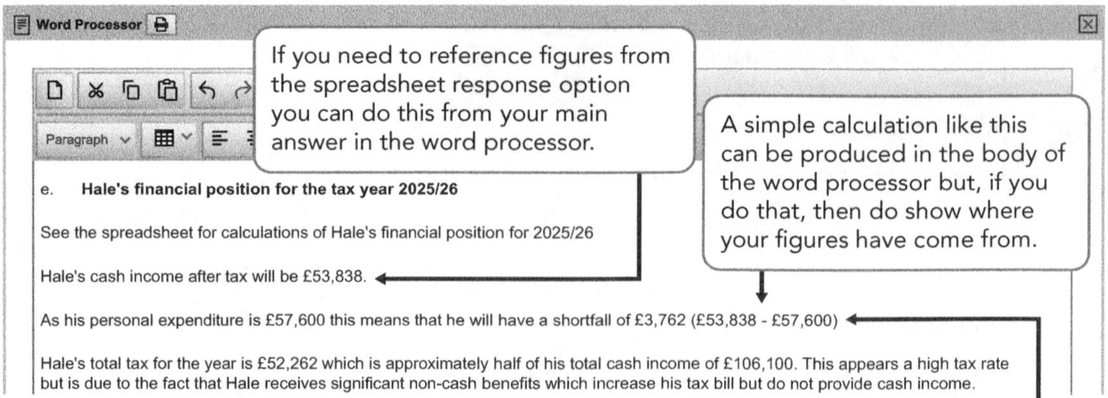

e. **Hale's financial position for the tax year 2025/26**

See the spreadsheet for calculations of Hale's financial position for 2025/26

Hale's cash income after tax will be £53,838.

As his personal expenditure is £57,600 this means that he will have a shortfall of £3,762 (£53,838 - £57,600)

Hale's total tax for the year is £52,262 which is approximately half of his total cash income of £106,100. This appears a high tax rate but is due to the fact that Hale receives significant non-cash benefits which increase his tax bill but do not provide cash income.

If you need to reference figures from the spreadsheet response option you can do this from your main answer in the word processor.

A simple calculation like this can be produced in the body of the word processor but, if you do that, then do show where your figures have come from.

As well as the calculations you are asked to explain why despite receiving substantial UK source income that he's short of cash and to summarise your findings. Make sure you do this as well as the numbers!

You could have also prepared the calculation of the shortfall of £3,762 in the spreadsheet response option (it would have saved you using a calculator). If you do this then just make sure that you do give the figures, explanation and summary in the main body of your note to client files.

Click on 'format' and 'cells'. Then select 'number' and 'currency.' You can then select £ and the negative style and your answers will display correctly rounded to the nearest £. (Click apply) Alternately, select 'number' which won't give you a '£' before each figure and use a '£' column header – either approach is acceptable.

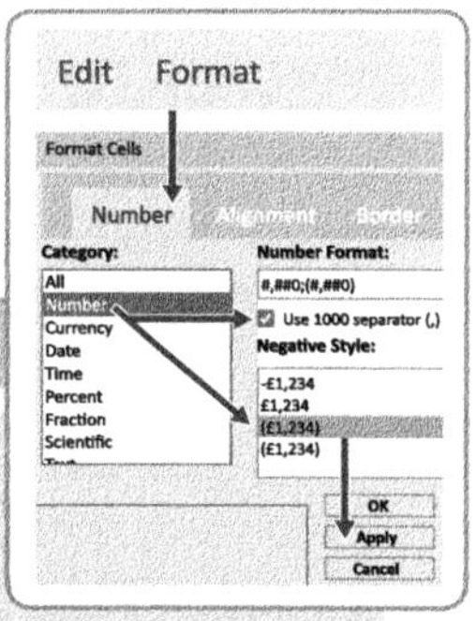

Spreadsheet

Edit Format

If you realise you don't have enough room you can't insert rows/ columns. However, you can copy and paste to move entries down/ right to be able to make more space if you need to.

Make sure you use the 'sum' formula to provide effective calculations.

	A	B	C	D	E	F
3	**Cash income after tax**					
4						
5	Salary	£87,800				
6	Dividend income	£18,300				
7	Total cash income	£106,100	=SUM(B5:B6)			
8	Less income tax (W1)	(£48,495)	=-B28			
9	Less NIC (W2)	(£3,767)				
10	**Cash income after tax**	£52,262				
11						
12						
13	**(W1) Income tax**			**(W2) NIC**		
14						
15	Salary	£87,800		Class 1 employee NIC		
16	Benefits	£26,230		(£50,270-£12,570)@8%	£3,016	
17	Shares in Jeg Ltd	£8,800		(£87,800-£50,270)@2%	£751	
18	Employment income	£122,830			£3,767	
19	Dividend income	£18,300				
20	Total income	£141,130				
21	Less PA (none)	£0				
22	Taxable income	£141,130				
23						
24	NSI 37700@20%	£7,540				
25	Balance @ 40%	£34,052	=(B18-37700)*.4			
26	DI: 500@0%	£0				
27	1810 @ 33.75%	£611				
28	Balance @39.35%	£6,292				
29	IT liability	£48,495				
30						

Cross reference cells through so that later corrections will automatically flow through your answer. Show the reference to the working (W1)

Again- look at the effective use of the formula to calculate the income tax. The marker can 'see inside the cell' and so you don't need to show full workings.

You can use 'format', 'cells' and then 'border' to access the menus to underline cells to show sub-totals

Videos can be viewed online by accessing your ebook version on VitalSource.

ANSWERS

Section B questions

Personal tax

13 Kesme and Soba

Course Book references

Property income is covered in Chapter 5 and taxable income in Chapter 2. Employment income is the subject of Chapter 4. Overseas aspects of income tax are covered in Chapter 9. Further aspects of the death estate for inheritance tax (IHT) are covered in Chapter 11. Overseas aspects of IHT are covered in Chapter 12.

Top tips

In part (b), make sure that you deal with the implications of the remittance basis for both Kesme and Soba.

Easy marks

There were easy marks in part (a) for a basic computation of taxable income.

ACCA examining team's comments

Part (a) required an explanation of the availability and operation of rent-a-room relief together with a calculation of an individual's taxable income. The basics of rent-a-room relief were reasonably well known by many candidates. However, a minority thought that the £3,750 could be deducted in addition to expenses incurred as opposed to instead of those expenses. Also, many candidates neglected to divide the £7,500 between the two owners of the property. Very few candidates mentioned the need to make an election for the relief to apply. The calculation of the individual's taxable income was done well by the majority of candidates.

Part (c) concerned inheritance tax and was done reasonably well. The difficulty was that most candidates wanted to calculate an inheritance tax liability when what was required was a calculation of the residue. The residue was calculated by deducting the legacy to the daughter and the inheritance tax liability from the estate. So a calculation of the inheritance tax liability was a necessary step on the way but was not an end in itself. The calculation of the inheritance tax liability also required the gift to the daughter to be grossed up because the residue of the estate was exempt. Very few candidates identified this point but it was possible to score a very good mark without it.

There are no Examining team's comments in relation to parts (b) and (d) as these requirements come from an earlier ATX–UK specimen exam and, as such, no comments are available.

Marking guide		Marks
(a) Rent a room relief		
– Availability	1	
– Operation	1.5	
– Claim	1.5	
Employment income	1	
Property business income	0.5	
Share options	3	
Personal allowance	0.5	
Marks Available	9	
Maximum		8

Marking guide		Marks
(b) Availability of remittance basis	1.5	
Kesme	3	
Soba	3	
Marks Available	7.5	
Maximum		6
(c) Value of residue of estate		
– Calculation of amount received by Soba	2	
– Inheritance tax liability	2	
Marks Available	4	
Maximum		4
(d) Spouse exemption available to Soba		
– No limit if both Kesme and Soba non-UK domiciled	1	
– Restriction if Soba UK domiciled	1	
Marks Available	2	
Maximum		2

Professional skills marks

Analysis and evaluation

- Appropriate use of information in the scenario to analyse the income tax implications regarding the shares in part (a)
- Appropriate use of information in the scenario to conclude on whether the remittance basis would be beneficial in part (b)
- Adoption of a logical approach to prepare the calculation of the residue of the estate in (c)

Commercial acumen

- Recognition of the implications of rent a room relief on Kesme and Soba's table property income in (a)
- Recognition that Soba as the residuary legatee will need to bear the IHT on the gift to the daughter
- Recognition that despite Kesme being non-domiciled that the UK plot of land will be liable to UK IHT as a UK asset in (c)

Maximum	5
Total	25

(a) **Income tax**

Availability and operation of rent a room relief

Rent a room relief is relevant because Kesme and Soba are letting furnished rooms in their main residence. The limit for each of them is £7,500/2 = £3,750.

Since gross rents exceed the limit, Kesme and Soba would be taxed under the normal property business income rules unless they elect for the 'alternative basis'. If they so elect, they will each be taxable on gross receipts less £3,750, with no deductions for expenses.

An election for the alternative basis must be made by 31 January 2027 (22 months after the end of the tax year 2024/25). The election will then continue to apply until it is withdrawn.

> **Tutorial note.** The election would also cease to apply in the unlikely event that the gross annual rent fell below £7,500.

ANSWERS

Taxable income for the tax year 2024/25

	£
Salary and benefits	48,500
Pension from former employer	24,100
Property business income £((17,650/2) – 3,750)	5,075
Shares acquired ((400 × £12) – £2,500)	2,300
Grant of non-tax advantaged share options – no tax on grant	0
Exercise of non-tax advantaged options (250 × £(12 – 0.5 – 3))	2,125
Net income	82,100
Less personal allowance	(12,570)
Taxable income	69,530

(b) **The remittance basis**

The remittance basis is available to UK resident individuals who are neither domiciled nor deemed domiciled in the UK. Accordingly, it is available to both Kesme and Soba (neither spouse will have yet been UK resident for at least 15 of the 20 years immediately preceding 2025/26).

Kesme will have unremitted overseas income of less than £2,000. Accordingly, the remittance basis will apply automatically, such that there will be no loss of his personal allowance, and the unremitted income will not be subject to income tax in the UK. There will also be no remittance basis charge. This is clearly beneficial for Kesme, as the income will also not be subject to tax in the country of Penne.

Soba will have unremitted overseas income of more than £2,000, such that the remittance basis will not apply automatically. In addition, because she has been resident in the UK for 12 of the 14 tax years prior to 2025/26, if Soba were able to claim the remittance basis there would be a remittance basis charge of £60,000 as well as the loss of her personal allowance. This is clearly not beneficial for Soba as it exceeds the amount of income which she would be sheltering from UK tax.

(c) **Soba**

Value of the residue of the estate

Soba will receive the residue of the estate, ie the estate less the gift to the daughter and the inheritance tax on that gift.

	£
Kesme's estate	1,280,000
Less: gross legacy to daughter (W)	(400,000)
Residue of estate received by Soba	880,000

Working

Gross legacy to daughter

	£
£325,000 × 0%	0
£45,000 × 40/60	30,000
£370,000	30,000
Gross legacy £(370,000 + 30,000)	400,000

Tutorial note. Note the following:

(1) Although Kesme is non-UK domiciled, the specific legacy to his daughter will be chargeable to UK IHT because it is a UK asset.

(2) The residence nil rate band does not apply because Kesme's share of the main residence passes to his spouse Soba.

(3) The inheritance tax due on the specific gift to the daughter will be paid out of the residue of the estate, such that it will be borne by Soba. Because the residue of the estate is exempt, due to the spouse exemption, the gift must be grossed up.

(4) **Proof of Kesme's IHT liability**

	£
Kesme's estate	1,280,000
Less: Legacy to Soba (part (c)) (spouse exemption)	(880,000)
Chargeable estate	400,000
£325,000 × 0%	0
£75,000 × 40%	30,000
£400,000	30,000

(d) **The spouse exemption available to Soba**

There is no limit on the 100% spouse exemption available to Soba where both Soba and Kesme are non-UK domiciled. However, if Soba were domiciled in the UK, the 100% spouse exemption in respect of transfers from her to Kesme would be restricted to the first £325,000 of total assets transferred.

14 Jessica

Course Book references

Redundancy packages and taxable benefits are covered in Chapter 4. Partnerships and losses dealt with in Chapter 15. Pension contributions are to be found in Chapter 3.

Top tips

In part (b), the ACCA examining team have helpfully split the requirement into two sub-parts. You are required to state the available loss reliefs in (i) and then apply them in (ii).

Easy marks

There were some easy marks in part (a) for dealing with the rules on termination payments as this is a frequently tested topic.

ACCA examining team's comments

This question concerned the receipt of a redundancy package on leaving employment, the reliefs available for an individual's share of a partnership trading loss, and the payment of contributions into a personal pension scheme.

The first part concerned the income tax implications of the receipt of a redundancy package comprising a statutory redundancy payment, an ex-gratia payment, and retention of a company provided laptop computer. Most candidates were clearly very comfortable with the availability of the £30,000 exemption. The majority of candidates included the laptop computer in their calculation, but did not know how to calculate its value, being an asset transferred to an employee who has previously been taxed on the provision of the benefit under the '20% × market value rule'. Termination payments are regularly tested in Advanced Taxation (ATX–UK), and should provide an opportunity for candidates to score well if they have practised these, and taken note of what has been required in previous model answers. [Note that this question has been amended since originally set to incorporate the NIC implications of redundancy payments which were not examinable when this question was originally set.]

The second part of this question required candidates to state the loss reliefs available to a partner who has just joined a loss making partnership. On the whole, candidates scored well on this part. The main issue seen was a lack of accuracy in identifying the available reliefs. The rules relating to trading losses are frequently examined, and candidates are expected to be precise in this sort of question. Candidates would do well to invest time at the revision stage of their studies memorising the rules concerning relief for trading losses, and ensuring that they are able to recognise those rules which apply in a given scenario. In particular, they should be able to identify those which apply in certain situations only, such as the opening years of a business, as here. It was disappointing to see that a number of candidates included consideration of the relief available by carrying the loss forward, when the requirement had specifically stated that the taxpayer did not want to do this. This wasted time, particularly if the candidate then went on to consider the tax savings in the next part.

The third part of the question required a calculation of the loss available to the partner, and determination of the loss relief strategy which would provide the highest income tax saving for the taxpayer.

Those candidates who scored well on this particular part:

- adopted a structured, methodical approach to considering in turn each of the reliefs for the trading loss which they had identified in the previous part, stating the taxpayer's total income in each year, and hence being able to identify the rate of tax which would be saved.
- didn't waste time considering irrelevant reliefs.

In order to gain a good mark in this type of question it is vital that candidates attempt past exam questions. Reading through model answers, while providing useful information, is often of limited help in these cases; candidates need to practise the structured approach necessary to produce a good, coherent answer.

The final part of the question concerned an explanation and calculation of the maximum amount of contributions which could be paid into the taxpayer's personal pension scheme without incurring an annual allowance charge. The majority of candidates were aware of the £60,000 allowance and the ability to bring forward unused allowances. However, a significant number failed to relate their knowledge to the scenario, bringing forward several years' worth of unused allowance, despite the fact that the taxpayer had not previously been in any pension scheme, and spending a considerable amount of time calculating whether or not the maximum amount of allowance would be restricted, when a quick calculation would have revealed that the taxpayer's income fell well below the income limits. In Advanced Taxation (ATX–UK), general rules are rarely required; candidates will invariably be asked to apply rules to a given scenario, so they must ensure they have taken this into consideration at every stage of their answer, to avoid wasting time.

Marking guide		Marks	
(a)	Cash amounts received	2.5	
	Laptop computer	2	
	NICs	1.5	
	Marks Available	6	
	Maximum		5
(b) (i)	Options for relief of Jessica's share of the partnership loss	3	
	Marks Available	3	
			3
(ii)	Relief in 2025/26	1.5	
	Relief in 2024/25	3	
	Relief in 2022/23	2.5	
	Conclusion	.5	
	Marks Available	7.5	
	Maximum		7
(c)	Maximum contribution 2025/26	2.5	
	Maximum contribution 2026/27	4	
	Marks Available	6.5	
	Maximum		5

Professional skills marks

Analysis and evaluation

- Appropriate use of data to determine suitable calculations of the amounts liable to income tax on Jessica in relation to the redundancy package
- Appropriate use of data to support discussion and draw appropriate conclusions regarding the maximum pension contributions possible without incurring an annual allowance charge
- Demonstration of ability to consider relevant factors applicable to each element of the redundancy package
- Use of information to support impact of loss relief options by reference to Jessica's tax status
- Demonstration of ability to consider all relevant taxes specified in the requirements (both income tax and NIC in relation to the redundancy package

Commercial acumen

- Recognition of constraints and opportunities related to choice of trading loss relief, for example, recognising that Jessica does not want to carry the loss forward, and carrying the loss back three years under early year relief results in the highest tax saving as the personal allowance is re-instated
- Practical considerations relating to the context relating to the amount of unused annual allowance available to bring forward, and Jessica's relevant earnings in each year.

Maximum	5
Total	25

(a) **Income tax implications of the redundancy package**

The one month payment in lieu of notice of £12,250 (£147,000/12) will be taxable on Jessica as normal employment income and class 1 employee and employer NIC will be due thereon. The statutory redundancy payment, the non-contractual *ex gratia* payment and the gift of the laptop are all taxable but the first £30,000 of their total value is exempt, the excess being taxable as specific employment income.

The cash equivalent of the gift is the higher of:

(1) the market value at 31 March 2025 ie £540; and

(2) the value of the laptop computer at the date it was first provided to Jessica, less the amounts subsequently taxed on her as a benefit, ie £680 (£850 – £170 (20% × £850)).

The total taxable amount of the package is therefore £20,680 £((18,000 + 32,000 + £680) – 30,000)). The package is taxed as the top slice of Jessica's income for the tax year 2024/25. Class 1A NICs will be due on the £20,680 so only Berens Ltd will suffer NIC.

(b) (i) **Reliefs available for Jessica's share of the partnership loss**

The 2025/26 trading loss can be relieved against Jessica's total income for 2025/26, the tax year of the loss, and/or 2024/25, the previous tax year. Alternatively, because the loss has arisen in one of the first four tax years in which Jessica will be a partner, it can be relieved against her total income of the three years prior to the year of the loss starting with the earliest year (ie 2022/23).

(ii) **Strategy for loss relief to maximise Jessica's income tax savings**

In 2025/26, Jessica's only source of income will be rental income of £6,000. As this will be covered by her personal allowance, relieving the loss in this year will not result in any tax saving.

In 2024/25, Jessica's taxable income before loss relief will be £186,100 (£147,000 + £6,000 + £170 + £12,250 + £20,680).

As Jessica is an additional rate taxpayer, the loss of £48,000 will generate a tax saving of £21,600 (£48,000 × 45%)

If, alternatively, Jessica carries the loss back to 2022/23 it will be relieved against her total income of that year of £147,000. As the resulting total income of £99,000 (£147,000 – £48,000) is below £100,000, the personal allowance will become available. Accordingly, the total income tax saving will be £25,321 ((£147,000 – £125,140) × 45% + ((£48,000 – £21,860) × 40%) + (£12,570 × 40%)).

Therefore the most beneficial claim is to carry back the loss and offset it in 2022/23 as this results in the highest tax saving, of £25,321.

(c) **Jessica – maximum pension contributions 2025/26 and 2026/27**

The maximum gross contribution which Jessica can make attracting tax relief each tax year is the higher of

(1) Jessica's relevant earnings in the tax year; and

(2) the basic amount of £3,600.

Jessica has no relevant earnings in the tax year 2025/26 as the Langley Partnership has made a loss in that year, and she has no other source of earned income. So the maximum contribution she can make in 2025/26 is £3,600.

In 2026/27, Jessica has relevant earnings of £122,000 (£305,000 × 40%) comprising her share of the partnership profit for the year ending 31 March 2027. Accordingly, she can make a contribution into the scheme of up to £122,000. This exceeds the annual allowance available of £60,000, but as she was a member of a registered pension scheme in 2025/26 she can bring forward her unused allowance from that tax year of £56,400 (£60,000 – £3,600).

Therefore the total amount of annual allowance available is £116,400 (£60,000 + £56,400), so this is the maximum (gross) contribution which Jessica can pay without incurring an annual allowance charge.

Tutorial note. No unused relief can be brought forward from years prior to 2025/26 as Jessica was not a member of a registered pension scheme until 1 May 2025.

15 Demeter

Course Book references

Employment income is the subject of Chapter 4. Capital gains tax reliefs are found in Chapter 8. Pensions are covered in Chapter 3.

Top tips

In part (b) use a table to show the exempt periods for private residence relief (PRR). Don't forget letting relief!

Easy marks

Part (a) should have been easy marks, but you needed to know the detailed rules in order to obtain them.

ACCA examining team's comments

Part (a) asked candidates to consider the extent to which an inducement package and relocation expenses would be taxable. Most candidates knew that the inducement package would be taxable but were not able to explain the reason why. Similarly most candidates knew that there was a relocation allowance of £8,000 but did not know the rules for qualifying relocation expenditure.

Part (b) required candidates to calculate and briefly explain the relief(s) available upon sale of a residence, which had been partially let to tenants. Many candidates were aware of the availability of private residence relief (PRR) in the scenario but made some mistakes in their calculations of the relief. Candidates should have known that periods of occupation are completely exempt and that the last 9 months are treated as 100% occupation and therefore exempt. Any remaining gain after private residence relief was eligible for letting relief although this proved to be a less well-known relief. Letting relief is restricted to the lowest of the following three values:

- The amount of the gain which is exempt under PRR
- The gain attributable to letting
- £40,000.

This is not a particularly tricky subject area and candidates should have been able to identify these points from the question.

Part (c)(i) considered the implications of an employer's contribution to an occupational pension scheme, when the employee is already making annual contributions to a personal pension scheme equal to the annual allowance. There was a general awareness of the rules in this area such as the £40,000 allowance but a lack of precision in relation to the detailed calculations required. The final part of the question, part (c)(ii), concerned the tax implications of a non tax-advantaged share option scheme, from option grant through to exercise and disposal. Candidates should have been able to identify the following tax points from the facts of the question:

- No income tax payable on grant of the options
- Income tax payable on exercise of the options
- No gain on sale of the shares because it immediately follows the exercise of the options and the shares will not have increased in value.

This part was not done particularly well since candidates did not have a sufficiently precise knowledge of the rules concerning a non tax-advantaged share option plan.

Marking guide

			Marks	
(a)	One-off lump sum payment		2	
	Financial assistance with relocation		3.5	
	Marks Available		5.5	
	Maximum			5
(b)	Private residence relief		4	
	Letting relief		3	
	Marks Available		7	
	Maximum			6
(c)	(i)	Poseidon Ltd's contributions	1.5	
		Annual allowance charge	4.5	
		Marks Available	6	
		Maximum		5
	(ii)	Grant of options	1	
		Exercise of options	2	
		Sale of shares	1	
		Consideration of impact on personal allowance/annual allowance charge	1	
		Marks Available	5	
		Maximum		4

Professional skills marks

Analysis and evaluation

- Appropriate use of data to support discussion and draw appropriate conclusions regarding the extent to which the lump sum inducement payment and relocation package would give rise to taxable employment income
- Appropriate use of data to determine suitable calculations of the reliefs available to Demeter to reduce his chargeable gain on the sale of his house in Manchester
- Demonstration of ability to consider relevant factors applicable to Demeter's situation to identify the reliefs available to Demeter to reduce the gain on the sale of his house in Manchester
- Use of information to determine the tax consequences for Demeter of participating in the non tax-advantaged share option scheme

Commercial acumen

- Effective use of calculations relating to the context to illustrate points being made relating to the tax consequences for Demeter of participating in the occupational pension scheme

Maximum	5
Total	25

(a) **Receipt of the one-off lump sum inducement payment and relocation package**

The one-off lump sum inducement payment of £20,000 paid on commencement of Demeter's employment is fully taxable as it wholly relates to future services to be performed by Demeter.

The total amount received by Demeter in relation to his relocation is £11,000 (£5,000 + (£1,500 × 4)). Demeter did not previously live within a reasonable daily travelling distance of his new employment, so is eligible for a maximum tax allowable amount of £8,000, provided he has spent at least this amount on qualifying expenditure.

Demeter's qualifying expenditure comprises all the costs relating to his move, including the estate agent fees on the sale of his house of £2,800, and the rent on his accommodation in London of £1,700 per month from 1 December 2025 until he purchases a new house on 1 April 2026. His total qualifying expenditure is therefore £12,800 (£6,000 + (£1,700 × 4)). This clearly exceeds £8,000, so the taxable amount of Demeter's relocation package is £3,000 (£11,000 – £8,000).

(b) **Reliefs available to Demeter to reduce the chargeable gain on the sale of his house in Manchester**

As the house was Demeter's only residence, private residence relief (PRR) will be available to exempt the proportion of the gain which relates to his actual or deemed occupation of the property. The relief is calculated as follows.

Demeter owned the house for 12.75 years (1 February 2013 to 31 October 2025).

Availability of PRR:

		Exempt years
1 February 2013 to 31 January 2015	100% occupation	2
1 February 2015 to 31 January 2025	70% occupation (10 years × 70%)	7
1 February 2025 to 31 October 2025	Last 9 months treated as 100% occupation	0.75
Total exempt years		9.75

The PRR will exempt £71,882 (£94,000 × 9.75/12.75) of the gain. The remainder of the gain, ie £22,118 (£94,000 × 3/12.75), is attributable to the let part of the property.

Letting relief provides an extension to the PRR exemption in relation to the gain arising on the part of Demeter's house which was let. The additional exemption is restricted to the lowest of:

(1) The amount of the gain which is exempt under the PRR exemption (£71,882).

(2) The gain attributable to the letting (£22,118).

(3) £40,000.

Therefore, the letting relief available is £22,118.

(c) (i) **Tax consequences for Demeter of participating in Poseidon Ltd's approved occupational pension scheme in 2026/27**

Poseidon Ltd's contribution into its occupational pension scheme on Demeter's behalf of £22,000 (10% x £220,000) will be an exempt benefit for Demeter, so no tax liability will arise on this.

However, the contributions will count towards Demeter's annual allowance. This will remain at £60,000 as Demeter's threshold income of £160,000 (net income (£220,000) less Demeter's personal pension contributions (£60,000)) does not exceed the £200,000 threshold.

Demeter has no unused annual allowance to bring forward from earlier tax years as he has made contributions up to the maximum amount each year. As the total contributions in 2026/27 of £82,000 (£22,000 + £60,000) will exceed the annual allowance, an annual allowance charge will be payable. Accordingly, as an additional rate taxpayer Demeter will pay an annual allowance charge of £9,900 (45% × £22,000 (£82,000 – £60,000)).

Tutorial note. There is no need to calculate Demeter's adjusted income as the amount of annual allowance will not be reduced regardless because his threshold income is below £200,000.

(ii) **Tax consequences for Demeter of participating in Poseidon Ltd's non tax-advantaged share option scheme**

No income tax will be payable by Demeter on the grant of the options on 30 November 2025.

When Demeter exercises the options on 6 April 2031, income tax will be payable on the excess of the market value of the shares at the date of exercise over the price paid by Demeter, ie £6,030 ((£6.00 – (£4.20 × 95%) × 3,000). The income tax payable is therefore £2,714 (£6,030 × 45%).

The exercise of the shares has no impact on Demeter's personal allowance because his personal allowance was already fully abated. There will also be no impact on Demeter's annual allowance charge because his threshold income remains below £200,000.

As Demeter will sell the shares immediately following the exercise of the options, the shares will not have increased in value and so no chargeable gain will arise.

Videos can be viewed online by accessing your ebook version on VitalSource.

16 Pedro

Course Book references

Inheritance tax is covered in Chapters 11 and 12 with gifts with reservation of benefit within Chapter 12. Property businesses are covered in Chapter 5.

Top tips

As usual, make sure you break down your time in this question across the three smaller sub-requirements. Part (c) is the longest and trickiest part so make sure you leave it until last.

In part (a) make sure you start with the basics. The gift would be a PET and so there is no life tax and only death tax if Marina dies within 7 years of the gift. Then, go on to discuss how we have to change this treatment because Marina continues to benefit from occupying the cottage rent-free.

Part (c) needs a logical approach to the large pension contribution. Start, by checking whether Pedro will get relief on the full £85,000 contribution- does he have sufficient relevant earnings? Once you know the size of the tax relievable contribution you can extend his bands of tax. When preparing his income tax computation and deciding whether to taper the personal allowance remember to deduct the tax relievable pension contribution in calculating his adjusted net income. Once you've calculated Pedro's income tax on his taxable income you need to compare total gross contributions by everyone into the pension scheme with the annual allowance available to determine whether an annual allowance charge will be due. Finally, don't forget that the question actually asks you to calculate the reduction in Pedro's IT liability due to the pension contribution- so compare your revised tax calculation to the £40,332 given in the question to see the reduction.

Easy marks

The explanation of the IHT consequences of the gift of the cottage should have been the source of some of the easier marks in this question. If you know the rules for calculating property income, the application of these rules to the scenario in part (b) would also have provided easy marks.

ACCA examining team's comments

This question concerned the IHT implications of a gift with reservation, a property business, and a calculation of the impact on an individual's income tax liability of them making a substantial contribution to their personal pension scheme.

The first part of the question required candidates to advise the client of the IHT implications of having received a lifetime gift following the death of the donor. Most candidates recognised that the lifetime gift was a potentially exempt transfer (PET) and also a gift with reservation. Significantly fewer knew the consequences of this as a result of the death of the donor, which was disappointing.

The second part of this question has been amended so the ACCA examining team's comments on the original question are no longer relevant.

The third part of this question was worth ten marks and involved a detailed income tax computation including both occupational and personal pension scheme contributions. There were few very good answers to this question part, although many managed to score half marks. Weaker candidates were clearly very confused about the rules for pension contributions relief and produced some very muddled answers. It appeared that quite a few candidates adopted a 'scattergun' approach, including parts of calculations, presumably as they occurred to them, which proved difficult to follow, and to mark, in some cases. It is important to adopt a logical approach to this sort of question, working through the income tax computation line by line, thinking through one stage at a time. Question practice, once again, is invaluable for this. Additionally, some candidates wasted time by calculating the individual's income tax liability prior to making the personal pension contribution, when this was given in the question. Others wrote a detailed explanation of some of the rules, instead of, or as well as, calculations. The only explanation required was in respect of the amount of personal allowance available to the taxpayer. Other explanations, sadly, didn't score marks.

Marking guide		Marks	
(a)	Gift treated as a PET	1	
	Recognition of gift with reservation	2	
	Implications of gift with reservation	3	
	Marks Available	6	
	Maximum		5
(b)	Calculation of property income	2	
	Mortgage interest	2	
	Furniture	1	
	Marks Available	5	
			5
(c)	**With pension contribution**		
	Total income	2	
	Personal allowance note	3	
	Tax calculation	1	
	Annual allowance charge	4	
	Tax on annual allowance charge	1	
	Impact on tax liability	0.5	
	Marks Available	11.5	
	Maximum		10

Marking guide	Marks
Professional skills marks	
Analysis and evaluation	
• Appropriate use of relevant information to determine that there are two alternative charges to IHT in part (a)	
• Demonstration of ability to consider the availability of the personal allowance in part (c)	
• Adoption of a logical approach to prepare suitable calculations in part (c)	
Commercial acumen	
• Appropriate use of information in the question to identify gift with reservation in part (a)	
• Effective application of the general rules to the specific facts of the scenario in part (b)	
• Recognition of the relevance of the property portfolio in part (a)	
Maximum	5
Total	25

(a) **Inheritance tax (IHT) implications of the gift of the holiday cottage to Pedro**

The gift of the holiday cottage was a potentially exempt transfer (PET), and therefore no tax was payable in Marina's lifetime. Although Marina died more than seven years after making this gift, IHT was payable as a result of her death as the gift constituted a gift with reservation. This is because Marina continued to derive benefit from the use of the holiday cottage following the gift, and she did not pay a market rent for staying in the cottage.

As the reservation was not lifted prior to her death, the IHT payable would have been calculated as the higher of (1) the total IHT payable if the cottage was included in her death estate at its value on death, and (2) the total IHT payable, if the cottage was taxed as a PET made in March 2015. As the latter liability is £nil, due to the date of the PET being more than seven years before Marina's death, the cottage would have been included in Marina's death estate. As the value of her death estate exceeded the nil rate band of £325,000 (as it included a portfolio of properties valued at £670,000), IHT was payable on the estate. The IHT attributable to the cottage, being a gift with reservation, was payable by the recipient of the gift, which, in this case, was Pedro.

(b) As total rental receipts for 2025/26 are less than £150,000, property income will be calculated on a cash basis being rental income received less allowable expenses paid from 6.4.2025 to 5.4.2026. However, an election can be made to use the accruals basis.

The mortgage interest will not be a deductible expense in calculating Pedro's future property income. Instead, tax relief will be available at the basic rate of income tax (20%) in respect of the interest paid on the residential property mortgage. This will be given as a tax credit, deducted from Pedro's income tax liability for the relevant tax year.

There will be no deduction for the cost of the new furniture. However, in the future any cost of replacing furniture will be deductible.

(c) **Reduction in Pedro's income tax liability for the tax year 2025/26 as result of making the planned contribution of £85,000 (gross) to a personal pension scheme**

Income tax liability with the pension contribution

		£
Employment income (£85,000)		85,000
Property income (£14,500 + £22,000)		36,500
Total/net income		121,500
Less: personal allowance (see note below)		(12,570)
Taxable income		108,930
Income tax liability (W1)		
£108,930 × 20%		21,786
Add: pension contribution additional charge (W2)		
£13,770 × 20%	2,754	
£7,230 × 40%	2,892	5,646
£21,000		
Income tax liability		27,432

Payment of the pension contribution leads to a reduction of £12,900 (£40,332 – £27,432) in Pedro's income tax liability for 2025/26.

Personal allowance

The pension contributions which qualify for tax relief cannot exceed Pedro's relevant earnings for the tax year. Pedro's relevant earnings for 2025/26 are £85,000 (employment income of £85,000). The whole of the £85,000 contribution is therefore eligible for tax relief.

Adjusted net income is £36,500 (£121,500 – £85,000), so there is no restriction of the personal allowance.

Workings

1 ***Increase in basic rate band***

The basic rate band threshold is increased to £122,700 (£37,700 + £85,000).

2 ***Annual allowance charge***

	£
Contribution by Pedro (gross)	85,000
Contribution by Loule Ltd to occupational scheme	28,000
Total contributions 2025/26	113,000
Less: annual allowance available	
– 2025/26 (W3)	(60,000)
– 2024/25 (W4)	(32,000)
Annual allowance charge	21,000

ANSWERS

3 ***Annual allowance available 2025/26***

Threshold income

	£
Net income	121,500
Less: pension contributions (gross)	(85,000)
Threshold income	36,500

As Pedro's threshold income does not exceed £200,000, the annual allowance for 2025/26 is not restricted. It is not necessary to calculate Pedro's adjusted income for the year.

4 ***Unused annual allowance brought forward***

The annual allowance brought forward from 2024/25 is £32,000 (£60,000 – £28,000).

The annual allowance is not available to bring forward from 2022/23 or 2023/24 as Pedro was not a member of a pension scheme in those years.

Videos can be viewed online by accessing your ebook version on VitalSource.

17 Caden and Amahle

Course Book references

Capital gains tax calculations are covered in Chapter 7 with inheritance tax administration in Chapter 12. IR35 is covered in Chapter 4 and overseas income in Chapter 9.

Top tips

In part (a)(i) note who Caden is disposing of the chairs to – is that significant? In part (b), note that you are asked to calculate Caden's taxable income not simply his deemed employment income. In part (c) it's important to notice the verbs in the question – you're asked to advise Amahle and then to explain, with supporting calculations. So make sure you're answer contains sufficient written explanation.

Easy marks

Provided you know the deemed employment income calculation, easy marks should be available for applying this in part (b) of the question. And then adding in Caden's actual salary and deducting the personal allowance to get taxable income will also provide easy marks. In part (c) try to make sure you state the basics to gain the easy marks. Amahle is resident and domiciled in the UK, so how will she be taxed? And what happens as she's taxed in Komor too?

ACCA examining team's comments

In part (a)(i) of this question, candidates were required to explain, with supporting calculations, the capital loss arising on the sale of four antique chairs, and how the loss could be relieved. The overall quality of responses to this part of the question was somewhat disappointing. Candidates needed to be aware of the requirement to both explain and calculate. Many went straight for the numbers without providing any form of written comment. As far as the explanation was concerned, it is important to note that because the chairs were being sold to the individual's son, it was a connected party disposal which meant that market value should be used as the sale proceeds. Very few candidates seemed to be aware of this rule and used actual proceeds instead. In addition, since a capital loss arises on a disposal to a connected person, that loss can only be used against gains arising on future disposals to exactly the same person.

When it came to performing the calculations, there appeared to be a certain degree of confusion. The cost of the four chairs to use in the capital loss calculation requires some thought. The four chairs were originally part of a set of six chairs, which were gifted to the individual by his mother when their total market value was £152,000; this figure therefore becomes the cost figure for the six chairs to use in future disposals. Some of this original cost will then have been allocated to the earlier disposal of two of the chairs. This will have been calculated in accordance with the part disposal formula of A/(A+B), and leaving the balance of the £152,000 to be used in the capital loss calculation on the disposal of the remaining four.

Part (a)(ii) involved advice on the availability and effect of the instalment option for the payment of an inheritance tax liability on certain gifts which had now become chargeable to IHT as a result of the death of the donor. Despite the requirement specifically stating that calculations were not required for this part, a significant number of candidates still provided them. It is very important for candidates to highlight such instructions in order to avoid wasting time in terms of doing things which are not required and for which credit cannot therefore be awarded.

Correct answers involved explaining that the instalment option would only be available on the property and not the chairs, and on the basis that the property was still owned at the time of the donor's death. Credit was also awarded for stating that the instalment option would involve 10 equal annual amounts, commencing 6 months from the end of the month of death. But if the property were sold by the recipient within the 10 year period, the remainder of the tax owing would become payable immediately. Many candidates discussed inheritance tax reliefs here which were not relevant to the scenario, such as taper relief; this wasted their time and failed to earn them any marks.

Part (b) involved the calculation of an individual's taxable income for 2025/26 on the basis that the personal services company (IR35) legislation applied to the budgeted fee income received by the company concerned. Although the requirement was to calculate, it is still important on such occasions for the logic behind the underlying calculations to be shown. Markers need to see how answers are derived so that appropriate credit can be awarded, even if the final answer is wrong. This means that each stage of the calculations needs to be shown, with a brief narrative explanation next to each number, so that the marker can follow the candidate's method.

Application of the IR35 legislation involves starting with the fee income of the personal services company from which a standard 5% is then deducted. Any salary already paid to the individual, as well as employer's NICs paid in respect of such salary, can then also be deducted. At this point, once employer's NICs on the remaining amount have been calculated and taken off, the balance that one is left with is the deemed employment income. Many candidates were able to successfully establish this amount. However, the requirement of the question was to calculate the individuals' taxable income for the tax year concerned and many candidates did not go on to work out this figure. This involved preparation of an income tax computation for the tax year. The employment income to be used in this computation was both the salary provided in the question and the 'deemed employment income' calculated above. There was no other income for inclusion since, under the personal service company rules, the dividend received from the company is effectively replaced by the 'deemed employment income'. The final stage was then to deduct the personal allowance in order to give taxable income for the tax year concerned.

Part (c) of the question related to the UK income tax liability arising on interest from an overseas bank account of an individual who was both UK resident and domiciled. The requirement was to advise the individual why the overseas interest will be subject to UK income tax and then to explain, with supporting calculations, why this would not actually result in any UK tax payable. With regard to the first part of the requirement, a UK resident individual is subject to UK income tax on their worldwide income, and because the individual is UK domiciled, the arising basis will always apply. Many candidates wrongly concluded that the remittance basis would be available on this occasion.

The key to answering the next part of the question, as to why no actual UK tax liability would arise on this occasion, was an understanding of how double tax relief (DTR) works. The individual's initial income tax liability will be based on all of their UK and overseas income. However, candidates then needed to explain that DTR would be available based on the lower of

UK tax and overseas tax suffered on the overseas source of income. On this occasion, since the overseas tax exceeded the relevant UK liability, DTR would equal the UK liability meaning that there would be no further tax to pay in the UK. Many candidates failed to draw appropriate conclusions at this point. Extra complexity was added to this question by including personal pension contributions, which impacted on the basic rate band when calculating the UK liability, and remembering to take advantage of the savings nil rate band which meant on this occasion, with the individual being a basic rate taxpayer, that the first £1,000 of the overseas savings income was taxed at the rate of 0%.

Marking guide		Marks	
(a)	(i) Calculation	2	
	Explanation	2.5	
	Marks Available	4.5	
	Maximum		4
	(ii) Availability of instalment option	1.5	
	Effect	3	
	Marks Available	4.5	
	Maximum		3
(b)	Deemed employment payment	3.5	
	Caden – taxable income	1.5	
	Marks Available	5	
			5
(c)	Explanation of liability to UK income tax	2.5	
	Explanation and calculation of UK tax	4	
	Double tax relief	1.5	
	Conclusion	1	
	Marks Available	9	
	Maximum		8

Professional skills marks

Scepticism

- Effective challenge of validity of advice provided by Caden's friend in part (a)

Analysis and Evaluation

- Appropriate use of information in the scenario to determine suitable calculations of the capital loss on the sale of the four antique chairs in part (a)(i)
- Appropriate use of information in the scenario to recognise the restriction on the use of the capital loss in (a)(i)
- Appropriate use of information in the scenario to determine suitable calculations of taxable income in part (b)
- Appropriate use of information in the scenario to explain why no actual income tax will be due on Amahle's overseas interest income in part (c)

Commercial Acumen

- Recognition of the availability of the savings income nil rate band in part (c) and its impact on the income tax due
- Recognition of the double tax relief available in part (c)

Maximum	5
Total	25

(a) (i) **Capital gains tax implications of the sale of the four antique chairs**

As Caden's son is a connected person to Caden, the market value of the chairs at 6 October 2025 will be used as proceeds.

The capital loss on the sale will be calculated as follows:

	£
Market value of the four chairs at 6 October 2025	99,000
Less: cost (working)	(104,711)
Allowable loss	(5,711)

Caden can relieve this loss only against gains arising on further disposals to his son in 2025/26 or future tax years. His friend's advice about using the loss to be able to save tax is therefore only true if Caden makes a disposal at a gain to his son in the future.

Working

	£
Market value of the six chairs at 3 March 2019	152,000
Less: used of disposal of first two chairs £152,000 × (£42,000 / (£42,000 + £93,000))	(47,289)
Cost of remaining four chairs	104,711

Here's a potential answer to this part in the spreadsheet response option. As it includes calculations the spreadsheet is a helpful tool to use.

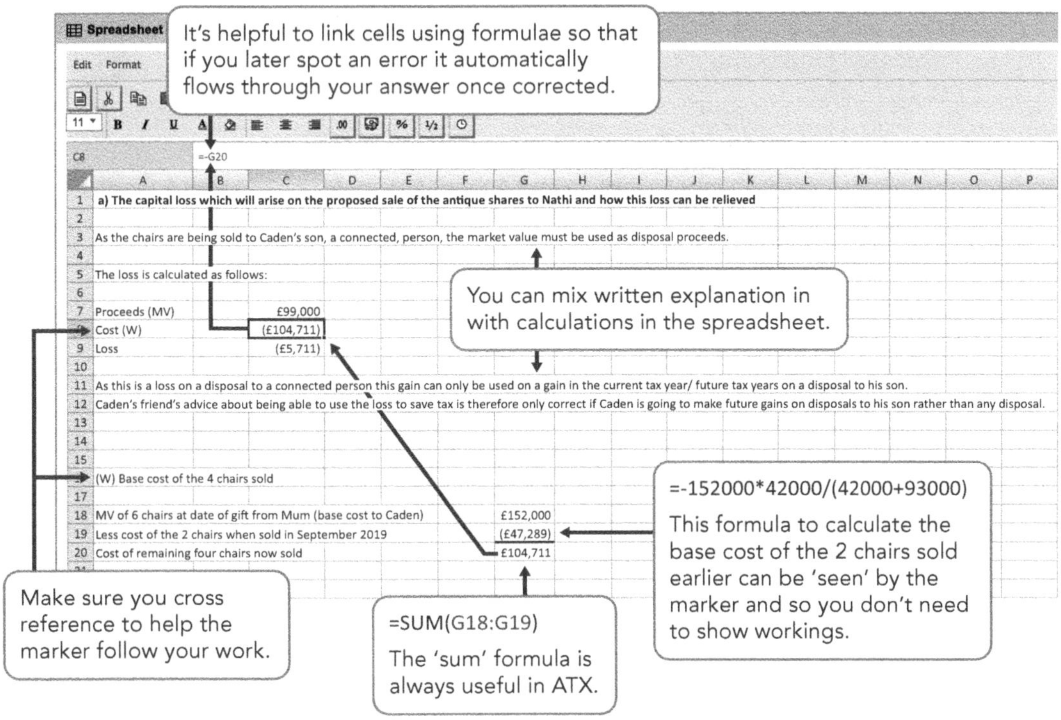

ANSWERS

(ii) **Availability and effect of the instalment option for payment of inheritance tax (IHT)**

Investment property

Land and buildings are qualifying assets for the instalment option for payment of IHT, so this will be available in respect of the IHT liability on the investment property, provided Nathi still owns the property on 20 March 2030, the date of his father's death. The IHT will be payable in ten equal annual instalments, commencing on 30 September 2030. However, if Nathi sells the house within the ten-year instalment period, the outstanding liability will become payable immediately.

Antique chairs

Antique chairs are not qualifying assets for the instalment option.

(b) **Implications of the application of the IR35 legislation for Caden**

Caden

Deemed employment payment:

	£
Budgeted fee income (all from relevant engagements)	65,000
Less: 5% deduction	(3,250)
	61,750
Less: salary (£1,500 × 12)	(18,000)
Employer's NIC ((£18,000 – £9,100) × 13.8%)	(1,228)
	42,522
Less: employer's NIC on deemed payment (£42,522 × 13.8/113.8)	(5,156)
Deemed employment payment	37,366
Total employment income (£18,000 + £37,366)	55,366
Less: personal allowance	(12,570)
Taxable income	42,796

Tutorial note. Note the following:

(1) As Caden is the only employee, and is also a director of Mandini Ltd, the employment allowance of £5,000 will not normally be available to deduct from the employer's NIC payable. However, even if available it cannot be used to reduce the employer's NIC on the deemed payment.

(2) As all the profits of Mandini Ltd are deemed to have been paid to Caden as employment income, the dividends of £35,000 paid to Caden are treated as exempt income in order to avoid a double tax charge.

Here's an example of how you could answer this part of the question in the spreadsheet response option.

Spreadsheet

> Clearly show which requirement you are responding to.

E31 =-.05*E30

	A	E
25		
26	**b) Caden's taxable income for 2025/26 on the basis IR35 applies**	
27		
28	Caden's deemed employment income will be calculated as follows:	
29		
30	Budgeted income from relevant engagements	£65,000
31	Less 5% deduction	(£3,250)
32		£61,750
33	Less salary (£1,500 x 12)	(£18,000)
34	Less employers NIC (£18,000-£9,100)x13.8%)	(£1,228)
35		£42,522
36	Less employer's NIC on deemed salary (£42,522 x 13.8/113.8)	(£5,156)
37	Deemed employment income	£37,366
38		
39	Caden's taxable income is therefore:	
40		
41	Total employment income	£55,366
42	Less personal allowance	(£12,570)
43	Taxable income	£42,796
44		
45		
46		

> Make effective use of the spreadsheet formulae. Here are some that are used in this answer:

- E31: =-.05*E30
- E32: =SUM(E30:E31)
- E33: =-1500*12
- E34: =-(18000-9100)*.138
- E36: =-E35*13.8/113.8
- E41: =18000+E37

> You don't need to show these workings if you don't want to. The marker can 'see inside' the cell to see the formula you have used to award you marks.

> If you can link your cells that is helpful. e.g. the formula for cell E36 references the figure from E35 and the formula for cell E41 references the cell E37.
> This means that if you later correct a figure it should flow through your calculations.

(c) **Interest arising on Amahle's bank account in Komor**

As Amahle is resident in the UK, she will be assessed to UK income tax on her worldwide income, including the interest on the bank account in Komor. The remittance basis is not available to her because she is UK domiciled. Accordingly, she will be assessed on the full amount of interest income arising regardless of whether or not she remits it to the UK.

In the tax year 2025/26, Amahle will make a contribution of £3,000 (net), to her personal pension scheme, so her basic rate band will be extended by £3,750 (£3,000 × 100/80) to £41,450 (£37,700 + £3,750).

Amahle's taxable income of £39,930 (employment income of £45,000 and interest income on the Komor bank account of £7,500 (£150,000 × 5%) less the personal allowance of £12,570) will all fall into her basic rate band. As a basic rate taxpayer, a savings income nil rate band of £1,000 is available to Amahle, so her UK income tax liability in respect of the Komor interest will be £1,300 ((£1,000 × 0%) + (£6,500 × 20%)).

As the interest income will have already been taxed in Komor, double taxation relief (DTR) will be available. This will equal the lower of the UK tax and the overseas tax payable on this income. As the overseas tax payable of £1,350 (£7,500 × 18%) exceeds the UK tax of £1,300, the DTR will equal the UK tax liability. Accordingly, there will be no tax to pay in the UK.

Capital tax

18 Luis

Course Book references

Inheritance tax can be found in Chapter 11 with tax efficient investments in Chapter 3. Tax on interest received is covered in Chapter 2 with tax relief for interest on investment properties covered in Chapter 5.

Top tips

Make sure you spot the 'command verbs' in each requirement to understand whether your answer should be written or calculational (or both). Part (b) of this question contains the most marks so make sure you allocate your time accordingly.

You will need to consider both income tax and CGT in part (b)(i) and in (b)(ii) make sure you answer the full question. You need (1) the relief(s) available, (2) the rate of tax the relief will save and then (3) a conclusion as to which relief will be most tax-advantageous. Remember that method marks will be given, so as long as you provide a conclusion based on your own logic you will be awarded credit.

In part (c)(ii) you need to think clearly about what the question is asking – you'll need to compare the relevant cashflows if Luis does not repay the mortgage (and so continues receiving and paying the interest) to the relevant cashflows if he repays the mortgage (and stops receiving and paying interest. Don't forget the tax consequences of the interest. Then to conclude you need to consider the difference in the relevant cashflows for the two courses of action.

Easy marks

The IHT calculation in part (a) of this question should be a source of straightforward marks. In addition, the explanation of the income tax treatment for the interest in part (c)(i) should also have been straightforward.

ACCA examining team's comments

Part (a)

Part (a) of this question asked for an explanation of the circumstances under which the maximum liability to inheritance tax (IHT) would arise in respect of a lifetime gift, and a calculation of the amount of IHT payable in this case.

The technical content of this part was quite straightforward, and overall candidates scored well. Most were able to cite the basic rules that IHT would be chargeable if Luis died within 7 years of making the gift, and that no taper relief would be available unless he survived for at least 3 years. However, fewer stated that additionally he would need to die within 7 years of making the earlier gift, such that this would use up part of his nil rate band. This gift was frequently included in the subsequent calculation of the IHT liability, but candidates omitted to include it as part of their explanation of the circumstances under which the maximum liability would arise.

The calculative aspects of this part were generally handled well, with the main issue being the omission of annual exemptions in respect of each of the gifts.

It is however important that candidates are not only able to produce good, accurate basic IHT computations, but are also able to provide written explanations where required to address the specific slant of the requirement.

Part (b)

There were two requirements within part (b). The first part asked for the income tax and capital gains tax (CGT) implications of the sale of qualifying enterprise investment scheme (EIS) shares. The sale gave rise to a loss, so the second part then went on to deal with the relief available in respect of this capital loss.

The command word in the first part of the requirement was 'Explain', so although some brief calculations were useful here, the emphasis needed to be on the written explanations. The majority of candidates knew that the immediate income tax implication was that the EIS relief given previously would be withdrawn as the shares had been held for less than three years. However very few were able to go on and explain that, since the sale had resulted in a loss, the relief withdrawn would, on this occasion, be based on 30% of the sale proceeds (as opposed to 30% of the original qualifying cost).

The CGT implications were not dealt with as well. In many cases candidates simply compared cost and sale proceeds to establish the amount of the capital loss. It was apparent that many candidates were struggling with the calculation of a capital loss in this situation, and also with the consequences of having made a claim for EIS reinvestment relief to defer a gain arising on the disposal of a previous asset. CGT reliefs can be quite tricky areas of the syllabus, but one or more are examined in almost every session, so candidates would be well advised to ensure that they do take the time to study all of them in some detail. The consequence of disposing of shares in respect of which reinvestment relief has been claimed, is that the deferred gain will crystallise and become chargeable to CGT in the tax year of the share disposal.

Answers to part (ii) were, in the main, rather imprecise. Candidates referred to relief against 'income' and 'gains' but needed to be more specific in terms of their explanations. The relief was available against general income of the tax years 2024/25 and/or 2023/24, and against chargeable gains of the tax year 2024/25 only.

Candidates are strongly encouraged to practise past exam questions which include explanations of loss reliefs in order to familiarise themselves with the level of specific detail that the ACCA examining team is typically looking for. Very few candidates stated that the relief was available against general income because the shares had qualified for EIS relief. It is not a relief that is otherwise ordinarily available for capital losses.

Many candidates did not address the final two parts of this requirement. This involved a discussion of the rate of tax savings in respect of each relief. The question stated that Luis was an additional rate taxpayer in 2023/24, and a higher rate taxpayer in 2024/25, so those who attempted this were able to deduce that the income tax saving in 2023/24 would be at the rate of 45%, and in 2024/25 at the rate of 40%. The gain on the residential property would be taxed at 24%. Those who did consider rates of tax were generally then able to go on and provide sensible advice to Luis regarding the most tax-advantageous relief. The command word here was 'advise' which meant that candidates had to consider and summarise the different options, and then go on to reach a conclusion. In situations such as this, there will always be credit available for a sensible conclusion/advice, based on the information the candidate has provided in their answer – it is therefore always advisable to attempt such parts, rather than leave them out completely.

Part (c)

Part (c) was also a two-part question. In the first part candidates were required to explain the tax treatment of both interest received on an investment, and interest payable on a residential mortgage. Most candidates had no problem with the interest received, identifying the availability of the £500 savings nil rate band, as Luis was a higher rate taxpayer in 2024/25. However, a fair number were not aware of the rules in relation to tax relief on mortgage interest, and said it was an allowable expense against income, rather than a tax reducer at the rate of 20%. The command word here was 'Explain'. It was therefore insufficient just to provide calculations, without any attempt at written explanation.

In the second part, many candidates were able to produce some form of computation, but unfortunately this did not always take into account the specific figure that was needed in order to address the requirement. The question asked for a calculation of the after-tax net interest saving from repayment of the mortgage. Candidates had to include four relevant figures here in order to derive this: the interest paid on the mortgage, which would be saved;

the tax relief on the mortgage interest which would be foregone; the interest received on the investment, which would also be foregone; and the tax payable in respect of the interest received, which would be saved.

Although the requirement here was simply to 'calculate', candidates should still ensure that they do clearly label their figures. Otherwise, it is not always clear to markers what the various figures represent, particularly if there are no accompanying workings. For any figure that does have to be calculated, workings should always be provided, either on the face of the answer or embedded in the relevant cell, so that markers are able to see what has been done, and award credit accordingly.

Marking guide

			Marks	
(a)	PET/death within seven years		1	
	Circumstances for maximum liability		3	
	Calculation of amount payable		3	
	Marks Available		7	
	Maximum			5
(b)	(i)	Withdrawal of EIS income tax relief	2.5	
		Capital gains tax implications	3.5	
		Marks Available	6	
		Maximum		5
	(ii)	Offset of loss	4.5	
		Marks Available	4.5	
		Maximum		4
(c)	(i)	Interest received – explanation	1	
		Interest paid – explanation	2	
		Marks Available	3	
				3
	(ii)	If mortgage not repaid – calculation	2	
		If mortgage repaid – calculation	1	
		Saving	0.5	
		Marks Available	3.5	
		Maximum		3

Professional skills marks

Analysis and Evaluation

- Appropriate use of information in the scenario to determine suitable calculations of the maximum IHT in part (a)
- Ability to evaluate information objectively to make a recommendation as to the most tax advantageous relief available in (b)(ii)
- Demonstration of ability to consider all relevant taxes specified in the requirements (eg both income tax and CGT in part (b)(ii))
- Adoption of a logical approach to prepare suitable calculations of the after-tax net interest saving in part (c)(ii)

Marking guide	Marks
Commercial Acumen	
• Recognition of the importance of timing with regard to the EIS share disposal in part (b)	
Scepticism	
• Acknowledgement of the uncertainties which exist concerning the potential dates of Luis' death and its impact on the maximum IHT payable	
Maximum	5
Total	25

(a) The answer could be effectively presented in the CBE spreadsheet response option like this:

Spreadsheet

Edit Format

100% 11

C12 =C11 *0.4

	A	B	C
1	**Circumstances which will give rise to the maximum inheritance tax (IHT) liability** The gift of Ivy Cottage to Silvia will be a potentially exempt transfer (PET) which will become chargeable to IHT if Luis dies within seven years of making this gift ie before 31 July 2032. However, the maximum IHT liability will arise if Luis dies before 31 July 2028 because: This date is within three years of gifting the investment property to Silvia on 31 July 2025, such that taper relief will not be available in respect of this gift; and It is within seven years of the gift of cash to Mario on 1 January 2022, such that this gift will also become chargeable as a result of Luis' death, and it will be accumulated in determining the nil rate band available in respect of the gift of Ivy Cottage to Silvia.		
2		£	£
3	Value of property at 31 July 2025		245,000
4	Less: annual exemptions:		
5	2025/26		(3,000)
6	2024/25		(3,000)
7			239,000
8	Nil rate band	325,000	
9	Less: chargeable transfer in the previous seven years	(244,000) [1]	
10		81,000	(81,000)
11	Taxable amount		158,000
12	IHT@40%		63,200

1 =(250,000 – (3,000 *2)

ANSWERS

(b) (i) **Sale of shares in Flores Ltd**

As Luis sold his Flores Ltd shares on 1 April 2025 he owned them for less than three years such that there will be a withdrawal of the income tax relief given when the shares were acquired. Enterprise investment scheme (EIS) relief was obtained on the acquisition of these shares at the rate of 30% ie £36,000 = (£120,000 x 30%).

As the shares were sold to an unconnected party at a loss, the amount of relief withdrawn will be calculated by reference to the sale proceeds ie £25,500 (£85,000 x 30%). A capital loss will arise on the sale of the shares.

The allowable cost for this calculation will be reduced by the EIS relief obtained and not withdrawn.

	£
Proceeds	85,000
Less: cost (£120,000 – (£36,000 – £25,500))	(109,500)
Allowable loss	(24,500)

In addition, this sale will result in the gain on the sale of Yew House, which was deferred on the acquisition of the Flores Ltd shares, being brought back in to charge. As the amount reinvested in qualifying shares (£120,000) exceeded the gain on disposal (£71,000), the full amount of the gain will have been deferred, as Luis elected to defer the maximum possible amount. This gain will become chargeable in 2024/25.

(ii) **Reliefs available for the capital loss**

Luis can offset the loss on disposal of his shares against the chargeable gain of £71,000 on the sale of Yew House. This would save CGT at the rate of 24%.

Alternatively, as the shares qualified for EIS relief, he can offset the loss against his general income of 2024/25 and/or 2023/24. In 2023/24 Luis was an additional rate taxpayer, so would save at least some income tax at the rate of 45%, with any balance at 40%. In 2024/25, Luis was a higher rate taxpayer, so would save at least some income tax at the rate of 40% with any balance at 20%.

Therefore, it will be tax advantageous for him to elect to offset the loss in 2023/24.

(c) (i) **Income tax on interest received**

As Luis will be a higher rate taxpayer in future tax years, a savings nil rate band of £500 will be available. Interest received in excess of £500 will be taxed at the rate of 40%.

Income tax relief on interest paid

Tax relief will be available at the basic rate of income tax (20%) in respect of the interest paid on the property mortgage loan. This will be given as a tax credit, deducted from Luis' income tax liability for the relevant tax year.

Here is how this part of the answer could be presented in the word processor response option:

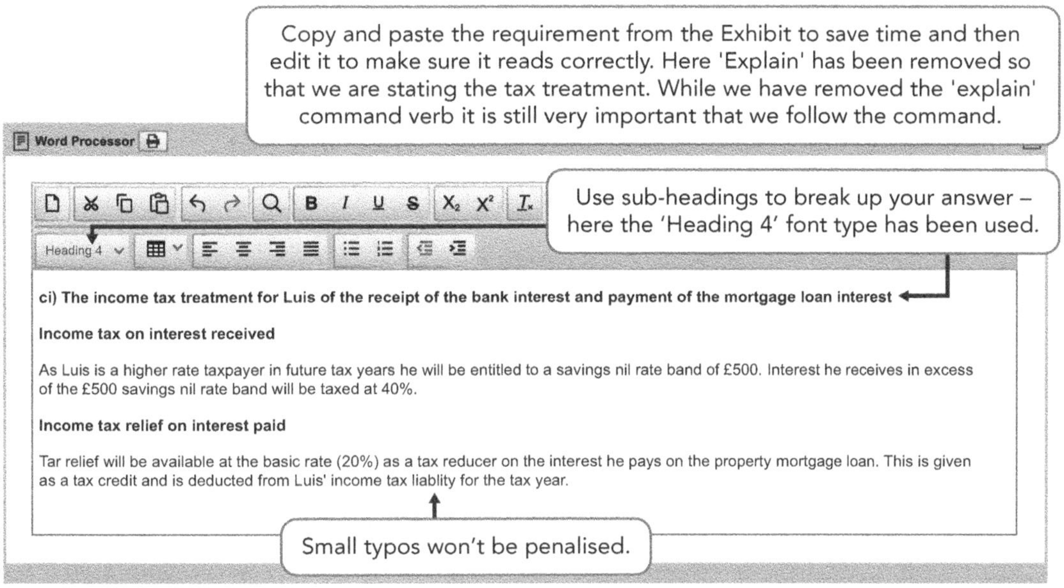

(ii) **After-tax net interest**

	Mortgage not repaid	Mortgage repaid
	£	£
Interest received:	850	nil
Income tax: (£850 - £500) x 40%	(140)	
Interest paid:	(1,275)	nil
Tax relief on interest paid: 20% x £1,275	255	
Net interest paid	(310)	nil

Therefore the after-tax interest saving will be £310.

19 Noah and Dan

Course Book references

The death estate for inheritance tax (IHT) and valuation of assets are covered in Chapter 11. Overseas aspects of inheritance tax are covered in Chapter 12. UK residence status and the overseas aspects of capital gains tax are covered in Chapter 9. Private residence relief is dealt with in Chapter 8.

Top tips

In part (a)(i) of this question you would need to ensure you present your answer clearly in terms of deciding Noah's domicile and how that would impact the IHT on the house located in Skarta. Make sure you follow the instructions in the question and include the main residence in Skarta in the death estate in (a)(ii). Part (b)(i) requires text-book knowledge about the sufficient ties tests. Make sure you clearly lay out your argument explaining each of the ties and concluding with how many ties you believe Dan has.

Easy marks

The basic rules about domicile and deemed domicile should have provided easy marks in this question together with the basics of the IHT computation in part (a)(ii). In part (b)(i) of the question the sufficient ties tests should allow you easy marks from stating and applying your text-book knowledge to the scenario. However, you need to know those rules to be able to state them – make sure you learn how to determine an individual's residence status if you don't know this already.

ACCA examining team's comments

Part (a) concerned inheritance tax on assets situated overseas. Candidates performed quite well and displayed a strong knowledge of the rules. However, a minority did not score as many marks as they could have done because they did not follow the instructions in the question sufficiently carefully. In particular, they failed to finish off their answers by calculating the value of the inheritance after deduction of all taxes and liabilities. (**BPP note**. The residence nil rate band was not relevant when this question was originally set so the ACCA examining team made no comments on this aspect.)

BPP note. Part (b) has been amended so the ACCA examining team's comments on the original question are no longer relevant.

Candidates who did well in this question:

- Applied their knowledge of the detailed rules to the facts of the question
- Managed their time carefully
- Read the requirements carefully and ensured that they answered the question set

Marking guide

			Marks	
(a)	(i)	Inclusion of house in Skarta in death estate	3	
				3
	(ii)	Chargeable estate	2	
		IHT liability	3.5	
		Value of Dan's inheritance	2	
		Marks Available	7.5	
		Maximum		6
(b)	(i)	Need three ties	1	
		Application of ties	4.5	
		Marks Available	5.5	
		Maximum		5
	(ii)	Gain on house before PRR exemption	1	
		PRR exemption	4	
		Gain on shop	2	
		Payment dates	1	
		Marks Available	8	
		Maximum		6

Marking guide	Marks

Professional skills marks

Analysis and Evaluation

- Appropriate use of information to determine suitable calculations of the value of Dan's inheritance after all taxes and liabilities, and the chargeable gains on Dan's disposal of the house and shop
- Appropriate use of information to support discussion and draw appropriate conclusions regarding Noah's deemed domicile status and the impact of this on his chargeable death estate
- Demonstration of ability to consider relevant factors applicable to an individual's situation to explain why Dan will not be resident in the UK in 2025/26
- Ability to evaluate information objectively to determine periods of actual and deemed occupation for PRR purposes
- Use of information to determine the IHT payable on Noah's death estate

Commercial acumen

- Other practical considerations relating to the calculation of Dan's inheritance (eg deduction of legal fees)
- Recognising that Dan is NR at the date of disposal of the shop and the tax consequences of this.

Maximum	5
Total	25

(a) (i) **Inheritance tax treatment of the house located in Skarta**

An individual who is not domiciled or deemed domiciled in the UK is liable to UK inheritance tax only in respect of assets located in the UK.

An individual is deemed domiciled in the UK if they have been resident in the UK for at least 15 of the 20 tax years immediately preceding the relevant tax year and for at least 1 of the 4 tax years ending with the relevant tax year, and accordingly are liable to UK inheritance tax on their worldwide assets.

Noah became resident in the UK on 1 April 2006, so by the time of his death on 31 May 2025, Noah had been resident in the UK for 19 tax years prior to the tax year 2025/26, so would be deemed domiciled in the UK for inheritance tax purposes. Therefore the house located in Skarta will be included in his chargeable death estate.

ANSWERS

(ii) **Value of Dan's inheritance**

Noah – death estate

	£
UK assets	460,000
House in Skarta (W1)	229,900
Chargeable estate	689,900
Residence nil rate band (max)	(175,000)
Nil rate band available on death	(325,000)
Taxable estate	189,900
IHT (£189,900 × 40%)	75,960
Less: Double tax relief – the lower of:	
– Overseas tax suffered £56,080	
– UK IHT on the house (£229,900 × 75,960/689,900)	(25,313)
IHT payable	50,647

Value of Dan's inheritance after all taxes and liabilities

	£
Value of assets in the estate (£460,000 + £242,000)	702,000
Less:	
– Legal and administration fees in Skarta	(12,400)
– IHT suffered (£56,080 + £50,647)	(106,727)
Value of inheritance	582,873

Working

House in Skarta

	£
Value of the house at 31 May 2025	242,000
Less: Legal and administration fees – the lower of:	
– The fees incurred £12,400	
– Maximum £12,100 (5% × £242,000)	(12,100)
Value to include in the estate	229,900

(b) (i) **Reasons why Dan will be classed as non-UK resident in the tax year 2025/26**

As Dan does not satisfy the criteria under either of the automatic tests for determining his UK residence status, the 'sufficient ties' tests must be considered. These take into account the number of days spent in the UK and the number of 'ties' Dan has to the UK.

As Dan has previously been resident in the UK in at least one of the previous three tax years, and will spend between 46 and 90 days in the UK during 2025/26 (15 May to 4 August 2025 inclusive, assuming he is not in the UK at midnight on 5 August), he would be considered to be UK resident in this tax year if he has at least three UK ties.

Dan will satisfy only one tie:

(1) He spent more than 90 days in the UK in the tax year 2023/24, as he did not leave the UK until 1 January 2024.

Dan will not satisfy the remaining four ties:

(1) Although he will have owned his house in the UK up to the date of its sale on 1 August 2025 (ie available to him for more than 91 days in 2025/26) he has not spent any nights there in 2025/26.

(2) He does not have any close family resident in the UK.

(3) He will not be present in the UK for the same number or more days in 2025/26 than in any other country.

(4) He will not have substantive work in the UK in 2025/26.

Accordingly, Dan will be classed as non-UK resident in 2025/26.

> **Tutorial note.** Note the following:
>
> (1) A parent (Noah) does not fall within the definition of close family for this purpose.
>
> (2) As Dan is planning to move permanently to Skarta on 5 August 2025, he will not be present in the UK for more days in 2025/26 than in any other country.
>
> (3) Dan will be working for up to 31 days in July 2025, which is insufficient to be regarded as 'substantive' (40 days or more).

(ii) **Dan – chargeable gains on disposal of UK land**

House – 1 August 2025

	£
Proceeds	361,000
Less: Cost	(286,000)
Gain before PRR	75,000
Less: PRR exemption (W) £75,000 × 60/70	(64,286)
Chargeable gain	10,714

ANSWERS

Working

PRR exemption

Because it is residential property, the CGT on this disposal (less the annual exempt amount) would be due within 60 days of completion, ie 30 September 2025.

	Total months	*Exempt months*	*Chargeable months*
Tax year			
2019/20			
– UK resident			
– Actual occupation 1 October 2019 to 5 April 2020	6	6	–
2020/21			
– UK resident			
– Actual occupation	12	12	–
2021/22			
– UK resident			
– Actual occupation	12	12	–
2022/23			
– UK resident			
– Actual occupation	12	12	–
2023/24			
– UK resident			
– Actual occupation 6 April to 31 December 2023	9	9	–
– Unoccupied 1 January to 5 April 2024	3	–	3
2024/25			
– Unoccupied (non-UK resident) but last 9 months of ownership exempt	12	5	7
2025/26			
– Non-UK resident but last 9 months exempt	4	4	—
	70	60	10

Shop – 1 October 2025

	£
Proceeds	165,000
Less: value at 5 April 2019	(150,000)
Chargeable gain	15,000

The CGT on this disposal would be due by 31 January 2027.

> **Tutorial note.** The shop is deemed to be disposed of and reacquired at 5 April 2019 so that only the gain arising after that date is chargeable on the disposal. Dan could elect to use the original cost but this election is clearly not beneficial in this case.

Videos can be viewed online by accessing your ebook version on VitalSource.

20 Max

Course Book references

The tests for residence and overseas aspects of chargeable gains will be found in Chapter 9. Chargeable gains reliefs are dealt with in Chapter 8. Lifetime transfers for inheritance tax and business property relief are covered in Chapter 11.

Top tips

Read all the information you are given in the question carefully. For example, for part (b) you were told that there is no split-year treatment which makes the discussion of Max's residence status fairly straightforward.

Easy marks

There were some easy marks in part (a) for stating basic inheritance tax principles such as the use of the annual exemption, cumulation of previous transfers of value and taper relief. In part (c) there is an easy half-mark for stating the increase in after-tax proceeds. You should gain this half-mark in relation to your own computations of tax even if they are not correct.

ACCA examining team's comments

This question concerned the capital gains tax and inheritance tax implications of a lifetime gift, and also the implications of a taxpayer moving abroad on his UK residence status, and his proposed sale of a UK asset.

The first part related to the availability of gift holdover relief in respect of a commercial building which has previously been used in a business, but which is now being rented out. Most candidates who attempted this question part were able to identify the issues and score 2 out of the 3 possible marks. Very few candidates went on to quantify the proportion of the gain which would be eligible for relief. Candidates should remember that where dates or figures are given in a question, they are usually required to use these in their answer.

The second part of the question required advice on the maximum potential inheritance tax liability which could arise in respect of the gift of the commercial building. The majority of candidates produced a good computation, but only a minority provided the necessary supporting explanations to fully satisfy the requirement – in this case, the fact that taper relief is available to reduce an inheritance tax liability if the donor of the lifetime gift survives for at least three years. Where an explanation or justification is needed for including or omitting figures, candidates must provide this.

(**BPP note:** the third part of this question has been rewritten and so the ACCA examining team's comments are no longer relevant.)

The final part of the question concerned an explanation of the availability of business asset disposal relief, and the calculation of the increase in after-tax proceeds if the individual delayed selling a further business asset to a date when he would not be UK resident. The main area of difficulty for this question was imprecise knowledge of the conditions for business asset disposal relief, and future candidates are reminded once again of the need to be very familiar with the precise rules in respect of all the capital gains tax reliefs. (**BPP note:** the answer to this part of the question has been rewritten to cover the new rules on a disposal UK non-residential land being chargeable even where the owner is non UK resident so this aspect was not commented on by the ACCA examining team.)

Marking guide

			Marks	
(a)	(i)	Gift holdover relief – one mark for each relevant point	4	
		Marks Available	4	
		Maximum		3
	(ii)	Gross chargeable value of the gift	2.5	
		Circumstances in which maximum liability arises	2.5	
		Calculation of maximum liability	1	
		Marks Available	6	
		Maximum		5
(b)		Max's residence status	2.5	
		Sale in June 2025	1	
		Sale in June 2026	2	
		Marks Available	5.5	
		Maximum		4
(c)		Business asset disposal relief	2.5	
		After-tax proceeds from sale in June 2025	3	
		After-tax proceeds from sale in June 2026	3.5	
		Increase in after-tax proceeds	.5	
		Marks Available	9.5	
		Maximum		8

Professional skills marks

Analysis and Evaluation

- Appropriate use of the information to determine suitable calculations of the maximum potential inheritance tax liability in respect of the gift of the office premises, and the CGT consequences on the sale of the warehouse
- Appropriate use of the information to support discussion and draw appropriate conclusions about the availability of gift holdover relief in respect of the gift of the office premises, the circumstances in which the maximum possible inheritance tax liability would arise, and the availability of business asset disposal relief on the sale of the warehouse
- Demonstration of ability to consider relevant factors applicable to an individual's situation in order to explain the effect of Max's period overseas on his UK residence status
- Use of information to determine impact on after-tax proceeds on sale of the warehouse if the sale happens in June 2025 or June 2026

Scepticism

- Identification of missing information in relation to whether Max will work full-time overseas, which may alter the analysis

Commercial acumen

- Effective use of calculations relating to the context to illustrate points being made relating to the amount of the gain and availability of business asset disposal relief on the sale of the warehouse

Maximum	5
Total	25

(a) (i) **Availability of gift holdover relief in respect of the gift of the office premises**

The office premises are eligible for gift holdover relief as they were used for the purpose of Max's trade. However, as they ceased to be used in the business on 31 May 2023, the proportion of the gain to be held over is restricted to the gain on disposal × period of business use/total period of ownership. Therefore the proportion of the gain eligible for gift holdover relief is 86/111 ((1 April 2016 – 31 May 2023)/(1 April 2016 to 30 June 2025)). The relief will be available whether or not the donee, Fara, is UK resident since it will be within the charge to tax even if she is non-UK resident as it is UK land.

(ii) **Maximum potential inheritance tax (IHT) liability in respect of the gift of the office premises**

No IHT is payable at the time the gift is made, but a liability may arise if Max dies within seven years of making the gift.

Business property relief is not available as this is a gift of an individual asset which has been used in an unincorporated sole trader business, rather than the gift of the business itself. However, annual exemptions are available for the tax years 2025/26 and 2024/25 such that the gross chargeable value of the gift will be £162,000 (£168,000 – £3,000 – £3,000).

Max has made one prior gift, on 6 May 2022, which will use part of his nil rate band if he dies before 6 May 2029. Taper relief will be available if Max dies after 30 June 2028 (three years after the date of the gift on 30 June 2025), so the maximum potential IHT liability will arise if Max dies before this date.

The maximum potential inheritance tax liability is therefore £12,400 (£162,000 – (£325,000 – £194,000) × 40%) and will arise if Max dies on or before 30 June 2028.

(b) **Effect of Max's period overseas on his UK residence status and the capital gains tax (CGT) consequences on the sale of the warehouse**

Max will leave the UK on 1 November 2025. As Max was resident in the UK for one or more of the previous three tax years, and he will spend at least 16 days in the UK in the tax year 2025/26 and does not appear to work full-time overseas, then he will **not** satisfy any of the automatic overseas tests.

Max **will** satisfy the first automatic UK residence test in 2025/26 as he will spend 183 days or more in the UK in that tax year.

In the tax year 2026/27 Max **will** satisfy the first automatic overseas residence test as described above since, although he was resident in the UK in one or more of the previous three tax years, he will spend less than 16 days in the UK.

(1) **Sale in June 2025**

As Max is resident in the UK in June 2025, the disposal will give rise to a chargeable gain in 2025/26.

(2) **Sale in June 2026**

Although Max is non-UK resident in 2026/27, he will be liable to CGT in the UK on this disposal of UK non-residential land. However, only the gain arising since 5 April 2019 will be chargeable.

(c) **Availability of business asset disposal relief on the sale of the warehouse**

The sale of the warehouse will satisfy two of the conditions for business asset disposal relief in that it was in use within Max's business at the date of cessation, and the business had been owned by Max for at least two years prior to cessation. However, the third condition, that the disposal must be within three years of the date of cessation, will only be satisfied if the disposal takes place before 1 June 2026. Accordingly, if the sale takes place in June 2025, business asset disposal relief will be available, but if it does not take place until June 2026 it will not.

Sale in June 2025

If the sale of the warehouse takes place in June 2025, this will give rise to a taxable gain of £31,000 (£84,000 – £50,000 – £3,000(AEA)).

As Max will be able to claim business asset disposal relief in respect of this chargeable gain, the after-tax proceeds will be £80,900 (£84,000 – (£31,000 × 10%)).

Sale in June 2026

If the sale of the warehouse is delayed until June 2026, this will give rise to a taxable gain of £17,000 (£90,000 – £70,000 (value at 5.4.19) – £3,000 (AEA)) in 2026/27.

As Max will not be able to claim business asset disposal relief in respect of this chargeable gain, the after-tax proceeds will be £86,600 (£90,000 – (£17,000 x 20%)).

The after-tax proceeds are £5,700 higher (£86,600 – £80,900) if he sells the warehouse in June 2026. It is therefore recommended that the sale is made in June 2026.

Videos can be viewed online by accessing your ebook version on VitalSource.

21 Liber and Vesta

Course Book references

The rules on chargeable gains for shares and capital gains tax computation are in Chapter 7. Business asset disposal relief and investors' relief are dealt with in Chapter 8. Inheritance tax computation is covered in Chapter 11. Capital tax advice is the subject of Chapter 13.

Top tips

In part (b), it was important to realise that the property being gifted was decreasing in value.

Easy marks

There were some easy marks in part (a)(ii) for identifying the reasons why the shares should be sold in the next tax year rather than the current tax year.

ACCA examining team's comments

When looking at the first part of the question concerning the takeover, candidates should have been able to identify the following tax issues from the facts of the question.

- At the date of the takeover, share-for-share rules automatically apply but there will be a gain on the cash element of the takeover consideration. When the new shares are eventually sold, a gain will arise on the sale.
- If the new shares are sold in the same tax year as the takeover, the gain on the cash element at takeover and the gain on the new shares will be added together and the annual exempt amount set against the total gains.
- If instead, the new shares are sold in a subsequent tax year for the same price, the gain on the new shares may be the same as calculated above but it will be offset by a new annual exempt amount. This will result in a tax saving.

Clarity of thought was critical here. Candidates needed to identify the tax implications of what had already happened and then consider the implications of the alternative sale date scenarios. Candidates should not be writing their answers immediately; they should be planning what points they need to make in their answer. Candidates who start preparing calculations in the hope that they will eventually arrive at the correct answer do not score well. For those candidates who took a moment to consider the facts and decide on a strategy for answering the question, the calculations were not very difficult and the two possible sale alternatives could be compared, scoring high marks.

A further issue in this part of the question was whether business asset disposal relief (BADR) would be available to the individual making the share disposals. Stronger candidates understood the BADR rules but more importantly, were able to apply them to the facts of the question and decide that BADR would not be available. Weaker candidates listed the BADR rules but were not able to apply them to the scenario. A significant minority of students considered the substantial shareholding exemption which is not relevant in the scenario of an individual disposing of shares. (**BPP note:** Investors' relief was not relevant when this question was originally set.)

The second part of the question required candidates to consider the capital gains tax and inheritance tax advantages of a lifetime gift rather than a death estate bequest. Candidates may have been familiar with this as a tax planning concept but once again, the key to answering this question was in applying knowledge to the facts given in this particular question. Candidates should have found the following tax issues arising from the facts of the question.

- A lifetime gift would result in a capital loss, not a capital gain, since the value of the asset had fallen since purchase. However the facts of the question were that the donor would not be able to use a capital loss. Since there is no capital gains tax on a death estate bequest, from a capital gains tax point of view, the donor would be indifferent between lifetime and death gifting.
- For inheritance tax purposes, a lifetime gift would be a potentially exempt transfer. However the facts of the question were that the potentially exempt transfer would become chargeable within three years, with neither taper relief nor annual exemptions available. Furthermore, fall in value relief would be available, meaning that once again the donor would be indifferent between lifetime and death gifting.

Candidates need to consider the scenario given *before* they start writing their answer and not simply state general tax rules. Each client has their own particular set of circumstances which the tax rules must be applied to. Once again, candidates would benefit from taking some thinking time to consider the scenario before they put pen to paper.

Marking guide			Marks	
(a)	(i)	Gain on cash at date of takeover	4.5	
		Gain on sale of Mercury plc shares on 1 January 2026	2.5	
		Capital gains tax payable	2	
		Marks Available	9	
		Maximum		8
	(ii)	2025/26 annual exempt amount available	1	
		Calculation of tax saving	3	
		Tax payable later	1	
		Marks Available	5	
		Maximum		4
(b)	Capital gains tax implications		4	
	Inheritance tax implications		5.5	
	Marks Available		9.5	
	Maximum			8

Professional skills marks

Analysis and evaluation

- Demonstration of ability to consider both capital gains tax and inheritance tax as specified in the requirement for part (b)
- Appropriate use of data to support discussion and draw appropriate conclusions regarding the availability of business asset disposal relief on the takeover of Vulcan Ltd, and the sale of the Mercury plc shares
- Appropriate use of data to determine suitable calculations of the capital gain on the takeover of Vulcan Ltd and the sale of the Mercury plc shares
- Appropriate use of data to support discussion and draw appropriate conclusions regarding the capital gains tax and inheritance tax advantages of gifting the investment property on 31 December 2025

Marking guide	Marks

Commercial acumen

- Effective use of calculations relating to the context to illustrate points being made relating to the advantages of delaying the sale of the Mercury plc shares until May 2026
- Recognising the key issue that the investment property was falling in value

Maximum	5
Total	25

(a) (i) **Capital gains tax implications of the takeover of Vulcan Ltd on 1 June 2025 and a subsequent sale of the Mercury plc shares on 1 January 2026**

Gain on the cash received in the takeover

The share-for-share exchange rules will automatically apply on the takeover of Vulcan Ltd on 1 June 2025, as this was a *bona fide* commercial transaction, and Mercury plc has acquired more than 25% of the ordinary shares in Vulcan Ltd. The shares in Mercury plc will 'stand in the shoes' of the shares in Vulcan Ltd and no gain will be chargeable in respect of these shares until they are sold. The receipt of cash is treated as a part-disposal of the Vulcan Ltd shares and a chargeable gain will arise at the date of the takeover.

The chargeable gain in respect of the cash received is £9,789 (£12,000 – £2,211 (W)).

Business asset disposal relief will not be available in respect of the gain arising on the cash consideration, as Liber was not a director or employee of Vulcan Ltd. Investors' relief is not available because Liber did not subscribe for the shares in Vulcan Ltd.

Gain on the sale of the Mercury plc shares

	£
Proceeds (3,200 × £28)	89,600
Less: cost (W)	(11,789)
Chargeable gain	77,811

Business asset disposal relief will not be available on the sale of the Mercury plc shares as Liber is not a director or employee of Mercury plc, and holds less than 5% of the ordinary shares in Mercury plc.

	£
Gain on cash received on takeover	9,789
Gain on sale of shares in Mercury plc	77,811
Total chargeable gains	87,600
Less: annual exempt amount	(3,000)
Taxable gains	84,600

Capital gains tax (CGT) payable is £16,170 (((£37,700 – £30,200) × 10%) + ((£84,600 – £7,500) × 20%)).

Working

Allocation of cost at time of takeover

	Market value	Apportioned cost
	£	£
Consideration received:		
Ordinary shares in Mercury plc		
– (800 × 4 × £20)	64,000	
– (£64,000/£76,000) × £14,000		11,789
Cash		
– (800 × £15)	12,000	
– (£12,000/£76,000) × £14,000		2,211
	76,000	14,000

(ii) **Reasons why it is beneficial to sell the Mercury plc shares on 1 May 2026 instead of on 1 January 2026**

The calculation of the gain on the sale of the Mercury plc shares will be the same, but the sale will be in the following tax year, 2026/27, so the following tax implications will arise:

The gain on the cash received on the takeover in 2025/26 will be partially covered by the annual exempt amount for that year and so there will be a CGT liability of £679 in 2025/26 ((£9,789-£3,000) × 10%).

The whole of the 2026/27 annual exempt amount will be available to be deducted from the gain on the sale of the Mercury plc shares. This will result in a CGT liability of £14,212 in 2026/27 (W). The overall tax saving if the Mercury plc shares are sold on 1 May 2026 is therefore £1,279 (£16,170 (as in (a)(i)) – (£679 + £14,212)).

> **Tutorial note.** Alternatively, delaying the sale of the shares until 1 May 2026 results in the gain on the cash received in the takeover of £9,789 having £3,000 covered by the annual exempt amount for 2025/26 with the remaining £6,789 being taxed at 10% rather than 20% and therefore a CGT saving of £1,279 (20% × £3,000 + £6,789 × 10%).

The tax relating to the sale of the Mercury plc shares will be due a year later on 31 January 2028, rather than 31 January 2027.

Working

CGT liability if Mercury plc shares disposed of on 1 May 2026

	£
Gain on sale of shares in Mercury plc	77,811
Less: annual exempt amount	(3,000)
Taxable gains	74,811

CGT payable is £14,212 (((£37,700 – £30,200) × 10%) + ((£74,811 – £7,500) × 20%)).

(b) **Vesta**

Capital gains tax and inheritance tax advantages of gifting the investment property on 31 December 2025

Capital gains tax (CGT)

If the property remains in Vesta's estate on her death, there will be no CGT implications, such that the fall in value of the property will not give rise to an allowable loss. If the property is gifted to Janus on 31 December 2025, an allowable loss will arise as a result of the fall in value. However, as Vesta will make no disposals for CGT purposes in 2025/26 (or 2026/27), she will not be able to relieve this loss.

Therefore, for CGT purposes, Vesta will be indifferent as to whether to gift the property to Janus in her lifetime, or to leave it to him in her estate on death. However, Janus's base cost of the property on a future disposal is its market value at the date it is transferred to him. Accordingly, as the property is expected to be worth less at the date of Vesta's death than it is currently, it will be advantageous from Janus's point of view if Vesta gifts the property to him on 31 December 2025 as he will then have a higher base cost for CGT purposes on a future sale.

> **Tutorial note.** As Janus and Vesta are connected persons, the CGT loss on the gift of the property to Janus on 31 December 2025 could only have been relieved against a gain arising on a later disposal by Vesta to Janus.

Inheritance tax (IHT)

If the property remains in Vesta's estate at the date of her death, it will be included at its value on death, which is expected to be lower than its current market value. If the property is gifted to Janus on 31 December 2025, it will be a potentially exempt transfer (PET), such that there will be no immediate charge to IHT. This PET will become chargeable as a result of Vesta's death within seven years.

As the value of the property is expected to have decreased between the date of the gift and the date of death, fall in value relief will be available (assuming that Janus still owns the property, or has sold it in an arm's length transaction), so the lifetime gift will not result in any more IHT being payable on the property than if it were left to Janus in the death estate.

No annual exemptions are available as they have been used on the cash gift to Janus on 1 June 2025. No taper relief will be available as Vesta will not have survived for three years after making the gift.

Therefore, for IHT purposes, both Vesta and Janus will be indifferent between a lifetime gift and leaving the property in her estate on death.

22 Yacon Ltd and Daikon

Course Book references

Share schemes are covered in Chapter 4, PRR and letting relief in Chapter 8 and the necessary IHT is covered in Chapter 12.

Top tips

Remember to check the command verbs in each requirement – do you need writing or numbers or both? Note that in (a) you're asked for income tax implications but not capital gains tax implications – no marks will be available if you provide something you've not been asked for.

Easy marks

Even if you can't provide all the necessary detail in part (a) there should be some easy marks available if you know your basics on share schemes. The basics of PRR relief should also provide some easy marks. Spotting the gift with reservation of benefit in (c) should also provide some easy marks even if you can't explain the full detail of how the IHT works.

ACCA examining team's comments

Requirement (a) asked for an explanation of whether two different share schemes, a company share option plan (CSOP) and a share incentive plan (SIP), would satisfy Yacon Ltd's criteria for a tax advantaged share scheme. In addition, the income tax implications for the employees of acquiring the shares in each case needed to be explained.

Those candidates who knew the rules for share option schemes were able to apply them to the facts of the question with relative ease. Those with only a superficial understanding of the rules struggled to score well on this part. A detailed knowledge of the underlying rules is required for ATX–UK and those who don't possess this will struggle to do well on questions where this needs to be demonstrated.

A number of candidates went on to discuss the capital gains tax consequences of disposing of the shares, despite the fact that the requirement only asked for the income tax implications on acquisition. It is vital to double check the precise scope of the requirement such that time is not wasted in terms of doing something that has not been requested.

Part (b) was to calculate, with brief explanations, the private residence relief (PRR) and potential letting relief, available to reduce the gain on the sale of a house.

It was encouraging to see that many candidates had a strong understanding of the PRR rules and were able to apply their knowledge to the facts of the question. However, common areas of confusion involved the first six month period when the owner was working overseas; this was a chargeable period because there had been no prior period of occupation. Also, it should be noted that the last nine months of ownership is always exempt, even if some of the property is rented out during that period (as long as it has been occupied as the private residence at some point in the past).

Some candidates only provided calculations, and others only explanations. The requirement did however stipulate 'a calculation, with brief explanations', so to score well a combination of the two was required.

Not all candidates were as familiar with letting relief, which is given after consideration of PRR. Those who did understand the rules were able to score the marks for knowing that it is the lower of three comparative amounts; namely £40,000, the gain already exempt under PRR and the gain attributable to the let period.

Part (c) of the question related to the inheritance tax implications of a gift of an apartment, on the assumption that the donor were to die within seven years.

The facts contained within the question are that when the apartment was first gifted, the donor retained the right to continue to live in it. Many candidates correctly identified this scenario as a 'gift with reservation of benefit' and a potentially exempt transfer (PET) at the time. The question then goes on to explain that, some time later, the donor removed the condition of her right to live in the property. Not all candidates realised that the removal of this 'reservation of benefit' created a further deemed PET at the date the condition was lifted.

Since the donor then went on to die within seven years of the first PET, both PETs in theory become chargeable but tax will only be due on the one giving rise to the higher liability.

Marking guide

			Marks
(a)	Company share option plan	4	
	Share incentive plan	5	
	Marks Available	9	
	Maximum		8
(b)	Private residence relief	5.5	
	Letting relief	2.5	
	Marks Available	8	
	Maximum		7
(c)	Original gift 5 June 2023	2	
	Reservation lifted	2	
	Death in December 2028	3	
	Marks Available	7	
	Maximum		5

ANSWERS

Marking guide	Marks
Professional skills marks	
Analysis and evaluation	
• Adoption of a logical approach to prepare suitable calculations of PRR and letting relief in part (b)	
• Appropriate use of the facts provided in order to reach relevant conclusions with respect to the suitability of the share plans in part (a)	
Commercial acumen	
• Appropriate use of information to identify the gift with reservation in part (c)	
• Demonstration of awareness that change in Jicama's circumstances will impact the inheritance tax position in part (c)	
Maximum	5
Total	25

(a) (1) **Company share option plan (CSOP)**

Ability to select employees

In a CSOP, Yacon Ltd would be free to select employees as it wishes to participate in the scheme.

Value of option granted

Yacon Ltd can choose to award options to purchase a different number of shares to each member of a CSOP. There is no annual maximum amount for the company, however, an employee can only be granted options over shares up to a total value of £60,000, as at the date of the grant. As Yacon Ltd only proposes to grant options over shares worth up to £3,000 per year for each employee, this is well within the limits.

Holding period required and tax implications for employees

There are no tax implications for employees on the grant of the options, or on their exercise after five years as the exercise will be between three and ten years of being granted.

(2) **Share incentive plan (SIP)**

Ability to select employees

Under the rules for a SIP, all employees must be offered the opportunity to participate in the plan. Yacon Ltd can specify a minimum period of employment in order to qualify, but this cannot exceed 18 months.

Value of free shares given

Yacon Ltd can give each employee free shares up to the value of £3,600 each tax year, and therefore, the proposal to offer shares with a value of up to £3,000 to each employee each year will be acceptable. The free shares must be offered on similar terms to all employees, such that different amounts of shares can be offered to different employees, depending on their meeting certain objective criteria, such as length of service or performance targets.

Holding period required and tax implications for employees

There are no tax implications for employees when the free shares are put into the plan.

As the free shares will be held in the plan for five years, there will be no income tax liability when they are withdrawn from the plan.

Here's an example of how (a) could be answered in the word processor response option.

'Headings' have been used to structure the response. This one uses 'Headings 3 & 4.'

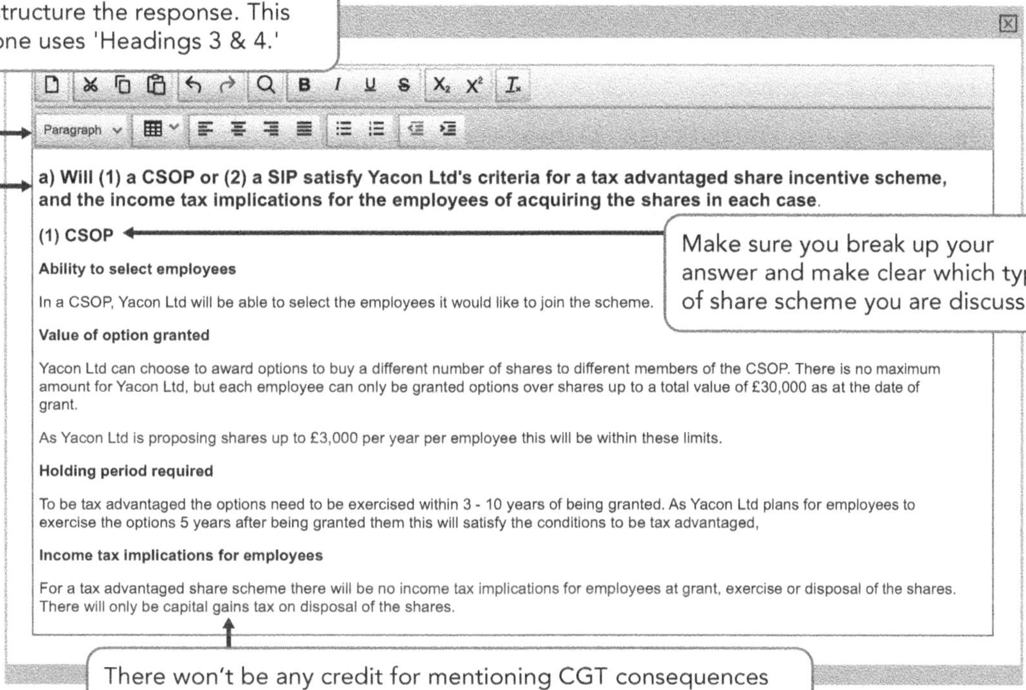

a) Will (1) a CSOP or (2) a SIP satisfy Yacon Ltd's criteria for a tax advantaged share incentive scheme, and the income tax implications for the employees of acquiring the shares in each case.

(1) CSOP

Ability to select employees

In a CSOP, Yacon Ltd will be able to select the employees it would like to join the scheme.

Value of option granted

Yacon Ltd can choose to award options to buy a different number of shares to different members of the CSOP. There is no maximum amount for Yacon Ltd, but each employee can only be granted options over shares up to a total value of £30,000 as at the date of grant.

As Yacon Ltd is proposing shares up to £3,000 per year per employee this will be within these limits.

Holding period required

To be tax advantaged the options need to be exercised within 3 - 10 years of being granted. As Yacon Ltd plans for employees to exercise the options 5 years after being granted them this will satisfy the conditions to be tax advantaged,

Income tax implications for employees

For a tax advantaged share scheme there will be no income tax implications for employees at grant, exercise or disposal of the shares. There will only be capital gains tax on disposal of the shares.

Make sure you break up your answer and make clear which type of share scheme you are discussing.

There won't be any credit for mentioning CGT consequences of the scheme as it's not asked for! It only asks for income tax implications. So this final sentence, while correct, isn't going to score. The author added this in to give a fuller answer.

(b) **Daikon – reliefs available on the sale of his house**

Private residence relief (PRR):

	Exempt years	*Chargeable years*
1 July 2017 to 31 December 2017 – Absent – no prior occupation		0.5
1 January 2018 to 30 June 2019 – Occupied	1.5	
1 July 2019 to 31 December 2020 – Absent but deemed occupation as employed overseas	1.5	
1 January 2021 to 31 March 2021 – Occupied	0.25	
1 April 2021 to 31 March 2025 Occupied (4 years × 75%)	3	1
1 April 2025 to 31 December 2025 – Last 9 months treated as 100% occupation	0.75	
	7	1.5

PRR is £119,412 (£145,000 × 7/8.5).

Letting relief

Letting relief is available to claim where part of individual's private residence is let out and so a proportion does not qualify for PRR. The property must be occupied both by the tenant and the owner during the let period to qualify for the relief.

The additional amount of the gain which will be exempt under letting relief is the lowest of:

(1) The amount of the gain which is exempt under the PRR exemption (£119,412).

(2) The gain attributable to the letting £17,059 (£145,000 × 1/8.5).

(3) £40,000.

Letting relief is therefore £17,059.

(c) **Inheritance tax implications of Jicama's gift of the apartment**

The gift of the apartment on 5 June 2023 was a potentially exempt transfer (PET), valued at the market value of the apartment on that date. The gift was also a gift with reservation of benefit, due to the condition imposed by Jicama that she would continue to live there.

However, the reservation of benefit was lifted on 12 March 2025, when Jicama went to live with her sister. This created a further PET, which would be valued at the market value of the apartment on that date.

On Jicama's death in December 2028, this is within seven years of the date of the original gift, so both the original PET and the later deemed PET become chargeable. The liability on each of these PETs would be subject to taper relief as both were made more than 3 years before the date of death.

To avoid a double tax charge, only the PET which results in a higher tax charge overall will actually be chargeable.

Owner managed businesses

23 Spike

Course Book references

Loss relief for sole traders is covered in Chapter 15. Chargeable gains, including the rates of capital gains tax (CGT), are to be found in Chapter 7. Value added tax (VAT) on cessation is covered in Chapter 23. Employment income is the subject of Chapter 4.

Top tips

In part (a), it is important to realise that the trading loss which can be relieved against general income (and gains) is computed differently from the terminal loss.

Easy marks

There were easy marks in part (c) in respect of the relocation expenses.

ACCA examining team's comments

Part (a)

Concerned losses realised on a cessation of trade and was in two parts.

Part (a)(i) was short and direct; it was intended to ensure that all candidates attempting this question addressed the two possibilities that needed to be considered when they went on to part (a)(ii) and had to explain the reliefs available in respect of the loss.

In part (a)(i) candidates were required to calculate the trading loss in the year of cessation and the terminal loss of the last 12 months. Very few candidates made a reasonable job of this; the majority of candidates simply did not know the rules.

Accordingly, many candidates simply did not appreciate the difference between the loss of the tax year and the terminal loss. Of those candidates who were aware that the terminal loss is calculated in its own particular way, very few knew how to do it.

In part (a)(ii) things did not really improve. Although many candidates were aware that there was the possibility of carrying back a loss on cessation to the three years prior to the loss, there was a general lack of precision as regards the rules and a confused approach to the figures.

When dealing with losses, there are only really two things that need to be known: the years in which the losses can be offset and the type of income or gains that the losses can be offset against.

Marks were available in part (a)(ii) for knowing these fundamental rules but they were not awarded as frequently as one might have expected. The approach of most candidates to part (a)(ii) was not as measured or considered as was necessary.

Candidates would have benefited from clearly defining the possibilities in their minds and then writing brief, precise points that addressed each of the possibilities. Instead, most candidates wrote too much that was confused and often contradictory.

In addition, because they did not give themselves sufficient time to consider the possibilities, many candidates did not consider the possibility of relieving the capital gains. Those that did often did so in general terms as opposed to addressing the particular gains in the question.

Part (b)

There are no Examining team's comments in relation to part (b) as this requirement comes from an earlier ATX–UK specimen exam and, as such, no comments are available.

Part (c)

Concerned the £8,000 exemption available in respect of relocation costs and was answered well.

Marking guide

			Marks	
(a)	(i)	Loss for tax year 2024/25	1	
		Terminal loss	1	
				2
	(ii)	**Relief of the loss for the tax year 2024/25**		
		The reliefs available	2	
		Tax savings 2024/25		
		– Business assets	1.5	
		– House	2	
		Tax savings 2023/24	1	
		Relief of the terminal loss		
		The reliefs available	3	
		Tax savings – terminal loss	1	
		Marks Available	10.5	
		Maximum		9
(b)		Requirement to deregister	2	
		Capital goods scheme adjustment	4	
		Output VAT on other assets	2	
		Marks Available	8	
		Maximum		7
(c)		Relocation payment	2	
				2

Professional skills marks

Analysis and evaluation

- Appropriate use of the information in the scenario to quantify the tax savings in (a)
- Appropriate use of the information the scenario to identify the option to convert the trade loss to a capital loss in (a)
- Adoption of a logical approach to prepare suitable calculations for the tax savings in part (a) and the capital goods scheme adjustment in part (b)

Commercial acumen

- Consideration as to the higher rate of tax savings by using trading losses against the residential property gain (if arising) in (a)
- Recognition of the timing- the deadline for Spike to notify his VAT deregistration is already passed

Scepticism

- Consideration as to whether the gain on Spike's house will be exempted by PRR

Maximum	5
Total	25

(a) (i) **Loss relief available on the cessation of the trade**

Trading loss for the tax year 2024/25

	£
6 April 2024 to 31 December 2024	
Loss	21,800

Terminal loss

	£	£
6 April 2024 to 31 December 2024		
– Loss £21,800		21,800
1 January 2024 to 5 April 2024		
– 1 January 2024 - 31 March 2024		
– Profit £22,850 x 3/12	5,712	
– Ignore as profit		0
		21,800

(ii) **The reliefs available in respect of the trading loss and the terminal loss**

Relief of the loss for the tax year 2024/25

The loss for the tax year 2024/25 can be offset against Spike's general income of 2024/25 and/or 2023/24.

Once the loss has been offset against the general income of a particular tax year, it can also be offset against the capital gains of that same year.

Spike has no general income in the tax year 2024/25. However, a claim can be made for the whole of the loss to be relieved against his 2024/25 capital gains.

Relieving the loss against the gains on the sale of the business assets would save capital gains tax at the rate of 10% due to the availability of business asset disposal relief. The tax saved would be £21,800 × 10% = £2,180.

Spike's sale of his house will be an exempt disposal of his private residence if he has always occupied it, or is deemed to have always occupied it. If part of the gain on the house is taxable, capital gains tax will be payable at 24% because it is residential property and the gains on the business assets will have used the basic rate band. Accordingly, if this is the case, the loss should be offset against any gain on the house in priority to the gain on the business assets.

In the tax year 2023/24, the loss would be offset against the general income of £22,850. The claim cannot be restricted in order to obtain relief for the personal allowance of that year. The tax saved would be £(22,850 – 12,570) = £10,280 × 20% = £2,056.

Relief of the terminal loss

The terminal loss can be offset against the trading profit of the business for 2024/25 and the three preceding tax years, starting with the latest year.

The trading profit in the tax year 2024/25 is nil, such that the terminal loss will be relieved in the tax year 2023/24 in full. This would save tax of £(22,850 – 12,570) = £10,280 × 20% – £2,056.

(b) **VAT**

Spike should have notified HM Revenue & Customs of the cessation of his business within 30 days of ceasing to make taxable supplies, ie by 30 January 2025.

He may be liable to a penalty if he failed to do so.

The capital goods scheme would have applied to the workshop. On its purchase, in the year ended 31 March 2021, 70% of the input VAT would have been recovered, ie 70% × 20% × £300,000 = £42,000.

As the workshop is sold within 10 years (in the year ended 31 March 2025, ie in year 5) there would be a sales adjustment. The workshop will be an old commercial building on sale and so will be an exempt supply meaning that 0% is used in the sales adjustment calculation. The sales adjustment would be:

$$\frac{60,000}{10} \times (0\%-70\%) \times 5 = (£21,000)$$

Thus Spike will have to make a repayment of £21,000 VAT to HMRC. Spike should have charged VAT on any machinery and inventory which he sold whilst he was still registered for VAT.

When Spike deregistered, he should have accounted for output tax on all business assets which he still owned in respect of which he had previously recovered input tax. There was no need to account for this output tax if it was less than £1,000.

(c) **The relocation payment**

The compensation in respect of the sale of the house at short notice at a low price will be regarded as having been derived from employment, so it will be taxable in full.

£8,000 of the payment in respect of the costs of moving house will be exempt; the remaining £(11,500 – 8,000) = £3,500 of the payment will be taxable.

24 Enid

Course Book references

Losses are covered in Chapter 15. CGT reliefs are dealt with in Chapter 8. Income tax computation is covered in Chapter 2. Class 1 national insurance contributions for employment are covered in Chapter 4. Owner managed business advice is the subject of Chapter 18. Value added tax is the subject of Chapter 23.

Top tips

When tackling a loss relief question, jot down the available reliefs and then decide which of them is relevant. Only deal with the loss relief(s) that can be used in your answer.

Easy marks

You should have been able to score well on the value added tax (VAT) aspects of registration tested in part (d). This was all brought forward knowledge from TX–UK. Make sure you don't discuss the TOGC rules!

ACCA examining team's comments

The first part related to the availability of loss relief for a trading loss brought forward. This question part was not well done, for two reasons. Firstly, the majority of candidates failed to realise that when a loss is given as being brought forward at a particular date, with no indication of the prior accounting period(s) or tax year(s) in which the loss arose, the current year/carry back reliefs against total income will not be relevant. Nor is terminal loss relief relevant, unless the loss arose in the last 12 months of trading, which was not the case here. So the only option is to carry the loss forward against the first available profits from the same trade, which here was just the profit of the final period of trading prior to incorporation. Secondly, the majority of candidates appeared to be unaware of incorporation relief, permitting the remaining loss to be carried forward against the former sole trader's income from the company. The rules relating to reliefs for trading losses for individuals are frequently examined, and candidates are expected to be precise in this sort of question. Candidates would do well to invest time at the revision stage of their studies in memorising the rules concerning relief for trading losses, and ensuring that they are able to recognise those rules which apply in a given scenario, so as not to waste time discussing reliefs which are not available.

The second part of the question focused on the CGT implications in respect of the assets transferred to the new company. It was pleasing to see that the majority of candidates knew the conditions for incorporation relief to apply, but, disappointingly, a significant number of these did not know how to apply it. More surprising, however, was the fact that relatively few candidates referred to business asset disposal relief (BADR) here. The issue of goodwill not qualifying for BADR in this situation, is, admittedly, quite a tricky one, but BADR is a very common, and frequently tested, relief available to individuals disposing of qualifying assets, so should be something that every candidate would be advised to consider, and comment on, in every situation where there is a disposal of business assets. It is important to be very familiar with the precise rules for this relief, so as to be able to ascertain whether or not it is available in any given scenario.

The third part of the question was a variation on the often-tested extraction of profits from a company, this time including withdrawal from a loan account, in addition to the more familiar dividend or salary. On the whole, this was done well, with most candidates adopting a marginal approach, and therefore being able to calculate the additional tax payable by both the individual and the company in a concise and efficient way. It is a useful skill for candidates to be able to recognise where a marginal approach will be appropriate, as in these cases it will usually prove to be much less time consuming than producing full computations, although full marks can still be obtained by a candidate who adopts this latter approach. The best way to develop this skill is, undoubtedly, question practice, in order to gain confidence in being able to identify when it is appropriate, and how to perform the marginal calculations. In relation to the withdrawal from the loan account, a significant number of candidates appeared not to have read the question properly, where it stated explicitly that there would be sufficient funds in the loan account to permit this withdrawal, and dived straight in to explaining the rules for close companies in relation to the tax charge payable on overdrawn director's loan accounts, with which they were clearly more familiar, but which unfortunately were not relevant.

The final part of the question concerned the administrative requirements in relation to deregistration for VAT by the unincorporated business, registration by the company, and the possibility of transferring the VAT registration. This was attempted well by the majority of candidates, who typically scored two out of the possible three marks.

Marking guide

		Marks	
(a)	Relief against future trading profit	1.5	
	Relief against income from Niche Ltd	3.5	
	Marks Available	5	
	Maximum		4
(b)	Availability of incorporation relief	1.5	
	Calculation of chargeable gain	2	
	Calculation of capital gains tax liability	3	
	Balance on loan account	2	
	Marks Available	8.5	
	Maximum		7
(c)	Tax on dividend	2.5	
	Tax payable on increased salary	3.5	
	Increased total tax liability	0.5	
	Tax on withdrawal from loan account	1	
	Tax saving from loan account withdrawal	0.5	
	Marks Available	8	
	Maximum		6

Marking guide		Marks
(d) Administrative requirements for VAT	3	
		3

Professional skills marks

Analysis and evaluation

- Appropriate use of the data to determine suitable calculations of the balance on Enid's loan account after deducting the cash to be withdrawn to pay any capital gains tax (CGT) due, and the impact on the total amount of tax payable if she receives additional salary of £15,000, or alternatively withdraws £15,000 from her loan account
- Use of information to support discussion of the impact of loss relief options by reference to Enid's tax status
- Appropriate use of the data to support discussion and draw appropriate conclusions about the availability of incorporation relief on the transfer of Enid's business to Niche Ltd
- Demonstration of reasoned judgement regarding the whether Enid is able to transfer the VAT registration from her unincorporated business to Niche Ltd.
- Demonstration of ability to consider relevant factors applicable to the situation regarding administrative obligations under the value added tax (VAT) legislation, arising from the transfer of Enid's business to Niche Ltd

Scepticism

- Acknowledgement of the need to confirm that the shares are retained until the end of 2025/26 for incorporation loss relief to be available

Commercial acumen

- Recognition of constraints and opportunities related to the choice of trading loss relief
- Other practical considerations regarding the transfer of the VAT registration to Niche Ltd (eg taking over the rights and liabilities of the business in respect of VAT)

Maximum	5
Total	25

(a) **Reliefs available for the trading losses brought forward at 6 April 2025**

Trading losses brought forward are automatically offset against the first available future profits from the same trade. Enid will therefore offset £42,000 of the trading losses brought forward against the profit of her unincorporated business in 2025/26 prior to its transfer to Niche Ltd. £9,000 (£51,000 – £42,000) remains unrelieved.

However, as her business has been transferred to a company, Enid can relieve the remainder of the loss against her income from the company. The loss will be relieved against the first-available income from the company, earned before unearned, which will be her salary of £37,500 (£75,000 × 6/12) in the tax year 2025/26. Enid qualifies for this relief as at least 80% of the consideration for the transfer of her business will be in the form of shares. She must retain these shares until the end of 2025/26 in order to make this claim.

(b) **Availability of incorporation relief and the balance on Enid's loan account**

Availability of incorporation relief

Incorporation relief will be available because:

- The business will be transferred as a going concern;
- All the assets will be transferred; and
- The consideration includes shares.

	Workshop (BADR)	Goodwill (no BADR)
	£	£
Gain on goodwill £(83,000 – 0)		83,000
Gain on workshop £(122,000 – 55,000)	67,000	
Less incorporation relief (85%)	(56,950)	(70,550)
Gains after incorporation relief	10,050	12,450
Less annual exempt amount (best use)	(0)	(3,000)
Taxable gains	10,050	9,450
CGT @ 10%/20%	1,005	1,890
Total CGT £(1,005 + 1,290)		£2,895

The funds left on loan account initially will be £30,000 (15% × £200,000 (£83,000 + £122,000 + £5,000 – £10,000)). The balance on Enid's loan account after deducting the cash to be withdrawn to pay the CGT liability will be £27,105 (£30,000 – £2,895).

Tutorial note. Note the following:

(1) Goodwill is not a relevant business asset for business asset disposal relief where it is transferred by an individual to a close company, and that individual is a related party to the close company, as is the case in this scenario.

(2) No SBAs are available on the workshop as it was not constructed after October 2018. If, however, Enid had been claiming SBAs on the workshop there would be no need for her to add the SBAs claimed to date to the proceeds in her gain calculation for the workshop. Instead Niche Ltd would continue to claim SBAs based on Enid's eligible cost and on a future disposal both Enid and Niche Ltd's SBAs claimed to date would be added to the consideration in Niche Ltd's gains calculation.

(c) **Replacement of Enid's dividend with increased salary or withdrawal from her loan account**

Enid is a higher rate taxpayer. She currently receives dividends of £500 each year, so the income tax payable on the dividend of £15,000 from Niche Ltd will be £5,063 ((£500 – £500) × 0%) + (£15,000 × 33.75%)).

There are no tax implications for Niche Ltd of payment of a dividend.

(1) **Increased salary**

Enid will pay income tax at the rate of 40% and class 1 employees' national insurance contributions (NIC) at the rate of 2% on the increased salary.

Niche Ltd will pay class 1 employers' NIC at the rate of 13.8%, but the increased salary and the NIC are deductible for corporation tax, providing a saving at the rate of 26.5% as Niche Ltd's TTP of approximately £200,000 means it will pay tax at 25% less marginal relief.

	£	£
Amount payable by Enid:		
Income tax (£15,000 × 40%)		6,000
NIC (£15,000 × 2%)		300
		6,300
Amount payable by Niche Ltd:		
NIC (£15,000 × 13.8%)	2,070	
Corporation tax saving ((£15,000 + £2,070) × 26.5%)	(4,524)	
Net corporation tax saving	(2,454)	(2,454)
Total tax payable		3,846

The increased salary will therefore decrease the tax cost by £1,217 (£3,846 – £5,063).

(2) **Withdrawal of £15,000 from Enid's loan account**

This will have no tax implications for either Enid or Niche Ltd.

Therefore there will be a tax saving of £5,063.

(d) The change in legal status of the business from an unincorporated business to a company means that Enid is required to cancel the business's value added tax (VAT) registration. Niche Ltd is required to register for VAT. The VAT registration number may be transferred from the business to Niche Ltd, in which case Niche Ltd will take over the rights and liabilities of the business in respect of VAT at the date of transfer.

25 Yacqui

Marking guide			Marks	
(a)		Specialist fixed machine	1.5	
		Warehouse	2.5	
		Increase/(decrease) in Yaqui's tax payable	2	
		Marks Available	6	
		Maximum		5
(b)	(i)	Sale of specialist fixed machine	3.5	
		Marks Available	3.5	
		Maximum		3
	(ii)	Business asset disposal relief availability	3	
		Chargeable gain	2	
		Structures and buildings allowance working	2.5	
		Marks Available	7.5	
		Maximum		6
(c)	(i)	Sale of the warehouse	2.5	
		Marks Available	2.5	
		Maximum		2
	(ii)	Renting out the warehouse	4.5	
		Marks Available	4.5	
		Maximum		4

Marking guide	Marks

Professional skills marks

Analysis and evaluation

- Appropriate use of information in the scenario to determine suitable calculations in relation to income tax and NIC in (a), CGT in part (b) and VAT in part (c)
- Appropriate use of information in the scenario to draw conclusions as to the tax treatment
- Demonstration of the ability to consider the VAT treatment on the sale/ rent of the warehouse and its impact on the recovery of input VAT in part (c)
- Appropriate use of information to calculate the change in Yaqui's tax due in part (a)
- Demonstration of the ability to consider all the taxes relevant eg income tax and Class 4 NIC in part (a)

Commercial acumen

- Recognising the impact of having claimed SBAs on the gain calculation in part (b)
- Recognising that the deferred gain would have already been taxed in part (b)

Maximum	5
Total	25

(a) **Income tax adjustments in respect of the disposal of the specialist fixed machine and the warehouse**

Specialist fixed machine

As the tax written down value of Yaqui's main pool was £nil, the sale of the machine will have given rise to a balancing charge of £23,000. This will increase Yaqui's taxable trading profit for the period ending 30 September 2025.

Warehouse

Structures and buildings allowances (SBAs) are available on the qualifying cost of the warehouse (ie excluding the cost of the land). This is £215,000 (£263,000 – £48,000). An allowance of £1,613 (£215,000 x 3% x 3/12) will be available for the three-month period ending 30 September 2025, which will reduce Yaqui's taxable trading profit for this period.

Increase/(Decrease) in Yaqui's tax payable

The net impact of the disposals on Yaqui's trade profits is that they will increase by £21,387 (£23,000 – £1,613).

As a higher rate taxpayer, Yaqui will pay income tax at 40% and Class 4 NIC at 2% on these increased profits. There will therefore be additional tax due of £8,983 (42% × £21,387).

(b) (i) **Sale of the specialist fixed machine**

No capital loss will arise on the sale of the specialist machine because it qualified for capital allowances.

As the specialist machine was a depreciating asset for capital gains tax purposes, the chargeable gain of £11,000 which was deferred against the purchase of this machine became chargeable on 31 March 2025, ie the earliest of:

- The date the machine will be sold (10 July 2025).
- The date the machine ceased to be used in Yaqui's business (10 July 2025).
- Ten years after the acquisition of the machine (31 March 2025).

This deferred gain would therefore have been chargeable to capital gains tax in 2024/25, and no chargeable gain or allowable loss will arise as a result of this sale on 10 July 2025.

ANSWERS

(ii) **Sale of the warehouse**

Availability of business asset disposal relief (BADR)

BADR will be available on the sale of the warehouse because:

(1) The business is ceasing and the sale is within three years of the cessation of trade.

(2) Yaqui will have owned the business for at least two years prior to ceasing to trade.

(3) The warehouse will still be in business use at the date of cessation.

> **Tutorial note.** It is irrelevant that the warehouse was used in the YP Trading business for less than two years (1 November 2023 to 30 September 2025). When determining the availability of BADR in respect of disposals of assets used in a business which has ceased, the business must have been owned for at least two years prior to cessation, not the asset being disposed of.

Chargeable gain

	£
Sale proceeds	296,000
Add: structures and buildings allowance (SBA) claimed (W)	12,363
	308,363
Less: cost	(263,000)
Chargeable gain	45,363

Working

	£
Qualifying cost for SBAs (from part (a))	215,000
SBAs: Year ended 30 June 2024 (£215,000 x 3% x 8/12)	4,300
Year ended 30 June 2025 (£215,000 x 3%)	6,450
3 months ending 30 September 2025 (from part (a))	1,613
Total SBAs	12,363

Here's an example of how the answer to part (b) could be produced in the CBE:

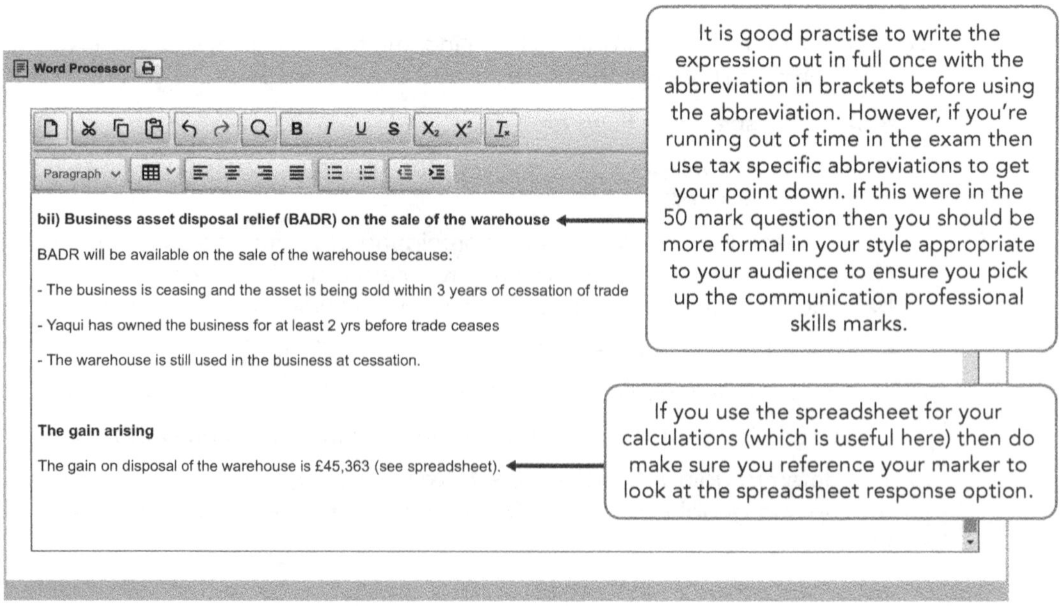

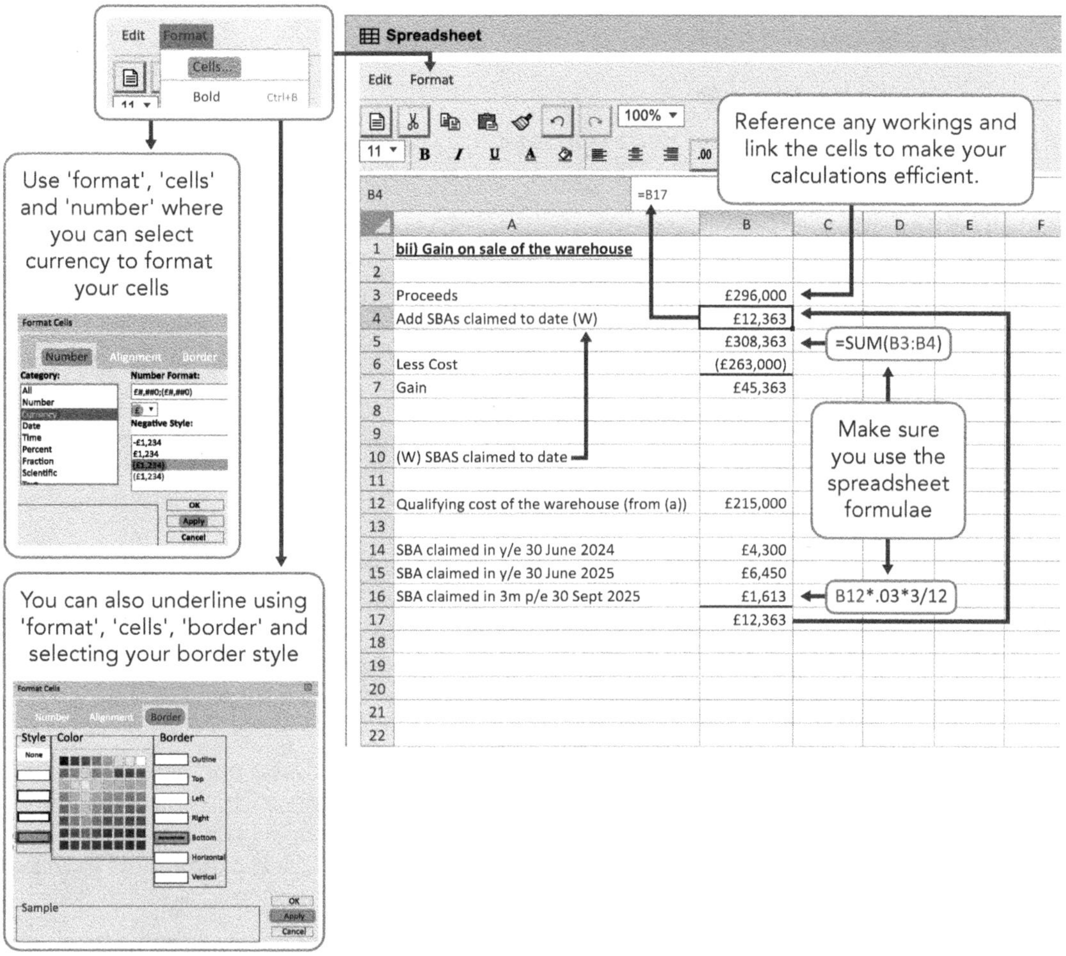

(c) **Value added tax (VAT) consequences of the sale or rental of the warehouse**

(i) **Sale of the warehouse**

If Yaqui sells the warehouse as planned on 30 September 2025, it will be less than three years since its construction so it will be a standard rated supply. Accordingly, Yaqui must charge output VAT of £59,200 (£296,000 x 20%) on the sale. No adjustment is required for the remainder of the ten-year adjustment period for capital goods scheme purposes, as 100% taxable use is assumed for this period.

(ii) **Renting out the warehouse**

The sale of a new freehold commercial building is standard rated such that Yaqui will have incurred input VAT of £52,600 (£263,000 x 20%) on the purchase of the warehouse. This input tax will have been reclaimed in full on acquisition, as the warehouse was wholly used in Yaqui's business making standard rated supplies.

Renting out the warehouse from 1 October 2025 would constitute an exempt supply for VAT, as Yaqui has not opted to tax it. Accordingly, as the warehouse is within the ten-year adjustment period, an annual adjustment of £5,260 (£52,600 x 1/10 (100% – 0%)) will be required to be repaid to HMRC in respect of each of the years within this adjustment period in which it continues to be rented out.

26 Rod

Course Book references

Employment income is covered in Chapter 4. Capital gains tax computation is dealt with in Chapter 7. Losses and partnerships are covered in Chapter 15.

Top tips

In part (b)(i) you only need to compute Rod's position, not that of the other partners. In part (b)(ii) remember to deal only with the loss reliefs which are relevant to Rod – there are no marks for discussing terminal loss relief!

Easy marks

There were some easy marks in part (a) for a basic gains computation even with the slightly unusual EMI element.

ACCA examining team's comments

Part (a) required a calculation of the after-tax proceeds from the sale of shares and also an explanation of the base cost of the shares. Many candidates were able to calculate the capital gains tax arising upon sale of the shares and then to calculate proceeds less tax, earning themselves many of the calculation marks. However unfortunately, many candidates appeared to lack knowledge of the detailed rules for the EMI scheme and so were unable to fully explain the base cost of the shares.

Part (b) required candidates to allocate a trading loss between partners in a partnership and then to calculate, for a new partner who had just joined the partnership, the share of the loss available over two tax years. [This question has been amended since it was originally set due to syllabus changes meaning basis of assessment rules not being examinable in this exam sitting].

Part (c) required candidates to state how the new partner could relieve his trading loss as early as possible and then to explain, with supporting calculations, the total amount of income tax which could be saved with this strategy. Most candidates were able to discuss a possible loss relief strategy although not all chose the loss relief strategy which would relieve the loss as early as possible. Many candidates were able to explain the subsequent tax saving and to support this with calculations. A minority of candidates recognised that claiming the loss relief would affect the amount of personal allowance available and went on to identify the tax implications of this.

Marking guide			Marks	
(a)	Calculation of chargeable gain		2	
	Calculation of after-tax proceeds		2	
	Explanations		3	
	Marks Available		7	
	Maximum			6
(b)	(i)	2024/25 loss	3	
		2025/26 loss	2.5	
		Marks Available	5.5	
		Maximum		5

Marking guide		Marks	
(ii)	Identification of earliest relief	3	
	Calculation of tax saving		
	– 2021/22	1.5	
	– 2022/23	4	
	Total saving	1	
	Marks Available	9.5	
	Maximum		9

Professional skills marks

Analysis and evaluation

- Adoption of a logical approach to prepare a suitable calculation of the after-tax proceeds from the sale of Rod's shares in Lumba plc
- Demonstration of ability to consider relevant factors applicable to the calculation of the base cost of the shares
- Use of information to determine Rod's share of the tax--adjusted trading loss in the Thora Partnership for the two tax years
- Recognition of the tax saving as a result of the re-instatement of the personal allowance after taking loss relief

Commercial acumen

- Effective use of calculations to illustrate the tax saving available to Rod as a result of taking the earliest possible relief for his share of the trading losses of the Thora Partnership
- Demonstration of the ability to identify the earliest possible relief for Rod's share of the trading losses

Maximum	5
Total	25

(a) **After-tax proceeds from the sale of the Lumba plc shares**

The capital gain on the sale of the Lumba plc shares is calculated as follows:

	£	£
Sale proceeds (£4.00 × 20,000)		80,000
Less:		
– exercise price (£2.30 × 20,000)	46,000	
– amount charged to income tax on exercise (see below)	6,000	
Base cost		(52,000)
Chargeable gain		28,000
Less: annual exempt amount		(3,000)
Taxable gain		25,000

The capital gains tax payable is £2,500 (£25,000 × 10%). The after-tax proceeds are £77,500 (£80,000 – £2,500).

As the options were granted at a discount to the market value at the date of grant, a charge to income tax will have arisen on 31 May 2024, when Rod exercised the options, on an amount of £6,000 (£0.30 per share × 20,000 shares), being the difference between the market value of the shares at the date of grant and the exercise price of the options £(2.60 –

ANSWERS

2.30). This is added to the price paid for the shares (£2.30 per share) in calculating the base cost of the shares.

(b) (i) **Rod's share of the tax-adjusted trading loss in the Thora Partnership for the tax years 2024/25 and 2025/26**

	Abe	*Bob*	*Rod*	Total
	£	£	£	£
Period 1 December 2024–31 March 2025 (4m)				
Salary (4/12 × £20,000)	6,667	6,667	0	13,334
Balance (PSR 1:1:1)	(9,667)	(9,667)	(9,667)	(29,001)
Loss to share (4/12 × £47,000)			(9,667)	(15,667)

Rod's 2024/25 trade loss is therefore £9,667.

	Abe	*Bob*	*Rod*	Total
	£	£	£	£
Period 1 April 2025–31 March 2026				
Salary	20,000	20,000	0	40,000
Balance (PSR 1:1:1)	(16,667)	(16,667)	(16,667)	(50,000)
Loss to share			(16,667)	(10,000)

Rod's 2025/26 trade loss is therefore £16,667.

(ii) **Tax saving available to Rod as a result of taking the earliest possible relief for his share of the trading losses of the Thora Partnership**

Rod has a trading loss of £9,667 in 2024/25 and a trading loss of £16,667 in 2025/26.

The losses can be carried back and offset against Rod's total income of the three years prior to the tax year of the loss in each case, on a FIFO basis. This is the earliest possible relief available to Rod.

The loss of 2024/25 will be carried back and offset against Rod's total income of 2021/22 of £82,000, which will result in a tax saving of £3,867 (£9,667 × 40%).

The loss of 2025/26 will be carried back and offset against Rod's total income of 2022/23 of £106,000 (£90,000 + £16,000). This will result in a tax saving of £6,667 (£16,667 × 40%), as the relief will be taken against the employment income in priority to the dividends. Additionally, as Rod's total income originally exceeded £100,000, his personal allowance was restricted to £9,570 (£12,570 – ((£106,000 – £100,000)/2)). After taking loss relief, his full personal allowance will be available, generating a further tax saving of £1,200 ((£12,570 – £9,570) × 40%).

Therefore Rod's total tax saving as a result of taking loss relief is £11,734 (£3,867 + £6,667 + £1,200).

Tutorial note. Note the following:

(1) Rod is eligible to claim opening years' loss relief as the trading loss arose within the first four years of him joining the partnership.

(2) In calculating an individual's income tax liability, losses are usually offset against non-savings income first, before savings income (if any), and then dividends. This will maximise the amount of tax relief obtained.

Videos can be viewed online by accessing your ebook version on VitalSource.

27 Rosa

Course Book references

Consideration of taking someone on as an employee or partner and tax savings from use of trade losses are both covered within Chapter 18 OMB tax planning and a similar question is also included in Skills Checkpoint 4. The capital goods scheme is covered in Chapter 23.

Top tips

While the calculations required in part (a) of this question are, in isolation, relatively straightforward pulling together the whole comparison can feel a little daunting. Make sure you set out which scenario you are considering by breaking down your answer with sub-headings.

In part (b) make sure you clearly set out Rosa's options for using her trade loss. As she's been trading for many years you can only consider the current year and / or prior year claims against total income and the extension to convert the trading loss to use against her gains. With losses it's always important that you apply them to the specific scenario so noticing that Rosa has no other current year income rules out discussion of a current year claim. It's also important that if you ever see a large loss that this triggers you to consider whether the amount of loss used needs to be restricted. Many students missed this in the real exam.

In (c) with the capital goods scheme it can be very helpful to 'tell the story' of the building to ensure you set out sufficient detail to score good marks. So starting with VAT recovery on purchase, considering any adjustments in the 10 year period and then considering the sale adjustment when the building is sold in year 8 is a good way to present your answer clearly. On sale the building will be an old commercial building and will therefore be an exempt supply in considering the sale adjustment.

Easy marks

The calculations in part (a) of this question as a whole may seem quite daunting but if you look at each calculation in isolation there were actually easy marks to be obtained here on a basic income tax calculation and basic employee and employer's NIC calculations. The capital goods scheme is also frequently tested and is therefore a topic which a well-prepared student should be able to score well on. If you've found these tricky you need to get more question practise in.

ACCA examining team's comments

This question was in three main parts, concerning an unincorporated business looking to bring someone else into the business, trading losses of an unincorporated business and VAT on sale of a property.

The first part of the question required advice, based on calculations, on whether an unincorporated business owner should bring a new person into the business as an employee or as a partner. The calculations required were the total amount of income tax and national insurance contributions for each scenario. There were some excellent answers to this part of the question, dealing with each of the relevant tax liabilities in a clear and logical manner. Those candidates who did not do so well would have benefited from taking time to plan their answer before they began, thinking about which taxes affect which individual.

The second part of the question required an explanation of the loss relief available to the unincorporated trader and a calculation of the maximum tax saving available as a result of such relief. Some candidates wrote very generally about loss reliefs, without applying their knowledge to the facts of the question, which lost them marks. A significant number of candidates seemed unaware of the technical rules on restriction of income tax reliefs against total income and were unable to factor these into their calculations. A thorough understanding of the technical rules from all areas of the syllabus is a requirement to do well in this exam.

The third part of this question dealt with disposal of a retail unit which was subject to the capital goods scheme. Some candidates spent time writing everything they knew about the capital goods scheme when only the implications upon disposal were required. Only knowledge which addresses the question requirements will earn marks; candidates should not waste their time writing out tax rules if they are not asked for in the question. Even if a candidate writes lots of correct information about a particular tax topic, if it has not been asked for, it cannot earn any marks.

Marking guide

		Marks	
(a)	Siena as partner	3	
	Siena as employee	4	
	Calculation of shares of loss	2	
	Conclusion	2	
	Marks Available	11	
	Maximum		9
(b)	Availability of loss relief	2	
	Relief against total income in 2025/26	3.5	
	Tax saving	3.5	
	Marks Available	9	
	Maximum		7
(c)	Disposal exempt	1.5	
	Initial reclaim	1.5	
	Implications of sale	2	
	Marks Available	5	
	Maximum		4

Professional skills marks

Analysis and evaluation

- Appropriate use of information to determine suitable calculations of the total amount of income tax and NIC payable if Siena becomes a partner or employee
- Appropriate use of information to support discussion and draw appropriate conclusions regarding the loss reliefs available to Rosa
- Demonstration of ability to consider relevant factors applicable eg cap on loss relief
- Use of information to determine the VAT impact of the disposal of the retail unit
- Demonstration of ability to consider all relevant taxes specified in the requirement regarding whether Siena should become a partner or an employee

Commercial acumen

- Recognition of constraints and opportunities related to whether Siena is taken on as a partner or employee, for example, the total tax liability will be lower if she is a partner, but the trading loss relief available is higher if she becomes an employee

Maximum	5
Total	25

(a) **Difference in the total amount of income tax and national insurance contributions (NICs) payable by Siena and Rosa for the tax year 2026/27 if Siena becomes a partner or an employee on 1 April 2026**

- **Siena becomes a partner**

If Siena becomes a partner in RS Trading on 1 April 2026, she will be allocated £2,800 of the partnership loss of the year ending 31 March 2027 (W), such that she will have no taxable income for the tax year 2026/27. Accordingly, she will have no liability to income tax or class 4 NIC.

Rosa will be allocated a trading loss of £59,200 in the tax year 2026/27 (W). As she will have no other source of income in that year, Rosa will have no liability to income tax or class 4 NIC.

- **Siena becomes an employee**

If Siena becomes an employee, on an annual salary of £22,000, she will have an income tax liability of £1,886 ((£22,000 – £12,570) × 20%), and a class 1 employee's NIC liability of £754 ((£22,000 – £12,570) × 8%).

In this case, RS Trading will also have a liability to class 1 employer's NIC of £1,780 ((£22,000 – £9,100) × 13.8%). As this is covered by the £5,000 employment allowance, no class 1 contributions would be payable.

Rosa will, again, have no personal liability to income tax or NIC, as she will incur a trading loss of £84,000 (£62,000 + £22,000).

Therefore, the total income tax and NIC payable by Siena and Rosa for the tax year 2026/27 will be reduced by £2,640 (£1,886 + £754) if Siena becomes a partner.

However, although the total tax and NIC payable by Siena and Rosa is lower if Siena becomes a partner, the amount of trading loss available for relief is higher if Siena becomes an employee (£84,000, rather than £62,000).

Working

Allocation of RS Trading loss for the year ending 31 March 2027

	Total	*Rosa*	*Siena*
	£	£	£
Budgeted loss	(62,000)		
Salary to Siena	(12,000)		12,000
Balance (80:20)	(74,000)	(59,200)	(14,800)
Total share of loss	(62,000)	(59,200)	(2,800)

Tutorial note. Although Rosa will have no personal liability to NIC, she can voluntarily continue to pay Class 2 contributions in order to ensure entitlement to contributions-based benefits.

(b) **Loss reliefs available to Rosa in respect of the budgeted trading loss of RS Trading**

Rosa will have a trading loss of £84,000 in the tax year 2026/27.

As Rosa has no other income in 2026/27, she can only carry back the loss to 2025/26, and offset the loss against her total income of that year, and then against the chargeable gains arising on the sale of the investment properties in 2025/26.

Rosa's total income in 2025/26 is £87,000 (£27,000 + £60,000). There is no restriction on the amount of loss which can be used against trading income from the same trade, but relief against the property income will be capped at the greater of £50,000 and 25% of Rosa's adjusted net income for the year, which is £21,750 (£87,000 × 25%).

Accordingly, a maximum of £50,000 can be offset against the property income. Therefore, a total of £77,000 (£27,000 + £50,000) can be offset against income leaving net income of £10,000 (£87,000 – £77,000), which will be covered by Rosa's personal allowance.

The balance of the loss of £7,000 (£84,000 – £77,000) can be relieved against the chargeable gains of £92,000 on the sale of the investment properties.

Maximum tax saving 2025/26

	£
Income tax (No liability to income tax remains, so the whole amount is repayable)	22,232
Capital gains tax (CGT) (Working)	4,662
	26,894

Working

CGT payable after taking loss relief

	£
Gains remaining chargeable (£92,000 – £7,000)	85,000
Less: annual exempt amount	(3,000)
Taxable gains	82,000
CGT:	
– £37,700 × 18%	6,786
– £44,300 × 24%	10,632
– £82,000	17,418

CGT saving is £4,662 (£22,080 – £17,418)

Tutorial note. Before taking loss relief, Rosa's taxable gains would all be taxed at 24% as Rosa's taxable income exceeded £37,700. After taking loss relief against Rosa's total income for 2025/26, the full amount of the basic rate band will be available to use against taxable gains.

(c) **Value added tax (VAT) implications of the disposal of the retail unit**

On 6 April 2026, when the retail unit is sold, it will be more than three years old. Accordingly, the sale will be exempt from VAT as Rosa has not opted to tax it.

On acquisition, the retail unit was newly constructed, so VAT of £58,000 (£290,000 × 20%) will have been charged. Rosa will have reclaimed the whole of this in the year ended 31 March 2020, as she used it in her business, making wholly standard rated supplies.

However, as the sale of the retail unit will be an exempt disposal, for the purpose of the capital goods scheme it is deemed to have 0% taxable use for the remainder of the ten-year adjustment period. As the warehouse is sold during the eighth year of the adjustment period, there are two years of the adjustment period remaining, and therefore a final VAT adjustment of £11,600 (£58,000 × 2/10 × (100% – 0%)) will be repayable by Rosa to HM Revenue and Customs (HMRC) in respect of the sale.

28 Tomas and Ines

Course Book references

Basic income tax and NIC calculations are assumed knowledge from TX but covered in Chapters 2 and 14. VAT is covered in Chapter 23 and EIS schemes are covered in Chapter 3.

Top tips

Part (b) in this question is more straightforward so you may like to attempt this to secure the easier marks before moving on to (a) and (c).

In part (a) it's important to spot that the question asks for **total** tax payable. This should remind you in the planning stage that you shouldn't only consider income tax. As a sole trader Tomas will pay Class 4 NICs on trade profits in addition to income tax and this will allow you to access more of the 5 marks available.

Part (c) of this question is probably the most challenging, looking at a sale of EIS shares within 3 years of acquisition. Using the verbs from the question start by trying to explain the tax issues- the gain on the EIS shares, withdrawal of the EIS IT relief and the deferred gain becoming taxable. Finally, don't forget that you're also asked to calculate Ines's after-tax proceeds. This is frequently asked in ATX and you must start with proceeds before deducting the tax - don't make the common mistake of starting your calculation with the gain! It's worth producing these calculations even if you're worried your tax is wrong- follow-on marks will be available.

Easy marks

The basic income tax and NIC calculations in part (a) of this question would have been the source of easy marks on the assumption that you realised that NIC in addition to income tax needed to be calculated.

ACCA examining team's comments

This question concerned the taxation of profits, voluntary registration for VAT for a new unincorporated business, and the sale of shares in respect of which enterprise investment scheme (EIS) relief had been claimed.

The first part of the question required candidates to explain the difference in the total amount of tax payable by the taxpayer due to his profits now being taxed as trading income rather than as chargeable gains. When specific taxes are not mentioned in the question, candidates need to think broadly. Although the majority of candidates correctly identified the income tax implications, very few considered that there would also be national insurance (NIC) implications as well. In relation to the CGT implications, only a minority recognised that the items being sold constituted chattels under £6,000, and so were exempt. So, the majority of candidates were only able to score two out of a possible five marks. The question did ask for supporting calculations, but many candidates produced detailed, comprehensive income tax and CGT computations, in addition to explaining the implications. Calculations were only needed to support the explanation, and so needed to only be brief. In particular, many candidates doing the CBE explained the position in the word processing document, referring the relevant numbers, and also produced comprehensive calculations in the spreadsheet, which did not gain them any additional marks.

[Part b(i)] of the question required candidates to explain two matters the taxpayer should consider in deciding whether it would be financially beneficial to register voluntarily for VAT. On the whole this was done well, although some candidates wasted time explaining more than two, and/or producing lengthy answers including what appeared to be all they knew about voluntary registration, without considering whether these would, in fact, have a financial impact. Candidates are encouraged to take time to read and understand the question fully before starting to write. A little more time spent reading the specific requirements here might have saved quite a bit of wasted effort in some cases.

[Note that part b(ii), the requirement relating to Tomas's purchase of overseas services, has been added to the question and so no ACCA examining team's comments are available in respect of this part].

The final part of the question (part (c)) tested the rules relating to the sale of shares, which qualified under the EIS scheme, being sold within three years of their acquisition. Many candidates were aware of the main principles relating to the taxation of the gain and the withdrawal of the EIS relief previously given but very few managed to get the calculation of the CGT right, particularly in relation to the treatment of the previously deferred gain, which was, admittedly quite a tricky aspect.

Marking guide		Marks	
(a)	Income tax implications	2	
	National Insurance implications	2	
	Capital gains tax - chattels <£6,000	1	
	Difference in tax payable	0.5	
	Marks Available	5.5	
	Maximum		5
(b) (i)	VAT status of suppliers	2	
	VAT status of customers	2	
			4
(ii)	VAT on overseas services supplied	3	
			3
(c)	Consequences of sale	5	
	Tax liabilities	3	
	After-tax proceeds	0.5	
	Marks Available	8.5	
	Maximum		8

Professional skills marks

Analysis and evaluation

- Appropriate use of information to summarise the net difference in tax cost between treating the profit as trading vs capital in part (a)
- Consideration of both income tax and NIC in part (a)
- Appropriate use of information to compare treatment of services provided by overseas supplier to treatment of services provided by a UK supplier in part (b)
- Recognition of more than one tax consequence of disposal of shares in part (c)
- Use of information to support discussion with respect to the implications of the sale of the Tavira Ltd shares

Commercial acumen

- Recognition of the need to consider the impact of voluntary registration for VAT on both suppliers and customers in part (b)
- Demonstration of the ability to make the most efficient use of the annual exempt amount when providing calculations in part (c)

Maximum	5
Total	25

(a) **Tax treatment of the sale of sporting memorabilia**

As Tomas is carrying on a trade of selling sporting memorabilia, the following liabilities will arise:

	£
Income tax	
(£14,000 – £12,570) = £1,430 x 20%	286
No tax will arise on the dividends, as they are covered by the dividend nil rate band	0
National insurance contributions (NIC)	
Class 4: (£14,000 – £12,570) × 6%	86
Total tax payable	372

If the sales were treated as capital disposals, there would be no capital gains tax to pay as the memorabilia are chattels, with cost and proceeds both less than £6,000.

The difference in the total tax which will be payable by Tomas for 2025/26 is an increase of £372.

(b) (i) **Matters to be considered by Tomas in deciding whether it is financially beneficial to register voluntarily for value added tax (VAT)**

The VAT status of his suppliers. If Tomas' suppliers are VAT registered, Tomas will be charged VAT on his purchases, which he will only be able to reclaim if he is registered for VAT himself. However, if he purchases from non-VAT registered businesses, or members of the public, he will not suffer any input VAT, so there will be no financial benefit from registering.

The VAT status of his customers. If Tomas' customers are registered for VAT, they will be able to reclaim the VAT charged by Tomas on the memorabilia. However, if they are not registered, the VAT will represent an additional cost for them, which may make Tomas' prices uncompetitive, or Tomas will have to bear the burden of the VAT himself.

Tutorial note. Marks were also awarded where candidates made other sensible comments.

(ii) **VAT implications of purchasing advice from the overseas supplier**

- The provision of this advice will be a business to business (B2B) service. It will be treated as supplied in the UK, because that is where Tomas' business is established.
- Tomas will be required to pay VAT at the UK standard rate of 20% to HM Revenue and Customs (HMRC) under the 'reverse charge' principle. The rate of VAT in the overseas country is irrelevant.
- The input VAT can be reclaimed on this expense in the same way as any other input tax incurred by the business.
- Accordingly, Tomas' VAT position will be the same as if the services had been purchased from a UK supplier.

(c) **Sale of shares in Tavira Ltd**

If the shares in Tavira Ltd are sold on 1 June 2025, Ines will have owned them for less than three years. The following consequences will therefore arise:

- A chargeable gain of £23,000 (£95,000 – £72,000) will arise on the sale; and
- The enterprise investment scheme (EIS) income tax relief obtained when the shares were acquired will be withdrawn. As the shares will be sold at a profit, the full amount of the tax credit originally given of £18,600 will be reclaimed by HM Revenue and Customs (HMRC).

In addition, the sale of the Tavira Ltd shares will result in the gain on the sale of the painting, which was deferred on the acquisition of the shares, being brought back into charge. The gain on this disposal was £86,000, but the maximum amount of the gain deferred was restricted to the qualifying expenditure of £72,000.

Ines will have a capital gains tax (CGT) liability in the tax year 2025/26, calculated as follows:

	Gain eligible for BADR	*Gain not eligible for BADR*
	£	£
Gain on Tavira Ltd shares	23,000	
Deferred gain on painting		72,000
Less: annual exempt amount (best use)	0	(3,000)
Taxable gains	23,000	69,000

Ines' CGT liability is £16,100 ((£23,000 × 10%) + (£69,000 × 20%)).

There will also be the clawback of the income tax relief previously obtained of £18,600.

Accordingly, Ines' after-tax proceeds from the sale of the Tavira Ltd shares is £60,300 (£95,000 – £16,100 – £18,600).

Tutorial note. Although unusual, there are certain real-life scenarios where both EIS income tax relief and BADR would both be available in relation to a shareholding. It is essential that you are able to follow the examiner's instructions in relation to the availability of reliefs (where given explicitly in a scenario), and to be able to apply them in order to accurately calculate the associated tax liabilities. You are not required to question the validity of statements given in a question unless specifically directed.

29 Sabin and Patan Ltd

Course Book references

Sole trader losses are covered in Chapter 15, capital gains tax and capital gains tax reliefs are covered in Chapters 7 and 8. The structures and buildings allowance is covered in Chapter 14 and research and development for companies in Chapter 16.

Top tips

In part (a) make sure you follow the requirement and ONLY consider terminal loss relief. To calculate the tax saving you'll need to think about Sabin's taxable income each tax year both before and after the trade loss offset.

In part (b) don't forget the second part of the requirement to calculate the post-tax proceeds from the sale of the assets.

Easy marks

Calculating the gain on the sale of the business premises in part (b) should be the source of easy marks and, given the method marks available, you should also be able to pick up marks by using your figures to calculate the post-tax proceeds. In part (c) there should be easy marks for you calculating the structures and buildings allowance available on the newly-constructed factory.

ACCA examining team's comments

Part (a) of the question was to calculate, with supporting explanations, the income tax saving for a sole trader if he claims terminal loss relief upon cessation of his loss-making business. Generally, answers to this part of the question were disappointing. Despite the wording used in the requirement, namely to 'calculate with supporting explanations' a common mistake made by many candidates was to produce only numbers and therefore miss out on the marks for providing the written explanations. Mistakes of this nature can be avoided if candidates make a point of highlighting the key words in the requirement and then subsequently go back and double check that they are doing exactly what has been required of them.

Many candidates demonstrated an understanding that the terminal loss could be carried back 36 months but made the offset against total income rather than trading profits. The best approach was to set up income tax computations (before taking account of any terminal loss) for the final four tax years of the sole trader, showing trading profits, any other sources of income, and deducting the personal allowance in order to give taxable income for all years concerned. In this scenario, there were no trading profits in the final tax year (2024/25) but there were trading profits in the previous 3 tax years (2021/22, 2022/23 and 2023/24).

The terminal loss can then be offset against the relevant trading profits of the past 36 months on a LIFO basis ie primarily against the trading profits of 2023/24 and then against 2022/23. There is insufficient terminal loss to use against the trading profits of 2021/22. When making the offset, it is important to remember that terminal losses of sole traders can only be carried back against the trading income of earlier years and not against any other sources of income.

Having shown the way in which the terminal loss would be offset, it was important to remember that the requirement asked for explanatory comment, as well as calculations. So candidates needed to explain what they had done, for example by stating that the terminal loss is carried back against trading income of the three preceding tax years, on a LIFO basis.

To fully address the requirement, it was also necessary to calculate and explain the income tax saving as a result of the terminal loss claim. In this respect, many candidates simply took the loss used and multiplied it by the basic income tax rate of 20%. However, to answer this part accurately, consideration of the sole trader's level of income before utilisation of the terminal loss was required in order to compare it with revised levels of income once the offset had taken place. This comparison should be quite straightforward if the pre-loss and post-loss computations are set up methodically. The tax saving is then the difference in the taxable income figures (for each year involved) multiplied by the appropriate tax rate, which is 20% in this scenario. [Note that this question has been amended since originally set due to syllabus changes. The Examiner's comments have been amended accordingly].

Part (b) of this question contains two requirements. The first involves an explanation of the capital gains tax (CGT) implications of the sole trader selling his business premises and a machine to a company. The second part asks for a calculation of the amount available to the sole trader from the sale of these two assets, after paying any CGT liability.

When dealing with the first part, many candidates recognised that there would be a capital gain on the building but fewer acknowledged that there would be no capital loss on the disposal of the machine by virtue of having claimed capital allowances on the asset. It was then necessary to consider business asset disposal relief (BADR) in respect of the gain on the building. This involved a discussion of the conditions for BADR in order to consider their applicability to the relevant asset; it had been held for more than two years, was in business use at the date of cessation of the trade and was sold within three years of date of cessation. Most candidates spotted the relevance of BADR and were able to pick up some of the marks for application of the relevant conditions.

The second part of the requirement involved calculation of the 'after-tax proceeds'. Regrettably, when addressing this part, a number of candidates simply stopped at the tax liability without thinking precisely about what it was they had been asked to do. It was first necessary to calculate the CGT liability on the building – this was at 10% due to the availability of BADR. This amount then needed to be deducted from the total proceeds on the sale of both assets in order to establish the amount of after-tax proceeds. In questions of this nature, candidates should always ensure that they are clear on what it is they are being asked to calculate – whether it is an actual tax liability only or, as in this case, the after-tax proceeds. The latter involves the extra step of deducting the tax liability from proceeds received. Many candidates overlooked this final stage.

The final part of this question involves an explanation of the tax deductions and reliefs available to a company in respect of the acquisition of a new factory and expenditure incurred on research and development (R&D). Responses to this part of the question were generally good. Although the requirement did not specifically ask for calculations, it is perfectly acceptable to provide these if they help to support the explanatory comment which had been requested.

Beginning with the factory, it was important to identify the availability of structures and buildings allowances (SBA) by virtue of its date of construction. A number of candidates were aware that SBAs were an issue, but could not explain with sufficient clarity precisely why this was the case. These allowances are available for commercial buildings constructed on, or after, 29 October 2018. It was also important to explain that the cost of land is excluded from SBAs and that the allowance is given at the rate of 3% per annum. However, on this occasion, because the building was only brought into use one month after the start of the accounting period, it needed to be pointed out that, for the accounting period concerned, the available allowance would be based on 11/12 of the full annual equivalent.

With regard to the R&D expenditure, it was important to note once again that explanations were required. Candidates were therefore expected to state how the R&D deduction works ie that a 20% credit is available for relevant expenditure, and then to go on to apply this to the facts of the question. This involved distinguishing between the employee costs which would qualify in their entirety for the additional relief and the subcontractor costs where only 65% would be eligible for the additional relief. A calculation of the total credit could be provided in support of the explanation, as long as it didn't replace it in its entirety.

Since the company was loss-making in the period concerned, it was also necessary to go on to consider the other relief options available in respect of the R&D tax credit. A significant number of candidates did not go on to think about this additional step. [Note that this question has been amended since originally set due to syllabus changes. The Examiner's comments have been amended accordingly].

Marking guide

		Marks	
(a)	Terminal loss relief – explanation	2	
	Calculation of tax relief	4.5	
	Marks Available	6.5	
	Maximum		6
(b)	Disposal of assets	1.5	
	Capital gains tax	3.5	
	After-tax proceeds	1	
	Marks Available	6	
	Maximum		5
(c)	New factory	4	
	Research and development		
	– Capital allowances	1	
	– Tax credit	5.5	
	Marks Available	10.5	
	Maximum		9

Marking guide	Marks

Professional skills marks

Analysis and evaluation

- Appropriate use of information in the scenario to determine suitable calculations of the income tax saving in part (a)
- Appropriate use of information in the scenario to support explanation of the tax deductions available re R&D in part (c)
- Demonstration of reasoned judgement when considering CGT on the sale of items in part (b)

Commercial acumen

- Effective use of information to calculate the after-tax proceeds in part (b)
- Recognition of the fact that, as a loss making company, Patan Ltd may choose to claim payment of the R&D expenditure in part (c)
- Recognition of the importance of timing in relation to availability of BADR in (b) and on the calculation of the SBA in part (c)

Maximum	5
Total	25

(a) **Income tax saving as a result of a terminal loss relief claim by Sabin**

Terminal loss relief is available for the loss arising in the final 12 months prior to cessation. The terminal loss is £32,800.

Sabin has no taxable trading income in 2024/25, such that he can claim terminal loss relief against his trading income of the three tax years prior to cessation on a LIFO basis, ie 2023/24, 2022/23, 2021/22, in that order.

Accordingly, the loss will be offset as follows:

	2021/22	2022/23	2023/24
	£	£	£
Trading income	44,000	32,000	21,000
Loss relief	nil	(11,800)	(21,000)

Tax relief

2023/24: Sabin's original income tax liability was £2,886 ((£21,000 + £6,000 – £12,570) x 20%). After terminal loss relief, his liability will be £nil as his employment income (£6,000) will be covered by his personal allowance. Accordingly, the income tax saving will be £2,886.

2022/23: Sabin's original taxable income was £25,430 (£32,000 + £6,000 – £12,570). Following the terminal loss claim, this will be reduced to £13,630 (£25,430 – £11,800), such that there will be a saving of £2,360 (£11,800 x 20%).

The total income tax saving as a result of the terminal loss claim is therefore £5,246 (£2,886 + £2,360).

Here's a potential answer to this part of the question in the CBE software. As it's quite numerical the spreadsheet response option has been used.

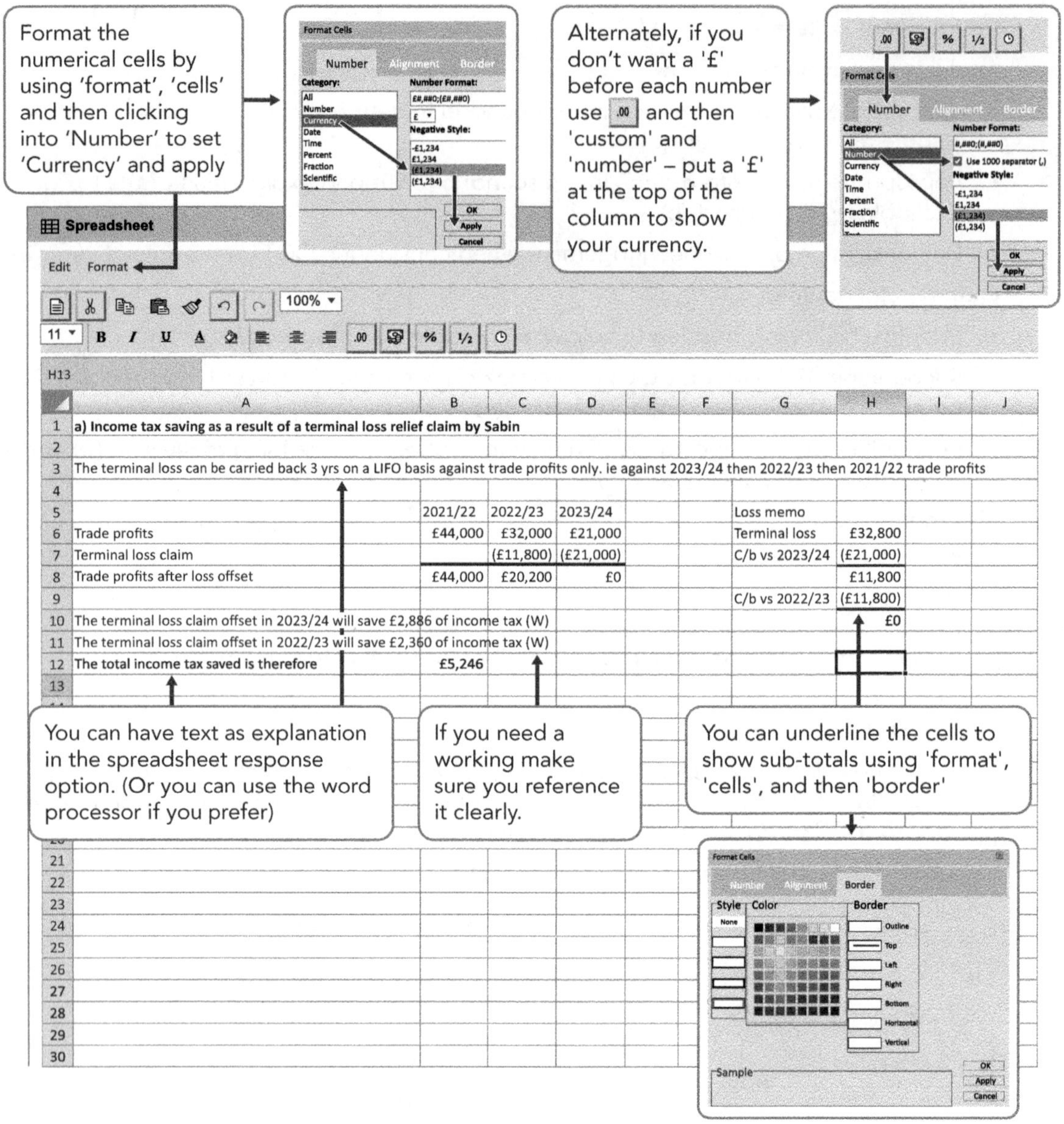

Here's the working referenced from the main answer.

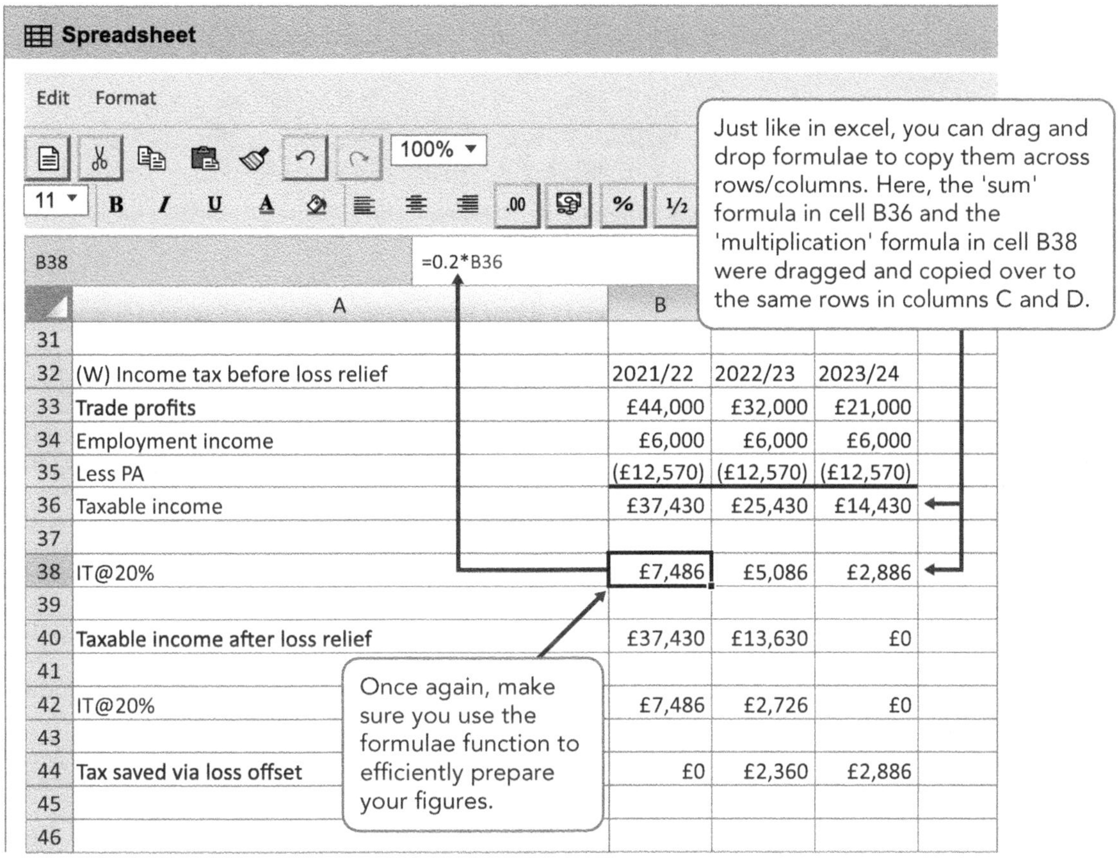

	A	B	C	D
31				
32	(W) Income tax before loss relief	2021/22	2022/23	2023/24
33	Trade profits	£44,000	£32,000	£21,000
34	Employment income	£6,000	£6,000	£6,000
35	Less PA	(£12,570)	(£12,570)	(£12,570)
36	Taxable income	£37,430	£25,430	£14,430
37				
38	IT@20%	£7,486	£5,086	£2,886
39				
40	Taxable income after loss relief	£37,430	£13,630	£0
41				
42	IT@20%	£7,486	£2,726	£0
43				
44	Tax saved via loss offset	£0	£2,360	£2,886
45				
46				

(b) **Capital gains tax (CGT) implications of the sale of the business premises and item of specialist machinery**

The sale of the business premises will give rise to a chargeable gain of £28,000 (£114,000 – £86,000).

No capital loss will arise on the sale of the specialist machine as capital allowances were claimed on this asset.

The gain on the business premises qualifies for business asset disposal relief (BADR) because Sabin carried on the business for more than two years prior to cessation, the premises were in business use at the date of cessation, and were sold within three years of the date of cessation. CGT payable is therefore £2,800 (£28,000 x 10%).

The amount available to Sabin from the sale of these assets

After-tax proceeds are £152,200 (£114,000 + £41,000 – £2,800).

This part of the question is more written and so may be more suited to the word processor response option.

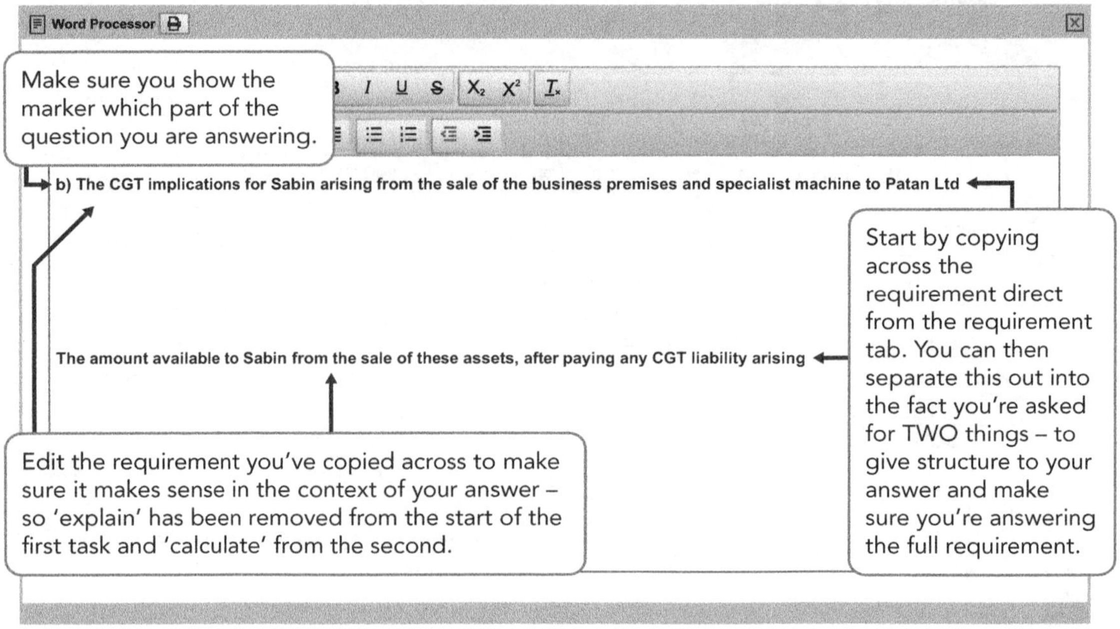

Once you have your structure you can then type in your answer. It could look something like this.

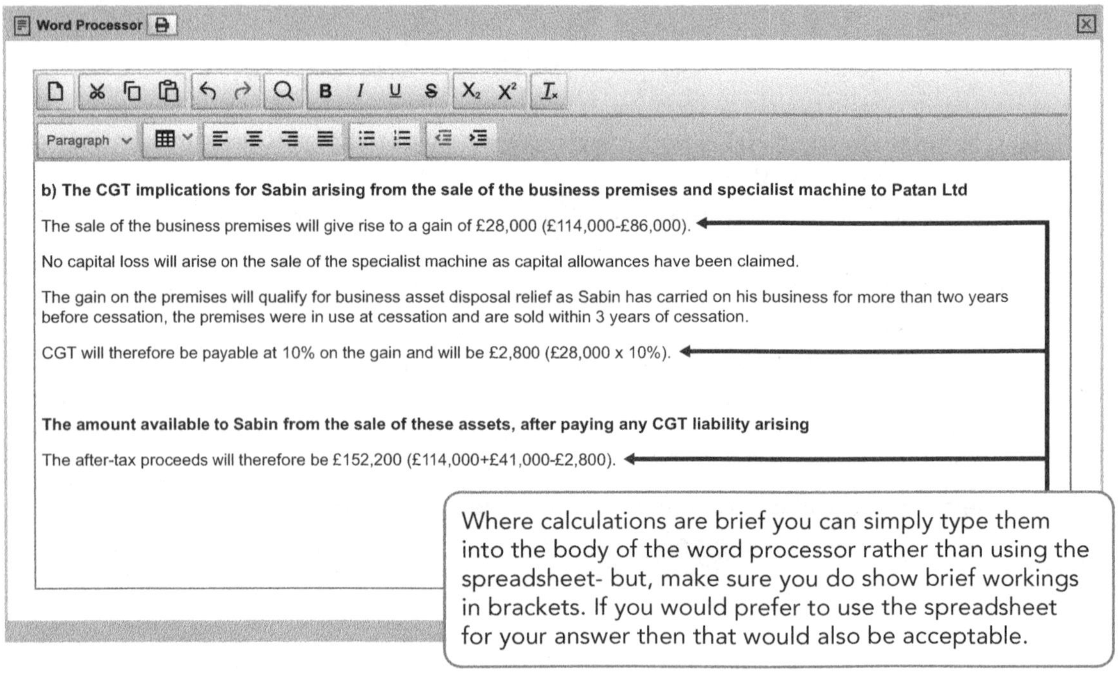

(c) **Patan Ltd**

(1) **Tax deduction available in respect of the acquisition of the new factory**

The new factory will qualify for the structures and buildings allowance (SBA) as it is a new commercial building. The cost of the land, planning permission, fees and stamp taxes are not eligible for the allowance, so Patan Ltd may claim an annual writing down allowance of £2,580 (3% x (£242,000 – £106,000 – £30,000 – £20,000)). As Patan Ltd only brought the building in to use on 1 May 2025, the SBA available in the year ending 31 March 2026 will be £2,365 (£2,580 x 11/12).

(2) **Tax deductions available in respect of the expenditure on research and development activities**

As Patan Ltd carries out R&D, the revenue expenditure which relates directly to undertaking research and development activities qualifies for a R&D expenditure credit (RDEC). The credit is 20% of the qualifying R&D. It is first added to Patan Ltd's taxable trading income and then it is offset against Patan Ltd's corporation tax liability. The whole of the employee cost qualifies, but only 65% of the cost of the external contractor, who is provided by an unconnected company. In addition, the computer software also qualifies.

While the specialist research equipment does not qualify for the RDEC it will qualify for a 100% first year allowance.

Accordingly, the expenditure qualifying for the RDEC is £55,300 (£40,000 + (65% x £22,000) + £1,000). The RDEC is therefore £11,060 (20% x £55,300).

As Patan Ltd will be a loss-making company in the year ending 31 March 2026, there is no corporation tax liability to offset the RDEC against. It can therefore choose to have it paid or carried forward and offset against the corporation tax liability of future periods.

Videos can be viewed online by accessing your ebook version on VitalSource.

Taxation of companies

30 Maria and Granada Ltd

Course Book references

Purchase of own shares will be found in Chapter 20. Loss relief is the subject of Chapter 17. Intangible assets are covered in Chapter 16. Value added tax (VAT) is dealt with in Chapter 23.

Top tips

Make sure you follow each requirement carefully in this question to ensure you are answering each sub-requirement fully. It's actually lots of smaller questions about separate topics which will make the question less intimidating. If you don't remember the rules for a purchase of own shares to be treated as capital then look them up quickly in your notes and then have a go at the calculations.

Easy marks

The tax treatment for companies for intangibles and the transfer of a going concern rules are commonly examined and thus should have allowed you easy marks in this question.

ACCA examining team's comments

Part (a)(i) of this question focused on the requirement for the sale of shares by an individual shareholder to the company to result in a 'substantial reduction' in their shareholding in order to receive capital treatment on the disposal. Unfortunately, it would appear that this is an aspect of a company purchasing its own shares which many candidates are not comfortable with. A small number of candidates just reproduced the conditions to be satisfied in order to obtain capital treatment, which was not required and so scored no marks.

Of those candidates who did try to answer this part of the question, the most common mistake was to forget that when a company repurchases shares from a shareholder, the shares are cancelled so that the total issued share capital of the company is reduced as a consequence.

Part (a)(ii) of this question required the calculation of after-tax proceeds on the disposal of two alternative numbers of shares from a shareholding, one of which did qualify for capital treatment and one of which didn't. This information was given in the requirements. In spite of this, a lack of technical knowledge or inadequate reading of the question meant that a significant number of candidates did not apply this and treated both disposals as giving rise to chargeable gains, rather than correctly treating one of them as a distribution. Additionally, many candidates failed to recognise that the disposal which attracted capital treatment would also qualify for business asset disposal relief. In any question regarding the disposal of shares by an individual, candidates should automatically consider the application of business asset disposal relief. This is an area where it is very important to know the precise conditions and to be able to state definitively whether or not the relief applies, and the reasons why or why not. Candidates who went on to calculate the after-tax proceeds generally identified the correct starting point on this occasion, which was pleasing.

Part (b)(i) concerned the tax deductions available to a company on the acquisition of an intangible asset. There were very few good answers to this part of the question. Intangible assets are examined frequently in Advanced Taxation (ATX – UK), so candidates need to be aware of their tax treatment as trading assets, rather than capital assets, for companies, and the consequential tax treatment of these for corporation tax purposes.

Part (b)(ii) required candidates to explain how the company could get tax relief for a loss incurred by a recently acquired trade. Several candidates incorrectly discussed group relief here. This was not the acquisition of shares in a company, which would have created a group, but the acquisition of trade and assets from a partnership. The two situations are completely different, and candidates must take care to ensure that they read and interpret the facts in this type of question correctly.

It appeared that many candidates would have benefited from pausing and thinking more before they started to write. It is important in any question dealing with relief for losses that a well-considered and logical approach is taken. Well-prepared candidates were able to identify that at least part of the trading loss would have to be carried forward, [relief for which would be restricted to profits from the same trade], and discussed the relevance of proposed changes to the trade in this context.

Part (c) required an explanation of the VAT implications of the acquisition of the business and additional information needed to fully clarify the VAT position in relation to a building. The majority of candidates were able to identify that the transaction would not be liable to VAT as it concerned the transfer of a going concern. Candidates who performed less well on this part, however, then went on to explain why the going concern rules applied, stating all the conditions, but reasons **why** a particular treatment applies aren't required in a discussion of the VAT implications of that treatment. The VAT rules relating to property are very frequently tested in Advanced Taxation (ATX – UK) and it was good to see that the majority of candidates were aware of the main facts here in relation to the age of the building and the existence, or otherwise of an option to tax.

Marking guide

			Marks	
(a)	(i)	Sale of 2,700 shares	3.5	
		Sale of 3,200 shares	1	
		Marks Available	4.5	
		Maximum		4
	(ii)	Sale of 2,700 shares	2.5	
		Sale of 3,200 shares	2	
		Marks Available	4.5	
		Maximum		4
(b)	(i)	Entitled to deduction	1	
		Writing down allowance	1	
		Impairment/consistent treatment	1	
				3
	(ii)	Current year relief	2	
		Carry forward	2.5	
		Relevance of change in nature of trade	2	
		Marks Available	6.5	
		Maximum		5
(c)	General implications of going concern transfer		1	
	VAT implications and additional information		4	
	Marks Available		5	
	Maximum			4

Marking guide	Marks

Professional skills marks

Analysis and evaluation

- Appropriate use of information to determine suitable calculations to demonstrate that the capital treatment will apply if Maria sells back 3,200 shares to Grenada Ltd, but not if she sells back 2,700 shares.
- Appropriate use of data to support discussion and draw appropriate conclusions regarding the corporation tax treatment of the acquisition of the patent by Granada Ltd if no charge for amortisation was required in its statement of profit or loss.
- Use of information to determine Maria's after-tax proceeds per share if she sells either 2,700 shares of 3,200 shares back to Grenada Ltd, and how Granada Ltd could obtain relief for the trading loss.

Scepticism

- Identification of additional information which may alter the VAT implications in relation to the acquisition of the trade and assets of Starling Partners in respect of the age of the building and the option to tax.

Commercial acumen

- Effective use of calculations relating to the context to illustrate points being made relating to the corporation tax treatment of the acquisition of the patent by Granada Ltd if no charge for amortisation was required in its statement of profit or loss.
- Recognition of constraints and opportunities related to the choice of trading loss relief.

Maximum	5
Total	25

(a) (i) **Sale of 2,700 shares back to Granada Ltd**

For capital gains tax treatment to apply, Maria's shareholding in Granada Ltd must be reduced to no more than 75% of her pre-sale holding.

Maria has a 25% shareholding before the sale. Therefore, after the sale her shareholding must be reduced to no more than 75% × 25% = 18.75%.

The total number of shares in issue after the sale will be reduced as the shares repurchased by the company are cancelled.

Maria will hold 10,000 – 2,700 = 7,300 shares out of (10,000 × 4) – 2,700 = 37,300 total shares in issue. This is a (7,300/37,300) × 100% = 19.6% holding, ie greater than 18.75%, so that the condition relating to the reduction in the level of shareholding will not be met.

Sale of 3,200 shares back to Granada Ltd

Maria will now hold 10,000 – 3,200 = 6,800 shares out of 40,000 – 3,200 = 36,800 total shares in issue. This is an (6,800/36,800) × 100% = 18.5% holding, ie less than 18.75%, so that the condition relating to the reduction in the level of shareholding will be met.

(ii) **Sale of 2,700 shares back to Granada Ltd**

The income tax payable in respect of each share is £(12.80 – 1.00) × 33.75% = £3.98.

The post-tax proceeds per share are therefore £(12.80 – 3.98) = £8.82.

> **Tutorial note.** Note the following:
>
> (1) As Maria does not satisfy all of the conditions for this sale to be dealt with under the capital gains tax rules, the disposal will be treated as an income distribution and Maria will have an income tax liability.
>
> (2) The dividend is the difference between the sale proceeds and the amount originally subscribed.
>
> (3) The dividend nil rate band of £500 has already been used.

Sale of 3,200 shares back to Granada Ltd

The capital gains tax payable in respect of each share is £(12.80 – 1.00) × 10% = £1.18.

The post-tax proceeds per share are therefore £(12.80 – 1.18) = £11.62.

> **Tutorial note.** The disposal will qualify for business asset disposal relief as Maria holds more than 5% of the ordinary shares of Granada Ltd and is a director of the company. The capital gain arising will therefore be taxed at 10%.

(b) (i) **Acquisition of the patent**

As the patent is an intangible asset which has been acquired as part of the Starling Partners' trade, it will be treated as a trading asset by Granada Ltd and an allowable deduction will be available in calculating the taxable trading income for each accounting period.

Although Granada Ltd has not made any charge for amortisation in its statement of profit or loss, it may take an annual writing down allowance for tax purposes equal to 4% of the cost of the patent, on a straight line basis. This would be £40,000 × 4% = £1,600 per year.

If an election is made to claim the 4% writing down allowance, any accounting debits for impairment would be disallowable for tax purposes. Such an election would be irrevocable.

(ii) **Relief for the expected loss from the former Starling Partners' trade**

As Starling Partners is an unincorporated business, Granada Ltd took over ownership of the assets and responsibility for the trade following its acquisition on 1 January 2025.

The forecast trading loss of £130,000 from Starling Partners' handbag trade could be offset against Granada Ltd's total income for the year ending 31 December 2025, comprising the trading profit from the knitwear business of £100,000 and the chargeable gain of £10,000.

So a loss of £20,000 (£130,000 – £110,000) will be left unrelieved.

As Granada Ltd does not want to carry any of the loss back, the unrelieved loss of £20,000 will be carried forward and automatically set against the first available future profits from the same trade. This is because the trading activities had become small or negligible in the loss-making period. Granada Ltd can make a claim for the whole or part of the loss not to be so relieved. Any remaining loss will be carried forward to the next accounting period and dealt with in a similar manner. This means that the losses cannot be relieved against Granada Ltd's total profits in future accounting periods which will include trading profits from Granada Ltd's knitwear manufacturing business.

Granada Ltd wishes to change the nature of the Starling Partners' trade, by starting to sell to the export market from 1 January 2026. Although this may be seen as a major change in the nature of the trade or the considerable revival of trading activities which had become small or negligible, it should not serve to prevent the loss incurred in the year ended 31 December 2025 from being carried forward providing HM Revenue & Customs (HMRC) agree that, essentially, the same trade is being carried on. The impact of a major change in the nature or conduct of a trade in restricting loss relief is only relevant where it precedes or follows a change in ownership of a company, not the acquisition of the trade and assets from an unincorporated business.

Accordingly, based on the expected profit, £15,000 of the carried forward loss may be relieved in the year ending 31 December 2026, and the remaining £5,000 will be carried forward for relief in future accounting periods as described earlier.

(c) **Value added tax (VAT) implications following the acquisition of the trade and assets of Starling Partners**

For VAT purposes, the transfer of Starling Partners' trade and assets qualified as a transfer of a going concern (TOGC). Therefore no VAT will have been charged on the transfer of the assets generally, and so there will have been no input VAT for Granada Ltd to reclaim.

However, additional information is needed in respect of the building, as its treatment will depend on its age and whether or not the option to tax has been exercised.

Age of the building: If the building was less than three years old at 1 January 2025, its sale would have been a taxable supply, chargeable to VAT at the standard rate.

Option to tax: If the building was more than three years old, its sale would have been exempt from VAT, unless Starling Partners exercised the option to tax.

If the building was less than three years old or Starling Partners had opted to tax the building, then the transfer would have been a taxable supply, chargeable to VAT at the standard rate. In either case, to bring the transfer of the building within the TOGC regime, so that no VAT is charged, Granada Ltd must also have opted to tax the building, prior to the date of transfer. Alternatively, if Granada Ltd did not opt to tax the building, but uses the building in its business, it may obtain an input credit for the VAT charged.

31 Acryl Ltd and Cresco Ltd

Course Book references

Liquidations are covered in Chapter 20. Chargeable gains for companies are dealt with in Chapter 16. Losses for companies are dealt with in Chapter 17. Value added tax (VAT) implications of cessation are covered in Chapter 23.

Top tips

Don't forget your basic taxation knowledge when tackling Advanced Taxation (ATX – UK) questions! Most candidates would have known that companies do not pay corporation tax on dividends but did not stop to think carefully when approaching part (a)(ii).

Easy marks

There were some easy marks in part (b)(ii) for explaining the VAT implications of ceasing business.

ACCA examining team's comments

Part (a)(i) required candidates to state the corporation tax implications arising for a company as a result of the appointment of a liquidator. The commencement of winding up/appointment of a liquidator is one of the factors which will bring a company's accounting period for corporation tax purposes to an end. This was worth only two marks, but most candidates appeared to not be aware of the impact on a company's accounting periods and so scored zero on this question part.

Part (a)(ii) was a 'textbook' question requiring an explanation of the tax implications for both an individual and a corporate shareholder of a distribution being made alternatively before the commencement of liquidation or on completion of the winding up. Answers were very mixed. A good number of candidates realised that the distribution would be taxed as a dividend prior to commencement of liquidation, but as a capital receipt once liquidation had commenced, although a surprising number were not aware of this distinction. For those candidates who realised this, the majority were able to go on and correctly identify the tax implications for the individual shareholder, but, disappointingly, not for the corporate shareholder. Many candidates referred to the corporate shareholder paying corporation tax on both of these, thereby failing to recognise that dividends are not taxable on corporate shareholders, and that the substantial shareholding exemption would apply in the case of the capital receipt. These are both fundamental points which candidates in Advanced Taxation (ATX – UK) need to be very familiar with, as they can be tested in a variety of different scenarios.

In part (b)(i) candidates were required to show how a company could relieve trading losses incurred in its last few periods of account. This involved consideration of loss relief in an ongoing company, in addition to the availability of terminal loss relief. It is important in any question dealing with relief for losses that a well-considered and chronological approach is taken. Precise explanations of the reliefs are required in these sorts of questions. Well-prepared candidates were able to deal correctly with the earlier losses in accounting periods prior to the final period, and were aware that, on cessation, an extended three year carry back is available, but almost all neglected to correctly calculate the loss which was available for this terminal loss relief. Nevertheless, those who adopted a sensible, logical approach scored well on this question part.

Part (b)(ii) required candidates to explain the VAT implications for the company of ceasing to trade. Many candidates were clearly confident with this situation and scored the full three marks available.

Marking guide

			Marks	
(a)	(i)	Effect on accounting periods	1	
		Two computations required	1	
				2
	(ii)	Distribution 31 December 2025	3	
		Distribution 31 March 2026	5	
		Recommendation with reason	1	
		Marks Available	9	
		Maximum		7
(b)	(i)	Loss year ended 31 March 2024	1.5	
		Loss year ended 31 March 2027	1.5	
		Terminal loss	5	
		Loss unrelieved	1	
		Marks Available	9	
		Maximum		8
	(ii)	Notify HMRC	1	
		Output tax on assets held on cessation	2	
				3

Professional skills marks

Analysis and evaluation

- Appropriate use of information to determine suitable calculations to show how Cresco Ltd will claim relief for the trading losses incurred and to identify the amount of trading losses which will remain unrelieved after all available loss reliefs have been claimed.
- Appropriate use of analysis to support discussion and draw appropriate conclusions regarding how Cresco Ltd will claim relief for the trading losses incurred.
- Ability to evaluate information objectively to make a recommendation of the most preferable date for the distribution to be made by Acryl Ltd.

Marking guide	**Marks**

- Use of information to determine the corporation tax implications for Acryl Ltd of the commencement of winding up.
- Demonstration of ability to consider all relevant taxes specified in the requirements in relation to the tax consequences for both Mambo Ltd and Alan depending on the timing of the distribution to be made by Acryl Ltd.

Commercial acumen

- Recognition of VAT consequences of cessation of trade.
- Recognition of the distinction between individual and corporate shareholders in a liquidation scenario.

Maximum	5
Total	25

(a) **Acryl Ltd**

(i) **Implications of the commencement of winding up**

The commencement of winding up will lead to the end of an accounting period on 31 December 2025 and the commencement of a new accounting period on 1 January 2026. Acryl Ltd will remain liable to corporation tax until the winding up is completed. Accordingly, a corporation tax computation is required for each of the two accounting periods: the first from 1 July 2025 to 31 December 2025, and the second from 1 January 2026 to 31 March 2026.

(ii) **Distribution on 31 December 2025**

In this case the distribution will be made prior to the commencement of winding up and therefore will be treated as an income distribution (ie a normal dividend) for tax purposes for both shareholders.

Mambo Ltd will not be subject to corporation tax on this dividend as companies are not subject to corporation tax on dividends. Alan will be subject to income tax on the dividend. It will be subject to income tax at 39.35% as Alan is an additional rate taxpayer to the extent that it exceeds his available dividend nil rate band.

Distribution on 31 March 2026

As the distribution will be made while the company is in liquidation, it will be treated as a capital receipt on disposal of the shares in Acryl Ltd for both shareholders.

Mambo Ltd should not be subject to corporation tax on the disposal as it should qualify as a disposal out of a substantial shareholding. Mambo Ltd will have held more than 10% of the shares in Acryl Ltd for more than 12 continuous months out of the 6 years preceding the disposal. Alan will be subject to capital gains tax on any gain arising. As Alan is eligible for business asset disposal relief on the disposal of his Acryl Ltd shares, capital gains tax will be charged at 10% on the taxable gain.

Conclusion

Mambo Ltd will not be subject to corporation tax under either alternative but Alan would probably prefer 31 March 2026 as he is likely to suffer a lower rate of tax if the distribution is made on this date.

> **Tutorial note.** It is not necessary to consider the possibility of a capital loss on receipt of the distribution on 31 March 2026. Mambo Ltd and Alan subscribed for the shares at par, so they will have a very low base cost and Acryl Ltd has substantial distributable profits.

(b) (i) **Cresco Ltd – relief for trading losses**

	Y/e 31 March 2024	Y/e 31 March 2025	Y/e 31 March 2026	Y/e 31 March 2027	P/e 31 October 2027
	£	£	£	£	£
Trading income	Nil	21,000	8,000	Nil	Nil
Bank interest receivable	1,000	3,000	3,000		
Total profits	1,000	24,000	11,000	Nil	Nil
Less:					
Loss for the year ended 31 March 2024 (note 1)	(1,000)				
Loss for the year ended 31 March 2024 (note 1)		(4,000)			
Loss for the year ended 31 March 2027 (note 2)			(11,000)		
Loss for the period ended 31 October 2027 (note 3)		(20,000)			
	Nil	Nil	Nil	Nil	Nil

Losses unrelieved:

	£
Year ended 31 March 2027: (£24,000 – £11,000 – £10,000)	3,000
Terminal loss: (£50,000 – £20,000)	30,000
Total unrelieved:	33,000

Tutorial note. £10,000 of the trading loss in the year ended 31 March 2027 is included as part of the terminal loss and used against the profits of the year ended 31 March 2025 (see note 3 below).

Notes.

1 The trading loss for the year ended 31 March 2024 of £5,000 will have been relieved against the £1,000 of bank interest (total profits) in the year, and then the balance of £4,000 (£5,000 – £1,000) will be carried forward and a claim can be made to relieve this against total profits in the following year. Total profits of £20,000 (£24,000 – £4,000) remain in the year ended 31 March 2025.

2 As there is no other income or gains in the year ended 31 March 2027, the trading loss of £24,000 will have been carried back and offset against the total profits in the year ended 31 March 2026 of £11,000 (£8,000 + 3,000). £13,000 of the loss remains unrelieved. However, £10,000 of this forms part of the terminal loss (see note 3).

3 As Cresco Ltd has ceased to trade on 31 October 2027, the loss of the last 12 months of trading is a terminal loss which is eligible to be carried back up to 36 months. The loss available for such relief is £50,000 (£40,000 + (£24,000 × 5/12), including the five months of loss for the period from 1 November 2026 to 31 March 2027. As there are no profits remaining in the years ended 31 March 2027 or 2026, the loss can be offset against the total profits of £20,000 in the year ended 31 March 2025.

ANSWERS

(ii) **Value added tax (VAT) implications of the cessation of trade**

Cresco Ltd must notify HM Revenue & Customs (HMRC) of the cessation of its business within 30 days of ceasing to make taxable supplies.

Output tax must be accounted for on any business assets it still holds at the date of cessation of trade in respect of which input tax was previously recovered. However, there is no need to account for this output tax if it is less than £1,000.

32 Achiote Ltd, Borage Ltd and Caraway Inc

Course Book references

Intangible assets for companies are covered in Chapter 16, transfer pricing in Chapter 22, chattels in Chapter 7, chargeable gains groups in Chapter 19, the chargeable gains for companies in Chapter 16, and value added tax (VAT) in Chapter 23.

Top tips

Each sub requirement in this question tested different topics so it would be key that you ensured you attempted each part of the question. It would also be important that you identified the group relationships existing between the companies in the question as some of the transactions were between group companies thus having special consequences.

Easy marks

The application, or otherwise, of the substantial shareholding exemption is frequently examined in Advanced Taxation (ATX – UK) and should have allowed you easy marks in part (c). In addition, the VAT in part (d) contains core topics which you must be able to answer.

ACCA examining team's comments

Part (a) required an explanation of the corporation tax implications of acquiring goodwill and a patent. The goodwill was a minor point and was handled well by the majority of candidates. The patent, however, was not handled so well. Many candidates treated it as a standard asset as opposed to being part of the intangible assets regime. As a result, the inter-group transfer was treated as a no gain, no loss transfer as opposed to a tax neutral transfer. This, in turn, caused problems when calculating the tax deductions available in the future.

Part (b) concerned transfer pricing. This part was not done particularly well because many candidates did not identify sufficient mark-scoring points. It was important to start the explanation at the beginning by identifying why the transfer pricing rules applied. This required a reference to the fact that one of the companies controlled the other and the lack of an arms' length price. Many candidates did not do this but simply took it for granted that the regime applied. Once the relevance of the rules had been established, candidates should then have explained the effect of the rules by reference to the need to increase the company's taxable profit and the amount of the increase. It was this part which most candidates focussed on. It was then necessary to consider any other relevant matters including the availability of the exemption where a group is not large and the possibility of obtaining advance approval of the arrangements from HM Revenue & Customs (HMRC).

Part (c) concerned the chargeable gains implications of the sale of an item of equipment and of some shares. Candidates needed to concentrate and take care in order to score well. The equipment was being transferred between two companies in a chargeable gains group. However, the company acquiring the property was not resident in the UK, such that the no gain/no loss treatment would not apply to the transaction. In addition, due to the availability of capital allowances, the loss arising on the disposal would not be available. When dealing with the sale of the shares, it was important to recognise that the substantial shareholding exemption would not be available because the vendor would not have owned the shares for a 12-month period in the [six] years prior to the sale.

Part (d) concerned various aspects of VAT. The aspects of this part relating to the option to tax a commercial building were generally handled well. However, candidates found the other aspect of this part more difficult. Candidates were asked to suggest reasons why a company which made taxable supplies did not charge VAT on sales made to an unconnected party. Stronger candidates stopped for a moment to gather their thoughts and then wrote about the registration limit and/or the making of zero rated supplies. Weaker candidates simply wrote about registration in general and often lengthy terms. Candidates need to be in a rhythm throughout the exam of reading, thinking and then writing.

Marking guide		Marks
(a) Goodwill	1	
Patent	4	
Marks Available	5	
Maximum		4
(b) Transfer pricing – reason why it applies	1	
Implications and action	5	
Marks Available	6	
Maximum		5
(c) Transfer of equipment	2.5	
Sale of shares	3	
Marks Available	5.5	
Maximum		5
(d) (i) Reasons why VAT is not charged	2	
		2
(ii) Beneficial due to input VAT incurred	1.5	
Implications of option to tax for Rye Ltd	3	
Marks Available	4.5	
Maximum		4

Professional skills marks

Analysis and evaluation

- Appropriate use of data to determine suitable calculations of the corporation tax treatment of the patent acquired by Borage Ltd
- Appropriate use of data to support discussion and draw appropriate conclusions regarding the rate of interest charged by Achiote Ltd on the loan to Caraway Inc
- Demonstration of reasoned judgement regarding reasons why Rye Ltd might not charge VAT on its sales to Achiote Ltd.
- Demonstration of ability to consider relevant factors applicable to Achiote Ltd's situation in order to advise of the chargeable gains implications arising from (1) the sale of the item of equipment to Caraway Inc; and (2) its proposed sale of the shares in Caraway Inc
- Use of information to determine the corporation tax treatment of the goodwill and the patent acquired by Borage Ltd, and the implications for Rye Ltd if Achiote Ltd chooses to opt to tax the commercial building.

Commercial acumen

- Recognising key issues and using judgement in proposing and recommending commercially viable solutions regarding the action which should be taken by Achiote Ltd for transfer pricing purposes
- Demonstrating an awareness of organisational and external factors which will affect the decision as to whether or not it would be financially beneficial for Achiote Ltd to opt to tax the commercial building.

	Marks
Maximum	5
Total	25

(a) **Goodwill**

No amortisation in respect of goodwill is deductible for corporation tax purposes, so the amortisation charged in the accounts for the year ended 31 March 2025 must be added back for tax purposes.

Patent

As the patent is transferred between two members of a capital gains group, it will be transferred at a price which is tax neutral. The written down value of the patent in Achiote Ltd at the date of its sale to Borage Ltd was £26,600 (£38,000 – (3 × 10% × £38,000)). Accordingly this will be the deemed acquisition price for Borage Ltd. Borage Ltd will continue to amortise the patent over the remainder of its ten-year life. In the year ended 31 March 2025 amortisation charged in its accounts will be £950 (£26,600/7 × 3/12). This amount is allowable for corporation tax purposes.

(b) **Loan to Caraway Inc**

It would appear that an arm's length rate of interest on the loan would be 8% as this is the rate at which Caraway Inc could have obtained an equivalent loan from an unrelated party. As Achiote Ltd controls Caraway Inc, they are connected companies and so the transfer pricing rules apply.

The interest receivable by Achiote Ltd is £2,000 (£100,000 × 2%) less than it would be under an arm's length agreement. This means that Achiote Ltd's non-trading loan relationship income is reduced by this amount, such that less tax is payable in the UK. Therefore, Achiote Ltd must adjust the figures within its corporation tax return to reflect the arm's length price.

As there is no double tax treaty between the UK and Nuxabar, Nuxabar will be regarded as a non-qualifying territory. As a result, the exemption which might otherwise have been available if a group is not large will not be available to the Achiote Ltd group.

Achiote Ltd can seek advance approval from HMRC in respect of any intra-group pricing arrangements, including the rate of interest to be charged on a loan.

(c) **Transfer of the item of equipment and the sale of shares in Caraway Inc**

Sale of item of equipment

The intra-group transfer of the item of equipment by Achiote Ltd to Caraway Inc will not be treated as a no gain, no loss transfer, because even though Achiote Ltd owns 80% of the company, such that the companies are in a capital gains group, the fact that Caraway Inc is not a UK resident company means that the asset will no longer be within the charge to UK taxation. This is therefore a chargeable disposal for Achiote Ltd at 1 March 2025. Although the equipment has fallen in value, no capital loss will arise as the asset qualified for capital allowances as it was used in Achiote Ltd's trade.

Sale of shares in Caraway Inc

The sale of the 8% holding in Caraway Inc will not be exempt from corporation tax under the substantial shareholding exemption (SSE) rules. This is because Achiote Ltd will only have held its shares in Caraway Inc for nine months prior to the proposed disposal date and so will not meet the criteria to have owned at least 10% of the shares in Caraway Inc for a continuous 12-month period out of the six years prior to disposal.

Accordingly, a chargeable gain will arise on the disposal, calculated as follows:

	£
Disposal proceeds	66,000
Less: Cost £258,000 × 8/80	(25,800)
Chargeable gain	40,200

Tutorial note. Note the following:

(1) The equipment is not exempt as a wasting asset as it qualified for capital allowances due to being used in a business.

(2) There is no indexation allowance as the shares were acquired after December 2017.

(d) (i) **Reasons why Rye Ltd might not charge value added tax (VAT) on its sales to Achiote Ltd**

Rye Ltd is a small company, and its taxable supplies may not yet have reached the registration threshold.

Rye Ltd's taxable supplies have reached the registration threshold, but its supplies to Achiote Ltd are zero rated.

(ii) **Option to tax the commercial building**

As the building purchased by Achiote Ltd was less than three years old, and a commercial building, it would have been a standard-rated supply. So Achiote Ltd will have incurred a significant amount of input value added tax (VAT) in relation to this expenditure. For this reason, it will be financially beneficial (at least in the short term), for Achiote Ltd to opt to tax the building in order to be able to reclaim this tax. This will also enable Achiote Ltd to recover the input tax in respect of the building's running costs.

However, VAT must then be added to the rent charged by Achiote Ltd to Rye Ltd. The impact of this on Rye Ltd will depend on its size and the nature of its supplies.

(1) If its taxable supplies are currently below the registration limit, Rye Ltd could voluntarily register for VAT purposes and reclaim the input VAT charged on the rent payments.

(2) If Rye Ltd's taxable supplies have reached the registration threshold, but its supplies are wholly or partially zero rated, provided it has registered for VAT purposes, the input VAT charged on the rent payments will, again, be reclaimable, and may lead to a (higher) repayment of VAT from HM Revenue and Customs (HMRC).

Tutorial note. In order to determine whether or not opting to tax the commercial building would be commercially beneficial, longer term implications, such as the impact on the building's future marketability, would also need to be considered. Credit was also available for candidates who made reference to partial exemption.

Videos can be viewed online by accessing your ebook version on VitalSource.

33 Kitz Ltd

Course Book references

The substantial shareholding exemption is covered in Chapter 16 and degrouping charges in Chapter 19. These are also summarised together in the context of a sale of company shares in Chapter 25 on Corporate Tax Planning. Transfer pricing is covered in Chapter 22 and tax on intangibles and rollover for intangibles are covered in Chapter 16.

Top tips

When you see a company selling shares in a scenario you must automatically consider whether the substantial shareholding exemption applies. Once you've spotted that you know you can score well in this section.

The fact that you're told that Kitz Ltd has made an intra group loan at an interest rate that is lower the market rate should be a trigger for you to realise that the transfer pricing rules are being tested. If you didn't spot it this time, make sure you do if you see it in another question.

Easy marks

The substantial shareholding exemption and degrouping charges are frequently examined in ATX and you must be able to spot them in scenarios. This should have been the source of the easier marks in this question.

ACCA examining team's comments

This question was in three main parts, dealing with a company selling shares in a subsidiary, transfer pricing and the sale of an intangible fixed asset.

The first part of the question asked for an explanation of the implications of a sale of shares in a subsidiary and many candidates were able to identify the availability of the substantial shareholding exemption and the associated conditions for this exemption. However a substantial number of candidates missed the further point regarding a degrouping charge arising, despite clues in the question pointing towards this. Candidates should practise as many questions as they can before sitting the ATX-UK exam so that they become accustomed to picking up relevant information given in exam questions.

This question part specifically asked for no calculations and yet a significant number of candidates gave calculations. Even if candidates' workings were correct, there were no marks awarded for calculations when they have been specifically asked not to provide them. Once again, the candidates are wasting their limited exam time and earning no marks. Candidates should read the requirement carefully and only answer what is being asked for.

The second part of the question dealt with the transfer pricing consequences for two group companies making an intra-group loan at an interest rate below market rate. This part of the question was generally very poorly answered. Many candidates were not aware of the most basic elements of the transfer pricing rules and very few could apply the rules to the facts of the question. The ATX-UK exams will seek to examine all areas of the syllabus and candidates need to have a solid understanding of all aspects of the syllabus.

The third part of the question dealt with the sale of an intangible fixed asset (IFA) and subsequent rollover relief. It was clear that very few candidates understood the detailed IFA rules and even less understood the IFA rollover relief and this part of the question was very poorly answered. Once again, candidates should be aware that any part of the syllabus can be tested and given that all questions are compulsory, candidates should aim to be prepared to answer questions on any topic.

Marking guide

Marking guide			Marks	
(a)	Availability of substantial shareholding exemption		3	
	Implications re degrouping charge		4	
	Marks Available		7	
	Maximum			6
(b)	Implications for Kitz Ltd		4	
	Implications for Feld Ltd		3.5	
	Marks Available		7.5	
	Maximum			7
(c)	(i)	Implications of the sale of the patent	2.5	
		Calculation of trading profit	1	
		Marks Available	3.5	
		Maximum		3
	(ii)	Reason for availability of rollover relief	2	
		Maximum rollover relief available	2.5	
		Calculation of reduction in corporation tax liability	0.5	
		Marks Available	5	
		Maximum		4

Professional skills marks

Analysis and evaluation

- Appropriate use of information to determine suitable calculations of the deductions available to Feld Ltd in relation to the loan interest, and the reduction in Kitz Ltd's corporation tax liability as a result of a rollover relief claim
- Appropriate use of information to support discussion and draw appropriate conclusions regarding the corporation tax implications for Kitz Ltd of the sale of the patent to Durn Ltd, and the impact on Kitz Ltd's corporation tax liability if the maximum rollover relief claim is made
- Demonstration of reasoned judgement when considering the chargeable gains implications arising from the sale of the shares in Mayr Ltd
- Demonstration of ability to consider relevant factors applicable to a company's situation in relation to the chargeable gains implications for Kitz Ltd arising from the sale of the shares in Mayr Ltd, the corporation tax implications of the interest charged on the loan, the sale of the patent, and the rollover relief claim
- Use of information to determine the corporation tax implications of the interest charged on the loan by Kitz Ltd to Feld Ltd

Commercial acumen

- Effective use of calculations relating to the context to illustrate points being made relating to the corporation tax implications for Kitz Ltd of the sale of the patent to Durn Ltd

Maximum	5
Total	25

(a) **Chargeable gains implications for Kitz Ltd arising from the sale of the shares in Mayr Ltd on 1 July 2025**

The sale of the 75% shareholding in Mayr Ltd on 1 July 2025 will be exempt from corporation tax under the substantial shareholding exemption (SSE). This is because Kitz Ltd owned more than 10% of the shares in Mayr Ltd for a continuous 12-month period out of the six years prior to sale, and Mayr Ltd is a trading company.

The sale of the warehouse to Mayr Ltd on 8 April 2020 was originally a no gain no loss transfer, because Kitz Ltd and Mayr Ltd were in a capital gains group, as Kitz Ltd owned 75% of Mayr Ltd. As Mayr Ltd left the group within six years of this transfer, still owning the warehouse, a degrouping charge will arise. This is added to the consideration received by Kitz Ltd on the sale of the Mayr Ltd shares. However, the SSE, which applies to sale of the shares, will also apply to the degrouping charge, such that this will also be exempt.

(b) **Corporation tax implications of the interest charged on the loan by Kitz Ltd to Feld Ltd for the year ending 31 March 2027**

Feld Ltd has been offered an interest rate of 10% per annum from a bank (which is an unrelated party), so this would appear to be an arm's length rate of interest.

As Kitz Ltd controls Feld Ltd, they are connected companies for the purpose of transfer pricing. No exemption is available as the companies are not small or medium-sized enterprises (SMEs).

As the interest receivable by Kitz Ltd is 7% per annum, ie lower than the arm's length rate, Kitz Ltd must make a transfer pricing adjustment, and include interest receivable in its corporation tax computation calculated at the rate of 10%. This will be an addition of £13,500 (£450,000 × (10% – 7%)) for the year ending 31 March 2027. Interest receivable of £45,000 (£450,000 × 10%) will be included as non-trading loan relationship (NTLR) income.

As Feld Ltd is also within the charge to UK corporation tax, it can make a claim to amend its computation to an arm's length basis, and deduct a total of £45,000 in respect of the interest payable on the loan.

The interest payable in respect of the proportion of the loan used to acquire assets for use in Feld Ltd's business will be deducted from trading income; the interest payable in respect of the proportion of the loan used to acquire shares in Durn Ltd will be deducted from NTLR income.

Accordingly, for the year ending 31 March 2027, £20,500 (£45,000 × 205/450) is deductible from Feld Ltd's trading income of £587,000, and £24,500 (£45,000 × 245/450) is deductible from its NTLR income of £48,100.

(c) (i) **Corporation tax implications for Kitz Ltd of the sale of the patent to Durn Ltd**

Durn Ltd will not be in a capital gains group with Kitz Ltd and Feld Ltd, as Feld Ltd will not have the minimum 75% holding in Durn Ltd which is required for this. Accordingly, the sale of the patent, which is an intangible asset, will give rise to a trading profit for Kitz Ltd, equal to the excess of the sale proceeds over the tax written down value of the patent at the date of sale. The profit on sale of the patent will therefore be £42,000 (£72,000 – £30,000). This will be included in Kitz Ltd's taxable trading profit for the year ending 31 March 2027.

(ii) **Impact on Kitz Ltd's corporation tax liability for the year ending 31 March 2027 if the maximum rollover relief claim is made**

As Feld Ltd is a UK resident, wholly owned subsidiary of Kitz Ltd, the two companies are in a capital gains group.

Feld Ltd will acquire an intangible fixed asset (goodwill of an unincorporated business) on 1 April 2026, which is within the 12 months prior to the sale of the patent by Kitz Ltd.

Accordingly, rollover relief will be available for part of the profit on the sale of the patent to be deferred against the cost of the goodwill. As the cost of the goodwill is less than the sale proceeds for the patent, the maximum profit which can be deferred is restricted to the excess of the amount invested in the goodwill over the original cost of the patent.

Therefore the maximum profit which can be deferred is £8,000 (£68,000 – £60,000).

This would lead to a reduction in Kitz Ltd's corporation tax liability of £2,000 (£8,000 × 25%).

34 Fox Ltd

Course Book references

Capital gains tax on a disposal of a lease is covered in Chapter 7 with CGT reliefs in Chapter 8. Corporate groups are covered in Chapter 19.

Top tips

In part (a)(i) spot that the rollover relief for the gain on the disposal of the office building is into the purchase of a 40 year lease – which type of rollover relief has been used? And when will the deferred gain become chargeable? In part (ii) you will need to be methodical in how you approach your answer. The verb here is to 'explain, with supporting calculations' so make sure your answer includes sufficient explanations. In both (a)(ii) and (b) you will need to be very clear about which companies in the group are in which type of tax group and in (b) make sure you spot that the trading loss that we are looking to relieve is for the period which includes the date Salas Ltd was purchased by the Fox Ltd group – this will be important in your answer.

Easy marks

The calculation of the gain on the assignment of the lease should be the source of easy marks given the lease percentages are given in the question. In addition, it is an essential ATX–UK skill that you can identify and explain which companies are in which type of loss group so these should be easy marks in part (a)(ii) and part (b).

ACCA examining team's comments

Part (a)(i)

Part (a)(i) involved the calculation of a chargeable gain arising on the assignment of a lease and an explanation of the tax treatment of a deferred gain.

The lease in the question had 26 years left to run (ie a short lease) which meant that candidates needed to consider two things in relation to its disposal:

(1) The fact that it was a wasting asset. Lease percentages were provided to enable candidates to restrict the cost figure in the computation of the gain.

(2) The fact that it was a depreciating asset (life of less than 60 years) for the purposes of rollover relief (ROR). This meant that, as the gain on the disposal of a previous asset had been deferred by virtue of investing in the lease, the deferred gain would not have been deducted from the base cost of the lease, but would crystallise on the earliest of three dates: the date of disposal of the lease, the date when the lease ceased to be used in the company's trade, or 10 years after its acquisition. In this scenario the gain would have already crystallised as the leasehold premises had been owned for more than 10 years.

Most candidates prepared a computation of the gain, but mistakes were frequently made. Candidates generally realised that they needed to use the lease percentages provided, but in many cases applied them incorrectly, or applied them to the gain, rather than the cost.

Failure to recognise that the lease was a depreciating asset meant that many candidates provided no explanation whatsoever, or only a very brief incorrect one, with regard to the treatment of the deferred gain. Candidates need to remember that, as was the case here, a deferred gain can sometimes become independently chargeable, rather than being deducted from the base cost of another asset. It is important for candidates to pay attention in their studies to situations where the relief operates in this manner.

Part (a)(ii)

There were two requirements within part (a)(ii). Candidates were required to provide an explanation, with supporting calculations of:

(1) The rollover relief (ROR) currently available within the Fox Ltd group in respect of the gain on the lease calculated in (a)(i); and then

(2) The minimum amount to be spent on a proposed new qualifying asset such that the full amount of the eligible gain could be rolled over.

Picking up on the reference to the 'group' in the first part, many candidates commenced with an explanation of which companies were members of Fox Ltd's gains group. This was a good place to start. It was encouraging to see that candidates generally appeared to have learnt the definitions of both gains groups and group relief groups, and were able to apply their knowledge to a given scenario. The ability to do this is fundamental at this level. It was then necessary to explain, and calculate, the amount of ROR currently available. A methodical approach was useful here:

(1) What were the requirements for ROR, and were they satisfied in this scenario?

Yes, Fox Ltd sold a qualifying asset, and Corro Ltd acquired a qualifying asset, within the required time period of four years commencing one year before the date of disposal.

(2) To what extent was the gain eligible for relief?

The full gain was eligible as the leasehold premises were wholly used in Fox Ltd's trade throughout its ownership of the property.

(3) To what extent were the proceeds on disposal invested in a qualifying asset(s)?

Corro Ltd had acquired a warehouse, which was a qualifying asset, but was going to use it only 70% for trading purposes. The qualifying expenditure therefore had to be restricted to 70%. The amount of the proceeds retained constituted the gain which would be immediately chargeable, and the remainder of the gain was the amount which was eligible for ROR.

Very few candidates adopted such a methodical approach. A majority spotted that the warehouse acquired by Corro Ltd would be a qualifying asset but didn't say why. Also, many picked up on the 70% trade use, but then applied this to the gain on the lease, rather than the cost of the replacement. Very few went on to consider the retained proceeds, and consequently the amount of ROR available, which was what they were specifically asked to do.

As a result of not completing the workings for the first part, many candidates were not then able to go on and get the mark for part (ii) by identifying the balance of the proceeds to be spent on the proposed new factory building. For those who did, the most common mistake was to deduct the amount spent by Corro Ltd from the gain, rather than the proceeds.

Part (b)

Part (b) related to a trading loss incurred by a new group member, Salas Ltd, in the accounting period in which it joined the group. Again, many candidates started, quite sensibly, by identifying the qualifying group for group relief purposes. Once again, this reinforces the necessity to learn these rules, and to be able to explain them and correctly apply them to a specific scenario.

The next step was to recognise that, as the company had joined the group part way through its accounting period, the loss had to be time apportioned into the pre-acquisition and post-acquisition elements, and then each part of the loss discussed separately. This step was key, however, many candidates missed it, suggesting that they had not taken enough time to read the question carefully. Dates are frequently provided in questions, and it is critical that candidates take the time to appreciate their relevance and any wider implications.

In respect of the pre-acquisition loss, group relief would potentially be available, but only after five years had elapsed, and then only to the extent that Salas Ltd had been unable to relieve this loss itself.

As for the post-acquisition loss, group relief was available in the corresponding accounting period for the other group companies, but only to the extent of their taxable total profits for this period. Any remaining loss could then be carried forward for group relief in the future.

Candidates need to be more accurate when discussing loss reliefs. Imprecise comments such as 'companies can take relief against their current profits' are not sufficient; candidates are expected to refer to 'taxable total profits' of the 'corresponding accounting period'.

Additionally, candidates should read the requirements very carefully to ensure that their answer is directed at what is specifically being asked. In this case, some candidates discussed the criteria for optimum relief within a group (surrendering the loss to a company which pays its corporation tax in instalments), or mentioned the possibility of consortium relief; neither of these points were relevant here. This wasted time and scored no marks.

Marking guide

			Marks	
(a)	(i)	Gain on lease	1.5	
		Explanation re deferred gain	4	
		Marks Available	5.5	
		Maximum		4
	(ii)	Existence of gains group	2	
		Extent to which rollover relief is available	4.5	
		Minimum amount to be spent on lease	2	
		Marks Available	8.5	
		Maximum		7
(b)	Qualifying group		1	
	Pre-acquisition Loss		4.5	
	Post-acquisition loss		4.5	
	Marks Available		10	
	Maximum			9

Professional skills marks

Analysis and evaluation

- Appropriate use of information in the scenario to realise that the deferred gain was in a depreciating asset and draw appropriate conclusions as to when the deferred gain would be taxed in (a)(i)
- Ability to evaluate information objectively to make a recommendation as to Fox's minimum spend to defer the full gain in (a)(ii)
- Appropriate use of information in the scenario to explain the basis for calculation of the maximum group relief in part (b)

Commercial acumen

- Recognising the key group relationships within the question and the relevant impact on the tax planning opportunities available
- Recognition of the fact that as Salas Ltd has no other income in any period and had an earlier trade loss that no current or carry back loss offset is possible in (b)
- Recognition of the importance of timing as to the pre-acquisition and post-acquisition parts of the trading loss of Salas Ltd in part (b)

Maximum	5
Total	25

ANSWERS

(a) (i)

Chargeable gain on the assignment of the lease

	£
Proceeds	180,000
Less: cost (£102,000 × 82.496/95.457)	(88,151)
	91,849

Tax treatment of the deferred gain

On acquisition the lease had less than 60 years remaining so was a depreciating asset for capital gains tax purposes. Accordingly, the gain on the factory building of £43,000 was deferred until the earliest of:

- The date the lease ceased to be used in Fox Ltd's business
- The date of disposal of the lease
- 1 October 2020 (ten years after the acquisition of the lease).

Therefore the deferred gain became chargeable on 1 October 2020 and not on the assignment of the lease of the factory. Accordingly the chargeable gain on disposal of the lease is just £91,849.

(ii)

Rollover relief available

As Fox Ltd acquired at least 75% of the ordinary shares in Salas Ltd on 1 April 2025, Salas Ltd became a member of a capital gains group with Fox Ltd, Bravo Ltd and Corro Ltd from that date. Corro Ltd is a member of the capital gains group as Bravo Ltd's holding in Corro Ltd is at least 75%, and Fox Ltd's effective holding in Corro Ltd is more than 50% (90% × 80% = 72%).

Qualifying assets acquired from outside the group by any of the members of the capital gains group within the period from 2 October 2023 to 1 October 2027 may be eligible assets for the purposes of a rollover relief claim. Qualifying assets include land and buildings, and items of fixed plant and machinery.

The whole of the gain on the disposal of the lease is eligible for relief as the leased factory was wholly used in Fox Ltd's trade. Therefore £180,000 needs to be reinvested in qualifying business assets.

Corro Ltd acquired a warehouse on 1 July 2024 for £168,000. This is a qualifying business asset, acquired within the qualifying reinvestment period, but as only 70% of the building will be used for trading purposes, only £117,600 (£168,000 × 70%) of its cost will be a qualifying acquisition for rollover relief purposes.

Accordingly, £62,400 (£180,000 – £117,600) of the proceeds from the disposal of the lease currently have not been reinvested, so this is the minimum amount that Fox Ltd must spend on acquiring the new freehold factory in order that the full amount of the eligible gain on the disposal of the lease can be deferred.

(b)

Word Processor

Group relief in respect of Salas Ltd's trading loss of the year ending 30 June 2025

As Fox Ltd acquired at least 75% of the ordinary shares in Salas Ltd on 1 April 2025, Salas Ltd became a member of a group for group relief purposes with Fox Ltd and Bravo Ltd from that date. Corro Ltd is not a member of the group for group relief purposes as Fox Ltd's effective holding in Corro Ltd is only 72%.

Pre-acquisition loss

Salas Ltd has no other sources of income in any accounting period, and generated a trading loss in the previous accounting period (which was its first accounting period), so there is no possibility of taking current period or carry back relief in Salas Ltd. Therefore the amount of the pre-acquisition loss available for group relief will be £168,750 (£225,000 × 9/12).

This pre-acquisition loss will not be eligible for group relief against the total profits of Fox Ltd or Bravo Ltd until after five years from the end of the accounting period in which the change in ownership occurred ie 30 June 2030, and then only to the extent that Salas Ltd has not been able to relieve it against its own taxable total profits.

Post-acquisition loss

The loss of the three months ending 30 June 2025 of £56,250 (£225,000 × 3/12) is a post-acquisition loss. This loss may be surrendered to Fox Ltd and/or Bravo Ltd for relief against these companies' taxable total profits of the corresponding period. The amount of the loss surrendered cannot exceed the claimant companies' taxable total profits for the corresponding period. Any remaining loss can be carried forward for group relief in future accounting periods. In future periods the loss must be relieved as far as possible by Salas Ltd against its own taxable total profits before any remaining loss can be surrendered.

35 Samphire Ltd and Kelp Ltd

Course Book references

Employment benefits and NIC calculations are covered in Chapter 4. The cost to a company of a proposal is covered in Chapter 18. Close companies are covered in Chapter 21. Calculations of gains are covered in Chapter 7 with rollover relief in Chapter 8.

Top tips

Make sure you take care analysing the requirements in part (a) – you're asked for an explanation with supporting calculations – so make sure you provide both. You're also asked for the 'total additional taxes payable' which implies there may be more than one tax for you to consider and that it's taxes payable 'by Samphire Ltd' not Nori. Do remember, however, that if an employee is provided with a benefit this will give the company a Class 1A NIC liability.

In (b)(ii), you need to consider carefully whether all of the gain on the sale of Factory 1 will be eligible for rollover relief before you then think about what proceeds need to be reinvested and whether all the necessary proceeds have been reinvested. Don't forget to state how much gain will remain chargeable to corporation tax as requested.

Easy marks

Provided you know your close company rules, there should be some easy marks available in (a)(ii). The gain calculation in (b)(i) should also be a source of some easy marks.

ACCA examining team's comments

Part (a) of the question concerned a UK resident close trading company which was looking to either make a gift of a computer to a director of the company or a loan to the same director to allow him to purchase the computer himself.

Part (a)(i)

The requirement here was to explain, with supporting calculations, the total additional taxes payable by Samphire Ltd if the company gifts the computer to the director.

It is important to focus on the requirement here and to break it down – first of all, 'explain, with supporting calculations' means providing a combination of words and numbers in the answer. Secondly, the reference to 'total' additional taxes implies that there will be more than one additional tax which is relevant and that therefore the sum of all of them should eventually be provided. Thirdly, the question refers to the total additional taxes 'payable by Samphire Ltd', and not by the director. Some candidates discussed the additional taxes payable by the latter; this did not earn credit because it was not what was required. It is always worth double checking a requirement to ensure that it is fully understood, perhaps by highlighting the key words in order to ensure that candidates are doing exactly what it is they are being asked to do.

The question stated that the written down value of the main pool, where the computer would originally have been allocated, was £nil and that the sale proceeds for the purpose of capital allowances were also £nil. This therefore indicated that there would be no balancing charge on the main pool as a result of the gift.

The gift of a capital asset should also lead to a consideration of the capital gains consequences for the company although on this occasion this was an exempt disposal, the cost and sale proceeds of the computer both being less than £6,000.

Since the gift of the computer was to a director of the company, this would also constitute a taxable benefit for the individual. However, it was only the tax implications for the company of making the gift which were relevant on this occasion. The provision of the asset by way of gift will mean that the company will have to pay Class 1A national insurance contributions (NIC) on the taxable benefit amount, which will then be tax deductible for the company when calculating its corporation tax liability.

Thus, the total additional taxes payable by the company are the Class 1A NIC cost less the 25% corporation tax relief thereon.

Part (a)(ii)

This part of the question required an explanation, together with supporting calculations, of the total additional taxes payable by Samphire Ltd if the company were to make a £1,500 loan to the director, and then to write off that loan two years later.

Once again, it is advisable to break down the requirement and highlight the key words. Candidates were being asked to explain and give supporting calculations, so both did need to be provided here. They were asked for total additional taxes, implying once again the need to consider more than one tax, and then total them all up. And finally, they were being asked for additional taxes payable by the company, not the director, so this should be kept in mind when preparing the answer.

Many candidates correctly identified that, since this was a loan from a close company to a director who is also a shareholder, this would result in a notional tax charge being payable by the company. Several then went on to discuss what would have happened if the loan was repaid, but in doing so failed to pick up on the facts of the question where they were specifically told that the loan would be written off in two years' time. This write-off would lead to repayment of the notional tax, meaning that the overall tax cost to the company will be £nil.

There would however be a cashflow impact because, having paid the notional tax, the company would have to wait two years for its repayment from HMRC.

The write-off of the loan itself would be classified as a distribution so there would be no corporation tax implications from the company's perspective.

There were however some further consequences which needed to be considered and many candidates did not go on to think about these. These involved the national insurance cost to the company.

The loan would not give rise to a taxable benefit for the director because, although interest free, it was below the £10,000 threshold. This means there will be no Class 1A NIC liability for Samphire Ltd.

However, when a loan to a director gets written off, Class 1 NICs will be payable by the company on the amount of the write-off; this will then be tax deductible for the company when calculating its corporation tax liability.

Therefore, in conclusion, the total additional taxes payable by the company under this alternative scenario are the Class 1 NIC cost of the write-off as reduced by the 25% corporation tax saving on that amount.

Part (b) of the question involved a different company, Kelp Ltd, which was disposing of a lease on a building and acquiring a factory and a warehouse.

Part (b)(i)

This requirement was to calculate the gain on the sale of the lease of Factory 1. Technically this is an 'assignment of a short lease'. The calculation of the chargeable gain involves the usual 'Sale proceeds less cost and (this being a company making the disposal) less indexation allowance' but, in view of the wasting nature of the asset involved, the cost figure needs to be restricted by reference to the lease percentages provided in the question.

A significant number of candidates didn't go on to calculate the indexation allowance, despite being given relevant indexation factors in the question.

Part (b)(ii)

This part of the question required an explanation, with supporting calculations, of the amount of the chargeable gain calculated in part (b)(i) remaining liable to corporation tax, after taking advantage of maximum rollover relief claims.

Once again, a full analysis of the requirement is important before starting to work on the answer. Explanations and calculations need to be provided. Having worked out the maximum rollover relief, it is then necessary to go to state how much of the gain will remain liable to corporation tax after the rollover relief claim has been made.

Firstly, before even considering the replacement assets acquired, it is necessary to consider how much of the gain arising on the disposal of the lease on Factory 1 is eligible for rollover relief.

The question states that Factory 1 was owned for 8 years but only used for trading purposes for 7 years and 6 months, having been rented out for the final six months of ownership. Consequently, only 7.5/8 of the gain is eligible for rollover relief ie £46,099 × 7.5/8 = £43,218.

This also means that Kelp Ltd must reinvest 7.5/8 of the sale proceeds from Factory 1, if this gain is to be rolled over in full ie £206,000 × 7.5/8 = £193,125.

So, to summarise, with regard to the asset being disposed of, there are two items which have to be pro-rated for non-trade use; namely the gain and the amount of sale proceeds which need to be reinvested.

Looking now at the assets in which Kelp Ltd has reinvested, these must be qualifying business assets purchased within the four year period commencing one year before the disposal of Factory 1.

In the scenario Kelp Ltd acquires Factory 2 from Samphire Ltd. Kelp Ltd and Samphire Ltd are both owned by the same individual, Nori. Many candidates thought that this therefore meant that they were in a single gains group but this would only have been correct if they had been owned by a company, and not an individual. As such, since Factory 2 is to be wholly used for trading purposes, its full cost of £138,000 counts as qualifying expenditure for rollover relief purposes.

Kelp also acquires a second property within the relevant four year time-frame, namely the warehouse. But this is only to be used 70% for trade purposes. Therefore, only 70% of the cost of the warehouse counts as qualifying expenditure for rollover relief purposes ie 70% × £78,000 = £54,600.

All of the above figures now need to be brought together in order to answer the question. The total qualifying acquisition cost of Factory 2 and the warehouse comes to £140,000 + £54,600 = £194,600. Since this amount is greater than the relevant sale proceeds from the sale of Factory 1 ie £193,125, it means that the whole of the eligible gain of £43,218 can be rolled over. However, it should be noted that the question actually asks for the amount of chargeable gain remaining liable to corporation tax, after a maximum rollover claim; given that £43,218 of the total gain of £46,099 is being rolled over, this leaves an amount of gain of £2,881 which is left in charge. This amount needed to be stated in order to answer the question fully.

Marking guide

			Marks	
(a)	(i)	Tax implications of transfer	1.5	
		Class 1A national insurance contributions (NIC)	2	
		Tax cost	1	
		Marks Available	4.5	
		Maximum		4
	(ii)	Loan to participator	4.5	
		NIC implications	3	
		Tax cost	1	
		Marks Available	8.5	
		Maximum		6
(b)	(i)	Calculation of chargeable gain	3	
				3
	(ii)	Gain eligible for rollover relief	1.5	
		Reinvestment required	2	
		Qualifying expenditure		
		– Factory 2	2	
		– Warehouse	1.5	
		Conclusion	1	
		Marks Available	8	
		Maximum		7

Marking guide	Marks
Professional skills marks	
Analysis and evaluation	
• Consideration of relevant taxes payable in part (a)	
• Appropriate use of information to determine the relationship between Samphire Ltd and Kelp Ltd and its relevance in the context of part (b)	
• Appropriate use of relevant information to consider the impact of non-trade use in part (b)	
• Appropriate use of information to support explanation of maximum rollover relief in part (b)	
Commercial acumen	
• Recognition of the potential taxable benefits which could arise in part (a)	
• Consideration of the cashflow implications of the notional tax in part (a)	
• Consideration of the capital gains tax implications arising from the disposal of the computer in part (a)	
Maximum	5
Total	25

(a) (i) **Alternative 1: Gift of a computer to Nori**

The transfer of the computer to Nori will not result in a balancing charge on the main pool, as the proceeds will be £nil. The transfer of the computer will also be a disposal of a chattel by Samphire Ltd, but this will be an exempt disposal as both cost and deemed proceeds are less than £6,000.

As Nori is a director of Samphire Ltd, the gift of the computer will give rise to a taxable benefit of £1,500, ie the market value of the computer at the date of the gift. Accordingly, there will be a Class 1A national insurance contributions (NIC) liability for Samphire Ltd of £207 (£1,500 × 13.8%). Corporation tax relief of £52 (£207 × 25%) will be available in respect of this.

Therefore, the total additional taxes payable in respect of this alternative for Samphire Ltd are £155 (£207 – £52).

(ii) **Alternative 2: Make a loan to Nori**

Samphire Ltd is a close company. Accordingly, on making a loan to Nori, a particular, it must make a payment of notional tax of £506 (£1,500 × 33.75%) to HM Revenue and Customs (HMRC). This payment will be due by 1 January 2028. Following the write off of the loan (on 6 April 2028), HMRC will repay all the notional tax to Samphire Ltd (by 1 January 2030).

Writing off the loan is treated as a distribution, so there will be no corporation tax implications for Samphire Ltd. Although the loan is interest-free, it will not give rise to a taxable benefit for Nori. This is because the total amount of the loan will not exceed £10,000 at any time. Accordingly, Samphire Ltd will not have any liability to Class 1A NIC.

However, a liability to Class 1 NIC will arise on writing off the loan on 6 April 2028, as Nori is also an employee of the company. Accordingly, Samphire Ltd will have a Class 1 NIC liability of £207 (£1,500 × 13.8%) and corporation tax relief in respect of this is £52 (£207 × 25%).

Therefore, the total additional taxes payable in respect of this alternative for Samphire Ltd is also £155 (£207 – £52).

(b) (i)

Spreadsheet

Edit Format

B6	=0.08*B4	
	A	B
1	**Gain on the sale of the lease on Factory 1** [1]	
2		£
3	Proceeds	206,000
4	Less: Cost (£165,000 × 95.457/99.289)	(158,632)
5	Unindexed gain	47,368
6	Less: Indexation allowance: (0.008 x £158,632) [2]	(1,269)
7	Chargeable gain	46,099

1 Make sure you clearly show which part of the question you are answering.

2 You don't need to show your workings as the marker can 'see inside' the cell to see your workings and award credit.

(ii) Here's an example of how you could answer (b)(ii) in the CBE software. The verb here is 'explain, with supporting calculations' so the answer has been produced in the word processor response option with supporting calculations referenced to the spreadsheet. Note the calculations have been included in brackets in the answer below for completeness of the solution. However, in your answer just a reference to the workings in the spreadsheet is sufficient.

Word Processor

Gain remaining chargeable after claiming the maximum amount of rollover relief.

Kelp Ltd owned the lease on Factory 1 for 8 years from 1 November 2017 to 1 November 2025. However, it did not occupy the building for trading purposes during the last six months of ownership from 1 May 2025 to 1 November 2025. Accordingly, only £43,218 (£46,099 × 7.5/8) of the gain is eligible for rollover relief.

In order to relieve the whole of this eligible gain, Kelp Ltd must invest £193,125 (£206,000 × 7.5/8) (see spreadsheet) in qualifying business assets within the four-year period commencing one year before the disposal of Factory 1.

The factory acquired from Samphire Ltd (Factory 2) is a qualifying business asset, acquired within the year prior to the disposal of Factory 1. Kelp Ltd and Samphire Ltd are not in gains group, as they are owned by an individual, not a company. Accordingly, the price paid by Kelp Ltd of £140,000 is its relevant acquisition cost. As Kelp Ltd will use Factory 2 wholly for trading purposes, the full amount of £140,000 is the qualifying cost for rollover relief purposes.

The warehouse to be acquired by Kelp Ltd is also a qualifying business asset, and it will be acquired within the three years following the disposal of Factory 1. However, as only 70% of the warehouse will be used by Kelp Ltd in its trade, only £54,600 (£78,000 × 70%) of its cost will be a qualifying acquisition for rollover relief purposes. Accordingly, £194,600 (£140,000 + £54,600) has been reinvested in qualifying business assets. As this exceeds £193,125, the whole of the eligible gain of £43,218 can be deferred, leaving an immediately chargeable gain of £2,881 (£46,099 – £43,218) (see spreadsheet for calculations).

ANSWERS

Mock Exams

ACCA

Advanced Taxation (ATX – UK) FA2024

Mock Exam 1

March/June 2023

Questions	
Time allowed	3 hours 15 minutes
ALL questions are compulsory and MUST be attempted	

DO NOT OPEN THIS EXAM UNTIL YOU ARE READY TO START UNDER EXAMINATION CONDITIONS

Section A

1 Hiromi (98 mins)

You should assume that today's date is 1 September 2025.

You are an ACCA student working for a firm of accountants. Your manager has asked for your assistance in drafting notes in preparation for a meeting with Hiromi in relation to her personal tax affairs.

In addition to some ethical considerations which have been raised by your manager, advice is required in respect of:

- The capital gains tax payable on the sale of a property and the sale of business assets;
- The availability of incorporation relief;
- The reliefs available in respect of a trading loss of a sole trader;
- The tax implications of the payment and receipt of a dividend; and
- The records to be kept by a company.

The following exhibits, available on the left-hand side of the screen, provide information relevant to the question:

(1) Hiromi's income and chargeable gains – memorandum from manager.

(2) Sale of unincorporated business – schedule from Hiromi.

(3) Work to be carried out – email from manager.

This information should be used to answer the question **requirement** within your chosen **response option(s).**

Required

You should assume that today's date is 1 September 2025.

Respond to the instructions in the email from your manager.

Note. The split of the mark allocation is shown in Exhibit 3 – Work to be carried out. **(40 marks)**

Professional marks will be awarded for the demonstration of skill in communication, analysis and evaluation, scepticism and commercial acumen in your answer. **(10 marks)**

(Total = 50 marks)

Exhibit 1: Extract from a memorandum from your manager (dated 1 September 2025) recording matters discussed in a meeting with Hiromi

Hiromi recently became a client of our firm. Her sources of income and chargeable gains for recent tax years are summarised below.

Sources of income

Hiromi has been in business as a sole trader since 2014. On 31 December 2025, Hiromi will incorporate her business by selling all of its assets to a newly formed company called HKR Ltd. The details of this transaction are set out in the schedule from Hiromi (Exhibit 2).

Hiromi's tax adjusted trading profits for her final periods of trading are set out below.

	£
2025/26 – loss	44,500
2024/25 – profit	8,000

Hiromi's only other source of income in recent years was a house which she rented out until she sold it on 28 February 2025 (see below). Hiromi's assessable property income for the final two tax years in which she owned the property is:

	£
2023/24	19,400
2024/25	15,500

Chargeable gains

Hiromi's only disposal in recent years was of her rental property on 28 February 2025. Hiromi sold this house for £265,000. She had inherited it from her uncle on 1 March 2011 when it had a market value of £221,500. Hiromi's uncle had purchased the house for £135,000 on 1 September 2004. Hiromi had never lived in the property.

Income tax refund

Hiromi has received an unexpected refund of income tax from HM Revenue and Customs (HMRC) in respect of the tax year 2021/22.

Exhibit 2: Schedule from Hiromi dated 1 September 2025

Sale of the assets of my business to HKR Ltd

I will sell all of the assets of my business to HKR Ltd for their market values on 31 December 2025. Details of the assets to be sold are set out below.

	Goodwill	Building	Current assets	Total
Market value	£4,000	£290,000	£21,000	£315,000
Cost	£4,000	£118,000	N/A	
Chargeable gain	0	£172,000	N/A	£172,000

I will receive 50,000 ordinary £1 shares in HKR Ltd (the whole of the company's issued share capital). The value of these shares will be £255,000, representing 81% of the total consideration. The remainder of the consideration will be left on loan account and will be paid to me in the future.

I will not make any further capital disposals in the tax year 2025/26.

Looking to the future

I expect the turnover of the business to increase considerably in 2026 and 2027. I anticipate the company will generate taxable total profits in the region of £100,000 – £200,000 in 2026 and 2027. As a result, HKR Ltd will be able to pay me a salary of £5,500 per month, beginning on 6 April 2026. I will also be paid a dividend of £7,000 each year. The first dividend will be paid on 1 November 2027.

Finally, I require advice on the record keeping requirements which will apply to HKR Ltd in relation to its business activities.

Exhibit 3: Extract from email from manager dated 1 September 2025

I need you to prepare some notes for internal use prior to our meeting with Hiromi. The notes should be set out in a manner which will make it easy for us to refer to them during our discussions and should address the following issues:

(a) **Refund of income tax (Exhibit 1)**

Summarise the actions which our firm should take, including the matters which we should bring to Hiromi's attention in relation to the refund she has received. **(5 marks)**

(b) **Chargeable gains (Exhibits 1 and 2)**

When carrying out this work in respect of Hiromi's chargeable gains you should ignore any relief which may be available to her in respect of her trading loss.

- Calculate the capital gains tax (CGT) payable by Hiromi as a result of the sale of the rental property on 28 February 2025.
- In respect of the proposed sale of Hiromi's business assets to HKR Ltd on 31 December 2025:
  - Explain whether or not each of the three conditions for incorporation relief will be satisfied; and
  - On the assumption that incorporation relief WILL be available, and that all available reliefs will be claimed where necessary, calculate the CGT which will be payable by Hiromi as a result of the sale of her business assets.

(13 marks)

(c) **Trading loss (Exhibits 1 and 2)**

For the purposes of this part (c) you should IGNORE terminal loss relief and national insurance contributions.

(i) State how Hiromi's budgeted trading loss for 2025/26 can be relieved. **(4 marks)**

(ii) Using the 2025/26 loss:

(1) Explain, with supporting calculations, the tax savings which would result from the following two alternatives:

- Relieving the loss as soon as possible assuming that NO relief is claimed in respect of the tax year 2025/26;
- Relieving the loss in the future.

(2) Set out the matters we should draw to Hiromi's attention in order to help her decide on how to relieve the loss.

(10 marks)

(d) **When HKR Ltd owns the business (Exhibit 2)**

- Explain with supporting calculations, the tax implications for HKR Ltd and Hiromi of HKR Ltd paying a dividend of £7,000 in the tax year 2027/28.
- State the matters you would draw to Hiromi's attention in relation to the requirement for HKR Ltd to maintain and retain the records relating to its business activities.

(8 marks)

Section B

2 Evora Ltd **(49 mins)**

You should assume that today's date is 1 June 2025.

The finance director of Evora Ltd has requested advice on the following:

- The tax implications of acquiring two assets from an unincorporated business;
- Commencing trading activities overseas; and
- The value added tax (VAT) consequences of purchasing goods and services from overseas.

The following exhibit, available on the left-hand side of the screen, provides information relevant to the question:

(1) Evora Ltd.

This information should be used to answer the question **requirements** within your chosen **response option(s)**.

Required

You should assume that today's date is 1 June 2025.

(a) Explain the corporation tax treatment for Silves Ltd in the year ending 31 March 2025 in relation to the acquisition of each of the two assets. **(6 marks)**

(b) (i) Explain, by reference to the relief(s) available for the forecast trading loss, why it will be advantageous for Evora Ltd to commence trading in Salema through a permanent establishment (PE) rather than an overseas subsidiary company.

You should assume for this part that Evora Ltd does not make an election to exempt the profits of its overseas PEs from UK corporation tax. **(3 marks)**

(ii) State the tax consequences for Evora Ltd of making an election to exempt the profits of overseas PEs from UK corporation tax, and advise the company whether or not it will be beneficial to make this election on the basis of the company's current forecast results, and its future plans. **(6 marks)**

(c) Explain how the following items will be reported on Evora Ltd's value added tax (VAT) return for the quarter ending 30 June 2025:

- the services purchased from the overseas legal firm; and
- the goods acquired from the overseas supplier.

State how these transactions will affect the amount of VAT payable declared on this return. **(5 marks)**

Professional marks will be awarded for the demonstration of skill in analysis and evaluation, commercial acumen and scepticism in your answer. **(5 marks)**

(Total = 25 marks)

Exhibit: Evora Ltd

Evora Ltd and Silves Ltd:

- Evora Ltd owns 100% of the ordinary shares in Silves Ltd.
- Evora Ltd and Silves Ltd are both UK tax resident trading companies.
- Both companies prepare accounts to 31 March each year.

Silves Ltd – acquisition of assets from an unincorporated business:

- On 1 April 2024, Silves Ltd acquired the following assets from an unincorporated business:

	Cost to Silves Ltd
	£
'Alte' brand	50,000
Specialist machine	30,000

- Silves Ltd is using both of these assets for the purposes of its trade.
- The 'Alte' brand will be amortised on a straight-line basis over an eight-year period.
- The specialist machine was previously used by the unincorporated business in its trade.
- Silves Ltd will adopt the most tax-efficient treatment which is available for these assets.

Evora Ltd – trading overseas:

- On 1 July 2025, Evora Ltd will start trading in the country of Salema.
- Evora Ltd has been advised that it will be advantageous for tax purposes to operate through a permanent establishment, rather than a subsidiary company incorporated and tax resident in Salema.
- The overseas operation will be loss-making for the first nine months of trading, after which it is expected to be profitable.
- Evora Ltd will take relief for the loss incurred by its operation in Salema as early as possible.
- Evora Ltd currently has no other overseas operations but plans to open additional permanent establishments overseas within the next few years.

The tax system in Salema:

- The rate of tax on the profits of permanent establishments in Salema is 28%.
- There is no double tax treaty between the UK and Salema.

Forecast trading results:

	Taxable trading profit/(loss)
	£
Evora Ltd	
– UK operations year ending 31 March 2026	610,000
– Salema operations period ending 31 March 2026	(240,000)
Silves Ltd year ending 31 March 2026	420,000

- Neither company has any other sources of income or gains.

Evora Ltd – value added tax (VAT):

- Evora Ltd is registered for the purposes of VAT in the UK and makes wholly taxable supplies.
- In April 2025, Evora Ltd engaged the services of a legal firm in Salema, to which it paid a fee of £3,500 in that same month.
- In May 2025, Evora Ltd purchased goods from a supplier in Salema costing £2,100 for sale in its UK operation.

3 Anya **(49 mins)**

You should assume that today's date is 1 June 2025.

Anya requires advice on:

- the capital gains tax (CGT) and inheritance tax (IHT) implications of a gift of a painting;
- the CGT and IHT reliefs available on a gift of shares; and
- the impact on post-tax income of the gift of shares.

The following exhibit, available on the left-hand side of the screen, provides information relevant to the question:

(1) Anya

This information should be used to answer the question **requirements** within your chosen **response option(s)**.

Required

You should assume that today's date is 1 June 2025 and Anya will die on 6 September 2026.

(a) Explain the capital gains tax and inheritance tax (IHT) implications of the proposed gift of the painting to Violette on 1 August 2025. **(6 marks)**

(b) In relation to Anya's proposed gift of the Chaski Ltd shares to Cara on 1 September 2025:

(i) Advise on the availability to Anya of gift holdover relief, and any consequences for Cara of this relief being claimed. **(5 marks)**

(ii) Advise on the availability of business property relief in calculating the IHT liability on this gift as a result of Anya's death, and any additional conditions for Cara attaching to this relief. **(4 marks)**

(c) Calculate the reduction in Anya's post-tax income for the tax year 2025/26 as compared with the tax year 2024/25, on the assumption that she gifts all of her shares in Chaski Ltd to Cara as planned. **(5 marks)**

Professional marks will be awarded for the demonstration of skill in analysis and evaluation, commercial acumen and scepticism in your answer. **(5 marks)**

(Total = 25 marks)

Exhibit: Anya

Anya:

- Is tax resident and domiciled in the UK.
- Has never been married, or in a civil partnership.
- Has one daughter, Cara, and two granddaughters, Flava and Violette, all of whom are tax resident and domiciled in the UK.
- Has made only one previous lifetime gift: on 31 March 2024, she gave Cara an investment property, valued at £390,000.
- You should assume that Anya will die on 6 September 2026.

Anya – proposed gifts:

- Anya is proposing to make the following gifts:
  - £50,000 cash to Flava on 1 July 2025.
  - A painting to Violette on 1 August 2025.
  - All of her ordinary shares in Chaski Ltd to Cara on 1 September 2025.

Proposed gift of painting:

- Anya purchased the painting on 8 July 2008 for £104,000.
- The value of the painting on 1 August 2025 will be £63,000.

Proposed gift of shares in Chaski Ltd:

- Anya acquired 100% of the ordinary shares in Chaski Ltd on 1 May 2009.
- Chaski Ltd is an unquoted trading company.
- The market values of the assets owned by Chaski Ltd at 1 September 2025 will be as follows:

	£
Land and buildings	853,000
Equipment (no item worth more than £6,000)	78,000
2% shareholding in RQ Ltd (held as an investment)	60,000
Inventory and cash	43,000
	1,034,000

Anya – income:

- Anya has gross annual taxable pension income of £65,000.
- Anya's only other source of income has been dividends from Chaski Ltd.
- Chaski Ltd paid a dividend of £40,000 in respect of its ordinary shares on 14 January 2025 and will pay a dividend of £34,000 on 13 January 2026.

Answers

DO NOT TURN THIS PAGE UNTIL YOU HAVE COMPLETED THE MOCK EXAM

A plan of attack

We've already established that you've been told to do it 101 times, so it is of course superfluous to tell you for the 102nd time to **take a good look at the exam before diving into the answers**.

What's the worst thing you could be doing right now if this was the actual exam? Wondering how to celebrate the end of the exam in about three hours' time?

Turn back to the exam and let's sort out a **plan of attack**!

First things first

Look through the exam and work out the order in which to attack the questions. You've got **two options**. Option 1 is the option recommended by BPP.

Option 1 (if you're thinking 'Help!')

If you're a bit worried about the exam, do the questions in the order of how well you think you can answer them. If you find the questions in Section B less daunting than the questions in Section A, start with Section B.

There are **two questions** in Section B. **Question 2** has three parts. Part (a) relates to the corporation tax implications of two assets acquired by Evora Ltd, a trading company. Both assets are used in the company's trade.

Part (b) has two sub-parts, both relating to the use of permanent establishments overseas as a way of expanding internationally. The first part asks for reasons why the use of PE would be advantageous in relation to anticipated losses of the overseas operation. The second asks about the election to exempt profits from overseas PEs.

Part (c) asks about the VAT treatment of goods and services acquired from overseas and how they would be reported on the VAT return.

Question 3 has three parts, the first two relating to the capital gains tax and inheritance tax treatment and potential reliefs in relation to several gifts. The third part asks about the impact on Anya's post-tax income of making a gift of shares to Cara.

Do not spend longer than about 97 minutes on Section B. When you've spent the allocated time on the questions in Section B turn to the **case-study question** in Section A.

Read the Section A question through thoroughly before you launch into it. Once you start make sure you allocate your time to the parts within the question according to the marks available and that, where possible, you attempt the easy marks first.

Question 1 has four parts concerning two different taxpayers. You are preparing separate memoranda for each client file.

Part (a) is a five-mark requirement on ethics in relation to a refund of income tax.

Part (b) relates to the capital gains arising from the disposal of rental property and also a trading business.

Part (c) asks about the reliefs available for a trading loss.

Part (d) asks about the tax implications for a company and a shareholder of a dividend payment.

Lastly, what you mustn't forget is that you have to attempt **the whole question in Section A and BOTH questions in Section B.**

Option 2 (if you're thinking 'This exam's alright')

It never pays to be overconfident but if you're not quaking in your shoes about the exam then **turn straight to the case-study question in Section A.**

Once you've done this question, **move to Section B**. The question you attempt first really depends on what you are most confident at. If you are undecided look at the requirements. It may be easier to obtain more marks if these are broken down into several smaller parts.

No matter how many times we remind you...

Always, always **allocate your time** according to the marks for the question in total and then according to the parts of the question. And **always, always follow the requirements** exactly. Answer the question that is set, rather than the one you wish had been set, and pay attention to verbs; 'explain' means there will be significant marks for your narrative and not just the figures –

you can assume that 'supporting' calculations will never be worth more than 50% of the available marks. Marks will not be available for you to discuss something which has been specifically excluded in the scenario. Not only will you not score marks but you will also be wasting valuable time if you write about something you've been asked not to.

You've got spare time at the end of the exam...?

If you have allocated your time properly then you **shouldn't have time on your hands** at the end of the exam. But if you find yourself with five or ten minutes to spare, check over your work to make sure that you have answered all the requirements of the questions and all parts of all requirements.

Forget about it!

And don't worry if you found the exam difficult. More than likely other candidates will too. If this were the real thing you would need to **forget** the exam the minute you leave the exam room and **think about the next one**. Or, if it's the last one, **celebrate**!

Section A

1 Hiromi

Course Book references

Ethics is covered in Chapter 1. Calculation of CGT is covered in Chapter 7 and CGT reliefs in Chapter 8. Sole trader loss relief is covered in Chapter 15 and personal tax admin in Chapter 10.

Top Tips

Make sure you break the question down into small parts and allocate your time accordingly. In part (c) it is important when explaining each loss option, you clearly state which tax years the loss can be relieved, specify what income/gains it can be relieved against and the rate of tax saved.

Easy marks

There should be easy marks for the ethics in part (a) as well as the calculation of CGT in part (b). Explaining the tax implications of a dividend payment in part (d) should also be a source of easy marks.

ACCA examining team's comments

Part (a)

The scenario here concerned an unexpected refund of income tax from HM Revenue and Customs (HMRC) and required a summary of the actions to be taken by the firm and matters which should be brought to the attention of their client. This was a fairly standard ethics requirement which has been tested frequently in the past.

Many candidates demonstrated a high level of familiarity with this area, and so scored full, or almost full marks. Many candidates knew the guidance on investigating the refund, informing and potentially repaying HMRC, and if the client refuses the firm should cease to act, notify HMRC, but not disclose the reason. However, the main issue for weaker candidates was in not recognising that if no valid reason for the refund can be found and the client fails to repay the amount to HMRC, the client should be informed that this would be a civil and/or criminal offence. In addition, it may be necessary for the firm to make a report under the money laundering rules.

There are a good number of past questions which have tested these ethical issues and candidates would be well advised to practise them. We were also looking to give a scepticism professional skills mark here for appropriate application of professional judgement in relation to the client's willingness to retain the refund. Very few candidates were able to earn this mark. Going forward, candidates should be prepared to challenge the information given in the scenario if it is clear that there are uncertainties in the information provided which could affect the conclusions reached.

Part (b)

The first element of part (b) required candidates to calculate the CGT payable as a result of the sale of a rental property. The majority of candidates were able to score full marks on calculating the gain.

Candidates often knew they had to apply residential rates to the gain but many simply said that because the client was a basic rate taxpayer, the whole gain would be charged at 18%. Better prepared candidates went a step further and calculated how much basic rate band was remaining and then applied 18% and 24% CGT rates to the gain accordingly. This is brought forward knowledge from TX – UK and candidates should be prepared to be tested on their brought forward knowledge. Analysis and evaluation marks may be awarded for appropriate use of relevant information to determine suitable calculations and this would be an example of this.

The second element of part (b) concerned the sale of the client's business assets to a newly formed company. Candidates were first asked to explain whether or not each of the three conditions for incorporation relief would be satisfied. There was some confusion over the conditions but lots of candidates were able to pick up one or two of the marks here. Many candidates suggested that the transfer must be in exchange for consideration made up of 80% shares. In fact, the requirement is that the consideration must include some element of shares but there is no specified amount. There are a multitude of reliefs to know about for ATX – UK but the precise details are important and candidates must ensure that they are clear on which rules relate to a particular relief.

Even when candidates correctly identified that 'transfer of a going concern' was a condition, virtually nobody went on to outline the meaning of going concern. In this case the client's sole trader business had been loss-making and so there may have been uncertainty regarding whether or not the business was a going concern. In order to earn scepticism marks, candidates should be prepared to challenge the information given in the question where it is clear there is some uncertainty.

Finally in this part of the question, candidates were asked to calculate the CGT payable upon transfer of the business assets, assuming that incorporation relief would be available. It was good to see most candidates following the instruction of the requirement and attempting the incorporation relief working. Similarly, most candidates knew that the annual exempt allowance would apply and that the gain should be charged at 10% due to the availability of business asset disposal relief.

Part (c)

Part (c)(i) required candidates to state how the loss can be relieved, ignoring terminal loss relief. Most candidates were able to score marks for current and prior year reliefs. Common errors were to not state the 'and/or' nature of these two reliefs, nor to state the loss would be used against total income. A reasonable number of candidates knew that the loss could also be used against gains. Candidates sometimes went on to state that the loss could be used against future business profits but should have recognised that the business was being incorporated and so the loss would have to be used against income from the company in the future. [**BPP Note.** The ACCA examining team's comments have been edited for this part as the question has been amended from its original form due to syllabus changes.]

Part (c)(ii) followed on from (c)(i) by requiring candidates to explain with supporting calculations, the tax savings which would result from relieving the loss as soon as possible (with no current year relief) and relieving the loss in the future. In ATX – UK, candidates are often required to apply rules and conditions to specific circumstances, such that a generic answer will not be sufficient to score well. It is very important to take the time to think and plan an answer to a fairly complex question like this in order to provide a comprehensive, well-structured answer. It is worth taking some time at the start of such a question part to read, and carefully consider how to approach that part. It is evident from their answers when candidates have done this, and invariably leads to a more logical, concise, and better-focused answer. Most candidates were able to explain and calculate the income tax saving from a prior year loss relief claim, ignoring a current year loss relief claim as instructed in the question. However, very few candidates then extended the prior year loss relief claim against the gain which they had calculated in part (b), even if they had identified this as a potential relief in part (c)(i). Candidates also had to relieve the loss against future income from the company and calculate the tax saving. Calculating the tax payable before and after loss relief and then taking the difference was an efficient way to present the workings for this. Candidates who tried to work 'at the margin' often chose the wrong income tax rate for the loss relief.

In order to earn professional skills marks of analysis and evaluation it was important to show a balanced appraisal of the loss relief options and by outlining the loss relief options in a methodical manner, with clarity as to which relief was being addressed.

The final requirement of part (c)(ii) was to set out matters which would help the client to decide how to relieve her loss. It was pleasing to see the majority of candidates attempting this requirement. Many candidates correctly concluded on their follow through tax savings, correctly identifying which of their reliefs gave the greater tax saving. Many also brought up the cashflow/delay issues regarding prior year or future year relief. And finally, a good number were able to point out that future profits, although predicted, were uncertain.

Effectively addressing the matters to be raised with the client regarding which loss relief to choose further enabled candidates to pick up professional skills marks as follows:

- Analysis and evaluation when addressing the advantages and/or disadvantages of a particular relief; and
- Commercial acumen when recommending which loss reliefs are practical and plausible and recognising the wider implications of the timing of any election for loss relief.

Part (d)

The first element of part (d) required candidates to explain with supporting calculations, the tax implications for the client and the newly incorporated company of paying a dividend.

It was good to see so many candidates follow the instructions to look at this from the point of view of both the company and the client. For the former, they tended to know that dividends are not allowable. For the latter they tended to score well by recognising that the client would be a higher rate taxpayer because of her future company salary and then following up with a nil rate band and 33.75% tax rate for dividends. Virtually no candidate mentioned that there would be no NIC which would have scored a mark.

A second element to part (d) was the requirement to state matters to draw to the client's attention in relation to maintaining business records. Lots of students correctly knew that the retention period for records was six years but there were also various wrong attempts of two, five and seven years. Only a few students mentioned possible penalties, and fewer still knew that there was a maximum £3,000 penalty.

As part of their overall preparation for this exam, candidates should be aware of the extent to which such detailed knowledge of rules contained within the ATX-UK syllabus can be tested. Candidates should expect tax administration issues to be tested and should not ignore these areas of the syllabus in their studies

Marking guide

			Marks	
(a)	Investigate and inform HMRC		2	
	Offence and penalties/interest		2	
	Unwillingness to return the money		2	
	Marks Available		6	
	Maximum			5
(b)	**Sale of the rental property**			
	Taxable gain		1.5	
	Capital gains tax liability		4	
	Proposed sale of business assets			
	Availability of incorporation relief		5	
	Capital gains tax liability		3.5	
	Marks Available		14	
	Maximum			13
(c)	(i)	Relief in year of loss and/or preceding year	3	
		Relief in the future	1.5	
		Marks Available	4.5	
		Maximum		4
	(ii)	**Relief in 2024/25**		
		Against income	1.5	
		Against chargeable gains	3	

ANSWERS

Marking guide

		Marks
Relief in 2026/27		
Original liability	2	
Effect of offsetting loss	2	
Conclusions	3	
Marks Available	11.5	
Maximum		10
(d) Payment of dividend	6.5	
Record keeping	3	
Marks Available	9.5	
Maximum		8

Professional skills marks

Communication

- General format and structure of meeting notes (eg use of headings/sub-headings to make meeting notes easy to refer to)
- Style, language and clarity (tone of meeting notes, presentation of calculations, appropriate use of the tools, easy to follow and more than a negligible amount of content)
- Effectiveness of communication (answer is relevant, specific rather than general and focused to the requirement)
- Adherence to specific instructions made in the scenario

Analysis and evaluation

- Appropriate use of relevant information to determine suitable calculations
- Balanced appraisal of the loss relief options available
- Demonstration of the ability to consider relevant factors when advising on the use of the trading loss

Scepticism

- Appropriate application of professional judgement in relation to Hiromi's willingness to retain the refund
- Critical assessment of the going concern status of Hiromi's business

Commercial acumen

- Recommendations in respect of loss relief are practical and plausible
- Recognition of wider implications regarding the timing of the election

Maximum	10
Total	50

Notes for discussion prior to meeting

For: The files

Client: Hiromi

Subject: Various matters

Prepared by: Tax senior

Date: 1 September 2025

(a) **Refund of income tax**

We should assist Hiromi in identifying whether or not there was a valid reason for the refund. If we are unable to find a valid reason, we would have to conclude that the refund was made as a result of an error on the part of HM Revenue and Customs (HMRC). In these circumstances:

- We should inform Hiromi that the amount should be repaid and that failing to do so would be a civil and/or a criminal offence.
- HMRC should be informed of their error as soon as possible in order to minimise any interest and penalties which may otherwise become payable.
- In the unlikely event that Hiromi is unwilling to return the money:
  - Hiromi's willingness to retain money which does not belong to her would require us to consider ceasing to act as her tax advisers;
  - We would then have to notify the tax authorities that we no longer act for her, although we would not provide them with any reason for our action;
  - our firm's money laundering reporting officer would also have to consider whether or not it is necessary to make a report under the money laundering rules.

(b) **Chargeable gains**

Sale of the rental property – 2024/25 capital gains tax (CGT) payable

	£	£
Proceeds		265,000
Less: cost (probate value)		(221,500)
Chargeable gain		43,500
Less: annual exempt amount		(3,000)
Taxable gain		40,500
Basic rate band		37,700
Trading income	8,000	
Property income	15,500	
	23,500	
Less: personal allowance	(12,570)	
Taxable income		(10,930)
Basic rate band remaining		26,770
CGT		
£26,770 × 18%		4,819
£13,730 (£40,500 – £26,770) × 24%		3,295
		8,114

Tutorial note. The chargeable gain on the sale of the rental property will have been reported by 29 April 2025 (ie within 60 days of completion of the sale) and a payment on account of the related CGT will have been paid at that time. However, the gain must also be included on Hiromi's 2024/25 tax return and the CGT paid in April will then be deducted from the finalised CGT liability.

Proposed sale of business assets

Incorporation relief

The following three conditions must be satisfied for the relief to be available:

(1) Hiromi's business is transferred as a going concern when it is sold to HKR Ltd.

(2) All of the assets of Hiromi's business (other than cash) are sold to HKR Ltd.

(3) The consideration received by Hiromi for the sale of her business includes shares in HKR Ltd.

The proposed sale will satisfy conditions 2 and 3.

The going concern condition will also be satisfied provided that, at the time of the sale, the business is operational and has everything it needs to carry out its business activities on a sound commercial basis. The lack of business profits in the 18 months prior to the sale does not automatically indicate that the business is not a going concern.

CGT payable

	£
Total gains:	172,000
Less: incorporation relief (£172,000 × 81%)	(139,320)
	32,680
Less: annual exempt amount	(3,000)
	29,680
CGT at 10% (business asset disposal relief)	2,968

(c) (i) **Reliefs available:**

The trading loss can be offset against:

- The total income of:
  - 2025/26 (the tax year of the loss); and/or
  - 2024/25 (the preceding tax year).
- the chargeable gains of either or both of the same two years provided a claim has been made against total income for the year(s) concerned.
- the first available income (eg salary and/or dividends) received from HKR Ltd.

(ii) **Evaluation of the reliefs available**

Relieving the loss as soon as possible

Offsetting the trading loss against Hiromi's income in 2024/25 would use £23,500 of the loss (£8,000 + £15,500). This would result in an income tax saving of £2,186 ((£23,500 – £12,570) × 20%). The remainder of the loss, £21,000 (£44,500 – £23,500), could then be offset against the chargeable gain on the sale of the rental property.

	£
Taxable gain (above)	40,500
Less: remainder of trading loss	(21,000)
	19,500
CGT (all within basic rate band) £19,500 × 18%	3,510
Reduction in CGT (£8,114 – £3,510)	4,604
Income tax saving (above)	2,186
Total tax saved	6,790

Relief in the future

The trading loss could be carried forward and offset against Hiromi's employment income in 2026/27.

	Original liability	Liability after loss relief
	£	£
Employment income (£5,500 × 12)	66,000	66,000
Less: trading loss brought forward		(44,500)
		21,500
Less: personal allowance	(12,570)	(12,570)
	53,430	8,930
Income tax payable		
£37,700/£8,930 × 20%	7,540	1,786
£15,730 (£53,430 – £37,700) × 40%	6,292	
	13,832	1,786

Summary of tax savings

	£
Relieving the loss as soon as possible	6,790
Relief in the future (£13,832 – £1,786)	12,046

Matters to be drawn to Hiromi's attention

- Carrying the loss forward for offset against income derived from HKR Ltd would save additional tax of £5,256 (£12,046 – £6,790).
- However:
  - Carrying the loss forward would result in the benefit of the loss relief being delayed;
  - In addition, HKR Ltd may not be as profitable as expected. This could have an effect on the salary to be paid to Hiromi, such that she would not be a higher rate taxpayer in 2026/27.
  - Fortunately, the election to offset the loss against total income of 2024/25 does not need to be made until 31 January 2028, by which time we will know whether or not Hiromi is a higher rate taxpayer for 2026/27.

(d) **When HKR Ltd owns the business**

Tax implications of paying a dividend of £7,000 in the tax year 2027/28

- The dividend will not be an allowable payment for the purposes of calculating HKR Ltd's taxable trading profit. With anticipated taxable total profits of £100,000 – £200,000 HKR Ltd will pay corporation tax at the main rate of 25% less marginal relief. This will give a marginal tax rate of 26.5%. Accordingly, in order to have £7,000 of post-tax profits available for distribution, HKR Ltd will have to pay corporation tax of £2,524 (£7,000 × 26.5/(100 – 26.5)).

- Hiromi will be a higher rate taxpayer due to her salary of £66,000 per year. Accordingly, she will have an income tax liability in respect of the dividend totalling £2,194, as set out below:

	£
£500 × 0% (nil rate band)	0
£6,500 × 33·75% (higher rate taxpayer)	2,194
	2,194

- Dividends are not liable to national insurance contributions.

Record keeping

- HKR Ltd must retain the records required to make a complete and correct corporation tax return. This will include:
  - Evidence of transactions, eg receipts, expenses, and sales and purchases of goods;
  - Supporting documents, eg accounts, books and contracts.
- The records must usually be retained until six years after the end of the relevant accounting period.
- HMRC may impose a penalty where insufficient records are retained. The maximum penalty is £3,000 for each accounting period.

Tax senior

Section B

2 Evora Ltd

Course Book references

Corporation tax is covered in Chapter 16 with overseas aspects of corporation tax in Chapter 22. Overseas aspects of VAT is covered in Chapter 23.

Top tips

Throughout this question you must ensure you apply your technical knowledge to the precise facts of the question and avoid generic comments.

Easy marks

Explaining the relief available for a trading loss of an overseas permanent establishment (PE) versus an overseas subsidiary company should be a source of easy marks as well as explaining consequences of making an election to exempt profits of a PE.

ACCA examining team's comments

Part (a)

This question part asked for an explanation of the corporation tax treatment in relation to the acquisition of two assets, one being a brand and the other a machine.

Some candidates scored full marks on the treatment of the brand, knowing that amortisation was allowed and that there was an alternative '4%' treatment, correctly concluding which one may be more advantageous. However, many candidates incorrectly discussed giving capital allowances on the brand.

Candidates generally knew that the machine would be eligible for capital allowances and many correctly identified that the machine would be eligible for the annual investment allowance (AIA). However, not all went on to discuss the annual £1m limit for the AIA and there were virtually no references to this limit applying to the group. In order to score an analysis and evaluation skills mark in this part, candidates needed to use relevant information to determine suitable calculations. By doing this, candidates are showing that they not only know the rules but that they can apply them to the facts of the question. In order to score a scepticism mark here, we were looking for candidates to challenge the uncertainty in the question of whether the annual investment allowance had been used by the group to any extent. In future questions, candidates should be looking to challenge uncertain information in the facts of the question to earn scepticism marks. [**BPP Note.** The ACCA examining team's comments have been edited for this part as the question has been amended due to syllabus update and only relevant comments have been given.]

Part b(i)

This part asked for an explanation of why it would be advantageous to trade through a permanent establishment (PE) rather than an overseas subsidiary company, with reference to the relief available for a loss in the overseas entity.

The majority of candidates were able to score at least two out of three marks on this part for recognising that, with an overseas PE, the loss could be used by the UK company but this was not the case if the loss arose in an overseas subsidiary. Some candidates lost out on a mark by only describing the consequence with a PE and not going on to describe the consequence with an overseas subsidiary. We were also looking for candidates to describe that a permanent establishment was not a separate legal entity but only a minority made this additional point.

A number of students wasted time discussing the treatment of profits in each of the two overseas entities which had not been asked for and so wasted time and earned no marks.

Candidates should take the time to read and re-read the requirements carefully, to ensure that they are not providing an answer beyond what is required. Highlighting key words within a requirement may help to maintain focus and to ensure that candidates do not lose sight of what it is they are being asked to do.

Part b(ii)

Part (b)(ii) asked candidates to state the tax consequences of making an election to exempt the profits of overseas PEs from UK corporation tax and further, to advise the company whether or not it will be beneficial to make this election (given the facts in the question).

A good number of candidates were able to state the consequences and scored well for doing this.

When candidates came to give advice, many knew that the election was not worthwhile while the overseas PE was loss-making. However, the facts of the question detailed that the overseas tax rate on PEs was higher than the UK tax rate and that there was no double tax treaty between the UK and the overseas jurisdiction. There was lots of confusion about the meaning of this.

Some candidates wrongly thought that in the absence of a treaty there would be no double tax relief (DTR). Some candidates mistakenly thought that by making the election the loss would remain in the overseas PE to be used to save tax at the overseas (higher) tax rate and that this would be beneficial. Only a minority of candidates correctly recognised that with a higher overseas tax rate, DTR would be equal to the UK tax charged on any future profits, so overall there would be no UK tax charged on overseas profits anyway (so no need to make the election to exempt profits). Many candidates just ignored the possibility of profits despite them being detailed in the question.

In order to recommend effectively, candidates needed to have assessed all aspects of the scenario ie current losses, future profits and plans for future PEs. Candidates needed to consider all the facts presented to them in the scenario and address them in their answers.

Another issue with this part of the question was that a number of candidates thought that they were still answering a question about PE versus overseas subsidiary company (as had been asked in part (b)(i)) instead of the PE election and so earned few or no marks.

Candidates should read and re-read the given requirement to ensure that they are clear on what they are being asked to do before they begin their answers.

In order to earn analysis and evaluation and commercial acumen marks for this part of the question, candidates needed to demonstrate that they had considered all the relevant factors relating to the election, such as losses, future profits and plans for future PEs. They needed to use appropriate information to draw conclusions, based on a balanced appraisal of the information and considering the possible consequences of an election.

Part (c)

This part asked candidates to explain how each of services and goods, both purchased from an overseas supplier, would be reported on a VAT return for a particular quarter.

Candidates fell into broadly three camps for this part. There were those who just didn't know any rules regarding VAT on goods and services from overseas and so earned no marks. They wasted time discussing zero rated and exempt goods and services and partial exemption rules.

The next group of candidates did have some understanding of the VAT rules but discussed the rules generally and did not discuss them in the context of what would be reported on a VAT return and so could only earn limited marks. The third group of candidates applied the rules to the context of submission of the VAT return and were able to score well.

In order to score well at ATX – UK, candidates need to be able to do more than state generic rules. They must be able to apply the rules to the facts of the question and what is being asked of them.

Marking guide

		Marks	
(a)	Brand	4	
	Machine	3.5	
	Marks Available	7.5	
	Maximum		6

(b)	(i)	Permanent establishment	2	
		Subsidiary company	2	
		Marks Available	4	
		Maximum		3
	(ii)	Consequences of election	3	
		Advice	4.5	
		Marks Available	7.5	
		Maximum		6
(c)		Value added tax (VAT) on overseas legal fees	3	
		VAT on imported goods	2	
				5

Professional skills marks

Analysis and evaluation

- Appropriate use of relevant information to determine suitable calculations
- Demonstration of the ability to consider all relevant factors in relation to the election
- Balanced appraisal of information to make a recommendation in respect of the election
- Appropriate use of information to draw conclusions

Commercial acumen

- Recognition of possible consequences of making the election

Scepticism

- Demonstration of the ability to identify missing information in respect of the annual investment scheme

Maximum	5
Total	25

(a)

Corporation tax implications of the acquisition of the assets of the unincorporated business

'Alte' brand

The amortisation charged in Silves Ltd's accounts will be an allowable deduction for corporation tax purposes. In the year ended 31 March 2025, the charge will be £6,250 (£50,000/8). An alternative treatment would be to claim an annual writing down allowance for tax purposes equal to 4% of the cost of the brand, on a straight-line basis, but clearly this would be less tax efficient for Silves Ltd.

Specialist machine

The 100% first-year allowance (full expensing) is not available in respect of this acquisition as the machine had been previously used in the unincorporated business, so was not new when it was acquired by Silves Ltd.

The acquisition of the machine is qualifying expenditure for the purpose of the 100% annual investment allowance (AIA). However, the AIA is limited to £1m in a 12-month accounting period, and this limit applies to a group of companies. As Evora Ltd owns 100%

of the shares in Silves Ltd, it has a majority of voting rights and so the two companies form a group for the purposes of sharing the AIA. So if the total qualifying assets acquired by the two companies exceed this limit, they may need to choose how to allocate the AIA between them in the most tax-efficient way.

(b) (i)

Tax advantage for Evora Ltd of commencing to trade through a PE

A PE does not constitute a separate legal entity, unlike a subsidiary company. Therefore, as the PE will incur a trading loss in the first nine months of trading, this can be offset against Evora Ltd's UK trading profit for the year ending 31 March 2026, thereby obtaining immediate tax relief for the losses.

However, trading losses incurred by a non-UK tax resident subsidiary company would not be available for relief in the UK, so loss relief would be delayed.

(ii)

Election to exempt the profits of overseas PEs from UK corporation tax

Tax consequences

- Trading profits generated in overseas PEs will not be liable to UK corporation tax.
- No relief will be available in the UK in respect of trading losses incurred in overseas PEs.
- No capital allowances can be claimed in the UK in respect of assets acquired for use in overseas PEs.
- The election is irrevocable.
- The election will apply to all future overseas PEs established by Evora Ltd.

Advice to Evora Ltd

There is clearly no advantage in Evora Ltd making this election at this point, as the PE in Salema will generate losses in its first nine months of trading, which, without making the election, can be relieved in the UK.

When the PE in Salema subsequently becomes profitable (after the first nine-month period), there will be no UK corporation tax liability in respect of these profits due to the availability of double taxation relief (DTR). This is because the rate of tax charged on profits in Salema is higher than the rate charged in the UK. So there is still no advantage to making the election at this point.

In addition, the election would prevent UK capital allowances being available in respect of expenditure on capital assets used in any overseas PEs, and no loss relief would be available in respect of any future trading losses incurred by any overseas PEs, including those which are yet to be set up.

Therefore, making this election would not appear to be beneficial for Evora Ltd.

(c)

Word Processor

Paragraph

Value added tax (VAT)

Overseas legal fees

The legal services provided to Evora Ltd will be regarded as being supplied in the UK, as this is Evora Ltd's place of business. Accordingly, Evora Ltd will be required to account for output tax in its VAT return for the quarter ending 30 June 2025. It can then recover this amount as input tax on the same VAT return. Therefore, this expense will not impact on the amount of VAT payable by Evora Ltd for this quarter.

Import of goods

On the assumption that Evora Ltd uses postponed accounting in respect of the import of goods from overseas suppliers, these goods will be reported on Evora Ltd's VAT return for the quarter ending 30 June 2025 in the same way as the legal services supplied (above). Therefore this expense will also not impact on the amount of VAT payable by Evora Ltd for this VAT quarter.

3 Anya

Course Book references

Capital gains tax and CGT reliefs are covered in in Chapter 7 and Chapter 8. IHT and IHT reliefs are covered in Chapters 11 and 12.

Top tips

Make sure you spot the 'command verbs' in each requirement to understand whether you answer should be written or calculational (or both). You will need to consider both IHT and CGT in parts (a) and (b) so structure you answer carefully, discuss each tax separately.

Easy marks

Stating the basic CGT and IHT implications of the gift of a painting should be a source of easy marks. In addition, there should be easy marks available for the calculation of income tax in part (c).

ACCA examining team's comments

Part (a) related to the tax implications for the client of gifting an asset to her granddaughter. It is quite common for CGT and IHT to be examined in this way, in relation to a single lifetime gift.

The gift will give rise to a loss for CGT purposes. The calculation of the loss was very straightforward, as there were only two figures given for this asset – the purchase price and the market value at the date of the gift. Most candidates did calculate this, and gained the 0.5 mark, and it then opened the door to go on and discuss the loss relief available to the donor. A few just stated that the painting had fallen in value, but didn't actually calculate the loss, and so were unable to score well on this part. Candidates should remember that where figures are provided to be able to calculate a chargeable gain or allowable loss in a question, they are usually required to be used for this purpose.

The key point to recognise when discussing the relief available for this loss was that the donor and donee were connected persons for CGT purposes (grandmother and granddaughter), such that relief for the loss was restricted to gains on future disposals to the same person. Candidates should learn the relationships between individuals which mean that they will be

ANSWERS

connected persons, and always note the relationship between the donor and the donee in any scenario so that they can apply this rule. In this question, there was both an analysis and evaluation mark available (for spotting the connected persons issue) and a technical mark for explaining the impact of this on the relief which would be available for the capital loss.

In general, performance was better on the IHT implications of the gift. Most candidates knew the basics – the gift was a potentially exempt transfer (PET), which would become chargeable as the donor's death would be within 7 years, and IHT would be charged at the rate of 40% – and it was pleasing to see that a good number did go on to explain why annual exemptions, the nil rate band, and taper relief wouldn't be available by reference to the facts in the question.

The command word for this requirement was to 'explain', so those candidates who provided written explanations of each of these latter three aspects – or at least two out of the three – scored well. However, there were still a number of candidates who just provided a calculation, with little to no accompanying explanation, and so were unable to score these marks. On the whole, in recent sittings, candidates' ability to address 'explain' requirements with a written answer has improved, with a majority clearly realising that if a question asks for an explanation, a calculation will not suffice, but unfortunately there are still a minority clinging to this approach, who consequently score only low marks. Sensible use of subheadings, as candidates are so often advised to utilise, ensured that in most cases they were able to score the analysis and evaluation professional skills mark for appropriate use of information to draw separate conclusions in relation to CGT and IHT.

Part (b) once again related to the CGT and IHT implications of a proposed gift; this time it was a gift of shares in a trading company, and the requirements related specifically to the availability of two reliefs – gift holdover relief for CGT in (b)(i) and business property relief (BPR) for IHT in (b)(ii). Performance on this part was disappointing. As in previous papers, candidates generally demonstrated a significant lack of knowledge and application skills in relation to CGT reliefs – in this case gift holdover relief – but, in the main, were a bit more confident with BPR for IHT. As has been said many times before, the reliefs available for both capital taxes are an important part of the ATX – UK syllabus and will continue to be tested on a very regular basis.

Part (b)(i) initially required candidates to essentially list the conditions for gift holdover relief to apply, relating them to this scenario.

A significant number of candidates managed to identify no more than the fact that this company satisfied the condition for the shares to be in an unquoted trading company. A few went on to correctly make reference to the donee's UK tax residence status, but only a minority picked up on the existence of investments (shares in another company) among the company's assets, which meant that relief would be restricted. This meant that these candidates were unable to score the analysis and evaluation mark for recognising that relief would be restricted in this case.

The information in the scenario in relation to these investments was presented in the same way as it has been in many past exam questions, which would suggest that these candidates are not undertaking sufficient question practice in their preparation for this exam. Time and again in these examiners' reports we emphasise the need for question practice as an integral part of candidates' preparation for this exam. Among other things, this helps to familiarise candidates with the way in which information is likely to be presented to them in the exam, and for them to learn how it should be utilised in their answer.

Answers to the second part of (b)(i) relating to the consequences of a gift holdover relief claim for the recipient of the shares were generally better, with many candidates recognising that there would be an impact on her base cost, and that, overall, gift holdover relief will only enable the gain to be deferred for a time. Most therefore managed to pick up the commercial acumen mark for recognising the consequences for the donee, in that the gain would only be deferred, but fewer gained the available technical mark for specifically identifying that the gain would be deducted from the base cost of the shares for the recipient. Virtually no candidates recognised that there would be an interaction between CGT and IHT for the recipient of the shares following the gift holdover relief claim, thereby not scoring the analysis and evaluation mark available for recognition of the potential IHT consequences.

As in previous papers, in part b(ii) candidates on the whole dealt better with the business property relief (BPR) for IHT, than with the CGT relief. Again, citing the basic rules for BPR at the time of the gift – the company was an unquoted trading company, the donor had owned the shares for at least 2 years, and relief would be available at the rate of 100% – meant that a good number were able to score at least half of the technical marks in this section, although, once again, the investments were ignored.

However, relatively few candidates completed the explanation by considering the BPR requirements for the donee ie that they must still hold the shares on the donor's death, if this is within seven years of the date of the gift, in order that BPR will be available in calculating IHT as a result of the donor's death. This meant that they were unable to access the commercial acumen mark for consideration of relevant factors in relation to available reliefs and the scepticism mark for identifying that further information would be required to confirm availability of the relief.

It was noticeable that few candidates appeared to gain many professional skills marks in part (b) overall except for the reference to gift holdover relief being merely a deferral relief for CGT, as mentioned above. This was primarily due to a lack of precise enough knowledge of the two reliefs being tested, meaning that candidates were unable to demonstrate their skills in applying this knowledge.

Candidates are advised to spend time learning the detailed conditions required for each of the reliefs for both CGT and IHT. Skill in identifying and applying these will continue to be rewarded with professional skills marks, in addition to technical marks for their correct applications. However, this requires a good, detailed knowledge of the reliefs in the first place.

Part (c) of this question involved the calculation and comparison of the client's post tax income for two consecutive tax years. The vast majority of candidates were clearly more comfortable with this part of the question.

As a result of this gift, the donor would no longer receive a dividend in respect of these shares, and consequently there would be a reduction in their income tax liability. The majority of candidates recognised that the requirement to calculate the reduction in the post-tax income between two consecutive tax years could be achieved by preparing a fairly straightforward income tax computation for each year to calculate the relevant tax liability in each case, which could then be deducted from the total income for the year, and a comparison made to determine the difference.

Marks were mainly lost due to a failure to read the question properly so, for example, picking up the wrong dividend figure, or for carelessness/lack of focus which, for example, caused candidates to miss the restriction in the personal allowance.

Most candidates were also able to pick up the analysis and evaluation mark for this part by at least making an attempt at a comparison of the difference in after tax income.

Marking guide

			Marks	
(a)		Capital gains tax implications	2.5	
		Inheritance tax implications	5	
		Marks Available	7.5	
		Maximum		6
(b)	(i)	Availability of gift holdover relief	4	
		Consequences of claim	2	
		Marks Available	6	
		Maximum		5
	(ii)	Availability of business property relief	3	
		Amount of relief	2	
		Marks Available	5	
		Maximum		4

ANSWERS

Marking guide		Marks
(c) Income tax liability 2024/25	3	
Income tax liability 2025/26	1	
Post tax income	1	
		5

Profession skills marks

Analysis and evaluation

- Appropriate use of information to draw conclusions in (a)
- Appropriate use of information to determine the consequences for Cara of a gift holdover relief claim
- Demonstration of ability to consider of relevant factors in relation to the availability of reliefs
- Appropriate use of information to determine restrictions to the reliefs
- Appropriate use of information to conclude on the reduction in post-tax income

Commercial acumen

- Effective use of information to determine the relevance of the disposal to Anya's granddaughter for capital loss relief purposes
- Recognition of the interaction between IHT and CGT in respect of a future disposal by Cara

Scepticism

- Demonstration of the ability to identify missing information in respect of business property relief

Maximum	5
Total	25

(a)

Word Processor

Tax implications of disposing of the painting

Capital gains tax (CGT)

This disposal will generate a capital loss of £41,000 (£63,000 – £104,000).

Violette is Anya's granddaughter, so is a connected person to Anya. Accordingly, this loss can only be relieved against gains made on any other asset disposals to Violette by Anya in the tax years 2025/26 or 2026/27 prior to her death.

Inheritance tax (IHT)

The gift of the painting will be a potentially exempt transfer (PET) for IHT, which will become chargeable as a result of Anya's death within seven years (on 6 September 2026).

No annual exemptions will be available as these will have been used against the gift of £50,000 cash to Flava on 1 July 2025. No nil rate band will be available as it will all be used against the gift of the investment property to Cara on 31 March 2024. No taper relief will be available as Anya's death occurs within three years of the gift.

Accordingly, the gift of the painting will give rise to an IHT liability of £25,200 (£63,000 × 40%), which will be payable by Violette.

(b) (i)

Availability of gift holdover relief on the gift of the Chaski Ltd shares

The gift of the shares in Chaski Ltd will be eligible for gift holdover relief as Chaski Ltd is an unquoted trading company, and Cara (the donee) is tax resident in the UK. However, because Chaski Ltd is Anya's personal company (ie she can exercise at least 5% of the voting rights), the gift holdover relief will be restricted by reference to the shares in RQ Ltd, which are not chargeable business assets. The proportion of the gain which will be eligible for gift holdover relief will be calculated as the value of the chargeable business assets divided by the value of the total chargeable assets. Accordingly, the proportion of the gain which will qualify for relief is 93.4% (£853,000/(£853,000 + £60,000)).

Consequences for Cara of the relief being claimed

When Cara subsequently disposes of the shares, her base cost will be reduced by the amount of the gift holdover relief, such that her gain on this sale will be higher. As the gift will be liable to IHT as a result of Anya's death on 6 September 2026, the gain arising on Cara's future disposal of the shares will be reduced by the amount of IHT payable in respect of them. However, this deduction cannot be used to create a loss.

(ii)

IHT reliefs available on the gift of the Chaski Ltd shares

Business property relief (BPR) will be available at the rate of 100% as Chaski Ltd is an unquoted trading company, and Anya will have held the shares for more than two years prior to the date of the gift. However, the fact that Chaski Ltd's assets include shares in RQ Ltd means that, as these shares fall within the definition of excepted assets, the relief will be restricted to the proportion: market value of business assets divided by market value of total assets. Accordingly, the relief available will be 94.2% ((£1,034,000 – £60,000)/£1,034,000) of the value of the shares.

Cara must still hold the shares (or replacement business property) at the date of Anya's death in order for BPR to be available, and the shares must still be relevant business property.

(c) **Reduction in Anya's post-tax income for the tax year 2025/26**

Spreadsheet

Edit Format

B6	=-B21		
	A	B	C
1		2024/25	2025/26
2		£	£
3	Pension income	65,000	65,000
4	Dividend from Chaski Ltd	40,000	nil
5	Total income	105,000	65,000
6	Less: personal allowance (Working 1)	(10,070)	(12,570)
7	Taxable income	94,930	52,430
8	Income tax:		
9	– £37,700 at 20%	7,540	7,540
10	– £17,230/£14,730 at 40%	6,892	5,892
11	– £(40,000 – 500) at 33.75%	13,331	nil
12	Total tax liability	27,763	13,432
13	Post-tax income:		
14	– £105,000 – £27,763	77,237	
15	– £65,000 – £13,432		51,568
16	Reduction in post-tax income is £25,669 (£77,237 – £51,568).		
17			
18	(W) Personal allowance in 2024/25		
19	PA	12,570	
20	Less ½ (£105,000 – £100,000	(2,500)	
21		10,070	

Tutorial note. Alternative presentation of answer using a marginal approach:

	£
Dividend received from Chaski Ltd in 2024/25	40,000
Dividend receivable from Chaski Ltd in 2025/26	nil
Reduction in dividend income	40,000
Less income tax payable on dividend income in 2024/25: ((£40,000 – £500) × 33.75%)	(13,331)
Less reduction in personal allowance available in 2024/25: (((105,000 – 100,000)/2) × 40%)	(1,000)
Reduction in post-tax income	25,669

ANSWERS

ACCA

Advanced Taxation (ATX – UK) FA2024

Mock Exam 2

Specimen exam

Questions	
Time allowed	3 hours 15 minutes
ALL questions are compulsory and MUST be attempted	

DO NOT OPEN THIS EXAM UNTIL YOU ARE READY TO START UNDER EXAMINATION CONDITIONS

Section A

1 REP Ltd **(98 mins)**

You should assume that today's date is 1 September 2025.

You are an ACCA student working for a firm of accountants. Your manager, Sheila Hughes, has asked for your assistance in drafting notes in preparation for an internal meeting to discuss issues raised by Lamar, who is the majority shareholder and managing director of REP Ltd, and his wife, Freya. Both Lamar and Freya are clients of your firm.

In addition to some ethical considerations which have been raised by your manager, advice is required in respect of:

- the corporation tax issues in relation to a proposed purchase of shares by REP Ltd in an overseas company;
- the value added tax (VAT) implications of the purchase of an investment property;
- the income tax consequences of ceasing to trade; and
- the inheritance tax consequences of a gift of shares to a trust.

The following exhibits provide information relevant to the question;

(1) REP Ltd – note of a conversation between Lamar and your manager

(2) Personal tax affairs – extract of an email received from Freya

(3) Manager's email – work to be carried out

This information should be used to answer the question **requirements** within your chosen **response option(s)**.

Required

You should assume that today's date is 1 September 2025.

Respond to the instructions in the email from your manager.

Note. The split of the mark allocation is shown in Exhibit 3 – Manager's email. **(40 marks)**

Professional marks will be awarded for the demonstration of skill in communication, analysis & evaluation, scepticism and commercial acumen in your answer. **(10 marks)**

(Total = 50 marks)

Exhibit 1: REP Ltd

Note of a telephone conversation between Lamar and Sheila Hughes (tax manager) on 1 September 2025

(1) **Potential investment in JAY Ltd**

The directors of REP Ltd are in discussion with the management of CRO Ltd (an unconnected company) regarding the establishment of a new company, JAY Ltd. Both REP Ltd and CRO Ltd are UK resident companies which prepare accounts to 31 March each year. CRO Ltd is part of a large multinational group which comprises of 19 companies.

JAY Ltd would commence trading on 1 April 2026 and carry on its business activities in the country of Garia, where it would manufacture computer components.

Business profits generated in Garia are subject to 13% business tax in that country. There is no double tax treaty between the UK and Garia.

Size of investment

CRO Ltd is proposing that REP Ltd would own 30% of the ordinary share capital of JAY Ltd, with CRO Ltd owning the remaining 70%. However, Lamar and his fellow directors regard this potential investment as somewhat risky, such that if they decide to proceed, they may prefer to own just 20% of JAY Ltd rather than 30%.

JAY Ltd will have no source of taxable income, other than its trading profits, and will not make any chargeable gains during the year ending 31 March 2027.

JAY Ltd's tax adjusted trading profit for the year ending 31 March 2027 is budgeted to be £135,000, all of which will relate to its activities in Garia. However, there is the possibility that it will be loss making in either that year, of in future years.

Additional information

REP Ltd has not been involved in a joint venture of this nature before and has no experience of carrying on a business outside the UK. Lamar told me that he had been provided with the following additional relevant information:

(i) It has not yet been determined whether JAY Ltd will be resident in the UK or in Garia.

(ii) If JAY Ltd is resident in the UK, it will be carrying on its business through a permanent establishment in Garia and will consider making an election to exempt its overseas trading profits from UK tax.

(iii) Confirmation has been received that if JAY Ltd is resident in Garia, this will not result in a charge under the controlled foreign company (CFC) rules

(2) **Purchase of investment property**

The directors are considering the purchase by REP Ltd of a new, unused commercial building, situated in the UK, for £200,000 plus 20% value added tax (VAT). REP Ltd would then grant a 20-year lease of this building to one of a number of different businesses they are currently in discussion with.

The directors are keen to recover the VAT charged by the vendor on the sale of this building. Lamar told me that one of his friends had suggested that they could do this by opting to tax the building before granting the lease, and that this would have no effect on their tenant or any potential future purchaser.

Exhibit 2: Personal tax affairs

Email extract from Freya dated 1 September 2025

Cessation of my business

I am intending to cease my unincorporated consultancy business on 31 October 2025. I began trading in 2013 and have always prepared accounts to 31 May each year. My business is my only source of income.

- I will prepare a single set of accounts for the 17-month period ending 31 October 2025. The budgeted tax adjusted profit for 2025/26, before the deduction of capital allowances, is £62,600.
- The only capital asset within my business is a car which has always been used 65% for business purposes. I will withdraw this car from the business on 31 October 2025 when it will have a market value of £11,100, which is less than its original cost. The tax written down value of this car as at 31 May 2024 was £8,700.

Proposed gift of shares to trust

- I established a discretionary trust for the benefit of my nieces and nephews on 1 August 2015.
- I own shares in Dexil Ltd and on 1 November 2025, I am planning to give 20,000 of these shares to the trust. After I have made the gift, I will still own 60,000 shares (60% of the company).

  You have already advised me that these shares are not relevant business property for the purposes of business property relief, due to the investment activities of Dexil Ltd. Accordingly, I am aware that the gift on 1 November 2025 may result in an inheritance tax (IHT) liability. If I decide to make the gift, I will pay any IHT due and I need to know by when such amount would fall due.
- I have made the following gifts in the past:

		£
1 August 2015	Cash to trustees on the creation of the trust	120,000
1 February 2021	Cash to brother	35,000
1 May 2021	Additional cash to trustees	170,000
1 July 2025	Cash to sister	45,000

- None of these gifts has resulted in an IHT liability.

Additional information provided by your manager:

These are the Dexil Ltd share valuations you should use:

Shareholding	Up to 25%	26% to 50%	51% to 74%	75% or more
Value per share	£8	£11	£17	£24

Freya currently owns 80% of the ordinary share capital of Dexil Ltd. The remaining shares in the company are owned by individuals who have no connection with Freya.

Exhibit 3: Manager's email – work to be carried out

To: Tax assistant

From: Sheila Hughes, Tax Manager

Date: 1 September 2025

Subject: REP Ltd

Hi

I need you to prepare some notes in preparation for an internal meeting with the rest of the engagement team. The notes should be set out in a manner which will make it easy for you to refer to them during the meeting and should address the following issues:

(a) **Knowledge obtained from advising other clients**

We have many existing clients which trade from permanent establishments situated overseas, and a few years ago we had a client with a presence in the country of Garia.

Identify the points which should be made in order to explain the extent to which REP Ltd can benefit from the knowledge our firm has gained from advising other clients. **(5 marks)**

(b) **Investment in JAY Ltd by REP Ltd (Exhibit 1).**

(i) **Residency of JAY Ltd**

Explanations of the relevance of the country of residency of JAY Ltd in relation to:

- the amount of corporation tax payable in the UK and Garia in respect of its profits; and
- the relief available to REP Ltd if JAY Ltd's business in Garia were to make a trading loss.

Before you start, take some time to identify the different possibilities which need to be addressed, recognising that we do not yet know what percentage of JAY Ltd will be owned by REP Ltd. **(9 marks)**

(ii) **Election to exempt the profits of JAY Ltd's overseas permanent establishment from UK tax.**

List the implications of JAY Ltd making this election. **(3 marks)**

(iii) **Controlled foreign company (CFC) rules.**

I can confirm that a CFC charge will not arise if JAY Ltd is resident in Garia. However, I want to provide Lamar with an explanation of the purpose of the CFC rules and the charge which can be levied under them. **(3 marks)**

(c) **Purchase of investment property by REP Ltd (Exhibit 1).**

- Explain how opting to tax the building would enable REP Ltd to recover the value added tax (VAT) charged by the vendor; and
- Explain whether or not the advice from Lamar's friend is correct.

There is no need for you to consider partial exemption or the capital goods scheme. **(5 marks)**

(d) **Personal tax affairs (Exhibit 2).**

(i) **Cessation of Freya's business on 31 October 2025.**

A calculation of Freya's estimated liability to income tax and Class 4 national insurance contributions in respect of her final tax year of trading. **(7 marks)**

(ii) **Proposed gift of shares to trust on 1 November 2025.**

- A calculation of the inheritance tax which would be payable by Freya if she were to give 20,000 shares in Dexil Ltd to the trust on 1 November 2025, as planned. Your calculation should indicate the availability or otherwise of all relevant annual exemptions.
- The payment date, together with a brief explanation of how it has been determined.

(8 marks)

I look forward to seeing your notes.

Sheila

Section B

2 Amelia (49 mins)

You should assume that today's date is 1 September 2025.

Amelia is a sole trader. She is seeking advice in respect of;

- a loss incurred by her business,
- the tax implications of replacing a warehouse, and
- deregistration for value added tax (VAT) purposes.

The following exhibit, available on the left-hand side of the screen, provides information relevant to the question;

(1) Amelia

This information should be used to answer the question **requirements** within your chosen **response option(s).**

Required

You should assume that today's date is 1 September 2025.

(a) (i) State the reliefs available to Amelia in respect of her trading loss of 2025/26, on the assumption that Amelia does not wish to carry forward any of the loss. **(3 marks)**

(ii) Explain, with supporting calculations, how much tax would be saved for each of the reliefs identified in requirement (a)(i). **(8 marks)**

(b) Explain, with supporting calculations, the capital gains tax and income tax implications for Amelia of the proposed sale of Warehouse 1, and the acquisition of Warehouse 2 and the forklift truck. **(6 marks)**

(c) Explain why Amelia can apply to voluntarily deregister for value added tax (VAT) purposes on 31 March 2026, from what date her VAT registration would be cancelled, and the immediate consequences for her of deregistering. **(3 marks)**

Professional marks will be awarded for the demonstration of skill in analysis and evaluation and commercial acumen in your answer. **(5 marks)**

(Total = 25 marks)

Exhibit: Amelia

Amelia:

- Has owned her unincorporated business, AS Trading, for many years calculating her taxable trading income using the accruals basis and has made the election to continue using this method from 2024/25.
- Has savings income of £6,000 each year.
- Had rental income of £11,600 from a UK residential property in the tax year 2024/25.
- Has no rental income in the tax year 2025/26 as the letting ceased on 31 March 2025.
- Sold this property on 30 April 2025.

AS Trading – tax adjusted trading profit/(loss):

	£
2024/25	30,000
2025/26 (forecast)	(14,000)

Amelia – recent capital disposals:

- Amelia's capital disposals are as follows:

Asset	**Date of disposal**	**(loss)/gain** **£**
Painting	1 June 2024	(11,000)
UK rental property	30 April 2025	45,000
Shares in Swartz Ltd	16 August 2025	28,000

- All of these disposals were made to unconnected persons.
- Amelia had never lived in the UK rental property.
- Swartz Ltd is an unquoted trading company.
- Amelia sold the whole of her 3% shareholding in Swartz Ltd. She had acquired the shares in 2023.

Proposed sale of Warehouse 1:

- Amelia acquired Warehouse 1 on 1 May 2018 for £86,000.
- Amelia will sell Warehouse 1 on 1 May 2026 for its expected market value at that date of £118,000.
- AS Trading occupies three out of the four floors of Warehouse 1.
- The remaining floor has been rented to tenants throughout Amelia's ownership of the building.

Proposed purchase of Warehouse 2:

- Amelia will purchase this warehouse on 1 March 2027. Structures and buildings allowance is not available in respect of this warehouse.
- She will also acquire a forklift truck for use in the warehouse on 1 March 2027.
- Amelia will pay £83,000 for Warehouse 2 and will pay £23,000 for the forklift truck.
- Amelia will start to use the whole of Warehouse 2 in her business from 1 May 2027.

AS Trading – taxable turnover for value added tax (VAT) purposes:

	£
Year ended 31 March 2025	92,000
Year ending 31 March 2026 (forecast)	65,000
Year ending 31 March 2027 (forecast)	79,000

- Amelia expects that the taxable turnover of the business will continue to increase gradually in the next few years.
- AS Trading makes wholly standard-rated supplies.
- Amelia wishes to apply for voluntary deregistration for VAT purposes on 31 March 2026.

3 Dorian (49 mins)

You should assume that today's date is 1 January 2026.

You have been asked to provide advice to Dorian, the managing director of Taupe Ltd, in relation to:

- Taupe Ltd's status as a close company
- the provision by the company of employment benefits to Dorian, and
- the late filing of the company's corporation tax return.

The following exhibit, available on the left-hand side of the screen provides information relevant to the question:

(1) Dorian and Taupe Ltd

This information should be used to answer the question **requirements** within your chosen **response option(s).**

Required

You should assume that today's date is 1 January 2026.

(a) Explain why Taupe Ltd is classed as a close company. **(4 marks)**

(b) Explain, with supporting calculations, the tax implications for both Dorian and Taupe Ltd, if Dorian repays the £7,500 loan on 30 April 2027 rather than on 30 June 2027. **(5 marks)**

(c) Explain, with supporting calculations, which of the two alternatives for providing assistance with travel costs, will produce the lower overall cost for Dorian. **(8 marks)**

(d) State, with reasons, the due date for filing Taupe Ltd's corporation tax return for the year ended 30 April 2024, and the implications for Taupe Ltd in respect of filing it late. **(3 marks)**

Professional marks will be awarded for the demonstration of skill in analysis and evaluation, and commercial acumen in your answer. **(5 marks)**

(Total = 25 marks)

Exhibit: Dorian and Taupe Ltd

Taupe Ltd:

- Is a UK resident trading company and is also a close company.
- Has six directors, Dorian and five other, unrelated, individuals.
- Has an accounting reference date of 30 April each year.
- Always pays all amounts due to HM Revenue and Customs (HMRC) by the due date.
- Is not a large company for the purpose of being required to pay its corporation tax liability in instalments.

Taupe Ltd – shareholders:

- The shares in Taupe Ltd are held as follows:

	Percentage of issued ordinary shares
Dorian	5%
The other five directors (each holding 5%)	25%
Basil (Dorian's father)	23%
Other, unrelated, shareholders (each holding less than 2%)	47%
	100%

Dorian:

- Has an annual salary of £78,000 from Taupe Ltd.
- Was provided with an interest-free loan of £7,500 from Taupe Ltd on 6 April 2024. Notional tax was payable on this loan by Taupe Ltd.
- Is due to repay this loan on 30 June 2027, but may repay it earlier, on 30 April 2027.
- Has no other income.
- Works full time at Taupe Ltd's office in London.

Taupe Ltd – assistance with Dorian's home to work travel costs:

- Taupe Ltd is considering two alternatives to assist Dorian with the costs of his daily travel from home to work for the tax year 2026/27.

Alternative 1:

- On 6 April 2026, Taupe Ltd will make an interest-free loan to Dorian of £4,800, equal to the cost of his annual travel season ticket.
- Taupe Ltd will write off this loan on 5 April 2027.
- Dorian will incur no additional travel costs under this alternative.

Alternative 2:

- Taupe Ltd will pay Dorian a mileage allowance for driving his own car to work, amounting to £3,600 for the year ending 5 April 2027.
- Taupe Ltd will pay an unconnected company an annual fee of £1,200 for a car parking space for Dorian near the company's London office.
- Dorian has estimated that his current annual cost of driving from home to work is £5,220, including £1,320 for parking.

Taupe Ltd – late filing of corporation tax returns:

- Taupe Ltd filed its corporation tax return for the year ended 30 April 2024 on 29 August 2025.
- HMRC issued a notice requiring the filing of this return on 8 June 2024.
- Taupe Ltd had filed its corporation tax return for the year ended 30 April 2023 on 6 July 2024.
- All previous corporation tax returns had been filed on time.

Answers

DO NOT TURN THIS PAGE UNTIL YOU HAVE COMPLETED THE MOCK EXAM

A plan of attack

We've already established that you've been told to do it 101 times, so it is of course superfluous to tell you for the 102nd time to **take a good look at the exam before diving into the answers.**

What's the worst thing you could be doing right now if this was the actual exam? Wondering how to celebrate the end of the exam in about three hours' time?

Turn back to the exam and let's sort out a **plan of attack**!

First things first

Look through the exam and work out the order in which to attack the questions. You've got **two options.** Option 1 is the option recommended by BPP.

Option 1 (if you're thinking 'Help!')

If you're a bit worried about the exam, do the questions in the order of how well you think you can answer them. If you find the questions in Section B less daunting than the questions in Section A, start with Section B.

There are **two questions** in Section B. **Question 2** has three parts. Part (a) concerns the reliefs available to Amelia in respect of her trading loss. In part (i) you're asked to state the reliefs available to her and then in part (ii) you need to explain, with supporting calculations how much tax each loss relief option will save. Make sure you're very clear about which tax year the loss relates to and which loss option you're discussing in your answer. Make sure you look at Amelia's other income in each tax year so that you can apply your answer to the specifics of the question.

Part (b) requires an explanation of the capital gains tax and income tax implications of the sale of warehouse 1 and the acquisition of warehouse 2 and a forklift truck. It should be obvious to think of the CGT implications and the possibility of rollover relief but don't forget to think about any income tax implications.

Part (c) deals VAT deregistration. Make sure you attempt each part of the requirement.

Question 3 has four parts. Part (a) asks for an explanation of why Taupe Ltd is a close company. This is new topic for Advanced Taxation (ATX–UK).

Part (b) asks about the tax implications for both Dorian and Taupe Ltd if Dorian repays a loan on 30 April rather than 30 June. This continues testing your close company knowledge and also your knowledge of beneficial loans which is a topic covered in Taxation (TX–UK).

Part (c) looks at the cost to Dorian of two alternative travel assistance proposals. Once again this combines Taxation (TX–UK) knowledge with close company knowledge which is new in Advanced Taxation.

Part (d) looks at implications of late filing of a corporation tax return and is a good reminder of the importance of administration in the syllabus.

Do not spend longer than about 97 minutes on Section B. When you've spent the allocated time on the questions in Section B turn to the **case-study question** in Section A.

Read the Section A question through thoroughly before you launch into it. Once you start make sure you allocate your time to the parts within the question according to the marks available and that, where possible, you attempt the easy marks first.

Question 1 has four parts and you are preparing notes for an internal meeting. Part (a) is the ethics question. There will always be five marks on ethics in Section A and they are relatively easy to obtain.

Part (b) has three sub-parts and which all relate to overseas corporation tax topics. The first part looks at the idea of residency, the second considers the election to exempt overseas permanent establishment's profits from tax and the final part looks at controlled foreign companies. These are all topics which are new at Advanced Taxation (ATX–UK) and you should expect some sort of overseas tax issues in your exam.

Part (c) looks at VAT on land and buildings - another topic which is frequently tested in ATX–UK.

Finally, part (d) has two sub-parts. The first asks for a calculation of an individual's liability to income tax and class 4 NICs in relation to her last year of trade and the second part looks at IHT on a lifetime gift of shares to a trust. These topics are all testing your assumed Taxation (TX–UK) knowledge and should be straightforward provided you've left time to attempt them.

Lastly, what you mustn't forget is that you have to attempt **the whole question in Section A and BOTH questions in Section B.**

Option 2 (if you're thinking 'This exam's alright')

It never pays to be overconfident but if you're not quaking in your shoes about the exam then **turn straight to the case-study question in Section A.**

Once you've done this question, **move to Section B**. The question you attempt first really depends on what you are most confident at. If you are undecided look at the requirements. It may be easier to obtain more marks if these are broken down into several smaller parts. In this exam each of questions two and three actually have four smaller parts so, in this situation, it may be easier to pick your question based on which topics you prefer.

No matter how many times we remind you...

Always, always **allocate your time** according to the marks for the question in total and then according to the parts of the question. And **always, always follow the requirements** exactly. For example in Question 1(b)(i) you are told to take some time before you start to identify possibilities to address including recognising that the percentage ownership of JAY Ltd is not yet decided. In 1(c) you are specifically told not to consider the partial exemption or capital goods scheme. Marks will not be available for you to discuss something which has been specifically excluded in the scenario. Not only will you not score marks but you will also be wasting valuable time if you write about something you've been asked not to.

You've got spare time at the end of the exam...?

If you have allocated your time properly then you **shouldn't have time on your hands** at the end of the exam. But if you find yourself with five or ten minutes to spare, check over your work to make sure that you have answered all the requirements of the questions and all parts of all requirements.

Forget about it!

And don't worry if you found the exam difficult. More than likely other candidates will too. If this were the real thing you would need to **forget** the exam the minute you leave the exam room and **think about the next one**. Or, if it's the last one, **celebrate**!

Section A

1 REP Ltd

Course Book references

Ethics is covered in Chapter 1 with overseas corporate issues in Chapter 22. VAT on land and buildings is covered in Chapter 23 and cessation of a sole trade business is within owner managed business tax planning in Chapter 18. IHT is covered in Chapters 11 and 12.

Top tips

Make sure you use your manager's email to break down your answer to cover each of the questions asked and structure your answer. In part (b) make sure you read your manager's email carefully as you're given specific instructions that you need to follow. Don't forget to keep moving through the question – there's a lot to cover and you need to make sure you have time for those final 8 marks on IHT in (d)(ii).

Easy marks

The ethical marks in part (a) should have been the source of some easy marks as well as Freya's income tax and class 4 NIC in part (d)(i). In addition, the IHT in (d)(ii) should also have provided easy marks as long as you didn't get bogged down earlier in the question and run out of time.

ACCA examining team's comments

This question related to a couple who required advice on various aspects of establishing a new company which will operate wholly overseas, the value added tax (VAT) implications of purchasing and leasing a new commercial building, personal tax advice about cessation of a sole trade business and the inheritance tax (IHT) implications of a proposed gift into a discretionary trust.

Candidates should note that the requirements for this question were clearly set out, using a series of subheadings, and the use of these subheadings in their answer, provides a useful structure in this type of question, which all candidates should consider adopting.

Part (a) focused on the firm's ability to use knowledge which it has gained from working with other clients to assist this company. The majority of candidates were able to recognise the ethical principles concerned here and apply them correctly to this scenario. Answers to this part were generally good.

Part (b) comprised three parts, each relating to specific aspects of establishing the new company. Candidates who scored well on this question part showed evidence of having carefully read each of the requirements and spent time thinking and planning their answer, which was then well structured and easy to follow. All candidates would be advised to do this in a question part like this, which was worth a significant proportion of the marks (15 marks), to demonstrate a well thought out and professional approach.

Part (b)(i) required candidates to consider the different UK tax implications of the new company being UK resident (and therefore operating through a permanent establishment overseas), or alternatively being an overseas resident company. Additionally, candidates had to consider the loss relief which would be available to the UK investing company in each of these situations. High scoring candidates adopted a logical approach to discussing the general UK tax implications of the new company being UK resident, or overseas resident, and then going on to address the relief available for trading losses in each of those situations. Use of several subheadings served to break up the information and make it easier for the reader to follow. Weaker answers tended to be more jumbled, so it was sometimes difficult to grasp which particular situation a candidate was talking about.

Part (b)(ii) required an explanation of the implications of making an election to exempt the profits of the overseas permanent establishment from UK tax. Answers to this part tended to polarise; some candidates were obviously very familiar with this area and appeared to easily score full marks. Others unfortunately didn't seem to be prepared for this and so were able to make no, or very little attempt at this part. Overseas aspects of taxation are very frequently tested areas in relation to both companies and individuals, and candidates would be well advised to spend time learning and practising these rules in quite some detail.

Part (b)(iii) related to controlled foreign company (CFC) legislation. The client specifically wanted an explanation of the purpose of the CFC rules, and the charge which can be levied under them. A majority of candidates were able to identify that the CFC rules comprise anti avoidance legislation to prevent overseas subsidiaries being used to avoid UK taxation on profits earned by the company.

However, a great many then went on to detail the exemptions from CFC status – which they were able to reproduce quite precisely – but were not relevant to what the client wanted to know. This wasted valuable time, for no marks. Candidates are once again reminded of the need to read the requirements very carefully, and to confine their answers to what is specifically being asked for in this particular question – which may not be the same as a past question which they have recently practised.

Part (c) concerned the recovery of input VAT in respect of the purchase of a commercial building which is to be immediately leased to a trader. Most candidates discussed the relevance of the option to tax the building in order to recover the input VAT, but relatively few referred to this being necessary on the grant of the lease, which would otherwise be an exempt supply. A minority of candidates confined their answers to this aspect of the requirement only, and did not fully address the requirement in the manager's email to explain more generally matters which the client should be aware of, which included the ramifications of opting to tax the building for both the company and the tenants of the building.

[Note that this requirement wording has been changed since it was originally set but these ACCA examining team's comments remain relevant.]

Part (d)(i) required a calculation of the individual's income tax and class 4 national insurance contributions (NIC) for the tax year of cessation of her business.

[Part of this question has been amended due to syllabus changes and so only the relevant ACCA examining team's comments remain].

The capital allowances computation proved to be a particular problem for candidates, with the main errors being calculating an annual investment allowance (AIA) and writing down allowance (WDA) for the final accounting period as well as, or instead of, a balancing adjustment. On the whole, candidates who sat the computer based exam (CBE) and chose to use the spreadsheet response space for this question part presented clearer, easier to follow answers than those who did not. Where detailed calculations are required, the use of the spreadsheet response option can provide valuable time savings and help candidates to present their workings more clearly.

Part (d)(ii) required a calculation of the immediate IHT payable by Freya on a proposed gift of shares into a discretionary trust. On the whole, this question part was done well. Many candidates recognised the need for application of the diminution in value approach and performed this correctly. The main issue was confusion over which of the previous lifetime gifts – which included both chargeable lifetime transfers (CLTs) and potentially exempt transfers (PETs) - to take into account in calculating the remaining nil rate band available to set against this lifetime gift. This is a fundamental concept, which is tested at TX–UK, but ATX–UK candidates must revise the rules and ensure they are confident with the principle of accumulation in calculating IHT payable on

CLTs in lifetime, as well as IHT payable as a result of the donor's death. A few candidates spent a considerable amount of time producing a table of all the lifetime gifts, deducting annual exemptions where appropriate. Such an approach is unlikely to be required in ATX–UK.

Candidates are advised to carefully read and think about requirements such as this to ensure that they focus on the relevant gifts which need to be considered, and not just take a blanket approach, by including all of them.

[The requirement asking for the payment date has been added to this question since it was originally set so no ACCA examining team's comments are given.]

Marking guide

			Marks	
(a)		One mark for each relevant point	5	
		Maximum		5
(b)	(i)	**Taxation of profits**		
		Subject to tax in Garia	1	
		JAY Ltd is UK resident	3	
		JAY Ltd is resident in Garia	2	
		Relief for losses		
		JAY Ltd is UK resident	4	
		JAY Ltd is resident in Garia	1	
		Marks Available	11	
		Maximum		9
	(ii)	One mark for each relevant point	4	
		Maximum		3
	(iii)	One mark for each relevant point	4	
		Maximum		3
(c)		Recovery of input VAT on purchase	2	
		Implications for the tenant	2	
		Implications for the future sale	2	
		Marks Available	6	
		Maximum		5
(d)	(i)	Capital allowances	2.5	
		Other aspects of taxable income	1	
		Income tax and Class 4 NIC liability	3.5	
				7
	(ii)	Taxable amount of transfer to trust	2.5	
		Nil rate band	2.5	
		Inheritance tax liability	1	
		Payment date	2	
				8

Professional skills marks

Communication

- General format and structure of meeting notes (eg use of headings/sub-headings to make meeting notes easy to refer to)
- Style, language and clarity (tone of meeting notes, presentation of calculations, appropriate use of the tools, easy to follow and more than a negligible amount of content)
- Effectiveness of communication (answer is relevant, specific rather than general and focused to the requirement)
- Adherence to specific instructions made in the scenario (eg limiting explanation of controlled foreign company rules to what was required, attempt to consider differing levels of investment in JAY Ltd).

Analysis and evaluation

- Use of information to determine impact of JAY Ltd's residence status
- Demonstration of reasoned judgement when considering impact of level of investment by REP Ltd
- Appropriate use of the data to determine suitable calculations of inheritance tax payable on Freya's proposed gift of shares into trust and income tax and class 4 national insurance contributions payable by Freya

Scepticism

- Effective challenge of validity of advice provided to opt to tax the investment property
- Demonstration of the ability to probe into the reasons for issues and problems with the advice to opt to tax the investment property, including the identification of uncertainty in respect of future tenant and purchaser.

Commercial acumen

- Recognition of external constraints and opportunities regarding the use of knowledge obtained from advising other clients
- Recognition of possible consequences of potential future decision to elect to exempt the profits of a permanent establishment from UK tax
- Demonstrating an awareness of purpose behind the controlled foreign companies legislation 10

Total 50

It's very important in all your ATX questions that you spend time planning before you start to write up your full answer. Here are some things to consider when you're planning:

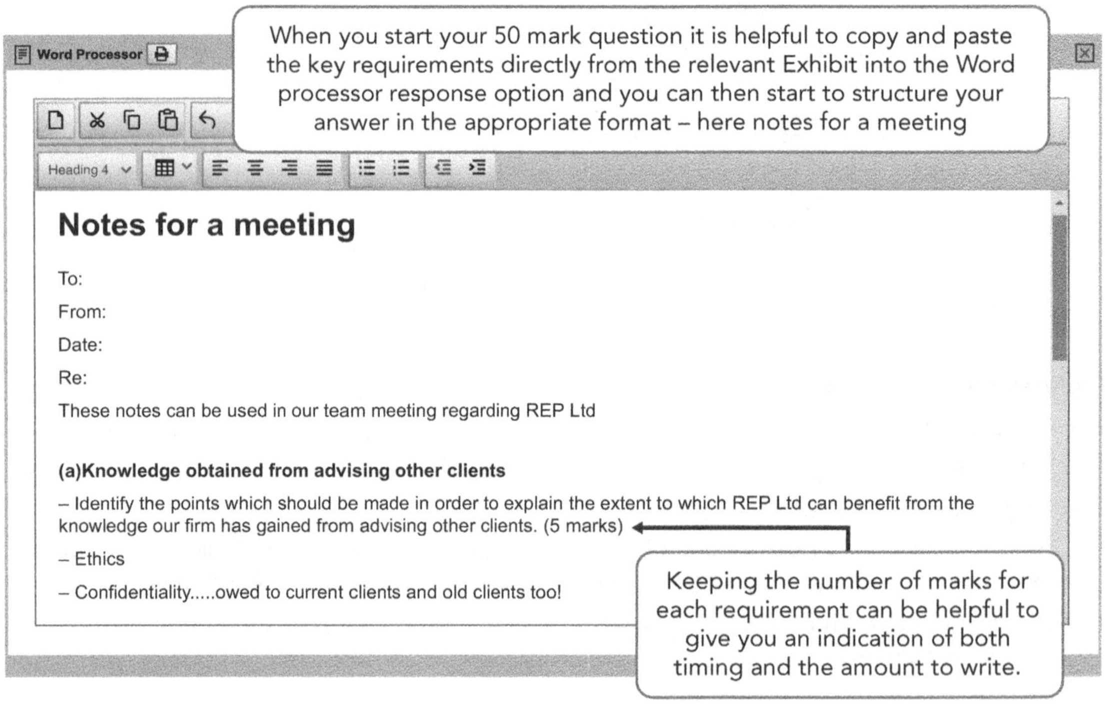

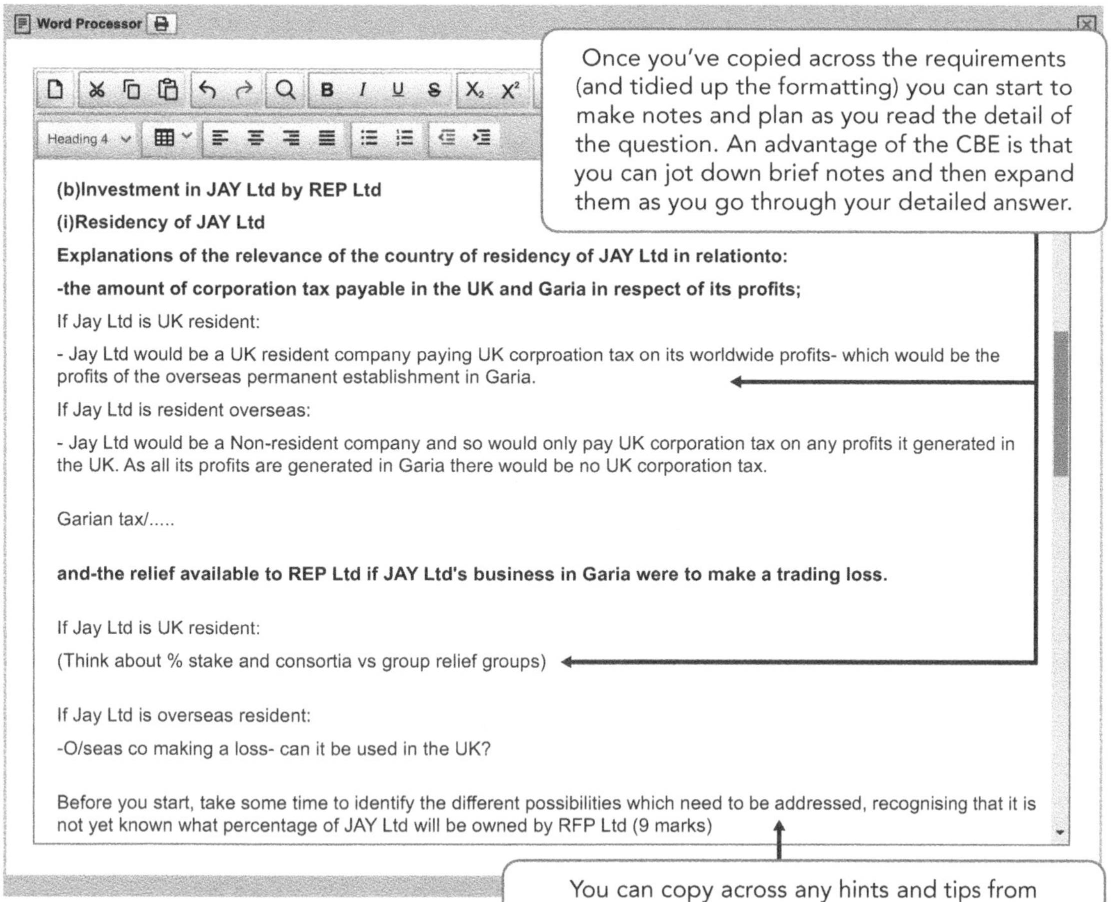
Word Processor

(b)Investment in JAY Ltd by REP Ltd

(i)Residency of JAY Ltd

Explanations of the relevance of the country of residency of JAY Ltd in relationto:

-the amount of corporation tax payable in the UK and Garia in respect of its profits;

If Jay Ltd is UK resident:

- Jay Ltd would be a UK resident company paying UK corproation tax on its worldwide profits- which would be the profits of the overseas permanent establishment in Garia.

If Jay Ltd is resident overseas:

- Jay Ltd would be a Non-resident company and so would only pay UK corporation tax on any profits it generated in the UK. As all its profits are generated in Garia there would be no UK corporation tax.

Garian tax/.....

and-the relief available to REP Ltd if JAY Ltd's business in Garia were to make a trading loss.

If Jay Ltd is UK resident:

(Think about % stake and consortia vs group relief groups)

If Jay Ltd is overseas resident:

-O/seas co making a loss- can it be used in the UK?

Before you start, take some time to identify the different possibilities which need to be addressed, recognising that it is not yet known what percentage of JAY Ltd will be owned by RFP Ltd (9 marks)

Once you've copied across the requirements (and tidied up the formatting) you can start to make notes and plan as you read the detail of the question. An advantage of the CBE is that you can jot down brief notes and then expand them as you go through your detailed answer.

You can copy across any hints and tips from your manager – the ACCA phrase these carefully to give you good advice so make sure you follow them!

Notes for meeting

Client: REP Ltd and Lamar

Purpose: Discussion of corporate and personal matters

Prepared by: Tax senior

Date: 1 September 2025

(a) **Knowledge obtained from advising other clients**

- We have experience of advising clients trading from permanent establishments situated overseas.

  We have also advised on trading in the country of Garia.

- We will be able to use this general experience and expertise for the benefit of REP Ltd.

- However, we must not use any confidential information obtained as a result of our professional and business relationships for the benefit of REP Ltd (or any other client).

  Confidentiality is one of the fundamental principles of ethics within ACCA's Code of Ethics and Conduct.

- This principle of confidentiality applies to confidential information obtained in respect of both ex-clients and continuing clients.

> **Tutorial note.** Candidates who mentioned the fundamental principle of professional competence and due care were also awarded credit.

ANSWERS

(b) (i) **Residency of JAY Ltd**

Taxation of profits

The profits of the business will be generated in Garia regardless of where JAY Ltd is resident.

Accordingly, the profits will always be subject to business tax at 13% in Garia.

If JAY Ltd is resident in the UK

The profits would be subject to UK corporation tax because the permanent establishment (PE) in Garia is not a separate legal entity and UK resident companies are subject to corporation tax on their worldwide profits. As JAY Ltd will be associated to the CRO Ltd group which consists of 19 other companies the upper profit limit for determining the rate of corporation tax will be £12,500 (£250,000/20). This means that JAY Ltd will pay main rate corporation tax.

However, double tax relief would be available in the UK: the amount payable in the UK would be 12% (25% – 13%) of the profits, as set out below:

	£
UK corporation tax (£135,000 × 25%)	33,750
Less: Unilateral double tax relief (£135,000 × 13%)	(17,550)
UK corporation tax payable	16,200

If JAY Ltd is resident in Garia

The profits will only be subject to tax in Garia at the rate of 13%, as noted above.

JAY Ltd would not have a UK corporation tax liability in respect of these profits.

Any dividends received by REP Ltd and CRO Ltd from JAY Ltd would be exempt from corporation tax.

Relief available in respect of trading loss

If JAY Ltd is resident in the UK

If REP Ltd owns 30% of JAY Ltd:

- JAY Ltd would be a consortium company because at least 75% of JAY Ltd would be owned by companies, each of which own at least 5%, and less than 75%, of the company.
- In these circumstances, REP Ltd would be able to offset up to 30% of JAY Ltd's trading loss against its taxable total profits.

If REP Ltd owns 20% of JAY Ltd:

- No relief would be available to REP Ltd in respect of any trading loss of JAY Ltd because CRO Ltd would own more than 75% of JAY Ltd.

If JAY Ltd is resident in Garia

No relief would be available in the UK for REP Ltd in respect of any trading losses realised by JAY Ltd in Garia.

(ii) **Election to exempt the profits of JAY Ltd's overseas PE from UK tax**

This election is available to UK resident companies which generate profits from PEs situated overseas. If JAY Ltd were to make this election:

- its profits in Garia would no longer be subject to corporation tax in the UK. If no election is made, UK corporation tax would be payable on the profits in Garia at the rate of 12% (25% – 13%) after double tax relief;
- no relief would be available in the UK in respect of any losses generated by the activities in Garia;
- it would be irrevocable;
- it would apply to all future overseas PEs of JAY Ltd.

(iii) **Controlled foreign company (CFC) rules**

The UK tax system charges corporation tax on the worldwide profits of UK resident companies. However, it does not charge corporation tax on the profits earned overseas by a non-UK resident company.

A UK resident company could seek to exploit the latter rule by establishing a non-UK resident subsidiary in which to generate its overseas profits. The CFC legislation is designed to prevent overseas subsidiaries being used to avoid tax in this way.

Where the rules apply (and no exemption is available), UK resident companies owning at least 25% of a CFC are charged UK corporation tax at the main rate of 25% on their proportionate share of the CFC's chargeable profits.

(c) **Purchase of investment property**

Recovery of input value added tax (VAT) on the purchase

When REP Ltd grants a lease of the building to a tenant, it will be making an exempt supply.

Therefore, REP Ltd will not be able to recover any VAT in relation to the purchase of the building unless it makes an election opting to tax it.

Suggestion from Lamar's friend

This statement is not necessarily correct for the following reasons:

'No impact on tenant'

If REP Ltd opts to tax the building, it would be required to charge VAT on the monthly rental payments due from the tenant. The effect on the tenant will depend on the type of supplies being made for VAT purposes. If the potential tenant is not making fully taxable supplies, then it will not be able to recover all of the VAT charged. This will represent an additional cost which may impact on the tenant's decision to rent the building and, if so, at what price.

'No impact on a future sale of the building'

Whilst the option to tax remains in place, REP Ltd would be required to charge VAT on a sale of the building. This could impact on any eventual sales price achieved if a future purchaser were not able to recover some, or all, of the VAT charged.

(d) (i) **Cessation of Freya's business on 31 October 2025**

Income tax and class 4 national insurance contributions (NIC): tax year 2025/26

	£
Trading profit before capital allowances for 2025/26	62,600
Add: balancing charge on sale of car (W)	1,560
Taxable trading profit	64,160
Less: personal allowance	(12,570)
Taxable income	51,590
£37,700 × 20%	7,540
£13,890 (£51,590 – £37,700) × 40%	5,556
Income tax liability	13,096
£37,700 (£50,270 – £12,570) × 6%	2,262
£13,890 (£64,160 – £50,270) × 2%	278
Class 4 NIC liability	2,540

ANSWERS

Working

Capital allowances

	Private use car	*Allowances*
	£	£
Tax written down value (TWDV) brought forward	8,700	
Disposals:		
– Market value	(11,100)	
	(2,400)	
Balancing charge	2,400	
	× 65%	(1,560)

Here is an example of how this numerical solution could be efficiently presented in the spreadsheet response option:

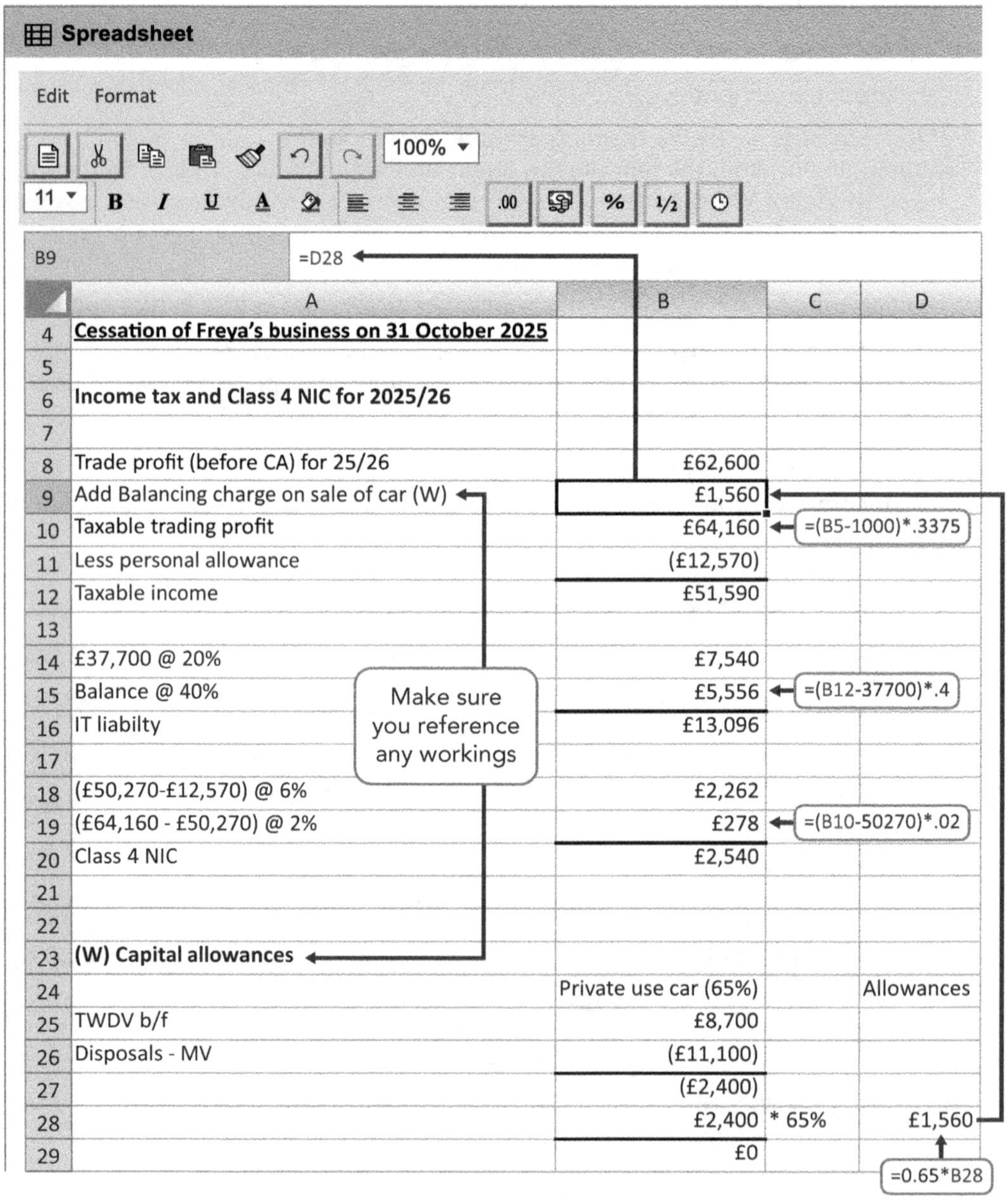

	A	B	C	D
4	**Cessation of Freya's business on 31 October 2025**			
5				
6	**Income tax and Class 4 NIC for 2025/26**			
7				
8	Trade profit (before CA) for 25/26	£62,600		
9	Add Balancing charge on sale of car (W)	£1,560		
10	Taxable trading profit	£64,160		
11	Less personal allowance	(£12,570)		
12	Taxable income	£51,590		
13				
14	£37,700 @ 20%	£7,540		
15	Balance @ 40%	£5,556		
16	IT liabilty	£13,096		
17				
18	(£50,270-£12,570) @ 6%	£2,262		
19	(£64,160 - £50,270) @ 2%	£278		
20	Class 4 NIC	£2,540		
21				
22				
23	**(W) Capital allowances**			
24		Private use car (65%)		Allowances
25	TWDV b/f	£8,700		
26	Disposals - MV	(£11,100)		
27		(£2,400)		
28		£2,400	* 65%	£1,560
29		£0		

(ii) **Proposed gift of shares to trust on 1 November 2025**

Inheritance tax (IHT) payable

	£	£
Transfer of value (W)		900,000
Annual exemptions for 2025/26 and 2024/25 (used by PET on 1 July 2025)		
Chargeable amount		900,000
Nil rate band		325,000
Less: chargeable transfer in the previous seven years		
1 May 2021	170,000	
Annual exemptions:		
– 2021/22	(3,000)	
– 2020/21 (used by PET on 1 February 2021)		
		(167,000)
		158,000
Taxable amount (£900,000 – £158,000)		742,000
IHT payable (£742,000 × 25%)		185,500

Since the transfer occurs in the second half of the tax year, the IHT will fall due six months after the end of the month of the transfer, ie by 31 May 2026.

Working

Transfer of value

	£
Value of shares held prior to the gift: (80,000 × £24 (80%))	1,920,000
Value of shares held after the gift: (60,000 × £17 (60%))	(1,020,000)
Transfer of value	900,000

Section B

2 Amelia

Course Book references

Sole trader losses are covered in Chapter 15. The capital gains tax computation is covered in Chapter 7 with CGT reliefs covered in Chapter 8. VAT is covered in Chapter 23.

Top tips

In part (a) precision is key. When considering each loss option you need to clearly specify:

(1) Which tax year(s) it can be relieved in – be specific to the scenario!

(2) Against what income/gains it can be used against – is it trading income, total income or capital gains?

(3) The rate of tax the relief will save.

Easy marks

Easy marks available for stating the loss options available in part (a)(i) and explaining the basis CGT implications of the sale of a building in part (b). In addition, stating the taxable turnover limit for voluntary deregistration of VAT should have been an easy mark as it is provided in the tax tables.

ACCA examining team's comments

This question concerned a sole trader whose business is currently loss-making, who is also going to replace a warehouse used in the business and is considering voluntarily deregistering for VAT.

Part (a)(i) asked candidates to state the reliefs available to the trader in respect of her trading loss, other than carrying it forward.

This is another area where precision is required. Candidates need to learn whether a loss can be relieved against total income, or trading income only. Candidates should also practise referring to the relevant tax years when dealing with an unincorporated business; just stating 'current year' or 'prior year' is not sufficient, without providing some context to this in terms of the tax years involved. If disposals of capital assets are included in the scenario, candidates are normally expected to consider extending the loss relief to any chargeable gains arising, which, surprisingly, many candidates omitted. Candidates are reminded that relief for trading losses, both for unincorporated businesses and companies, remains a frequently tested area, and would be advised to ensure that they learn the precise rules applicable in each situation.

Part (a)(ii) required candidates to explain and calculate the tax saving for each of the reliefs that they had identified in (a)(i).

This type of question requires a structured, organised approach, and candidates should spend a little time planning an efficient way to address the requirement. The standard of the explanations and calculations was very mixed. Candidates who were well-prepared chose to use a marginal approach to calculate the tax saving, which is an efficient approach to use when tax savings are required. This approach has been used in many past exam questions involving the tax implications of taking loss relief, which candidates would be well advised to practise. Additionally, these candidates had identified the available chargeable gains, and were able to score well on this part by including an explanation and calculation of the CGT saved, in addition to the income tax saving.

Weaker answers often comprised full tax computations, before and after taking loss relief, and, in some cases without actually calculating the tax saving at the end. Additionally, the CGT implications were overlooked by a number of candidates.

Part (b) required an explanation, together with relevant calculations, of the CGT and income tax implications of replacing a warehouse and acquiring moveable equipment.

The CGT implications were the more obvious, and most candidates recognised that the disposal of the original warehouse qualified for rollover relief, and that the replacement had been acquired within the required time period. However, the details of the computation proved to be trickier. A good number restricted the eligible gain correctly, by reference to the proportion of the building which had been used in the trade, but relatively few also restricted the qualifying sale proceeds and then went on to calculate the correct chargeable gain. The most common error in this question part, was the failure to recognise that the moveable equipment was not a qualifying asset for rollover relief purposes. Many candidates appeared to forget, or ignore, the income tax element, but those who did address this correctly recognised that the moveable equipment would qualify for the AIA, to reduce the individual's income tax liability.

Part (c) required an explanation of the immediate consequences of the individual deregistering for VAT.

Many candidates were able to score at least half of the three marks available here, although there were a number of inaccuracies in the detail again here, relating to the level of 'profits' rather than sales, or turnover, and a lack of knowledge regarding the date from which the deregistration would be effective.

Marking guide		Marks
(a) (i) Reliefs available	3.5	
Marks Available	3.5	
Maximum		3
(ii) Relief in 2025/26		
– against income	1.5	
– against gains	5	
Relief in 2024/25	2.5	
Relief in 2025/26 and 2024/25	1	
Marks Available	10	
Maximum		8
(b) Availability of rollover relief	2.5	
Calculation of rollover relief	3.5	
AIA on fork-lift truck	1	
Marks Available	7	
Maximum		6
(c) Deregistration for VAT	4	
Maximum		3

Professional skills marks

Analysis and evaluation

- Use of information to support impact of loss relief options by reference to Amelia's tax status
- Appropriate use of the data to determine suitable calculations of tax savings associated with available trading loss relief options and the tax implications of the proposed sale of Warehouse 1 and acquisition of Warehouse 2 and the forklift truck.
- Appropriate use of the data to support discussion and draw appropriate conclusions about the availability of rollover relief on the proposed sale of Warehouse 1.
- Demonstration of ability to consider all relevant taxes specified in the requirements.

Marking guide	Marks

Commercial acumen

- Recognition of constraints and opportunities related to choice of trading loss relief, for example, trading loss offset may not be desirable, but allows offset against gains.
- Recognition of possible consequences of potential future decision to voluntarily deregister for value added tax.

Maximum	5
Total	25

Once again, it's important that you use the CBE functionality to plan your answer effectively:

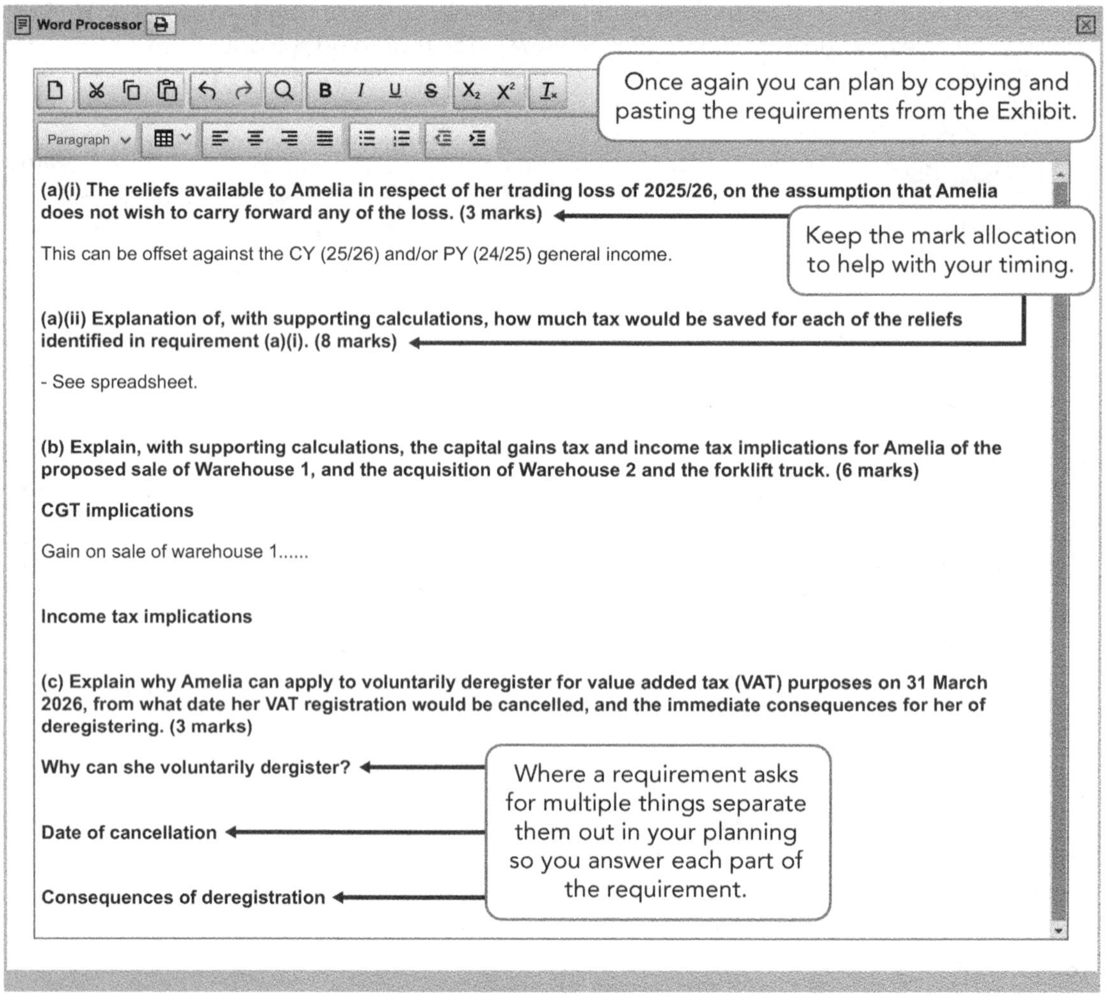

(a)(i) The reliefs available to Amelia in respect of her trading loss of 2025/26, on the assumption that Amelia does not wish to carry forward any of the loss. (3 marks)

This can be offset against the CY (25/26) and/or PY (24/25) general income.

(a)(ii) Explanation of, with supporting calculations, how much tax would be saved for each of the reliefs identified in requirement (a)(i). (8 marks)

- See spreadsheet.

(b) Explain, with supporting calculations, the capital gains tax and income tax implications for Amelia of the proposed sale of Warehouse 1, and the acquisition of Warehouse 2 and the forklift truck. (6 marks)

CGT implications

Gain on sale of warehouse 1......

Income tax implications

(c) Explain why Amelia can apply to voluntarily deregister for value added tax (VAT) purposes on 31 March 2026, from what date her VAT registration would be cancelled, and the immediate consequences for her of deregistering. (3 marks)

Why can she voluntarily dergister?

Date of cancellation

Consequences of deregistration

(a) (i)

Reliefs available in respect of Amelia's trading loss of 2025/26

Amelia can offset the loss against her total income of 2025/26 and/or 2024/25. If she chooses to offset the loss against her total income of 2025/26, she can then offset any remaining loss against her chargeable gains of that year.

(ii)

Relief against income and chargeable gains in the tax year 2025/26

In the tax year 2025/26, Amelia's only income will be savings income of £6,000. This will be covered by her personal allowance, such that she will have no liability to income tax for this year. Accordingly, if she chooses to take relief for the loss against this income, there will be no income tax saving. However, the remaining loss of £8,000 (£14,000 – £6,000) could then be offset against her chargeable gains for the year.

Amelia's chargeable gains comprise total gains less the capital loss brought forward ie £62,000 (£45,000 + £28,000 – £11,000). Accordingly, the full £8,000 of trading loss could be offset.

Ignoring offset of the trading loss, Amelia would have taxable gains of £59,000 after deducting the annual exempt amount of £3,000. As Amelia will have no taxable income in 2025/26, £37,700 of her taxable gains will fall within her basic rate band, and the remaining £21,300 will be taxed at the higher rate.

The trading loss should therefore be offset against the gain on the UK rental property, as this will be taxed at the higher, residential property rates of 18%/24% (working). The capital gains tax (CGT) saving will be £1,920 (£8,000 × 24%).

Working

Offset of remaining trading loss against chargeable gains

	Residential property gain	*Other gain*	*Total gains*
	£	£	£
Gain on UK rental property	45,000		45,000
Gain on Swartz Ltd shares		28,000	28,000
Less:			
– trading loss converted to capital loss	(8,000)		(8,000)
– annual exempt amount	(3,000)		(3,000)
– capital loss brought forward	(11,000)		(11,000)
Taxable gains after loss relief	23,000	28,000	51,000

Relief against income in the tax year 2024/25

In the tax year 2024/25 Amelia's total income is £47,600 (£30,000 + £11,600 + £6,000), so the full amount of the loss of £14,000 can be offset. Amelia's taxable income was £35,030 (£47,600 – £12,570), such that she was a basic rate taxpayer. The loss offset (which is against her non-savings income of this year) would generate a tax saving of £2,800 (£14,000 × 20%).

Relief against income in the tax years 2025/26 then 2024/25

Amelia could offset the loss against her income of £6,000 in 2025/26, with the remaining £8,000 offset against her income in 2024/25. This would save no tax in 2025/26, and only £1,600 (£8,000 × 20%) in 2024/25.

Tutorial note. Note the following:

(1) After taking relief for the trading loss, only £13,300 (£51,000 – £37,700) of Amelia's taxable gains will be taxed at the higher rate, instead of £21,300.

(2) The trading loss would be treated as a current year capital loss in the CGT computation, (ie it would be deducted from Amelia's chargeable gains before deducting the annual exempt amount and the capital loss brought forward), as shown above. However, candidates were awarded full credit regardless of the order in which they deducted the trading loss.

(b)

Word Processor

Capital gains tax and income tax implications of the sale of Warehouse 1 and the acquisition of Warehouse 2 and the forklift truck

The sale of Warehouse 1 will give rise to a chargeable gain of £32,000 (£118,000 – £86,000). Rollover relief will be available to defer part of this gain because Amelia acquired a qualifying replacement asset, Warehouse 2, during the three years following the sale. The acquisition of the forklift truck does not qualify for rollover relief as it is a moveable asset.

The gain which is eligible for rollover relief is restricted to £24,000 (£32,000 × ¾) because Amelia only occupied three of the four floors of Warehouse 1 for business purposes. The rollover relief available will be further restricted because not all of the proceeds relating to the business use of Warehouse 1 have been used to acquire Warehouse 2:

	£
Proceeds of business element (£118,000 × ¾)	88,500
Cost of replacement	(83,000)
Gain remaining chargeable	5,500

The balance of the eligible gain of £18,500 (£24,000 – £5,500) will be available for rollover relief. Amelia's chargeable gain in respect of the sale of Warehouse 1 will therefore be £13,500 (£32,000 – £18,500). The gain of £18,500 will be rolled over and deducted from the base cost of Warehouse 2. The base cost of Warehouse 2 will be £64,500 (£83,000 – £18,500).

The cost of the forklift truck of £23,000 will be eligible for the annual investment allowance in AS Trading's year ending 31 March 2027.

(c)

Word Processor

Why can she voluntarily deregister?

Amelia is able to apply voluntarily to deregister for VAT on 31 March 2026 as the value of her taxable supplies in the following year are not expected to exceed the deregistration limit of £88,000.

Date of cancellation

Her registration will be cancelled from 31 March 2026, or from a later date if agreed with HMRC.

Consequences of deregistration

On deregistration, output VAT will be payable on all non-current assets and inventory held by Amelia on which input VAT was previously reclaimed. If the total VAT payable does not exceed £1,000, no payment is needed.

As a result of deregistration, Amelia will not be able to reclaim input VAT on the acquisition of Warehouse 2 and the forklift truck.

3 Dorian

Course Book references

Close companies are covered in Chapter 21 and employment income is covered in Chapter 4. Corporation tax admin is covered in Chapter 16.

Top tips

Make sure you spot the 'command verbs' in each requirement to understand whether you answer should be written or calculational (or both). Part (c) of this question contains the most marks so make sure you allocate your time accordingly.

Easy marks

Explaining the definition of a close company and the notional tax payable on loans to participators of a close company should have been a source of easy marks.

ACCA examining team's comments

The question focused on a close company, its transactions with one of the directors and the late filing of its corporation tax return.

This question was not at all well attempted by candidates, as there appeared to be a considerable lack of knowledge of close company legislation. In ATX–UK candidates are expected to be able to accurately define a close company and be able to explain the consequences of close company status in respect of loans made, and benefits provided, to participators. Candidates would be well advised to learn these rules, and practise questions in relation to their application in any given scenario.

Part (a) required candidates to explain why the company in the scenario was classed as a close company.

Nearly all candidates knew that it was something to do with the number of directors and shareholders, but relatively few were able to correctly state the rules, relating to the need for control, the relevance of associates, and concluding on the reason why this company fell within the definition. Candidates therefore struggled to score any marks on this question part or scored only one mark out of a possible four.

Part (b) related to the repayment of a loan made by the company to a participator, and the implications for both the participator and the company of it being repaid early.

Despite being told in the question that notional tax was payable by the company on this loan, a number of candidates discussed why the loan would be exempt from this notional tax charge, which clearly could not be relevant here. A reasonable number of candidates recognised that the notional tax would be repayable to the company when the participator repaid the loan, but were not able to elaborate on this, and, in particular, to recognise that early repayment would mean that the repayment would fall into an earlier accounting period for the company, and therefore bring forward the repayment of the notional tax by 12 months. Many answers were extremely brief and rather general.

Part (c) involved a comparison of two alternative ways of the company providing the participator with assistance with travel costs, to determine which of the two would result in the lower cost for the participator.

Alternative 1 comprised the provision of an interest-free loan to purchase a season ticket. Candidates needed to pause and think about this in context. The original loan to this participator was still outstanding, so the total loans would exceed £10,000, and there would be a taxable benefit, calculated by reference to the official rate of interest. Also, as this loan was to be written off at the end of the tax year, candidates had to consider the income tax implications of this write off. The majority of candidates identified either the beneficial interest implications, or the implications arising from the write off, but only a minority identified and dealt with both. Fewer still appeared to realise that the loans needed to be considered in total, not individually.

Alternative 2 included the payment of a mileage allowance and provision of a free car-parking space. Many candidates recognised that the provision of the car-parking space would be an exempt benefit, but fewer identified that the mileage allowance would be fully taxable as it related wholly to non-business (home to work) travel. Workings to calculate the additional costs to be borne by the participator were often muddled, and insufficiently explained. In particular a number of CBE candidates who chose to use the spreadsheet response option for this question part – which was fine – just provided numbers with no accompanying labels or explanations. Candidates are reminded that their workings should be clearly presented and explained, in order that a marker can follow them. Finally, the majority of candidates did provide a sensible conclusion re the lower cost for the participator, which was pleasing to see.

Part (d) required a brief explanation of the implications for the company of the late filing of its corporation tax return.

A significant number of candidates did not know that the normal filing date for a company's corporation tax return is 12 months after the end of its accounting period. The most popular incorrect answer was nine months and one day after the end of this period, which is, of course the due date for payment of tax by non-large companies. Additionally, many appeared to guess at the late filing penalty which would apply, without giving a reason.

Marking guide		Marks	
(a)	General definition	2	
	Associates	1	
	Application to scenario	1.5	
	Marks Available	4.5	
	Maximum		4
(b)	Tax implications for Dorian	1	
	Tax implications for Taupe Ltd	4	
			5
(c)	Interest benefit	3.5	
	Loan written off	2	
	Mileage allowance alternative	4	
	Marks Available	9.5	
	Maximum		8
(d)	Filing date	1.5	
	Penalty	2	
	Marks Available	3.5	
	Maximum		3

Professional skills marks

Analysis and evaluation

- Appropriate use of the data to arrive at conclusion regarding Taupe Ltd's close company status
- Appropriate use of the data to determine suitable calculations of the overall cost to Dorian of Alternatives 1 and 2 and draw appropriate conclusions.

Marking guide | **Marks**

- Use of information to determine impact for Dorian and Taupe Ltd of early repayment of the loan.
- Demonstration of reasoned judgement regarding implications of late filing.

Commercial acumen

- Recognition of other possible consequences of late filing of corporation tax return.
- Other practical considerations related to the calculation of cost to Dorian of Alternative 2 (eg additional non-tax travel costs)

Maximum	5
Total	25

Once again, it's important that you use the CBE functionality to plan your answer effectively:

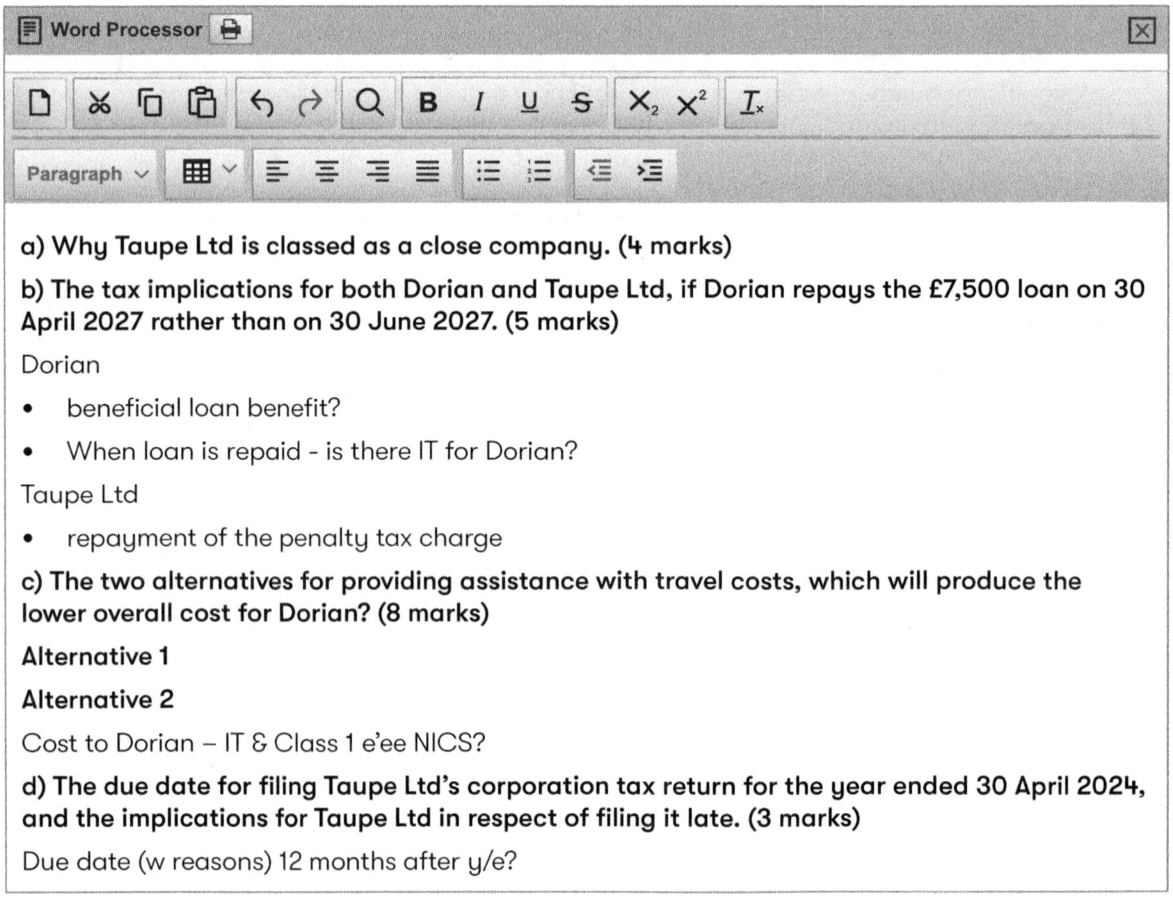

(a)

Reason for close company status

A company is a close company if it is controlled by:

- Any number of shareholders who are also directors, or
- The five largest shareholders in the company.

Control is exercised by shareholders who own more than half of the company's issued share capital.

For the purpose of determining control, a shareholder is regarded as owning any shares owned by their associates, in addition to the shares which they own personally. Associates include direct relatives, so Dorian is associated with his father.

Dorian is regarded as owning 28% of the shares (his own 5% plus his father's 23%). The remaining five directors own a total of 25%, so that overall the six directors own 53% of the issued share capital, and control the company.

Tutorial note. There are additional complexities when determining whether or not a company is a close company, but the above points were sufficient to score full marks.

(b)

Tax implications for Dorian and Taupe Ltd of early repayment of Dorian's £7,500 loan

There will be no tax implications for Dorian. This will be the only loan outstanding in 2027/28, so there will be no loan interest benefit arising as it does not exceed £10,000.

As Taupe Ltd is a close company, it will have paid notional tax of £2,531 (£7,500 x 33.75%) to HM Revenue and Customs (HMRC) in respect of the loan to Dorian, who is a participator in the company.

HMRC will repay the £2,531 to Taupe Ltd nine months and one day after the end of the accounting period in which the loan is repaid.

Accordingly, if Dorian repays the loan on 30 April 2027, Taupe Ltd will receive the repayment by 1 February 2028, one year earlier than it would if the loan were repaid on 30 June 2027.

Tutorial note. Notional tax will have been payable in respect of the £7,500 loan made to Dorian as Dorian (including his associate (Basil)) has a material interest (>5%) in Taupe Ltd.

(c)

Word Processor

The cost to Dorian of the two alternative travel assistance proposals

Alternative 1: Provision of an interest-free loan to purchase a season ticket

Dorian already has an existing interest-free loan from Taupe Ltd of £7,500. If he receives a further loan from Taupe Ltd of £4,800, the total amount outstanding will exceed £10,000, such that a taxable benefit will arise in respect of the whole of these loans.

Both of the loans are interest-free, so there will be a taxable benefit, calculated by reference to the official rate of interest, of £277 ((£7,500 + £4,800) × 2.25%). This will be subject to income tax at 40%, as Dorian will be a higher rate taxpayer in 2026/27, but the loans will not result in a liability to Class 1 national insurance contributions (NIC) for Dorian. The income tax payable would be £111 (£277 × 40%).

When the loan is written off on 5 April 2027, the amount written off will be treated as a distribution, and therefore liable to income tax at the rate of 33.75%. As Dorian has no other dividend income, the dividend nil rate band would be available, such that Dorian would incur an income tax liability of £1,451 ((£4,800 – £500) × 33.75%)).

The cost to Dorian of this alternative will be £1,562 (£111 + £1,451).

Alternative 2: Payment of a mileage allowance and provision of a free car-parking space

The mileage allowance will be subject to income tax at 40% and Class 1 NIC at 2%. This will give rise to a total tax cost of £1,512 (£3,600 × 42%).

Dorian will have additional travel costs, not covered by the mileage allowance of £300 ((£5,220 – £1,320) – £3,600).

Provision of a car parking space at, or near, an employee's normal place of work is an exempt benefit for income tax and NIC.

The total cost to Dorian of this alternative is therefore £1,812 (£1,512 + £300).

Provision of the interest-free loan to purchase a season ticket results in the lower overall cost for Dorian.

Tutorial note. Note the following:

(1) Although Dorian is an employee of Taupe Ltd, the loan written off is still treated as a distribution, rather than employment income. However, the amount written off will be liable to Class 1 NIC and candidates who were aware of this were awarded credit.

(2) The approved mileage rates are not relevant in this case as the driving costs are not related to journeys made in the course of Dorian carrying out his duties of employment.

(d)

Implications for Taupe Ltd of the late filing of its corporation tax return

Taupe Ltd's corporation tax return for the year ended 30 April 2024 should have been filed by 30 April 2025 (12 months after the end of the period of account), as the notice requiring the filing of this return was issued before 1 February 2025. As the return was filed more than three months late, a fixed late filing penalty of £200 will arise. Although the return for the year ended 30 April 2023 was also filed late, the penalty will not be increased to £1,000 as the return for the year ended 30 April 2022 was filed on time.

ACCA

Advanced Taxation (ATX – UK) FA2024

Mock Exam 3

September/December 2023

Questions	
Time allowed	3 hours 15 minutes
ALL questions are compulsory and MUST be attempted	

DO NOT OPEN THIS EXAM UNTIL YOU ARE READY TO START UNDER EXAMINATION CONDITIONS

Section A

1 Jake **(98 mins)**

You should assume that today's date is 1 January 2026.

You are an ACCA student working for a firm of accountants. Your manager has asked you to prepare a memorandum concerning the personal tax affairs of Jake, a new client of your firm.

In addition to some ethical considerations which have been raised by your manager, advice is required in respect of:

- the capital gains tax (CGT) implications of the replacement of a destroyed building;
- the relief available for revenue and capital expenditure incurred by an unincorporated trader;
- the value added tax (VAT) capital goods scheme; and
- the inheritance tax and CGT implications of a sale of shares which were originally acquired by way of a gift.

The following exhibits, available on the left-hand side of the screen, provide information relevant to the question:

(1) Jake's new unincorporated business – letter from Jake

(2) Sale of shares in POL Ltd – schedule from Jake

(3) Work to be carried out – email from manager

This information should be used to answer the question **requirements** within your chosen **response option(s)**.

Required

Respond to the instructions in the email from your manager.

Note. The split of the mark allocation is shown in Exhibit 3 – Work to be carried out. **(40 marks)**

Professional marks will be awarded for demonstration of skill in communication, analysis & evaluation, scepticism and commercial acumen in your answer. **(10 marks)**

(Total = 50 marks)

Exhibit 1: Extracts from a letter from Jake (dated 1 January 2026)

New unincorporated business

I will begin trading on 1 May 2026 and will elect to use the accruals basis to calculate taxable trading profit. I will also register for the purposes of value added tax (VAT) from that date. I will prepare accounts to 30 April each year.

Construction of business premises

As you know, I owned the Vol Building (a commercial building that I rented out to a business tenant for many years) until it was destroyed in a fire on 1 August 2025. I understand from our discussions that the insurance proceeds of £380,000 resulted in a chargeable gain of £130,000. This will be my only chargeable gain in the tax year 2025/26.

I have now decided to use some of the insurance proceeds to have a new building (the Yak Building) constructed on the site where the Vol Building was situated. The construction of the Yak Building will cost £335,000 plus 20% VAT. The cost of £335,000 includes £75,000 in respect of electrical systems, heating systems and other integral features.

I plan to use the whole of the Yak Building for the purposes of carrying on my unincorporated business from 1 May 2026.

Expenditure to be incurred in relation to the new business

I will incur the following expenditure in relation to the new business:

- On 1 February 2026 I will complete the purchase of the newly-constructed Yak Building.
- Any post tax insurance proceeds remaining after construction of the Yak Building will be invested in my new business as follows:
  - Between now and 30 April 2026, I will travel extensively throughout the UK in order to visit potential customers and persuade them to place advance orders for my products.
  - On 1 May 2026 I will purchase a new car, which I will use 65% for business purposes and 35% for private purposes. This will NOT be a car with zero CO_2 emissions.

Alternative plan for the use of the Yak Building

I am considering an alternative plan for the use of the Yak Building, as follows.

For a period of four years from 1 May 2026, I would use 70% of the Yak Building for the purposes of carrying on my unincorporated business and I would rent out the remainder of the building from that date. By the end of the four-year period my business should have grown sufficiently to require the use of the whole building.

Sale of shares in POL Ltd

I am also considering selling the whole of my shareholding in POL Ltd, consisting of 6,000 ordinary shares. I enclose a schedule setting out additional information in respect of these shares (Exhibit 2).

Exhibit 2: Schedule from Jake dated 1 January 2026

Details of the possible sale of all of my shares in POL Ltd

- This sale would not take place until the tax year 2026/27.
- I would sell the shares for their full market value, which I would expect to be £470,000.

POL Ltd

- POL Ltd is an unquoted manufacturing company.
- I have never been an employee of POL Ltd and will not become one in the future.

Acquisition of the shares from my aunt

1 May 2017	My aunt purchased 6,000 ordinary shares in POL Ltd for £295,000.
1 October 2023	My aunt gave all of her shares to me. At that time they had a market value of £420,000. My aunt and I made a joint election for the purposes of gift holdover relief. This resulted in £112,500 of the gain being held over. For the purposes of inheritance tax, I was advised (and you have subsequently confirmed) that: • this gift qualified for the 100% rate of business property relief at that time because my aunt had owned the shares for more than two years; and • 12% of the value of POL Ltd's total assets consisted of excepted assets.

In the tax year 2023/24, my aunt also made a gift of an investment property to my sister. This occurred on 1 September 2023 when the property had a market value of £360,000.

Exhibit 3: Email from your manager

To: Tax senior

From: Tax manager

Date: 1 January 2026

Subject: Jake

Please prepare a memorandum for the client file which addresses the following issues:

(a) **Becoming tax advisers to Jake**

I have not identified any threats to compliance with the fundamental principles of professional ethics which would arise as a result of becoming tax advisers to Jake.

- Explain why it is important that we contact Jake's previous tax advisers.
- State any other actions we should take before we agree to become Jake's tax advisers.

(5 marks)

(b) **New unincorporated business (Exhibit 1)**

When carrying out tasks (i) and (ii) below you should ignore the alternative plan for the use of the Yak Building and simply assume that the whole of the Yak Building will be used for the purposes of carrying on Jake's unincorporated business. You should also ignore value added tax (VAT).

(i) **Insurance proceeds available for investment in the business**

(1) On the assumption that the construction of the Yak Building will be completed and paid for on 1 February 2026, explain the relief available to Jake in respect of the chargeable gain resulting from the destruction of the Vol Building.

(2) On the assumption that Jake claims the relief you have identified in (1), and will have total income in the tax year 2026/27 of £30,000, calculate the amount of post-tax insurance proceeds which will be available, after the construction of the Yak Building, for investment in the new business.

(8 marks)

(ii) **Tax deductions in respect of the expenditure to be incurred**

(1) Explain when, if at all, Jake will be able to obtain a tax deduction for the costs he is likely to have incurred in respect of visiting potential customers.

(2) Explain the tax deductions which will be available in Jake's first trading period ending on 30 April 2027 in respect of the costs of:

- the construction of the Yak Building; and
- the purchase of the car.

(8 marks)

(iii) **Alternative plan for the use of the Yak Building**

When carrying out this task (iii), you should assume that the alternative plan for the use of the Yak Building is followed.

I can confirm that the supplies to be made by Jake's unincorporated business will be wholly standard rated for VAT purposes. However, due to the application of the capital goods scheme, Jake's ability to recover the full £67,000 of input tax over the life of the building will be restricted unless he opts to tax the building.

Calculate the maximum amount of ADDITIONAL input VAT which Jake could recover if he were to elect to opt to tax the Yak Building on 1 May 2026. Your calculations should indicate the years in which the input tax would be recovered.

(6 marks)

(c) **Sale of shares in POL Ltd (Exhibit 2)**

On the assumption that Jake sells the POL Ltd shares in the tax year 2026/27 for £470,000, and that his aunt dies between now (1 January 2026) and 30 September 2030 (ie within seven years of the potentially exempt transfer):

(1) Explain, without carrying out any calculations, Jake's potential liability to inheritance tax (IHT) at the time of the sale of the shares and on the subsequent death of his aunt.

(2) Calculate the chargeable gain resulting from the sale, before the deduction of any available reliefs, and explain whether or not the following reliefs would be available:

- business asset disposal relief; and
- rollover relief.

(3) Explain the relief which would be available in respect of any IHT payable following the death of Jake's aunt.

(13 marks)

Thank you,

Tax manager

Section B

2 Rabo Ltd **(49 mins)**

You should assume that today's date is 1 December 2025.

Nali has entered into an agreement to purchase the whole of Rabo Ltd's ordinary share capital from its parent company, Morada Ltd.

He has requested advice on the following:

- the tax implications of Rabo Ltd selling an asset it acquired from Morada Ltd;
- the reliefs available in respect of a trading loss incurred before Rabo Ltd leaves the group; and
- the corporation tax implications of the acquisition of capital assets.

The following exhibit, available on the left-hand side of the screen, provides information relevant to the question:

(1) Rabo Ltd

This information should be used to answer the question **requirements** within your chosen **response option(s)**.

Required

(a) In relation to Rabo Ltd's sale of the freehold factory:

- Calculate the after-tax proceeds; and
- Explain how the base cost of this factory is calculated.

Note. You should ignore Rabo Ltd's capital acquisitions and trading loss for this part of the question. **(6 marks)**

(b) (i) Explain the maximum possible amount of Rabo Ltd's trading loss for the year ending 31 December 2025 which can be transferred to Morada Ltd; and

(ii) Explain the tax consequences for Rabo Ltd of using some, or all of the loss itself, and explain any potential issues associated with such a course of action. **(7 marks)**

(c) Explain with supporting calculations:

- The rollover relief and capital allowances which may be claimed as a result of the planned capital acquisitions on 1 June 2026; and
- The total corporation tax savings which these will give rise to in the year ending 31 December 2026.

(7 marks)

Professional marks will be awarded for the demonstration of skill in analysis & evaluation and commercial acumen in your answer. **(5 marks)**

(Total = 25 marks)

Exhibit: Rabo Ltd

Morada Ltd and Rabo Ltd

- Morada Ltd has owned 100% of the ordinary shares in Rabo Ltd for many years.
- Both companies are UK tax resident trading companies.
- Both companies prepare accounts to 31 December.
- On 31 October 2025, Morada Ltd entered into an arrangement to sell all the ordinary shares in Rabo Ltd to Nali, who is an unconnected individual.
- This sale of shares will take place on 31 December 2025.

Rabo Ltd – sale of factory

- Rabo Ltd will sell a freehold factory building on 1 April 2026 for £395,000.
- Rabo Ltd acquired this factory from Morada Ltd on 1 September 2022 for its market value of £302,000.
- Morada Ltd had acquired the factory on 1 June 2020 for £266,000.
- The factory has always been used for trading purposes.

Forecast results for the year ending 31 December 2025

	Rabo Ltd £	Morada Ltd £
Trading (loss)/profit	(72,000)	840,000
Property income	nil	43,000

- Rabo Ltd is not able to relieve its trading loss in an earlier accounting period.
- Rabo Ltd is expected to make a trading profit of around £530,000 in the year ending 31 December 2026.

Rabo Ltd – future plans and capital acquisitions

- Nali is considering making significant changes to the company's operations, over the next few years.
- The following assets will be acquired by Rabo Ltd on 1 June 2026 from an unconnected seller:
- A second-hand warehouse costing £312,000, including £71,000 for the land. The seller had acquired the land in May 2012, and the warehouse had been constructed on it later that year.
- An additional five delivery vans, each costing £35,000.
- These acquisitions will all be brought into immediate use in the company's trade.

3 Pinto **(49 mins)**

You should assume that today's date is 1 December 2025.

Pinto has requested advice on the following:

- his tax residence status for the tax year 2025/26;
- the capital gains tax implications of selling his house; and
- the UK tax implications of receiving overseas income.

The following exhibit, available on the left-hand side of the screen, provides information relevant to the question:

(1) Pinto

This information should be used to answer the question **requirements** within your chosen **response option(s)**.

Required

(a) Assuming that Pinto does not satisfy any of the automatic tests in relation to tax residence, explain whether or not he will be resident in the UK for tax purposes in the tax year 2025/26.

Note. You should not consider the split year rules. **(5 marks)**

(b) Explain, by reference to Pinto's tax residence status, why the sale of his house in the UK on 30 April 2024 will have been subject to UK capital gains tax, and calculate the chargeable gain arising. You should include an explanation of any relief(s) available. **(7 marks)**

(c) Calculate Pinto's property income, after all taxes, in respect of his house in Vicia for the tax year 2026/27. **(8 marks)**

Professional marks will be awarded for demonstration of skill in communication, analysis & evaluation, scepticism and commercial acumen in your answer. **(5 marks)**

(Total = 25 marks)

Exhibit: Pinto

Pinto:

- Is domiciled in the UK.
- Is neither married, nor in a civil partnership, and has no children.

Travel to the country of Vicia – Pinto:

- Had always been tax resident in the UK until, on 1 May 2023, he left to travel and work part-time in the country of Vicia.
- Visited the UK for only two weeks in each of the tax years 2023/24 and 2024/25, such that he was not tax resident in the UK in either tax year.

Return to the UK – Pinto:

- Will return to the UK on 20 December 2025, where he intends to remain permanently.
- Will live with his sister following his return to the UK.
- Will work part-time in the UK from 1 March 2026 until 5 April 2026.

Sale of UK house:

- On 30 April 2024, Pinto sold his UK house; there was an excess of proceeds over cost of £47,000.
- Pinto bought the house on 1 May 2019 and had lived in it himself from 1 May 2019 to 30 April 2023 (48 months).
- Pinto let the house to tenants from 1 May 2023 until its sale on 30 April 2024 (12 months).
- Pinto did not own any other property in the period from 1 May 2019 to 30 April 2024 (60 months).

Pinto's income for the tax year 2026/27:

- On 6 April 2026, Pinto will incorporate a new company, Fava Ltd.
- Pinto will take a salary of £10,000 and dividends of £2,500 from Fava Ltd in the tax year 2026/27.
- Pinto's only other source of income in the tax year 2026/27 will be rental income from his house in Vicia.

Overseas rental income:

- Pinto acquired a house in Vicia on 1 June 2024.
- Pinto will rent out this house from 1 May 2026.
- In the tax year 2026/27, Pinto will receive rental income of £8,375, after allowable expenses but before deduction of Vician tax.

The tax system in the country of Vicia:

- The rate of tax on property income in Vicia is 16%.
- There is no double tax treaty between the UK and Vicia.

Answers

DO NOT TURN THIS PAGE UNTIL YOU HAVE COMPLETED THE MOCK EXAM

A plan of attack

We've already established that you've been told to do it 101 times, so it is of course superfluous to tell you for the 102nd time to **take a good look at the exam before diving into the answers.**

What's the worst thing you could be doing right now if this was the actual exam? Wondering how to celebrate the end of the exam in about three hours' time?

Turn back to the exam and let's sort out a **plan of attack**!

First things first

Look through the exam and work out the order in which to attack the questions. You've got **two options**. Option 1 is the option recommended by BPP.

Option 1 (if you're thinking 'Help!')

If you're a bit worried about the exam, do the questions in the order of how well you think you can answer them. If you find the questions in Section B less daunting than the questions in Section A, start with Section B.

There are **two questions** in Section B. **Question 2** has three parts. Part (a) asks for the calculation of the after-tax proceeds on sale of a factory and also for an explanation on how the base cost is calculated considering the fact that it has been transferred between two group companies with the recipient company having been sold.

Part (b) is in two parts. Part (b)(i) asks for an explanation of the maximum loss that can be group relieved. Part (b)(ii) asks you to consider if the company does not group relieve the loss and instead uses it itself.

Part (c) asks you to explain and calculate the rollover relief which may be claimed as a result of the purchase of a warehouse and vans, including a calculation of the tax saving in respect of these.

Question 3 has three parts. Part (a) asks you determine and explain the residency status of an individual, remember to consider the information you have available to you in the tax tables.

Part (b) asks you to explain why the individual will be liable to capital gains tax on disposal of their house by reference to their tax residence status determined in part (a). It is also asks you to include an explanation of any reliefs available so you need to consider private residence relief here.

Part (c) asks you to calculate the property income after all taxes of an individual.

Do not spend longer than about 97 minutes on Section B. When you've spent the allocated time on the questions in Section B turn to the **case-study question** in Section A.

Read the Section A question through thoroughly before you launch into it. Once you start, make sure you allocate your time to the parts within the question according to the marks available and that, where possible, you attempt the easy marks first.

Question 1 has three parts and you are preparing a memo for the client file. Part (a) is the ethics question. There will always be five marks on ethics in Section A and they are relatively easy to obtain. This time it relates to actions to take when taking on a new client.

Part (b) has three sub-parts worth 22 marks in total. The first six marks ask you to explain the relief available on a gain resulting from the destruction of a building and a subsequent purchase of a replacement including a calculation of the post-tax insurance proceeds. The next 8 marks relate to the deductibility of pre-trading expenditure. The last 6 marks of this part is asking you to calculate the additional input VAT recovered if an election to opt to tax is made.

Part (c) relates to the sale of shares by the client. You need to consider both the IHT and CGT on the sale including the availability of any reliefs (specifically BADR and rollover relief for CGT).

Lastly, what you mustn't forget is that you have to attempt **the whole question in Section A and BOTH questions in Section B.**

Option 2 (if you're thinking 'This exam's alright')

It never pays to be overconfident but if you're not quaking in your shoes about the exam then **turn straight to the case-study question in Section A.**

Once you've done this question, **move to Section B**. The question you attempt first really depends on what you are most confident at. If you are undecided look at the requirements. It may be easier to obtain more marks if these are broken down into several smaller parts. In this exam question 2 actually has four smaller parts and question 3 has three so, in this situation, it may be easier to pick your question based on which topics you prefer.

No matter how many times we remind you...

Always, always **allocate your time** according to the marks for the question in total and then according to the parts of the question. And **always, always follow the requirements** exactly.

You've got spare time at the end of the exam...?

If you have allocated your time properly then you **shouldn't have time on your hands** at the end of the exam. But if you find yourself with five or ten minutes to spare, check over your work to make sure that you have answered all the requirements of the questions and all parts of all requirements.

Forget about it!

And don't worry if you found the exam difficult. More than likely other candidates will too. If this were the real thing you would need to **forget** the exam the minute you leave the exam room and **think about the next one**. Or, if it's the last one, **celebrate**!

Section A

1 Jake

Course Book references

Ethics is covered in Chapter 1. CGT and CGT reliefs are covered in Chapters 7 and 8. Sole traders are covered in Chapter 15 and VAT on land and buildings in Chapter 23. IHT is covered in Chapters 11 and 12.

Top Tips

Treat this question as four smaller parts to help make the information more manageable and use your manager's email and the requirements set out to structure your answer. Make sure you stick to time and attempt each of the requirements in full.

Easy marks

In part (a) there are easy marks for actions to be taken when taking on a new client. In part (b) there should be easy marks for the calculation of capital gains tax. In addition, the basic CGT and IHT implications of the sale of the shares and subsequent death of Jake's aunt should also have provided easy marks.

ACCA examining team's comments

Part (a)

Candidates were told that the tax manager had not identified any threats to compliance with the fundamental principles of professional ethics which would arise as a result of becoming tax advisers to this potential client. In light of this, candidates were asked to explain why it was important to contact Jake's previous advisers. Reasons were to discover any matters which may influence the decision to take on the work, such as the client's ethics, and to obtain information necessary to avoid administrative errors in the transfer of the client's affairs, such as details of outstanding claims. Many candidates struggled to pinpoint reasons for contacting the previous tax advisers, with some wasting valuable time detailing the fundamental principles but not actually detailing any reasons.

Candidates were generally much better at identifying other actions to take, with most candidates aware of the importance of obtaining evidence of the client's identity and address and many candidates aware that money laundering checks should be performed.

Given that ethics will be tested in every exam and that there are plenty of past exam questions which have tested these ethical issues, candidates would be well advised to practise questions on this topic.

Part (b)(i)

The client was planning to use the insurance proceeds from a destroyed building to construct a new building and the requirement was to explain the relief available in respect of the destroyed building. Most candidates correctly identified that a relief would be available for the resulting gain on the destroyed building because the proceeds were being invested in a new building. They also generally knew that there would be a restriction on the relief available because not all the proceeds were being reinvested in the new building. However, a significant number of candidates thought that this relief was restricted by calculating the 'proportion' of proceeds not reinvested. In fact the rule is that the gain chargeable immediately, which cannot be relieved, is equal to the amount of insurance proceeds not spent on the new building.

Virtually all candidates included the annual exemption for gains, but weaker candidates struggled with the rate of tax to charge on the gain. The question requirement detailed the client's total income for the tax year. From this, candidates should have been able to calculate how much basic rate band remained and then tax the gain accordingly at 10% and 20%. However weaker candidates merely noted that the client was a basic rate taxpayer and taxed the whole gain at 10%, irrespective of how large the gain was and which tax bands it fell into.

An analysis and evaluation professional skills mark was available here for attempting to calculate the remaining income tax rate band in order to determine the rate(s) of capital gains tax to charge. Candidates often need to apply their technical knowledge appropriately to facts given in the question in order to earn this type of analysis and evaluation mark.

Finally, candidates were asked to calculate the amount of post-tax insurance proceeds available, after the construction of the new building, for investment in the business. This required candidates to calculate proceeds less two deductions ie tax and the cost of the new building. Most candidates were able to deduct tax but only a minority went on to deduct the cost of the new building. Candidates are advised to read the precise wording of the requirement very carefully, highlighting the key points, so that they don't just assume they know what is required. A few weaker candidates continue to wrongly calculate the gain less deduction(s), instead of proceeds less deduction(s), despite this being regularly tested and commented on in ACCA examining team's reports.

There was a further analysis and evaluation mark available for deducting both tax and the cost of the new building from proceeds and only candidates who provided all these three elements were able to earn this mark.

Part (b)(ii)

This question part related to tax deductions available for costs incurred before setting up an unincorporated business and costs incurred on the first day of trading. Only a minority of candidates seemed aware of the technical rules for allowing pre-trading expenditure, namely that it is allowable if incurred in the seven years prior to commencement of trade, it must be allowable under the normal rules of what is allowable and it is treated as incurred on the first day of trading.

The question stated that the client was going to travel extensively to visit potential clients and persuade them to place orders with him. A scepticism professional skills mark was available here for interpreting the available question information and including a relevant illustrative pre trading expense such as the fact that any client entertaining costs would be disallowable. When presented with detailed information in a question, candidates should pause to consider why they are being given the detail. Knowing the rules is vital for this but so too is question practice which will help candidates to start making connections between information given and possible impact on their answers.

A significant number of candidates treated Jake as an employee, despite him planning to set up his own unincorporated business and earned no marks for discussing allowances and benefits from an employee's point of view. Candidates need to be very clear that someone who sets up their own unincorporated business is a sole trader and not an employee and as such the rules for employees do not apply to their tax calculations. Most candidates knew that the structures and buildings allowance would be available for the new building at 3%. Fewer candidates knew that the building's integral features would qualify for a 100% annual investment allowance.

The question stated that the client was going to buy a new car for 65% use in his business and that the car would not have zero CO_2 emissions. Again, candidates needed to take a moment to consider why they were being given this information about the CO_2 emissions. It meant that there was more information required before capital allowances could be computed because depending on whether the CO_2 emissions were above 50g/km or not, this would decide whether the capital allowance writing down allowance would be at 18% or 6%. There was another scepticism mark available for recognising that the CO_2 emissions of the car would need to be known before computing capital allowances. As has been said above, advice to candidates is that they must focus not only on learning the details of the tax rules but also on question practice, so that they improve at being able to spot the clues being given in questions and can then apply their knowledge.

Part (b)(iii)

The scenario here required candidates to calculate the maximum amount of additional input VAT which the client could recover if he were to elect to opt to tax his new building, compared to not making the election. This was the part of the question which candidates were weakest at, with many candidates obviously very confused over what it means to opt to tax a building. Lots of candidates were unable to reach an answer for 'additional' input VAT recoverable.

The client was planning to use 70% of the building for business purposes for the first four years of his business and then at the end of the four-year period, use 100% of the building for business purposes. This meant that if the client did not opt to tax the building, he will initially only be able to recover 70% of the input VAT on the building in the first year.

For years 5-10 of ownership of the building he will then be able to recover 30% x input VAT/10 years, for each of those six years. However, if the client opts to tax the building, he is able to recover 100% of the input VAT on the building in the first year. Hence the additional amount he can recover by opting to VAT will be the difference between these two scenario calculations.

In order to earn the available analysis and evaluation mark, candidates needed to consider both possibilities of opting to tax and not opting to tax. However, many candidates did not consider both possibilities and were not able to earn this mark. VAT is a part of the syllabus which is often ignored by candidates, particularly this area of opting to tax. However, candidates should be clear that VAT will be tested in the exam and this syllabus area of opting to tax will be returned to.

Part (c)

The first part of this requirement asked for an explanation, with no calculations, of the potential IHT liability on two occasions: firstly, if the client sells the shares he was given by his aunt and secondly on the death of his aunt. Overall candidates appeared confident on this area of the syllabus and were able to score well.

Most candidates missed the easy mark of stating that there would be no inheritance tax on a sale of shares at market value. However, it was good to see that a lot of candidates recognised that selling the shares would result in a withdrawal of business property relief. Most candidates knew that the PET would become chargeable upon the death of the aunt and referred to the availability of taper relief.

Analysis and evaluation marks may be awarded for appropriate use of relevant information, and this was the case here. Better prepared candidates spotted that the annual exemptions and nil rate band would have been used already by earlier lifetime gifts, earning technical marks and a commercial acumen mark.

The second part of this requirement asked candidates to calculate the chargeable gain resulting from the sale of shares and whether business asset disposal relief and rollover relief would be available. The calculation of the gain was generally performed well.

Many candidates correctly identified that business asset disposal relief would not be available as the client was not an employee but fewer candidates knew that shares are not a qualifying asset for rollover relief purposes.

There was a final part to this requirement asking for an explanation of the relief which would be available in respect of any IHT payable following the death of the aunt.

Only a very small minority of candidates knew that IHT payable could be deducted from the gain and that this was because gift holdover relief had been claimed in respect of the gift.

Marking guide

		Marks	
(a)	Contact previous tax adviser	4	
	Actions to take	2	
	Marks Available	6	
	Maximum		5
(b) (i)	Explanations	3	
	Calculations		
	Gain subject to CGT	1	
	Basic rate band available	2	
	Post-tax proceeds	2	
			8

(ii)	Visiting potential customers	5.5	
	Purchase of the Yak Building	2	
	Purchase of car	3	
	Marks Available	10.5	
	Maximum		8
(iii)	**Calculation of recoverable input tax**		
	If no option to tax	4	
	If opt to tax	2	
	Marks Available	6	
			6
(c)	**Inheritance tax**		
	At time of sale	1	
	As a result of death of aunt:		
	– Chargeable amount	5	
	– IHT liability	3.5	
	Capital gains tax		
	Chargeable gain	2	
	Reliefs available	4	
	Marks Available	15.5	
	Maximum		13

Communication

- General format and structure of memorandum (eg from/to etc, use of headings)
- Style, language and clarity (tone of memorandum, presentation of calculations, appropriate use of the tools, easy to follow and more than a negligible amount of content)
- Effectiveness of communication (answer is relevant, specific rather than general and focused to the requirement)
- Adherence to specific instructions made in the scenario

Analysis and evaluation

- Appropriate use of information in the question to determine suitable calculations
- Appropriate use of information in the question to draw conclusions
- Demonstration of ability to consider all relevant factors in relation to the sale of shares in POL Ltd
- Critical assessment of information re ownership of the POL Ltd shares

Scepticism

- Identification of missing information in relation to the car
- Critical assessment of the deductibility of pre-trading expenditure

Commercial acumen

- Recognition of the possible consequences of making the gift to Jake's sister
- Recognition of the consequences of the gift holdover relief claim
- Recognition of the possibility of relieving the inheritance against the chargeable gain

Maximum	10
Total	50

Memorandum

For: The files

Client: Jake

Subject: New unincorporated business and related matters

Prepared by: Tax senior

Date: 1 January 2026

(a) **Becoming tax advisers to Jake**

Contacting Jake's previous tax advisers

Reasons for contacting Jake's previous tax advisers:

- To discover any matters which may influence our decision to take on the work.

  For example, Jake's attitude to disclosure of information to HM Revenue and Customs (HMRC) and the reasons Jake has decided to change his tax advisers.

- To obtain the information necessary to ensure that Jake's affairs are transferred without any administrative errors.

  For example, details of any outstanding elections and claims.

If Jake were to prevent us from discussing his affairs with his previous advisers, the ACCA's Code of Ethics and Conduct states that we should not accept him as a client.

Other actions to take

- We should obtain evidence of Jake's identity and address.
- We should carry out our procedures in order to assure ourselves that Jake is not involved in any form of money laundering.

(b) **New unincorporated business**

(i) **Insurance proceeds available for investment in the business**

(1) **Relief available in respect of the gain on the Vol Building**

A relief will be available in respect of the gain on the Vol Building because Jake will use part of the insurance proceeds to acquire a replacement asset within 12 months of receipt.

As a result of this relief:

- The gain charged now is reduced to the amount of insurance proceeds not spent.
- The balance of the gain will be deducted from the capital gains tax (CGT) base cost of the new building, such that it will be deferred until the new building is disposed of.

(2) **Insurance proceeds available for investment in the business**

	£
Insurance proceeds	380,000
Less: CGT payable (W1)	(6,373)
Post-tax proceeds	373,627
Less: Cost of new building	(335,000)
Available to invest in the business	38,627

ANSWERS

Workings

1 ***CGT payable***

	£
Insurance proceeds	380,000
Cost of replacement	(335,000)
Gain charged (proceeds not spent)	45,000
Less: Annual exempt amount	(3,000)
Taxable gain	42,000

	£
£20,270 (W2) × 10%	2,027
£21,730 (£42,000 – £20,270) × 20%	4,346
	6,373

2 ***Basic rate band available***

	£	£
Basic rate band		37,700
Income	30,000	
Less: Personal allowance	(12,570)	
		(17,430)
Basic rate band available		20,270

(ii) **Tax deductions in respect of the expenditure to be incurred**

Visiting potential customers

- A tax deduction is available for qualifying expenditure incurred during the seven years prior to commencing to trade.
- For the purpose of this rule, qualifying expenditure is expenditure which would normally be allowable when calculating the tax adjusted trading profits of a business.
- For example, it should be recognised that:
  - travel expenditure would have to be incurred wholly and exclusively for the purposes of the trade in order to be allowable; and
  - no deduction would be available for any amounts incurred in respect of entertaining customers.
- The total of the qualifying pre-trading expenditure will be treated as having been incurred on 1 May 2026, the first day of trading.

Tutorial note. Credit was given for alternative relevant examples of allowable and/or disallowable expenditure (for example, gifts).

Construction of the Yak Building

- The cost of the integral features will qualify for a tax deduction of £75,000 in full in the first period of trading due to the availability of a 100% annual investment allowance.
- The balance of the cost of the building will qualify for structures and buildings allowances (SBAs).

  SBAs are given at the rate of 3% per year. Accordingly, the SBAs in the year ending 30 April 2027 will be: £260,000 (£335,000 – £75,000) x 3% = £7,800.

Purchase of the car

- For income tax purposes the car will be written down on a reducing balance basis by reference to its CO_2 emissions; either 18% (if its CO_2 emissions do not exceed 50 g/km) or, otherwise, by 6%.
- Jake will obtain a tax deduction equal to the amount written off multiplied by 65% to reflect his use of the car for business purposes.

(iii) **Alternative plan for the use of the Yak Building**

Under the alternative plan, the maximum amount of additional input value added tax (VAT) which Jake would recover if he were to elect to opt to tax the Yak Building would be calculated as follows:

	£	£
No option to tax		
Year 1		
Year ending 30 April 2027		
£67,000 × 70%		46,900
Years 5–10		
Six years ending 30 April 2036		
Each year: £67,000/10 × 30% (100% – 70%)	2,010	
Total in six years: £2,010 × 6		12,060
Total input VAT recovered		58,960
Opt to tax		
Year 1		
Year ending 30 April 2027		
£67,000 × 100%		67,000
Additional amount recovered due to opting to tax		8,040

Tutorial note. If an option to tax is made, the supply of the building becomes a standard rated supply. VAT is therefore charged at 20% on the rent and any future sale of the property. If Jake elects to opt to tax, the letting of the building is now a taxable supply and therefore the building is now 100% being used in making taxable supplies. 100% of the VAT on purchase can be recovered.

(c) **Sale of shares in POL Ltd**

Liability to inheritance tax (IHT)

At the time of the sale

- The sale will be at full market value, such that there will be no immediate IHT implications.

As a result of the death of his aunt

Chargeable amount

- If Jake does NOT own the shares at the time of his aunt's death:
  - Business property relief (BPR) will NOT be available, such that the full value of the shares at the time of the gift of £420,000 will be subject to IHT.
- If Jake does own the shares at the time of his aunt's death:
  - 100% BPR will be available.
  - However, the relief will be restricted due to the excepted assets owned by the company. Accordingly, BPR will be £369,600 (£420,000 x 88%).
- There would be no annual exempt amounts available in either situation. This is due to the gift to Jake's sister on 1 September 2023 (or due to other, earlier gifts in the tax year 2023/24).

IHT liability

- There would be no nil rate band available, as it will have been applied against the gift to Jake's sister on 1 September 2023 (or against other, earlier gifts).
- Accordingly, the value of the shares, less BPR where available, will be subject to IHT at the rate of 40%.
- The IHT liability will be reduced by 20% taper relief if Jake's aunt does not die until 1 October 2026 (ie more than three years after the gift of the shares). An additional 20% relief will be available for each additional full year that she survives the gift.

CGT implications

Chargeable gain on sale

	£	£
Sale proceeds		470,000
Less: Cost		
Market value on 1 October 2023	420,000	
Gift relief claimed	(112,500)	
		(307,500)
Chargeable gain		162,500

Availability of reliefs

- Business asset disposal relief will not be available because Jake is not an employee of POL Ltd.
- Rollover relief will not be available because shares are not qualifying assets for the purposes of rollover relief.
- Relief will be given, against the chargeable gain, in respect of any IHT payable following the death of Jake's aunt. This is because gift holdover relief was claimed in respect of the gift

Section B

2 Rabo Ltd

Course Book references

Corporation tax is covered in Chapter 16 and corporate groups are covered in Chapter 19.

Top Tips

It is important to identify the verb used in parts (b) and (c) which is to 'explain with supporting calculations' so you need to make sure you answer include sufficient explanations. Wherever detail is given, then you need to consider the relevance and why it is important. For example, why are we told the date the arrangement for sale of the Rabo Ltd took place? Why are we told Nali plans to make significant changes to Rabo Ltd's operations in the future?

Easy marks

The calculation of the gain on sale of the factory should be a source of easy marks. Also, the explanation and calculation of the loss to surrender to Morada Ltd in part (b) should also be easy marks.

ACCA examining team's comments

Part (a)

The scenario for part (a) involved a factory being transferred between two group companies, the recipient company then being sold, and finally the recipient company selling the factory to a third party. The requirement was to calculate the after-tax proceeds upon sale of the factory and to explain how the base cost of the factory was calculated.

Most candidates recognised that the two companies were in a gains group and that the original asset transfer was a no gain no loss transfer. However, most candidates then wrongly thought that when the recipient company sold the asset, its base cost would be its original cost to the transferor company.

Only better prepared candidates recognised that since the recipient company would leave the group within six years of the transfer, still owning the asset, a degrouping charge would arise. This would mean that the base cost of the asset would be the market value at the time of the no gain no loss transfer. By picking up the clues in the question and applying their knowledge, these candidates were able to earn a commercial acumen mark for recognising that a degrouping charge would arise in this situation.

This question part was a good example of candidates needing to be able to do more than just state generic rules in order to score high marks at ATX–UK. They must be able to apply the rules to the facts of the question and what is being asked of them.

Once again, the advice to candidates is that they must focus not only on learning the details of the tax rules but also on question practice, so they that begin to see the links between information given in questions and can then apply their knowledge.

Most candidates were able to earn the capital gain calculation marks but as mentioned many times before, there still remain some candidates who wrongly calculate after-tax proceeds as 'gain less tax' instead of 'proceeds less tax'.

Part (b)

Part (b)(i) asked candidates to explain the maximum amount of trading loss which a subsidiary could transfer to its parent, in an accounting period where the subsidiary was being sold.

Most candidates correctly identified that the two companies were in a losses group and knew that losses could only be transferred up to the date that 'arrangements' to sell the subsidiary were made, which was 10 months into a 12-month accounting period.

Unfortunately, some candidates lost a few easy marks by not explaining that the maximum loss which could be transferred was the lower of 10/12 x taxable total profits in the claimant company and 10/12 x loss in the loss-making company.

Part (b)(ii) required candidates to explain the tax consequences if the loss-making company used some or all of the loss itself.

It was good to see that most candidates could apply the facts of the question and realise that current year and prior year relief would not be available due to lack of available profits in these two years.

Candidates correctly went on to discuss carry forward relief, with better candidates correctly stating that this could lead to a delay in loss relief.

In the question, candidates were told that the purchaser of the subsidiary company planned to make 'significant changes' to the subsidiary's operations 'over the next few years'. This was a clue in the question that carry forward relief may be restricted due to the application of the 'major change in the nature or conduct of the trade' (MCINOCOT) rules.

This is often the sort of wording used, in a situation where there has been a change in ownership of a company, to try and suggest to candidates that more information is required in order to determine whether or not the MCINOCOT rules apply.

Those candidates who picked up on this 'MCINOCOT' point, were able to earn the technical marks for spotting this and the commercial acumen mark for identifying that this was an issue. A further scepticism mark was awarded to those candidates who were able to make the point about needing more information about the planned changes to operations.

There was an analysis and evaluation mark available to those candidates who considered both group relief and the company using its own loss and many candidates earned this mark.

Part (c)

Part (c) tested candidates' knowledge of rollover relief and capital allowances available on given capital acquisitions. Finally, candidates were asked for the corporation tax savings that these would give rise to.

Most candidates recognised that the gain on the sale of the factory in part (a) could be rolled over into the purchase of a warehouse in part (c). There was some confusion over how to calculate how much of the gain is chargeable immediately and how much can be rolled over. The rule is that the amount of gain which is chargeable immediately corresponds to the amount of proceeds not reinvested and then the balance of the gain can be rolled over.

Lots of candidates failed to state that rollover relief is not available on vans because they are not qualifying assets. They possibly knew this rule but neglected to state it. Highlighting key words within a requirement may help to maintain focus and to ensure that candidates do not lose sight of all aspects of the requirement that they are being asked to do.

Many candidates calculated structures and buildings allowance (SBA) for the warehouse, but this was not available because the warehouse was constructed in 2010 and no capital allowances or SBAs were available for this asset.

In terms of capital allowances for the vans, the 100% annual investment allowance was available and not, as a significant number of candidates thought, 18% writing down allowance in the main pool.

It was pleasing to see most candidates attempt to calculate the corporation tax saving based on their figures and earn technical marks for this and an analysis and evaluation mark.

A further analysis and evaluation mark was given to those candidates who attempted to explain both rollover relief and capital allowances for both assets.

Marking guide

		Marks	
(a)	Calculation	2	
	Explanation of choice of base cost	5	
	Marks Available	7	
	Maximum		6

(b) (i) Maximum surrender to Morada Ltd	5	
(ii) Relief in Rabo Ltd only	3.5	
		7
(c) **Rollover relief**		
Warehouse	4.5	
Delivery vans	1	
Capital allowances		
Warehouse	1	
Delivery vans	1	
Corporation tax saving	1	
Marks Available	8.5	
Maximum		7

Professional skills marks

Analysis and evaluation

- Appropriate use of relevant information to consider the full picture for group loss relief
- Appropriate use of relevant information to draw conclusions regarding the availability of both rollover relief and capital allowances
- Appropriate use of relevant information to determine suitable calculations

Scepticism

- Critical assessment of the information provided to determine the need for more information regarding the change in conduct of the trade

Commercial acumen

- Recognition of possible consequences of actions and decisions

Maximum	5
Total	25

(a)

After-tax proceeds from the sale of the freehold factory

	£
Sale proceeds	395,000
Cost (market value at 1 September 2020)	(302,000)
Chargeable gain	93,000

Corporation tax payable is £23,250 [(£93,000 × 25%)

After-tax proceeds are £371,750 (£395,000 – £23,250).

ANSWERS

Base cost of the factory

The sale of the warehouse to Rabo Ltd by Morada Ltd was originally a no gain no loss transfer as Morada Ltd owned at least 75% of the ordinary shares in Rabo Ltd, such that the two companies were in a gains group at that time. However, as Rabo Ltd will leave Morada Ltd's group within six years of this intra-group transfer, whilst still owning the factory, a degrouping gain will arise.

This will be calculated by treating Rabo Ltd as having sold the factory for, and immediately reacquired it at, its market value at the date of the intra-group transfer. The degrouping gain is then added to the proceeds received on the sale of the shares in Rabo Ltd for Morada Ltd. If the share disposal qualifies for the substantial shareholding exemption (SSE) the gain on disposal of the Rabo Ltd shares including the degrouping gain will be exempt. Accordingly, Rabo Ltd is then deemed to have acquired the factory on 1 September 2022 for £302,000. Therefore, this will be Rabo Ltd's base cost on disposal.

(b) (i)

Max amount of Rabo Ltd's trading loss which can be surrendered to Morada Ltd

Rabo Ltd's trading loss can be surrendered to Morada Ltd for relief against its taxable trading profits of the corresponding accounting period. Although Rabo Ltd will not leave the Morada Ltd group until 31 December 2025, the agreement to sell all the ordinary shares on 31 October 2025 constitutes 'arrangements' for the company to leave, such that a corresponding accounting period for group relief purposes ends on that date. Accordingly, the maximum amount of the loss which can be surrendered to Morada Ltd is the lower of:

- 10/12 of Rabo Ltd's trading loss for the year ending 31 December 2025; and
- 10/12 of Morada Ltd's taxable total profits for this period.

Accordingly, the max amount which can be surrendered is £60,000 (£72,000 × 10/12).

(ii)

Tax consequences of taking relief for the trading loss only in Rabo Ltd

The main consequence of this decision would be that tax relief would be delayed, or even lost. Rabo Ltd has no other sources of income in the current accounting period, and also has no available profits in the previous accounting period, so there is no possibility of taking either current period or carry back relief in Rabo Ltd. Following the change in ownership of the company, the loss can only be carried forward for relief providing there is not a major change in the nature or conduct of the trade within a period of five years, starting no more than three years before the date of the change in ownership. Further information is required in relation to Nali's plans to make significant changes to the company's operations to ascertain whether or not this will apply to Rabo Ltd. At best, this means that loss relief will be delayed; at worst it may mean that no relief will be available.

(c)

Corporation tax savings as a result of the planned capital expenditure

Rollover relief

Second hand warehouse

Land and buildings are qualifying assets for the purpose of rollover relief. Accordingly, as the warehouse was acquired within the three years after the sale of the factory building, (part of) the gain on the sale of the factory can be deferred as a result of this acquisition. The land and building constitute a single asset for the purpose of rollover relief, so the amount of the qualifying reinvestment is £312,000.

Proceeds not reinvested are £83,000 (£395,000 – £312,000). This amount of the gain will remain chargeable. Rollover relief of £10,000 (£93,000 – £83,000) will be available to reduce the corporation tax liability in respect of this gain.

Delivery vans

The delivery vans are not qualifying assets for the purpose of rollover relief as they are moveable (rather than fixed) plant and machinery.

Capital allowances

Warehouse

As the warehouse was constructed in 2012, it will not be eligible for the structures and buildings allowance.

Delivery vans

This expenditure will qualify for the annual investment allowance. A total of £175,000 (£35,000 x 5 x 100%) is available.

Accordingly, the total corporation tax saving is £46,250 ((£10,000 + £175,000) x 25%).

3 Pinto

Course Book references

Overseas personal taxation is covered in Chapter 9.

Top Tips

Make sure you pay careful attention to the verbs in each requirement. Part (c) only asks you to 'calculate' so don't waste time providing any explanations for this part.

Easy marks

Easy marks are available in part (a) for identifying the number of ties required to be satisfied for Pinto to be UK resident using the tax tables available in the exam. In addition, the calculation of the gain and private residence relief in part (b) and the calculation of income tax in part (c) should also be a source of easy marks.

ACCA examining team's comments

Part (a)

Part (a) tested candidates' knowledge of the 'ties' to be considered to determine the taxpayer's tax residence status when none of the automatic tax residence tests are satisfied.

Most candidates recognised that discussion of the ties was what was required and were able to identify at least a couple of them, but very few were able to identify all five. As a conclusion was going to be required here (whether or not the taxpayer will be UK tax resident), a good starting point would have been to explain the number of ties which would need to be met in order to establish UK tax residence status. This should not have posed too much of a problem for a well-prepared candidate, who was aware that relevant information needed for this was included in the tax tables. Candidates are advised to ensure that they are familiar with the information which is provided in the tax tables, and when this is likely to be useful in the exam. A surprising number of candidates did not undertake this first step, which meant that they were unable to conclude as to whether the requisite number of ties had been met, and consequently, whether or not the taxpayer will be tax resident in the UK.

The majority of the technical marks in this question were awarded for correct descriptions of the different ties. Precision was required here in order to score well. However, many candidates did not have this level of detailed knowledge. For example, most identified broadly the family, accommodation and work ties. But far fewer knew that 'family' in this context relates only to a spouse/civil partner or minor children; that the requirement in relation to accommodation was only that it had to be available, not necessarily owned by the taxpayer; and that the work performed had to be 'substantive' ie for at least 40 days in the tax year. Recognition of the remaining two ties, relating to the amount of time spent in the UK, was poor. As is so often the case at ATX, candidates need to pay close attention to the details of relevant conditions and reliefs in order to score a good mark.

An analysis and evaluation professional skills mark was available for reaching an appropriate conclusion in respect of the taxpayer's tax resident status, based on the number of ties satisfied compared to number of ties required. Most of the candidates who had stated the required number of ties were able to go on and get this mark. There were also up to two further analysis and evaluation marks available for applying the rules to the facts of this scenario. Overall, this question part was a good example of candidates needing to be able to do more than just state basic, generic rules in order to score high marks at ATX-UK. They must be able to provide the requisite amount of detail and apply the rules to the facts of the question and what is being asked of them.

Part (b)

Part (b) firstly required candidates to explain why an individual, who they have been told was not UK resident at the time, would nevertheless be liable to capital gains tax (CGT) on the sale of his UK house, and then to identify, explain, and calculate the effect of, any relief which was available. It appeared that many candidates were not aware of the specific rule which states that the disposal of property which is situated in the UK will be liable to UK CGT regardless of the tax residence status of the vendor. Instead, a good number of these candidates discussed the implications of temporary non-residence – which is a more frequently tested topic – but was not what was in point in this scenario.

The vast majority of candidates recognised that private residence relief (PRR) would be available in respect of this disposal, and thereby opened the door to being able to score well in respect of the remainder of this question part. As is normally the case, a commercial acumen professional skills mark was available for identifying this relevant relief. Candidates are advised to pay close attention to the wording of the requirement; where there is a reference to available relief(s) (in respect of any tax, not just CGT), they will be rewarded for being able to identify which relief(s) are available in the given scenario. Tax reliefs are a very important aspect of the ATX–UK syllabus, and candidates should be prepared for these to be regularly tested in every exam.

Most candidates continued to score well on the calculation marks available here, being able to correctly – or almost correctly – identify the periods which would qualify for PRR and apply the relevant fraction to the gain on disposal. The explanation of the availability of PRR was less well done, with many candidates restricting their comments to reference to actual occupation, and, in a good number of cases, recognition that the last nine months of ownership would also qualify. The inclusion of information relating to the taxpayer's recent absence from the property was intended to draw discussion of the concept of 'deemed occupation', but few candidates picked up on this. Where a requirement includes both a calculation and an explanation of something – as for PRR here – candidates should take the time to address both.

Separate marks are available for both elements, so in order to score well, both elements need to be addressed.

Part (c)

Part (c) required candidates to calculate after-tax income – a common requirement at ATX-UK – which primarily involved the production of a relatively straightforward income tax computation, including both UK and overseas sources of income, and a deduction for double taxation relief (DTR).

Most candidates performed well overall on this question part, showing clear familiarity with the basics of DTR. However, the majority were not able to correctly calculate the amount of the UK income tax liability which was attributable to the property income when calculating the DTR available. This should be calculated as the difference between the taxpayer's total income tax liability, including the overseas income in the computation, and then the total liability excluding it from the computation. So two computations are required.

The taxpayer in this question was a basic rate taxpayer, and in many cases like this, a shortcut can be taken, whereby the UK tax attributable to the overseas income can be calculated by just applying the appropriate basic rate of income tax to the gross amount of the income included in the computation. But in this question, candidates had to recognise that the inclusion of dividend income, which is taxed at different rates, including a nil rate band, meant that the shortcut would not work, and that they therefore needed to use the two computation approach. Very few candidates did this. In any question involving the calculation of DTR in respect of overseas income, candidates would be well advised to recheck the sources of taxable income included in the computation for those sources – savings and dividends – which attract different rates of tax, before calculating the DTR. Those who did were rewarded with a professional skills mark in addition to the technical marks available.

There were two other main observations in relation to this question, both of which demonstrated a failure on the part of some candidates to read the requirements carefully enough:

- The requirement was to 'calculate' only. There was no requirement for any supporting explanations in this part. Candidates are reminded to pay careful attention to the 'command' word(s) in each requirement and ensure that they address what is required. Quite a considerable amount of time appeared to have been wasted by some candidates in this question part, providing unnecessary explanations, which attracted no marks.
- The requirement was to calculate 'property income after all taxes'. A minority of candidates ignored this altogether, while others deducted only the UK tax liability which they had calculated, which, in both cases, cost them straightforward follow through technical marks.

As has been said many times before, candidates would be well advised to reread the requirement while they are in the process of answering it, to ensure that they are directing their answer at the specific question which has been set. Highlighting key words within a requirement may help to maintain focus and to ensure that candidates do not lose sight of what it is they are being asked to do.

Marking guide

		Marks	
(a)	Number of ties required	1	
	Consideration of ties	5	
	Marks Available	6	
	Maximum		5
(b)	Reason chargeable	2	
	Calculation of chargeable gain	2	
	Explanation of PRR	4	
	Marks Available	8	
	Maximum		7

Marking guide		Marks
(c) Overseas tax suffered	0.5	
UK tax suffered	6.5	
After-tax income	1	
		8

Professional skills marks

Analysis and evaluation

- Appropriate use of relevant information to draw conclusions regarding Pinto's residency status
- Appropriate use of relevant information to determine suitable calculations

Commercial acumen

- Recognition of the relevance of the residence status of the three preceding tax years
- Appropriate use of relevant information to determine tax reliefs available

Maximum	5
Total	25

(a)

Word Processor

Pinto's tax residence status in the tax year 2025/26

As Pinto does not satisfy any of the automatic tax residence tests, his tax residence status will be determined by the number of ties he has with the UK.

As Pinto was previously tax resident in the UK in at least one of the previous three tax years (2022/23), and will be in the UK for between 91 and 120 days in the tax year 2025/26, he will be UK tax resident in this tax year if he satisfies at least two ties.

Pinto will satisfy the following tie:

- He will have accommodation available to him for a continuous period of more than 90 days, and he will make use of this accommodation for more than 16 nights in the tax year 2025/26.

Pinto will not satisfy the remaining four ties:

- He does not have any close family (spouse/civil partner or child under 18) who are resident in the UK.
- He will not have substantive work (at least 40 days) in the UK in 2025/26.
- He was not in the UK for more than 90 days in either 2023/24 or 2024/25.
- He has not spent more time in the UK than in any other country in 2025/26.

Accordingly, as Pinto satisfies only one tie, he will not be UK tax resident in the tax year 2025/26.

(b)

Word Processor

Pinto's sale of his UK house on 30 April 2024

	£
Gain before relief	47,000
Less: Private residence relief (PRR) (W)	(43,867)
Chargeable gain	3,133

PRR

	Months
Total period of ownership (1 May 2019 to 30 April 2024)	60
Actual occupation (1 May 2019 to 6 April 2023)	47
Add: Last 9 months	9
Actual and deemed occupation	56

PRR relief available is £43,867 (£47,000 × 56/60).

PRR is available for the period for which Pinto occupied the property prior to travelling to Vicia, with the exception of the period from 6 April 2023 to 30 April 2023. This is because Pinto was not UK tax resident in 2023/24, and did not satisfy the 'day count test' (staying overnight at the property for at least 90 days) in that tax year.

Pinto's period of absence from 1 May 2023 to 30 April 2024 will not be treated as deemed occupation as Pinto did not return to live in the property prior to sale.

PRR is also available for Pinto's final nine months of ownership.

(c)

Spreadsheet

Edit Format

B4	= C24		
	A	B	C
1	**Pinto's income after all taxes from his house in Vicia**		
2		£	
3	Tax suffered in Vicia (£8,375 × 16%)	1,340	
4	UK tax suffered (W)	nil	
5	Property income after taxes (£8,375 – £1,340 – £0)	7,035	
6		With overseas income	Without overseas income
7		£	£
8	Employment income	10,000	10,000
9	Property business income	8,375	nil
10	Dividend	2,500	2,500
11		20,875	12,500
12	Less: Personal allowance	(12,570)	(12,570)
13	Taxable income	8,035	nil
14			
15	**Income tax with overseas income**		
16		£	£
17	Property business income (£8,375 – (£12,570 – £10,000) × 20%)		1,161
18	Dividends (£2,500 – £500) × 8.75%		175
19	Total tax		1,336
20	Additional UK tax due to inclusion of overseas income (£1,336 – £nil)		1,336
21	Less: Double taxation relief, lower of:		
22	– Overseas tax suffered	1,340	
23	– UK tax attributable to overseas income	1,336	(1,336)
24	UK tax payable		nil

ACCA

Advanced Taxation (ATX – UK) FA2024

Mock Exam 4

March/June 2024

Questions	
Time allowed	3 hours 15 minutes
ALL questions are compulsory and MUST be attempted	

DO NOT OPEN THIS EXAM UNTIL YOU ARE READY TO START UNDER EXAMINATION CONDITIONS

Section A

1 Lark Ltd (98 mins)

You should assume that today's date is 1 February 2026.

You are an ACCA student working for a firm of accountants. Your manager has asked you to carry out some work in relation to both Lark Ltd and Lark Ltd's managing director, Rosetti.

In addition to some ethical considerations which have been raised by your manager, advice is required in respect of:

- the sale of a wholly-owned subsidiary company;
- the sale by a company of a building and an intangible asset;
- group registration for the purposes of value added tax (VAT);
- the VAT implications of the sale of a building;
- the pricing strategy between the group companies; and
- gifts of shares to a trust and to an individual.

The following exhibits, available on the left-hand side of the screen, provide information relevant to the question:

(1) Lark Ltd group – memorandum from manager

(2) Tax reduction strategies – email from Rosetti

(3) Gifts of shares in Lark Ltd – email from Rosetti

(4) Work to be carried out – email from manager

This information should be used to answer the question **requirement** within your chosen **response option(s).**

Required

You should assume that today's date is 1 February 2026.

Respond to the instructions in the email from your manager.

Note. The split of the mark allocation is shown in Exhibit 4 – Work to be carried out. **(40 marks)**

Professional marks will be awarded for the demonstration of skill in communication, analysis and evaluation, scepticism and commercial acumen in your answer. **(10 marks)**

(Total = 50 marks)

Exhibit 1: Extract from a memorandum from your manager dated 1 February 2026

This memorandum records discussions with Rosetti, the managing director of Lark Ltd.

The Lark Ltd group

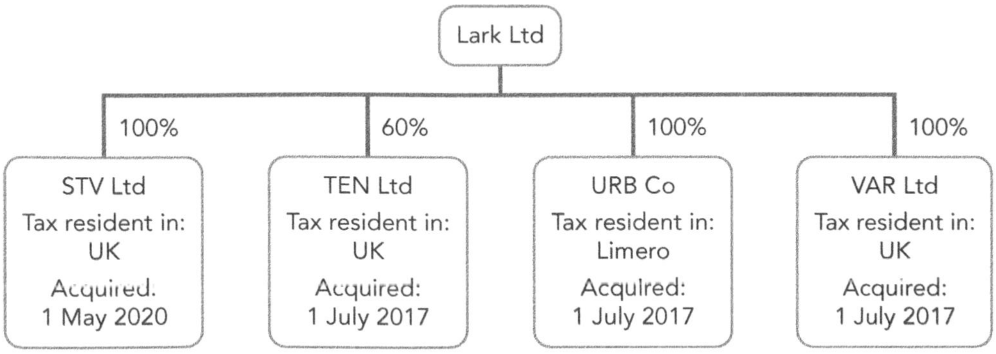

- All five companies are trading companies which prepare accounts to 31 March each year.
- URB Co trades in the country of Limero and is resident there for tax purposes. There is no double tax treaty between the UK and Limero.
- All of the other four companies are tax resident in the UK and pay UK corporation tax at the main rate.

STV Ltd – background information

Lark Ltd acquired the whole of the ordinary share capital of STV Ltd on 1 May 2020 for £550,000.

STV Ltd trades from the Strick Building, which it purchased from an unconnected person on 1 October 2021 for £430,000. The Strick Building is not eligible for structures and buildings allowances.

On 1 April 2024, STV Ltd purchased a registered trademark (the 'S' trademark) for £30,000. You should also be aware that, on 1 May 2025, VAR Ltd purchased a registered trademark (the 'V' trademark) for £40,000. Both trademarks were acquired from unconnected persons for use within the respective companies' trades. They are being written off over a twenty-year period in the companies' financial statements. Total amortisation in respect of the 'S' trademark for the two years ended 31 March 2026 will be £3,000.

STV Ltd is a profitable company. It has no trading losses or capital losses brought forward as at 1 April 2025.

Sale of STV Ltd

A sale of either STV Ltd's share capital (Option 1) or the company's assets (Option 2) will take place on 31 March 2026.

Option 1

Under this option, Lark Ltd would sell the whole of the ordinary share capital of STV Ltd to an unconnected company for £920,000.

Option 2

Under this option, STV Ltd would sell its assets and would cease trading. It would then pay a dividend to Lark Ltd equal to the post-tax proceeds realised.

The following transactions would occur:

- The Strick Building would be sold to VAR Ltd for its market value of £700,000. VAR Ltd would use the building for trading purposes.
- The 'S' trademark would be sold to an unconnected company for £50,000.
- Other assets:
  - Equipment and inventory would be sold to various unconnected companies for market value. This would result in additional taxable profits of £20,000.
  - Receivables would be collected, and trade and other payables would be paid.
- In total, the sale/realisation of these other assets would result in a net cash surplus of £130,000.

Value added tax (VAT)

I agreed to provide advice to Rosetti on applying for a group VAT registration, and on the VAT implications of the sale of the Strick Building if Option 2 is chosen.

Reducing the corporation tax payable by the group companies

Rosetti asked for my advice on two possible strategies to reduce the corporation tax payable by the Lark Ltd group companies. These strategies are summarised in an email from him which is attached to this memorandum (Exhibit 2).

Rosetti – personal tax matters

I also attach a further email from Rosetti setting out some matters he wishes to discuss in relation to his personal tax affairs (Exhibit 3).

Exhibit 2: Tax reduction strategies – email from Rosetti

To: Tax manager
From: Rosetti
Date: 1 February 2026
Subject: Tax reduction strategies

I have been looking for ways to reduce the corporation tax payable by the group. I set out below two strategies which have come to my attention, and I would be interested to hear your views. I would emphasise that, as you would expect, the group would never do anything illegal or attempt to conceal the actions of the companies in any way.

Pricing strategy

Lark Ltd buys some of the components it uses from URB Co. The price currently charged by URB Co to Lark Ltd is the same as that which would be charged by an independent third-party supplier. If Lark Ltd were to pay a higher price for these components, its profits, and therefore its corporation tax liability, would be reduced. The profit of URB Co would increase but, as you know, the rate of corporation tax in the country of Limero is lower than the main rate in the UK, such that the total corporation tax payable by the group would be reduced.

Strategy suggested by business adviser

A business adviser has suggested a strategy to reduce the group's corporation tax payable. It would involve Lark Ltd making payments to VAR Ltd, which would result in a tax deduction for Lark Ltd, but would not give rise to taxable income in VAR Ltd.

We would need to incorporate two new subsidiary companies which would enter into a number of inter-related contracts with Lark Ltd. There would then be a series of payments and repayments by the companies involved.

Rosetti

Exhibit 3: Gifts of shares in Lark Ltd – email from Rosetti

To: Tax manager
From: Rosetti
Date: 1 February 2026
Subject: Gifts of shares in Lark Ltd

As you know, I purchased 70,000 ordinary shares in Lark Ltd (a 70% holding) in June 2016 for £1.50 per share and I have made gifts from this shareholding in the past.

On 1 May 2026, I will make two further such gifts: 1,500 shares to a discretionary trust established for the benefit of my sister's children and 1,500 shares to my brother. These will be my only gifts in the tax year 2026/27.

My brother has been living in the country of Limero since 2017. Unfortunately, he is in poor health, such that he has not visited the UK since 2019 and will not be able to do so in the future.

When I have made gifts in the past, I have claimed gift holdover relief. I would like to do this again in respect of the gifts to be made on 1 May 2026. I recall that when I last made a gift of shares in Lark Ltd, the relief was restricted to 94% of the gain arising due to the undeveloped land owned by the company. When advising me on these gifts, please assume that this percentage has not changed.

Rosetti

Exhibit 4: Extracts from email from manager dated 1 February 2026

Please carry out the following work.

(a) **Corporate matters (Exhibit 1)**

Write a memorandum for the Lark Ltd group client file to assist us in preparing for a meeting with Rosetti. When carrying out this work you should note that the Lark Ltd group claims all possible tax deductions and deferrals in respect of both tangible and intangible assets as soon as possible.

The memorandum should cover the following matters:

(i) **Sale of STV Ltd (Exhibit 1)**

You should ignore value added tax (VAT) when carrying out this task (i).

(1) **Tax implications of the sale** (10 marks)

In respect of Option 1:

(i) Explain the corporation tax implications for Lark Ltd of a sale of the shares.

In respect of Option 2:

(ii) Explain the corporation tax implications for STV Ltd and the stamp duty land tax implications of a sale of the Strick Building; and

(iii) Calculate the taxable profit resulting from a sale of the 'S' trademark.

(2) **In order to assist Rosetti in deciding on which option to proceed with** (7 marks)

(i) Prepare calculations to show which option would generate the greater amount of post-tax proceeds for Lark Ltd.

(ii) In respect of both options, set out any other tax and/or commercial matters directly related to this proposed sale which we should draw to Rosetti's attention.

(17 marks)

(ii) **VAT (Exhibit 1)**

You should note that Rosetti intends to include all eligible companies in the group VAT registration and that the UK tax resident companies in the group make standard rated supplies only. However, Rosetti will need to resolve certain administrative issues before the application can be finalised, such that the group registration will not be in place until 1 May 2026.

- Explain which of the companies in the Lark Ltd group could be included within a group VAT registration with Lark Ltd.
- On the assumption that the sale of STV Ltd is carried out in accordance with Option 2, explain why the sale of business assets would NOT qualify as a transfer of a going concern (TOGC) and, consequently, whether or not STV Ltd would be required to charge VAT on the sale of the Strick Building to VAR Ltd.

(7 marks)

(iii) **Reducing the corporation tax payable by the group companies (Exhibit 2)**

Pricing strategy (4 marks)

- Explain the corporation tax implications for the Lark Ltd group of adopting the pricing strategy suggested by Rosetti.

Strategy suggested by business adviser (5 marks)

I have reviewed this strategy and concluded that it would fall within the general anti-abuse rule (GAAR).

- Distinguish between tax evasion and tax avoidance and state the purpose of the GAAR.
- Explain why the GAAR would apply to the strategy suggested by Rosetti's business adviser.

(9 marks)

(b) **Rosetti – gifts of ordinary shares in Lark Ltd (Exhibit 3)**

Write a memorandum for Rosetti's client file. When carrying out this work you should assume that:

- On 1 May 2026 the market value of 1,500 shares in Lark Ltd will be £27,000.
- Rosetti is a higher rate taxpayer and business asset disposal relief will be available in respect of the gifts.

For each of the two proposed gifts:

- Explain whether or not gift holdover relief will be available.
- Calculate Rosetti's capital gains tax (CGT) liability (if any), and the recipients' CGT base cost in the shares received.

(7 marks)

Section B

2 Risa **(49 mins)**

You should assume that today's date is 1 June 2025.

Risa has requested advice in respect of:

- the after-tax amount of an inheritance and the reliefs available to reduce an inheritance tax liability;
- the reliefs available for her share of a partnership trading loss; and
- the tax relief available for interest payable on two loans.

The following exhibit, available on the left-hand side of the screen, provides information relevant to the question:

(1) Risa

This information should be used to answer the question **requirements** within your chosen **response option(s)**.

Required

You should assume that today's date is 1 June 2025.

(a) (i) Explain the relief available in respect of the lifetime gift made by Fiera to Perla, as a result of Fiera's death. **(2 marks)**

(ii) Calculate the amount of Risa's inheritance from Fiera's death estate, after deducting any inheritance tax payable. You should include an explanation of the relief available to reduce the taxable value of the estate. **(6 marks)**

(b) (i) State the options available to Risa to relieve her share of the loss of Perro & Co for the year ended 31 March 2025, on the assumption that she does not wish to carry any of this loss forward. **(3 marks)**

(ii) Explain which of the available options for relieving the loss (as identified in (i) above) will result in the highest income tax saving for Risa and calculate the amount of this tax saving. **(5 marks)**

(c) Explain how income tax relief will be given for the interest payable on the loans taken out by Risa on 6 April 2025, and calculate the total amount of any income tax saving for the tax year 2025/26 in respect of this relief. **(4 marks)**

Professional marks will be awarded for the demonstration of skill in analysis and evaluation, and commercial acumen in your answer. **(5 marks)**

(Total = 25 marks)

Exhibit: Risa

Risa

- Has recently inherited the residue of her aunt Fiera's estate.
- Left her previous employment on 30 September 2024.
- Became a partner in Perro & Co on 1 October 2024.
- Has not made any disposals for capital gains tax purposes since the tax year 2021/22.

Fiera

- Died on 8 February 2025.
- Had always been tax resident and domiciled in the UK.
- Gave Risa's sister, Perla, an investment property on 1 March 2021. This was Fiera's only lifetime gift.

- Perla still owns this investment property, which was valued at £210,000 on 1 March 2021, and at £182,000 on 8 February 2025.
- Left the whole of her estate to Risa, except for a specific bequest of £90,000 cash to Perla.

Fiera – assets owned at death on 8 February 2025

	£
House (Fiera's own residence)	370,000
20,000 shares in Gato Ltd, an unquoted trading company	240,000
Personal chattels	160,000

Additional information

- Fiera had inherited the shares in Gato Ltd (a 20% holding) from her husband, Marco, on his death on 21 November 2023.
- Marco had acquired the shares on 2 May 2015.
- Marco had used the whole of his nil rate band for inheritance tax purposes.

Perro & Co

- Prepares accounts to 31 March each year.
- Has a tax-adjusted trading loss for the year ended 31 March 2025.
- Risa's share of this loss is £32,000.

Risa – other income

- Risa earned an annual salary of £96,000 (£8,000 per month) throughout her previous employment which terminated on 30 September 2024.
- She also received a bonus of £34,000 in each of the tax years 2022/23 and 2023/24.

Risa – loans

- On 6 April 2025 Risa took out the following bank loans:
  - A loan of £50,000 in order to provide additional capital to Perro & Co. Interest payable in the tax year 2025/26 will be £4,000.
  - A loan of £80,000 to finance the acquisition of a residential investment property. Interest payable in the tax year 2025/26 will be £5,020.
- The residential property will generate taxable rental income of £24,000 in the tax year 2025/26.
- Risa will be a higher rate taxpayer in the tax year 2025/26.

3 Iker (49 mins)

You should assume that today's date is 1 June 2025.

Iker has requested advice in respect of:

- the income tax payable on his overseas property income;
- the capital gains tax implications of two gifts to his daughter; and
- the provision of rent-free living accommodation by his employer.

The following exhibit, available on the left-hand side of the screen, provides information relevant to the question:

(1) Iker

This information should be used to answer the question **requirements** within your chosen **response option(s)**.

Required

You should assume that today's date is 1 June 2025.

(a) (i) Calculate the amount of UK income tax Iker would have to pay in respect of his overseas property income for the tax year 2025/26 on the assumption that it will be taxed on the arising basis.

(ii) Explain whether or not Iker is eligible to claim for his overseas property income to be taxed on the remittance basis. **(8 marks)**

(b) In respect of the gifts of the two paintings to Arama:

(i) Explain, by reference to Iker's tax residence status, why the disposal of Painting 1 will be subject to UK capital gains tax (CGT); and

(ii) Explain whether it would be preferable for Iker to gift Painting 2 on 1 April 2026 or 1 May 2026 in order to minimise his liability to CGT. **(7 marks)**

(c) Calculate the additional disposable income available to Iker for the tax year 2026/27 as a result of being provided with living accommodation by Laudio Ltd. You should include an explanation of your treatment of the expenditure on the construction of the conservatory. **(5 marks)**

Professional marks will be awarded for the demonstration of skill in analysis and evaluation, and commercial acumen in your answer. **(5 marks)**

(Total = 25 marks)

Exhibit: Iker

Iker

- Was born in the country of Tassia and is of Tassian domicile.
- Was tax resident in the UK throughout the 19 tax years from 2003/04 to 2021/22.
- Was tax resident in Tassia in the three tax years 2022/23 to 2024/25.
- Returned to the UK on 6 April 2025 to take up employment with Laudio Ltd and became UK tax resident again from that date.
- Inherited a house in Tassia on the death of his father in 2019.
- Started to rent out this house for one year commencing 6 April 2025 following his return to the UK.

The tax system in Tassia

- Income tax is charged on income in respect of property situated in Tassia at the rate of 25%.
- There is no capital gains tax (CGT) in Tassia.
- There is no double tax treaty between the UK and Tassia.

Iker's income in the tax year 2025/26

- £45,000 salary from his employment with Laudio Ltd.
- £24,000 rental income (net of expenses) from the property in Tassia.
- Iker will not remit any of this property income to the UK.

Gifts of two paintings – Iker

- Purchased two paintings in 2016, both of which are situated in the UK.
- Gave Painting 1 to his daughter Arama on 1 January 2025, when he was still in Tassia.
- Will give Painting 2 to Arama on either 1 April 2026 or 1 May 2026.
- Painting 1 gave rise to a chargeable gain of £33,000; Painting 2 will generate a capital loss of £17,000.
- Has no plans to make any further gifts to Arama.
- Makes disposals each year to use his annual exempt amount for CGT.

Iker's income in the tax year 2026/27

- Iker will be a higher rate taxpayer and will have no overseas income.
- Laudio Ltd will also provide beneficial living accommodation for Iker (see below).

Provision of beneficial accommodation – Laudio Ltd

- Will provide Iker with an unfurnished house, rent-free, from 6 April 2026. The annual value of the house is £6,100.
- Purchased this house in June 2021 for £426,000. Its market value on 6 April 2026 will be £455,000.
- Will pay £68,000 for the construction of a conservatory on the house in May 2026.
- Will not contribute to any of the running costs of this house.
- This house will not constitute job-related accommodation for Iker.

Iker's cost savings

- On 6 April 2026, when his rental agreement ends, Iker will move out of his current living accommodation and into the house provided by Laudio Ltd.
- Iker's regular monthly outgoings in the tax year 2026/27 in respect of his current accommodation would have been:

	£
Rent	1,100
Running costs (heat, light etc)	700

- Iker estimates that the equivalent running costs of the house to be provided by Laudio Ltd will be 5% higher than those of his current accommodation.

Answers

DO NOT TURN THIS PAGE UNTIL YOU HAVE COMPLETED THE MOCK EXAM

A plan of attack

We've already established that you've been told to do it 101 times, so it is of course superfluous to tell you for the 102nd time to **take a good look at the exam before diving into the answers.**

What's the worst thing you could be doing right now if this was the actual exam? Wondering how to celebrate the end of the exam in about three hours' time?

Turn back to the exam and let's sort out a **plan of attack**!

First things first

Look through the exam and work out the order in which to attack the questions. You've got **two options**. Option 1 is the option recommended by BPP.

Option 1 (if you're thinking 'Help!')

If you're a bit worried about the exam, do the questions in the order of how well you think you can answer them. If you find the questions in Section B less daunting than the questions in Section A, start with Section B.

There are two questions in Section B. Question 2 has three parts.

Part (a) is in two parts. Part (a)(i) asks you to explain the IHT reliefs available on a lifetime gift and part (a)(ii) asks you to calculate IHT on an individual's death and explanation of the relief available to reduce the taxable estate.

Part (b) is also in two parts. Part (b)(i) asks you to state the options available to relieve a partner's share of a partnership's trade loss and part (b)(ii) then asks you to explain and calculate the option that will result in the highest tax saving.

Part (c) asks you to explain and calculate the relief available in respect of the interest payable on two loans taken out by an individual.

Question 3 has three parts. Part (a) asks you calculate income tax on overseas property income and to explain whether the individual is eligible to claim the remittance basis. Part (b) asks you to explain, with reference to their residence status, whether the individual is liable to CGT on their disposals.

Part (c) asks you to calculate the additional disposal income for an employee of being provided with living accommodation by their employer.

Lastly, what you mustn't forget is that you have to attempt **the whole question in Section A and BOTH questions in Section B.**

Option 2 (if you're thinking 'This exam's alright')

It never pays to be overconfident but if you're not quaking in your shoes about the exam then **turn straight to the case-study question in Section A.**

Question 1 has two parts and you are preparing a memo for the client file.

Part (a)(i) is asking you to compare the sale of shares vs sale of trade and assets and prepare calculations to show which option would generate the highest post-tax proceeds. Part (a)(ii) is about considering which companies should be included within a VAT group and also asks you to explain why the sale of trade and assets in part (a)(i), would not qualify as a TOGC.

Part (a)(iii) includes the ethics question. There will always be five marks on ethics in Section A and they are relatively easy to obtain. This time it requires you to distinguish between tax evasion and tax avoidance and state the purpose of the general anti-abuse rule.

Part (c) relates to the gift of shares by the client. You need to determine and explain whether or not gift holdover relief is available and then calculate the CGT payable.

Once you've done this question, **move to Section B**. The question you attempt first really depends on what you are most confident at. If you are undecided look at the requirements. It may be easier to obtain more marks if these are broken down into several smaller parts.

No matter how many times we remind you...

Always, always **allocate your time** according to the marks for the question in total and then according to the parts of the question. And **always, always follow the requirements** exactly. Answer the question that is set, rather than the one you wish had been set, and pay attention to verbs; 'explain' means there will be significant marks for your narrative and not just the figures –

you can assume that 'supporting' calculations will never be worth more than 50% of the available marks. Marks will not be available for you to discuss something which has been specifically excluded in the scenario. Not only will you not score marks but you will also be wasting valuable time if you write about something you've been asked not to.

You've got spare time at the end of the exam...?

If you have allocated your time properly then you **shouldn't have time on your hands** at the end of the exam. But if you find yourself with five or ten minutes to spare, check over your work to make sure that you have answered all the requirements of the questions and all parts of all requirements.

Forget about it!

And don't worry if you found the exam difficult. More than likely other candidates will too. If this were the real thing you would need to **forget** the exam the minute you leave the exam room and **think about the next one**. Or, if it's the last one, **celebrate**!

Section A

1 Lark Ltd

Course Book reference

For Lark Ltd, corporation tax is covered in Chapter 16 with overseas aspects covered in Chapter 22. VAT groups and VAT on land and buildings is covered in Chapter 23. Ethics is covered in Chapter 1. For Rosetti, CGT reliefs are covered in Chapter 8.

Top Tips

Treat this question as four smaller parts; sale of STV Ltd, VAT, suggested pricing strategy and gift of shares by Lark. This will help make the information more manageable and provides a clear structure for your answer. You need to be careful to allocate your time to each part of the requirement accordingly.

Easy marks

An explanation of the basic corporation tax implications of a sale of shares and sale of a building in part (a) should be a source of easy marks as well as the ethics in this part. In addition, there should be easy marks available for your capital gains tax calculation in part (b).

ACCA examining team's comments

Part (a)(i)

When one company disposes of shares in another company, the substantial shareholding exemption (SSE) is applied to any gain arising if certain conditions are met. The facts of the question confirmed that the conditions were met in this case and as such, the SSE would be automatic. However, weaker candidates incorrectly calculated a gain on the sale of shares by Lark Ltd, often referring to business asset disposal relief at 10%, which is not available to companies selling shares but only available to sole traders disposing of their businesses. For those candidates who correctly identified that the SSE would apply, very few explained why. Candidates are reminded that there can be different rules for companies and sole traders and they need to be clear on these.

Most candidates identified that the two companies were in a 'group' but candidates should state that they are in a 'gains group' and refer to the 75% ownership required for a gains group. Lots of candidates knew that the building would be transferred at nil gain nil loss but then wasted time discussing a potential future degrouping charge which was not relevant.

Many candidates incorrectly calculated stamp duty land tax (SDLT) on the intra group transfer, when in fact SDLT does not apply on a 75% intra group transfer such as this. Most candidates were able to calculate the profit on sale of the trademark intangible asset but very few identified the potential for rollover relief. Candidates needed to take a moment to consider why they were being given information about the purchase of a trademark as well as the sale of a trademark. Advice to candidates is that they must focus not only on learning the details of the tax rules but also on question practice, so that they improve at being able to spot the clues being given in questions and can then apply their knowledge.

There were three commercial acumen professional skills marks available for this part of the question; for recognising that the SSE was available and consideration of rollover relief and the SDLT exemption.

Some candidates produced calculations which were difficult to follow. Candidates must label calculations appropriately and show all steps in their workings. Also, candidates should consider when it is appropriate to use the spreadsheet for calculations and not automatically use the word document for their whole answer leaving the spreadsheet blank. Overall, this question part was a good example of candidates needing to apply the detailed ATX rules to the facts of the question and what is being asked of them. A superficial knowledge of the rules is not enough. Candidates are advised to practise questions to help them with this required skill.

Many candidates were able to produce reasonable calculations comparing which option would generate the greater amount of post-tax proceeds. They were also often able to earn two analysis and evaluation professional skills marks for producing these calculations and identifying the better option. However, most candidates did not score well when asked to consider any other relevant tax or commercial matters. This required candidates to use their analysis skills and apply their tax and commercial knowledge to the facts presented to them. To get better at doing this kind of analysis, candidates are once again advised to practise questions and think about how they can apply their knowledge to the facts of the question.

Part (a)(ii)

A number of candidates thought that 75% ownership was required for companies to be in a VAT group when in fact the rule is more than 50% ownership is required. Also, a number of candidates thought that a company had to be UK resident to be in a VAT group, but the rule is that the company must be 'established in the UK' or have 'a fixed establishment in the UK'. These detailed rules are important to know for the ATX exam and VAT is a topic which will continue to be tested.

A lot of candidates stated that the sale of the business assets would not qualify as a transfer of a going concern (TOGC) because the company itself was not continuing to trade. This was not the correct rule. The rule is that for the sale to qualify as a TOGC, the whole business (or part of the business) must be sold and continue to trade. At the time of the building transfer the two companies would not be in a VAT group and for that reason, candidates should have considered whether an option to tax had been made on the building. It was pleasing to see many candidates refer to the option to tax and understand the consequences.

There was an analysis and evaluation professional skills mark for recognising that any VAT group registration will not be in place at the date of sale of the building, but few candidates stated this point, even though they may have known it. Candidates are advised to state any assumptions or rules that they are applying to the facts of the question in order to maximise the marks earned.

Part (a)(iii)

The vast majority of candidates were able to earn a mark for stating that profits should be calculated using the lower arms-length price rather than the price paid. However, there were more transfer pricing marks available which fewer candidates mentioned. These included stating that the companies were connected companies for this purpose and that there is a possible exemption within the transfer pricing rules which should be considered.

The ethics part of this question was generally well answered with many candidates able to discuss tax avoidance, tax evasion and the general anti-abuse rule (GAAR). Those that were able to discuss all three areas were also rewarded with an analysis and evaluation professional skills mark. This is an ethics area which will continue to be tested and candidates should ensure they understand this area and know when the GAAR would be applied.

Part (b)

The majority of candidates were able to calculate the gain on the gift of the shares correctly. Lots of candidates knew that gift holdover relief would be available on the gift to a discretionary trust, but fewer knew that relief would be on 100% of the gain, rather than the 94% applicable to business assets, which would have earned a scepticism professional skills mark.

Similarly, many candidates knew that gift holdover relief would not be available on the gift to the brother because he was not resident in the UK. The requirement asked for the recipients' base cost in the shares received and lots of candidates failed to answer this part of the requirement, losing an analysis and evaluation professional skills mark.

Candidates would be well advised to reread the requirement while they are in the process of answering it, to ensure that they are directing their answer at all the specific question parts which have been set. Highlighting key words within a requirement may help to maintain focus and to ensure that candidates do not lose sight of all the elements of the question they are being asked to address.

Marking guide

			Marks	
(a)	(i)	(1) Sale of shares	2.5	
		Sale of assets		
		Strick building		
		– Corporation tax	2	
		– Stamp duty land tax	2	
		S trademark	4	
		(2) Post-tax proceeds	4.5	
		Bringing it together	4	
		Marks Available	19	
		Maximum		17
	(ii)	Group registration	2.5	
		Sale of the Strick building	5	
		Marks Available	7.5	
		Maximum		7
	(iii)	Purchase of components from VAR Co	5	
		Strategy to reduce corporation tax	7.5	
		Marks Available	12.5	
		Maximum		9
(b)	Chargeable gain		1	
	Gift to trust			
	– Gift holdover relief		2	
	– Trustees' base cost		1	
	Gift to brother			
	– Gift holdover relief		2.5	
	– Capital gains tax liability		1	
	– Brother's base cost		1	
	Marks Available		8.5	
	Maximum			7

Professional skills marks

Communication

- General format and structure of memorandum (eg use of headings/sub-headings)
- Style, language and clarity (tone of memorandum, presentation of calculations, appropriate use of the tools, easy to follow and more than a negligible amount of content)
- Effectiveness of communication (answer is relevant, specific rather than general and focused to the requirement)
- Adherence to specific instructions made in the scenario

Analysis and evaluation

- Appropriate use of information to determine suitable calculations
- Consideration of relevant factors in drawing conclusions
- Appropriate use of information to determine tax rates and reliefs applicable on the gifts

Scepticism

- Application of professional judgement to draw conclusions

- Critical assessment of the information to determine the tax consequences of choosing alternative options

Commercial acumen

- Effective use of information in relation to identifying the availability of rollover relief and SSE
- Effective use of information in relation to determining whether the SDLT exemption is available — 10

Total — 50

(a) **Memorandum**

Client Lark Ltd group

Subject Corporate matters

Prepared by Tax senior

Date 1 February 2026

This memorandum has been prepared to assist our preparation for a meeting with Rosetti, the managing director of Lark Ltd.

(i) (1) **Tax implications of the sale**

Option 1 – Lark Ltd sells the shares in STV Ltd

Corporation tax implications for Lark Ltd

- The gain realised by Lark Ltd on the sale of the shares would be exempt from corporation tax due to the substantial shareholding exemption (SSE).
- The SSE would be available because:
  - STV Ltd is a trading company; and
  - Lark Ltd would have owned at least 10% of the ordinary share capital of STV Ltd for at least 12 months in the six years prior to the date of sale.

Option 2 – STV Ltd sells its assets

Sale of the Strick Building

Corporation tax implications

- STV Ltd and VAR Ltd are members of the Lark Ltd chargeable gains group because Lark Ltd owns at least 75% of the ordinary share capital of both companies.
- Accordingly, the sale of the building to VAR Ltd will take place automatically at no gain, no loss for the purposes of corporation tax, such that it will not give rise to a corporation tax liability.

Stamp duty land tax implications

- Stamp duty land tax will not be due in respect of the sale of the Strick Building. This is because Lark Ltd owns at least 75% of the ordinary share capital of both companies.

Taxable profit from the sale of the 'S' trademark

	£	£
Proceeds		50,000
Cost	30,000	
Less: amortisation	(3,000)	
		(27,000)
		23,000

	£	£
Intangible asset rollover relief		
Lower of:		
– disposal proceeds	50,000	
– amounts reinvested by VAR Ltd	40,000	
Lower figure	40,000	
Less: cost of the 'S' trademark	(30,000)	
		(10,000)
Trading profit		13,000

Tutorial note. The Lark Ltd group companies claim tax deductions and deferrals as soon as possible. Accordingly, intangible asset rollover relief will be claimed in respect of the 'V' trademark purchased by VAR Ltd.

(2) **Assisting Rosetti in deciding on which option to proceed with**

Lark Ltd's post-tax proceeds

		Post-tax proceeds
	£	£
Option 1: Lark Ltd sells the company		
Post-tax proceeds equals amount received		920,000
Less: corporation tax due (SSE)		(0)
Lark Ltd's post-tax proceeds		920,000
Option 2: STV Ltd sells its assets		
Proceeds:		
– Strick building	700,000	
– 'S' trademark	50,000	
– Other assets	130,000	
Total proceeds	880,000	
Less: corporation tax due in respect of:		
– 'S' trademark (£13,000 × 25%)	(3,250)	
– Other assets (£20,000 × 25%)	(5,000)	
STV Ltd's post-tax proceeds paid as dividend to Lark Ltd		871,750
Less: corporation tax payable by Lark Ltd		(0)
Lark Ltd's post-tax proceeds		871,750

- Option 1 would generate the greater amount of post-tax proceeds for Lark Ltd.

Matters to draw to Rosetti's attention

Under Option 1:

- The Strick Building would be owned by STV Ltd when the company is sold.
- Accordingly, VAR Ltd would not be able to acquire the building and would have to find a suitable alternative for use in its trade. This could turn out to cost more, or less, than £700,000.

Under Option 2:

- Option 2 generates a lower amount of post-tax proceeds. In addition, the majority of the proceeds would not be new money in relation to the group, as the building would be sold to VAR Ltd.
- Option 2 also results in the following tax disadvantages:
  - VAR Ltd's base cost in the Strick Building would be equal to STV Ltd's base cost of £475,000 as opposed to the building's current market value of £700,000. Accordingly, VAR Ltd's taxable gain on a future sale of the building would be greater than the profit it makes.
  - Claiming intangible asset rollover relief would reduce the total tax deductions available to VAR Ltd in respect of the 'V' trademark by the amount of profit relieved, ie £10,000.

> **Tutorial note.** Credit was given for other relevant points.

(ii) **Value added tax (VAT)**

Group registration

- The companies which could be included in a group VAT registration with Lark Ltd are those which are:
  - controlled by Lark Ltd (ie Lark Ltd owns more than 50% of the company's ordinary share capital); and
  - established in the UK (eg their headquarters are in the UK) or have a fixed establishment in the UK (eg they have a genuine trading presence in the UK).
- Accordingly, the group registration could include Lark Ltd, TEN Ltd and VAR Ltd.

Sale of Strick Building under Option 2

- STV Ltd's sale of its business assets would NOT qualify as a transfer of a going concern (TOGC) for the purposes of VAT because no single purchaser will be acquiring an operational business.

  Accordingly, it may be necessary to charge VAT on the sale of the Strick Building.
- As STV Ltd and VAR Ltd will not be members of a VAT group registration when the sale takes place, we need to know whether or not an option to tax has been made in respect of the building.
  - If an option to tax has been made:

    STV Ltd will be required to charge VAT at 20% on the sale of the building.
  - If no option to tax has been made:

    The sale will be an exempt supply because the building is more than three years old.

(iii) **Reducing the corporation tax payable by the group companies**

Pricing strategy

- Lark Ltd and URB Co are connected companies for the purposes of the transfer pricing rules.

  This is because Lark Ltd controls URB Co, such that it directly participates in the management, control, or capital of the company.

  Accordingly, the transfer pricing rules would apply to the purchase of components from URB Co.

- Under the transfer pricing rules, Lark Ltd would obtain a tax advantage (reduced taxable profits in the UK) if it were to pay more for components purchased from URB Co than the price charged by an unconnected company. Consequently, it would be required to calculate its profits for UK corporation tax purposes using the lower arm's length price rather than the price paid.

- The exemption within the transfer pricing rules for small and medium-sized enterprises would not be available, regardless of the size of the Lark Ltd group.

  This is because there is no double tax treaty between the UK and Limero, such that Limero is classified as a non-qualifying territory.

Strategy suggested by business adviser

Tax evasion and tax avoidance

- Tax evasion is unlawful. It involves the provision of false information or the withholding of information in order to evade tax.
- Tax avoidance involves the use of legal methods in order to reduce the amount of tax payable.
- The general anti-abuse rule (GAAR) is intended to counteract tax advantages, obtained via what would otherwise be legal tax avoidance methods, where the arrangements can be considered to be abusive.

The GAAR would apply to this plan because:

- a 'tax advantage' would be obtained where payments result in a tax deduction for Lark Ltd but do not give rise to taxable income in VAR Ltd;
- the formation of the subsidiary companies together with the inter-related contracts and the series of payments and repayments which are intended to obtain the tax advantage would be regarded as 'tax arrangements'; and
- these arrangements appear to have been designed to give rise to additional tax deductions and/or non-taxable income rather than for genuine commercial reasons, such that they are likely to be regarded as 'abusive'.

(b) **Memorandum**

Client Rosetti

Subject Gifts of ordinary shares in Lark Ltd

Prepared by Tax senior

Date 1 February 2026

This memorandum has been drafted to assist our preparation for a meeting with Rosetti.

Rosetti – gifts of ordinary shares in Lark Ltd

Each of the two gifts will result in a chargeable gain of £24,750, as set out below.

	£
Proceeds deemed to be market value	27,000
Less: cost (1,500 × £1.50)	(2,250)
Chargeable gain	24,750

Gift to discretionary trust

- Rosetti is incorrect; gift holdover relief will be available in respect of the whole of the gain, as opposed to 94% of it.
- This is because a gift to a trust is immediately chargeable to inheritance tax.
- The trustees' base cost in the shares received will be £2,250 (£27,000 – £24,750). This is the market value of the shares less the chargeable gain held over.

Gift to Rosetti's brother

- Gift holdover relief will not be available in respect of this gift because Rosetti's brother will not be UK tax resident in the tax year 2026/27.
- He will be non-UK tax resident automatically because he will be in the UK for less than 16 days in the tax year.

	£
Chargeable gain	24,750
Annual exempt amount	(3,000)
Taxable gain	21,750
CGT at 10% (BADR)	2,175

- Rosetti's brother's base cost in the shares received will be the market value of the shares on 1 May 2026 of £27,000.

Section B

2 Risa

Course Book reference

IHT computations and reliefs are covered in Chapters 11 and 12. Sole trader losses are covered in Chapter 15. Qualifying interest is covered in Chapter 2 and relief for interest on loans to buy residential property are covered in Chapter 5.

Top Tips

Make sure you spot the 'command verbs' in each requirement to understand whether you answer should be written or calculations (or both). In part (b) you need to be very specific to the scenario when considering each loss option. You need to for each option state; (1) which tax year(s) it will be used in and (2) the rate of tax saved. Don't forget to then explain which option results in the highest tax saving as well as calculating it.

Easy marks

The IHT calculation in part (a) of this question should be a source of straightforward marks. In addition, the explanation of the income tax treatment of the interest payable on the loans in part (c) should also have been straight forward.

ACCA examining team's comments

Part (a)(i)

Many candidates wrongly thought that taper relief would be available on this lifetime gift. However, the gift was made within three years of the date of death, so even if the gift became chargeable on death, no taper relief would be given. Well prepared candidates recognised that if the value of the gift was lower at the date of death than at the time of the gift, then fall in value relief would be available. However few candidates went on to explain that fall in value relief would be ignored when calculating the remaining available nil rate band for the death estate. Once again candidates should take a moment to think why information about the valuation of the gift has been given to them in the question and then apply this in their answers. For those better prepared candidates there was a commercial acumen professional skills mark available for applying fall in value relief rules to the scenario.

Part (a)(ii)

Many candidates scored well on this part of the question although a few lost easy marks by simply calculating the inheritance tax payable and not taking the further step to calculate the client's inheritance after deducting any inheritance tax payable. Candidates should watch out for this further step required, which is often tested at ATX, and earned an analysis and evaluation professional skills mark in this question. Common mistakes included applying the residence nil rate band to the death estate property when it was unavailable because the property was not left to a direct descendant. Also, a number of candidates gave annual exemptions in the death estate which are only available on lifetime gifts. Many candidates correctly identified that business property relief (BPR) would be available on the unquoted shares, but few were able to explain that the husband's ownership could be included to reach the required two-year threshold for BPR. There were two commercial acumen professional skills marks available for considering BPR and being aware of how the two-year threshold could be met using the husband's ownership as well as his wife's.

Part (b)(i)

Generally, this part of the question was well answered with many candidates aware of the possible loss reliefs. Unfortunately, a large number of candidates wasted time discussing possible loss relief against gains when the question made it clear that the client had not made any disposals resulting in gains. This question part was a good example of candidates needing to be able to do more than just state generic rules in order to score high marks at ATX-UK. They must be able to apply the rules to the facts of the question and what is being asked of them. Once again, the advice to candidates is that they must focus not only on learning the details of the tax rules but also on question practice, so that they begin to see the links between information given in questions and can then apply their knowledge.

Part (b)(ii)

A number of candidates lost out on marks because they simply calculated the optimum tax saving when they were asked to explain which option would result in the highest tax saving and then to calculate the tax saving. If the requirement asks for an explanation, simply producing calculations, even if they are correct, cannot score full marks. Those candidates who offered an explanation and identified an optimum based on tax savings were awarded two analysis and evaluation professional skills marks. Once again candidates are advised to highlight key command words at the beginning of a requirement such as 'advise' or 'calculate' so that they are clear as to exactly what they are being asked to do.

Part (c)

A large number of candidates thought wrongly that the loan interest would be deductible from partnership income and property income respectively. The requirement was to calculate the total amount of any income tax saving but not all candidates earned the easy analysis and evaluation professional skills mark, which simply required them to add together the two individual interest payable tax savings to produce a total. There was a commercial acumen professional skills mark available for recognising that the tax treatment was different for each loan, which many candidates were able to achieve

Marking guide

			Marks	
(a)	(i)	Fall in value relief	2	
				2
	(ii)	Fiera's taxable estate	3	
		After-tax amount	1.5	
		Business property relief	2.5	
		Marks Available	7	
				6
(b)	(i)	Loss reliefs available	3.5	
		Maximum		3
	(ii)	Optimum	6.5	
		Maximum		5
(c)		Loan to provide partnership capital	2	
		Loan to purchase residential property	2	
				4

Professional skills marks

Analysis and evaluation

- Appropriate use of relevant information to determine suitable calculations
- Demonstration of ability to consider all relevant factors to determine loss relief options available
- Appropriate use of information in the question to draw conclusions

Commercial acumen

- Appropriate use of relevant information in the question to determine tax reliefs available
- Recognition of the specific rules for the tax reliefs applicable
- Recognition that the tax treatment is different for each loan

Maximum	5
Total	25

(a) (i)

Word Processor

Relief available in respect of the lifetime gift to Perla

Fall in value relief

The investment property which had been given to Perla had fallen in value between the date of the gift and the date of Fiera's death. This fall in value would have been taken into account in calculating the tax payable by Perla following Fiera's death. However, it is ignored when calculating the value of the gift for the purpose of calculating the remaining available nil rate band.

(ii)

Spreadsheet

C21 =-C13

	A	B	C
1	**Risa's after-tax inheritance from Fiera's death estate**		
2	**Fiera – death estate at 8 February 2025**		
3		£	£
4	Shares in Gato Ltd		240,000
5	Less: 100% business property relief (BPR)		(204,000)
6			nil
7	House and personal chattels (£370,000 + £160,000)		530,000
8	Total chargeable estate		530,000
9	Less: available nil rate band		
10	– Nil rate band	325,000	
11	– Less: used on lifetime gift (£210,000 – £3,000 – £3,000)	(204,000)	(121,000)
12	Taxable estate		409,000
13	IHT at 40%		163,600
14			

C21	=-C13		
	A	B	C
15	**Risa's after-tax inheritance**		
16			£
17	Shares in Gato Ltd		240,000
18	House and personal chattels		530,000
19			770,000
20	Less: specific bequest		(90,000)
21	IHT borne by Risa		(163,600)
22	After-tax inheritance		516,400
23	**Relief available** BPR is available at the rate of 100% on the Gato Ltd shares. This is because: – the company is an unquoted trading company; and – although Fiera did not personally hold the shares for two years prior to her death, she inherited them on the death of her husband, such that his period of ownership will be included, and therefore the aggregate ownership period exceeds the requisite two years.		

(b) (i)

Word Processor

Reliefs available for Risa's share of the trading loss

Risa's trading loss of £32,000 is in respect of the tax year 2024/25.

It can be relieved against Risa's total income for 2024/25, the tax year of the loss, and/or 2023/24, the previous tax year.

Alternatively, because the loss has arisen in one of the first four tax years in which Risa will be a partner, it can be relieved against her total income of the three years prior to the year of the loss starting with the earliest year (ie 2021/22, 2022/23, 2023/24).

(ii)

Word Processor

Strategy for loss relief to maximise Risa's income tax saving

Relief against total income of the current and/or previous tax year

In 2024/25, Risa's total income will comprise only her salary up to 30 September 2024 of £48,000 (£8,000 × 6). She is a basic rate taxpayer in this tax year, such that claiming relief for the loss of £32,000 will result in an income tax saving at the rate of 20% with no loss of personal allowance.

In 2023/24, Risa's taxable income before loss relief was £130,000 (£96,000 + £34,000), such that she was an additional rate taxpayer in this tax year. She would have had no entitlement to a personal allowance for this tax year as her net income exceeded £125,140.

Claiming relief for the loss in this tax year will generate an income tax saving partly at the rate of 45% and partly at 40%. In addition, Risa's total income will be reduced to £98,000 (£130,000 – £32,000), which is below £100,000, such that the full amount of her personal allowance will become available.

Opening years loss relief

If, alternatively, Risa carries the loss back to 2021/22, it will be relieved against her total income of that year of £96,000. She was a higher rate taxpayer in this tax year, such that the rate of tax saved will be 40% on the full £32,000.

Conclusion

Therefore, the most beneficial claim is to carry back the loss and offset it in 2023/24 as this results in the highest tax saving of £18,071:

	£
At additional rate: £4,860 (£130,000 – £125,140) × 45%	2,187
At higher rate:	
– £27,140 (£32,000 – £4,860) × 40%	10,856
– £12,570 (personal allowance) × 40%	5,028
	18,071

ANSWERS

(c)

Tax relief available in respect of the loans

Loan to provide capital to the partnership

This is a qualifying loan for the purpose of income tax relief. Accordingly, the interest paid on this loan will be deducted from Risa's total income for 2025/26. Therefore, as Risa will be a higher rate taxpayer in 2025/26, this will result in an income tax saving of £1,600 (£4,000 × 40%).

Loan to acquire a residential property

Tax relief is available in respect of the interest payments on this loan at the basic rate of income tax only, and will be given as a tax reducer in calculating Risa's income tax liability for the tax year 2025/26. Accordingly, the amount of tax saved will be £1,004 (£5,020 × 20%).

The total amount of tax saved will be £2,604 (£1,600 + £1,004).

3 Iker

Course Book reference

Overseas aspects of personal tax in Chapter 9 and taxable benefits are covered in Chapter 4.

Top Tips

It is important to adopt a logical approach for each part of this question. For part (a)(ii) explain first the rules that need to be satisfied to claim the remittance basis and then conclude if they are met in this scenario. Then in part (b)(i) first explain the impact of an individual's residency status in determining whether a disposal is liable to CGT and then apply those rules to the individual in the question. When calculating the additional disposable income in part (c) break it down into small steps showing your workings of each clearly to pick up the follow through marks.

Easy marks

The calculation of income tax on overseas property income in part (a) should be the source of easy marks as well explaining the basis impact of being UK resident for CGT purposes in part (b).

ACCA examining team's comments

Part a(i)

Part (a)(i) tested candidates' ability to calculate the UK income tax payable in respect of overseas property income, including consideration of the availability and amount of double tax relief (DTR). Candidates were told that the arising basis applied, so this should have been a fairly straightforward question part, very much in line with previous questions on this area of the syllabus, several of which are available to candidates in the workbooks and question banks. Well prepared candidates, who were clearly familiar with this type of question, produced a full, clearly labelled, income tax computation, including both UK and overseas sources of income, and a deduction for double taxation relief (DTR). Consequently, these candidates scored full, or almost full marks on this question part.

The majority of candidates were confident with the basics of DTR, correctly applying the principles to calculate the relevant tax credit, for which they were rewarded with both a commercial acumen mark, for recognition of its application, and technical marks for correctly identifying the relevant figures. However, a very significant number of candidates were not able to correctly calculate the amount of the UK income tax liability which was attributable to the property income when calculating the DTR available. Technically, this should be calculated as the difference between the taxpayer's total income tax liability including the overseas income in the computation, and then the total liability excluding it from the computation. This is achieved by producing two computations, which some candidates did, and this almost always produced the correct answer.

However, it was possible in this question to shortcut this, but care was needed. The taxpayer in this question was a higher rate taxpayer, and their income was all non-savings income, such that the UK tax on the overseas income could be calculated by treating the overseas income as the top slice of the total. Those who had already produced an income tax computation including both the UK and overseas sources of income were able to fairly easily identify that the overseas income would actually fall partly into the basic rate band and partly into the higher rate band, and correctly calculate the amount of UK tax attributable to the overseas income to include in the DTR calculation.

However, as stated above, care is needed when adopting a 'marginal' approach. A significant minority of candidates adopted this approach from the start of their answer. They identified, from looking at the total amount of income of the taxpayer, that they would be a higher rate taxpayer, so, recognising that the overseas income would be taxed as the top slice, just applied the rate of 40% to the full amount of this income. This ignored the fact that the personal allowance would reduce the total income figure such that part of the overseas income would fall into the basic rate band, so they omitted part of the detail of this calculation, which necessarily restricted their mark. The marginal approach can provide a useful shortcut in some cases, but caution and discretion must be used in its application; a full computation approach will often be a safer option.

A final observation on candidates' performance in this question part is that a good number appeared not to have read carefully what they were required to do. The command word here was 'calculate' only. No explanations were required, so unfortunately, candidates – and there were many -- who decided to provide these wasted their time for no marks.

Part a(ii)

In part (a)(ii), as a conclusion was going to be required here (whether or not the taxpayer will be eligible to claim the remittance basis in respect of his overseas income), a good starting point would have been to explain the rules to be satisfied in order to be eligible to claim the remittance basis. A surprising number of candidates did not undertake this first step, which meant that they were unable to satisfactorily conclude as to whether or not the remittance basis was available.

An analysis and evaluation professional skills mark was available for reaching an appropriate conclusion in respect of the eligibility to claim the remittance basis. The key point here was to recognise that eligibility for the remittance basis depends on an individual's tax residence and domicile status. Those who concisely stated the rules, including consideration of deemed domicile status, and then related them to the taxpayer, were able to score full marks on this question part. However, a very significant number of candidates went on to provide further information - sometimes in great detail – in relation to the application of the remittance basis, such as reference to its automatic application if the amount of unremitted overseas income was less than £2,000, or the rules relating to loss of the personal allowance, or the potential liability to the remittance basis charge. As the requirement was merely to address the taxpayer's eligibility to claim the remittance basis, the consequences of doing so were not relevant, and, once again, served to just waste time. Candidates are reminded that it is often useful to reread the requirement while they are in the course of writing their answer to ensure that they are confining their answer to precisely what is required.

Part b(i)

In part (b)(ii), the two dates given were carefully chosen – only one month apart – but the key point is that they fall into two different tax years. This fact is of fundamental importance to the decision regarding which date to choose, but few candidates stated this. In any question relating to an individual taxpayer in which a decision is to be made between two potential dates for a transaction, consideration of the tax year(s) involved is likely to be very important. Frequently candidates refer to the 'year' of a transaction, but this could often be ambiguous as it could refer to a calendar year, or, in the case of a business, the business's accounting year. Candidates are encouraged to be more precise; to note where the term 'tax year' is used in model answers, and to practise using it when working questions.

A good number of candidates recognised that 1 April 2026 would fall into the same tax year as the gift of painting 1, such that the loss arising could be relieved against the gain on this earlier gift. However, the full impact of this choice was recognised only by very few. The fact that the recipient of these gifts was the taxpayer's daughter means that they are connected persons for the purposes of CGT, such that relief for the loss will be restricted to gains on disposal(s) to her in the same or future tax years. Hence it will not be available if the gift of painting 2 is made on 1 May 2026 as this will mean that the loss arises in the following tax year. Further, as the taxpayer is not planning to make any further gifts to his daughter in the future, the loss on painting 2 would remain unrelieved.

Candidates should always take note of the relationship between individuals in any given scenario. The nature of the relationship between any two individuals will very often be relevant to the requirements, and recognition of this will frequently be rewarded with a commercial acumen mark, as here, in addition to opening the door to further technical marks for relevant explanations of the consequences.

Part (c)

Part (c) moved forward to the next tax year, 2026/27, when the taxpayer will have been provided with living accommodation by his employer, such that he is able to make considerable cost savings in respect of rent, albeit having to pay some additional living expenses. Candidates were required to calculate the additional income after all taxes and expenses ('disposable income') which would be available to the taxpayer as a result of this. A good approach to this calculation would have been to break it down into small logical steps. For example:

- Calculate the total rent payments saved.
- Calculate the additional running costs to be incurred.
- Calculate the cost to the taxpayer of being provided with the beneficial living accommodation. This involved calculating the taxable benefit, then recognising that the relevant cost would be the tax payable in respect of this. It was stated in the scenario that the taxpayer would be a higher rate taxpayer in 2026/27, with no overseas income, such that candidates were expected to just take 40% of the value of the taxable benefit.
- Bring these three elements together, deducting the costs from the saving on the rent payments, to arrive at the additional disposable income figure.

A significant number of candidates did not do this. Many candidates realised that a calculation of the taxable benefit would be required but did not go on to calculate the tax cost of this, nor to put it into context with consideration of the tax savings on rent payments and additional expenses. Others provided calculations relating to the rent payments and expenses, but without making it clear whether their figures represented savings or costs, such that these were difficult to follow.

This question part involved a very practical situation in which the client wishes to know how much more disposable income he will have as a result of receiving a benefit from his employer. In this sort of question, candidates need to stop and think about the practicalities of the situation before starting their calculations, to ensure that their efforts are directed towards the specific requirement.

Candidates were also required to explain their treatment of the expenditure on the construction of the conservatory. Many candidates did not attempt this. However, those that did were usually able to gain 1–2 fairly straightforward marks.

Marking guide

			Marks	
(a)	(i)	Income tax liability before double tax relief	3	
		Double tax relief	2	
		Calculation of tax on overseas income	0.5	
	(ii)	Availability of remittance basis	3	
		Maximum		8
(b)	(i)	Painting 1	5	
	(ii)	Painting 2	4	
		Maximum		7
(c)		Additional disposable income 2026/27	1.5	
		Income tax on accommodation benefit	2.5	
		Explanation of construction of conservatory	2	
		Marks Available	6	
		Maximum		5

Professional skills marks

Analysis and evaluation

- Appropriate use of relevant information in the question to draw conclusions
- Demonstration of the ability to both explain and conclude on the impact of the date of the gift
- Appropriate use of relevant information in the question to determine suitable calculations

Commercial acumen

- Recognition of relevance of domicile status
- Appropriate use of information in the question to determine whether temporary non-residence rules apply
- Recognition of connected persons rules for CGT

Maximum	5
Total	25

(a) (i)

Spreadsheet

Edit Format

	A	B	C
1	**UK income tax payable on Iker's overseas property income**		
2		£	£
3	UK employment income		45,000
4	Tassian property income		24,000
5	Net income		69,000
6	Less: personal allowance		(12,570)
7	Taxable income		56,430
8	**Income tax liability**		
9	UK employment income: £32,430 (£45,000 – £12,570) × 20%		6,486
10	Tassian property income:		
11	– £5,270 (£37,700 – £32,430) × 20%		1,054
12	– £18,730 (£24,000 – £5,270) × 40%		7,492
13	UK income tax liability		15,032
14			
15	UK tax on overseas income (£1,054 + £7,492)		8,546
16	Double tax relief – lower of:		
17	– UK tax on overseas income	8,546	
18	– Overseas tax on overseas income (£24,000 × 25%)	6,000	(6,000)
19	UK income tax payable on overseas property income		2,546

(ii)

Availability of the remittance basis

The remittance basis is available to individuals who are tax resident, but not domiciled or deemed domiciled in the UK.

Iker will be tax resident in the UK throughout 2025/26, and he is not domiciled in the UK. However, he will be deemed UK domiciled in this tax year due to having been resident in the UK for 15 of the previous 20 tax years. Therefore, Iker will not be eligible to claim the remittance basis.

(b) **Disposal of the two paintings**

(i)

Painting 1

Individuals who are tax resident in the UK are liable to capital gains tax (CGT) in respect of disposals of their worldwide assets.

Although Iker was tax resident in Tassia in the tax years 2022/23 to 2024/25, Iker will be treated as only temporarily non-resident in the UK for CGT purposes because:

- he was UK tax resident for at least four of the seven tax years prior to the year he left the UK; and
- he was non-UK tax resident for no more than five years.

Accordingly, as the painting which he gifted to Arama while he was in Tassia was owned by him when he left the UK, it will be subject to CGT in 2025/26, the tax year he returns to the UK and resumes UK tax residence.

(ii)

Painting 2

Iker and Arama are connected persons for CGT purposes. Accordingly, the loss arising on the gift of Painting 2 can only be relieved against gains arising on other disposals to Arama in the same, or future, tax years.

If Iker gifts this painting to Arama on 1 April 2026, the loss can be offset against the gain arising on Painting 1.

However, if the gift is not made until 1 May 2026, the loss will arise in the tax year 2026/27, such that Iker will have a CGT liability in respect of the full amount of the gain on Painting 1, and an unrelieved loss on Painting 2, which may never be relieved if Iker makes no future gifts to Arama.

Therefore, it is preferable for Iker to gift Painting 2 on 1 April 2026.

(c)

Word Processor

Additional disposable income from the provision of the rent-free house 2026/27

	£
Rent payments saved (£1,100 × 12)	13,200
Less: additional running costs (£700 × 12 × 5%)	(420)
Less: income tax on the accommodation benefit (W)	(5,599)
Additional disposable income	7,181

	£
Accommodation benefit	
– Annual value	6,100
– Additional charge ((£426,000 – £75,000) × 2.25%)	7,898
	13,998
	5,599

Tax treatment of the expenditure on the conservatory

For the purpose of calculating the additional charge, the original cost of the property is increased by the cost of any capital improvements made prior to the start of the relevant tax year. Accordingly, the improvement expenditure of £68,000 in relation to the construction of the conservatory which will be incurred in May 2026 will be ignored in the calculation of the additional charge for 2026/27.

Tutorial note. The original cost of the property (rather than the market value at the date Iker moves in) is used for the purpose of calculating the additional charge in respect of the provision of the accommodation as the company will have owned the property for less than six years at this date.

Tax Tables

Supplementary information

(a) You should assume that the tax rates and allowances for the tax year 2024/25 and for the financial year to 31 March 2025 will continue to apply for the foreseeable future unless you are instructed otherwise.

(b) Calculations and workings need only be made to the nearest £.

(c) All apportionments may be made to the nearest month.

(d) All workings should be shown.

Tax rates and allowances

The following tax rates and allowances are to be used in answering the questions.

Income tax

		Normal rates	Dividend rates
Basic rate	£1 – £37,700	20%	8.75%
Higher rate	£37,701 – £125,140	40%	33.75%
Additional rate	£125,141 and over	45%	39.35%
Savings income nil rate band	Basic rate taxpayers		£1,000
	Higher rate taxpayers		£500
Dividend nil rate band			£500

A starting rate of 0% applies to savings income where it falls within the first £5,000 of taxable income.

Personal allowance

	£
Personal allowance	12,570
Transferable amount	1,260
Income limit	100,000

Where adjusted net income is £125,140 or more, the personal allowance is reduced to zero.

Residence status

Days in UK	Previously resident	Not previously resident
Less than 16	Automatically not resident	Automatically not resident
16 to 45	Resident if 4 UK ties (or more)	Automatically not resident
46 to 90	Resident if 3 UK ties (or more)	Resident if 4 UK ties
91 to 120	Resident if 2 UK ties (or more)	Resident if 3 UK ties (or more)
121 to 182	Resident if 1 UK tie (or more)	Resident if 2 UK ties (or more)
183 or more	Automatically resident	Automatically resident

Remittance basis charge

UK resident for:	Charge
Seven out of the last nine years	£30,000
12 out of the last 14 years	£60,000

Car benefit percentage

The relevant base level of CO_2 emissions is 55 grams per kilometre. The percentage rates applying to petrol cars (and diesel cars meeting the RDE2 standard) with CO_2 emissions up to this level are:

51 grams to 54 grams per kilometre	15%
55 grams per kilometre	16%

The percentage for electric cars with zero CO_2 emissions is 2%. For hybrid-electric cars with CO_2 emissions between 1 and 50 grams per kilometre, the electric range of the car is relevant:

Electric range	
130 miles or more	2%
70 to 129 miles	5%
40 to 69 miles	8%
30 to 39 miles	12%
Less than 30 miles	14%

Car fuel benefit

The base figure for calculating the car fuel benefit is £27,800.

Company van benefits

The company van benefit scale charge is £3,960, and the van fuel benefit is £757.

Vans producing zero emissions have a 0% benefit.

Individual savings accounts (ISAs)

The overall investment limit is £20,000.

Rent a room relief

The rent a room limit is £7,500.

Pension scheme limits

Annual allowance	
– 2021/22 and 2022/23	£40,000
– 2023/24 and 2024/25	£60,000
Minimum allowance	£10,000
Threshold income limit	£200,000
Income limit	£260,000

The maximum contribution that can qualify for tax relief without any earnings is £3,600.

Approved mileage allowances: cars

Up to 10,000 miles	45p
Over 10,000 miles	25p

Capital allowances: rates of allowance

Plant and machinery

Main pool	18%
Special rate pool	6%

Cars

New cars with zero CO_2 emissions	100%
Second-hand cars with zero CO_2 emissions	18%
CO_2 emissions between 1 and 50 grams per kilometre	18%
CO_2 emissions over 50 grams per kilometre	6%

Annual investment allowance

Rate of allowance	100%
Expenditure limit	£1,000,000

Enhanced capital allowances for companies

Main pool first year allowance (full expensing)	100%
Special rate pool first year allowance	50%

Structures and buildings allowance

Straight-line allowance	3%

Cap on income tax reliefs

Unless otherwise restricted, reliefs are capped at the higher of £50,000 or 25% of income.

Corporation tax

Financial year	2022	2023	2024
Small profits rate	N/A	19%	19%
Main rate	19%	25%	25%
Lower limit	N/A	£50,000	£50,000
Upper limit	N/A	£250,000	£250,000
Standard fraction	N/A	3/200	3/200

Marginal relief

$$(\text{Upper limit} - \text{Augmented profits}) \times \text{Standard fraction} \times \frac{\text{Taxable total profits}}{\text{Augmented profits}}$$

Quarterly instalments

Profit threshold	£1,500,000

Value added tax (VAT)

Standard rate	20%
Registration limit	£90,000
Deregistration limit	£88,000

Penalties for late VAT payments

Days late	Penalty
Up to 15 days	None
16 to 30 days	2%
More than 30 days	4% plus a daily penalty at an annual rate of 4%

Inheritance tax: nil rate bands and tax rates

Nil rate band	£
Nil rate band	325,000
Residence nil rate band	175,000
Rate of tax on excess	
– Lifetime rate	20%
– Death rate	40%

Inheritance tax: taper relief

Years before death	Percentage reduction
More than 3 but less than 4 years	20%
More than 4 but less than 5 years	40%
More than 5 but less than 6 years	60%
More than 6 but less than 7 years	80%

Capital gains tax

	Normal rates	Residential property
Rates of tax:		
– Lower rate	10%	18%
– Higher rate	20%	24%
Annual exempt amount		£3,000

Capital gains tax: business asset disposal relief and investors' relief

Lifetime limit	
– business asset disposal relief	£1,000,000
– investors' relief	£10,000,000
Rate of tax	10%

National insurance contributions

Class 1 Employee	£1 – £12,570 per year	Nil
	£12,571 – £50,270 per year	8%
	£50,271 and above per year	2%
Class 1 Employer	£1 – £9,100 per year	Nil
	£9,101 and above per year	13.8%
	Employment allowance	£5,000
Class 1A		13.8%
Class 4	£1 – £12,570 per year	Nil
	£12,571 – £50,270 per year	6%
	£50,271 and above per year	2%

Rates of interest (assumed)

Official rate of interest	2.25%
Rate of interest on underpaid tax	7.75%
Rate of interest on overpaid tax	4.25%

Standard penalties for errors

Taxpayer behaviour	Maximum penalty	Minimum penalty – unprompted disclosure	Minimum penalty – prompted disclosure
Deliberate and concealed	100%	30%	50%
Deliberate but not concealed	70%	20%	35%
Careless	30%	0%	15%

Stamp duty land tax on non-residential properties

Up to £150,000	0%
£150,001 – £250,000	2%
£250,001 and above	5%

Stamp duty

Shares	0.5%

Additional CBE Mock Exam

Please find below information and a link relating to an additional CBE Mock Exam. This Mock Exam has been written by the BPP team and built in the ACCA exam software. Please sit this exam at home at a time convenient to you and self-review using the model answers available at the end of the assessment.

It is extremely important to follow the below guidelines when attempting this Mock Exam:

- Please make sure that you launch the exams using **Google Chrome** in order to enjoy the full functionality of the Software.
- Only launch the exam once you are ready to fully complete it.
- Remember to retain a copy of the pdf output of your script as this will be useful for you to self-review and self-mark the script.
- The Mock Exam is set to time out after 4 hours. There will be a timer on the top right of the screen. You will be warned if the 4 hours is about to expire.
- We recommend that you use a wired internet connection wherever possible to reduce the likelihood of any internet outage during the Mock Exam.
- In the same way as the real exam environment, this Mock Exam must be sat in one attempt. Once you close out of the exam it will save your output to pdf. You will not be able to re-enter the exam or pick it up where you left off.

Link here:

https://ondemand.questionmark.eu/delivery/open.php?session=0445029000445029&customerid=612294&NAME=x&GROUP=x

Tell us what you think

Got comments or feedback on this book? Let us know.
Use your QR code reader:

Or, visit:
https://www.smartsurvey.co.uk/s/BFO4OC/

Need to get in touch with customer service?

www.bpp.com/request-support

Spotted an error?

https://learningmedia.bpp.com/pages/errata